THE TRADE GAME

Engaging with Central Asia

"Om Namaha Shivaya..."

i offer to Shiva a respectful invocation of His Name
thee omni present, the only one
true thy name, doer of all deeds
thee supreme lord, keeper of the time, oh the fearless one
boundless thy creations, unlimited thy games
mysterious amongst the mysterious, oh the enchanted one
infinite thy names and infinite thy blessings
slayer of fears, oh divine light
thee my true master, my true guru
thee in my heart, your servant tread on the path thee ask
my saviour, oh the compassionate one
i bow before you a thousand time, a million time as a beggar before the king
Shivaya, Shivaya, Shivaya
Om Namaha Shivaya

Amiya Chandra

THE TRADE GAME

Engaging with Central Asia

Amiya Chandra

PENTAGON PRESS

THE TRADE GAME: Engaging with Central Asia

Amiya Chandra

First Published in 2017

ISBN 978 93-86618-09-2

Published by
PENTAGON PRESS
206, Peacock Lane, Shahpur Jat
New Delhi-110049
Phones: 011-64706243, 26491568
Telefax: 011-26490600
email: rajan@pentagonpress.in
website: www.pentagonpress.in

Printed at Aegean Offset Printers, Greater Noida, U.P.

Dedicated to My Parents

Contents

Acknowledgements

I owe immense gratitude to Shri Ajay Bisaria, the then Joint Secretary (Eurasia Division) and now the Ambassador of India to Poland, who cajoled me to write this book and gave valuable inputs and moral support.

My sincere gratitude goes to Prof. Sharad K Soni of Central Asian Studies Programme, Centre for Inner Asian Studies, School of International Studies, Jawaharlal Nehru University, New Delhi, who provided constant support and enthusiastic encouragement for the intellectual framework of this study.

I am grateful to H.E. Mr Durdyyev Parahat Hommadovich, the Ambassador of the Republic of Turkmenistan toIndia, for his valuable guidance, insights and vision.

I am grateful to Ms Tanu Singh, Deputy DGFT, Ministry of Commerce and Industry, for compilation of latest trade statistics.

I am also grateful to Shri Gagan Malhotra, Director General- CHL International, my old friend and a young entrepreneur based in Dushanbe, the Republic of Tajikistan.

Special mention for invaluable support provided by my dear friend Pervinder Singh, who was a great assistance and helped me in completing and compiling my study.

I am grateful to Smita for her detailed proof reading of the final manuscript.

Emotional support and love of my children and parents are of immense value and source of encouragement.

A special note of appreciation goes to the staff of the Central Library of Jawaharlal Nehru University, Nehru Memorial Museum and Library, Central Secretariat Library, Institute for Defence and Strategic Analyses (IDSA) Library, Indian Council of World Affairs (ICWA) Library, Ministry of External Affairs Library, all in New Delhi, for extending their generous assistance in searching for resource material.

I owe tremendous gratitude to Shri Rajan Arya,who will set the deadline and will always believe that I shall honour it. He also happens to be my publisher.

AMIYA CHANDRA

Preface

Time changes, and so do many things with time. When you look back through the mirror of time, you are able reflect upon and see, what all has been left behind and who all were travelling besides you on the same long journey. It is also time which substantiates to a man, who all has surged miles ahead of him, leaving him behind, and yet the destination is not in sight, it is only time which will again tell who reached the destination completing their long journey. As a student of history and foreign trade, it is important for me to reflect upon the trade relationship between India and the five Central Asian Republics namely Kazakhstan, Tajikistan, Turkmenistan, Uzbekistan and Kyrgyzstan. It's been over quarter of century when the five nations gained independence in 1991 with the collapse of Soviet Union. Since 1994, when I was actively involved in establishing and improving India's trade relationship with relatively very young Central Asian nations, my keen interest and desire has been to see the cultural, political, economical and trade relationship to flourish to its real potential. "The Great game", which was once being played out between the colonial British and Russia, to control the fate of Central Asia is now being re-played as the "New Great Game", between Russia and China with the same objective.

Since 1994, it's been twenty three years, and it is very painful to note that despite sustained excellent rapport at top political level and mutual respect for each other, the trade relationship between India and Central Asia Republics is still at miniscule level. The challenges and obstacles are yet to be overcome. Whereas China has surged way ahead in establishing their trade relationship, so much so that it is one of the important external factor in Central Asia. India's trade share is around 1% of the overall Chinese trade share with Central Asia. Many of the challenges that India faced are genuine as geo-political events as well as geographical barriers hampered the growth of trade relationship. Yet two decades time and yet we are nowhere close to our trade objectives and still at discussion stage, leaves a big question mark.

The previous edition of this study, "India-Central Asia Relations, The Economic Dimension" published in 2015 delved into the economic dimensions of the India- Central Asia relations. The completion of research study and compilation for the book was undertaken in year 2014, and it was finally published in 2015. Two years later, it gives me satisfaction that my previous edition was well received and acknowledged. During the last two years I have received many comments from the readers, largely in appreciation and few pointing out discrepancies that they brought to my notice and few critical of my study. I very humble accept all their comments & views and also thank my critics to whom I may not whole heartedly agree, though I admit they inspired me to view my subject from many other perspectives and it helped me while revising my last edition into this new book. Many major events also occurred in the last two-three years, which are surely to influence the trade relationship between India & Central Asia republics. One such important event has been election of Shri. Narendra Modi as the Indian Prime Minister, he has wholeheartedly extended his support and instructed for urgent action on resolving all pending issues and increase pace of trade negotiations and engagement. India also became a full member of SCO during his tenure. The other key events have been election of President Trump as the American President, Brexit and Launch of China's One Belt One Road initiative and re-elevation of Russia as a power center.

The interest of the US and the EU is driven strategically from the standpoint of energy and security. Though EU is one of the three largest trade partner of the Central Asia Republics, but that is mostly driven by the import of Hydrocarbon & Gas, which they import. The Brexit event is not going to be adversely impacting India's relationship with central Asia. Similarly Trump is following his election rhetoric of America First and he has moved miles away from the Globalization and Free Trade policy that was followed by the US until now. He has chosen to follow more protectionist and more America centric trade policies, which rules out the US playing any dominant role in Indo-Central Asian trade relationship. Though for now the US is still committed in Afghanistan and still has strategic interest in Central Asia, but that interest is again driven by security reasons, rather than economic or trade reasons. The rise of China trade and its OBOR initiative is one of the factors which have an impact on the ambitions of India with respect to Central Asia. China and Russia are engaged in the" New Great Game ", in Central Asia and trying to edge out the other from retaining their control and clout over Central Asia. With all these new developments, the idea occurred to me to revise my previous edition and view them from the event occurred in immediate history. It also provided me the opportunity to add one whole new chapter (Chapter Nine) to my previous edition on key actionable recommendations to build upon the lost opportunities. The chapter suggests a shift from existing approach so that the trade relationship can be meaningful. It is not to suggest that we abandon the existing initiatives altogether, what it does is suggest is a shift.

The study is my tribute to the people working tirelessly towards improving India Central Asia trade relations and to those who are assigned the responsibility of taking this forward. The book is purely from an academic pursuit and a personal attempt to share and contribute my personal insights. It has no relationship with professional or official positions held. The suggestions, comments, recommendations are personal and do not reflect the official stand of the Indian Government or any of its department.

Apart from my own personal experience and understanding gained through multiple extensive tours and travel into Central Asian heartland, I have studied the research and study material available on online digital platform as well as in print form, through books & journals. I have tried to list references wherever I have referred the works of other. The same has been done purely to substantiate a point of view. The critique is also based on personal assessments and understanding, from a positive viewpoint to understand the gap. If any reference is omitted or there is a discrepancy it is purely unintentional and regrettable from my end. The sole purpose of this book is to initiate a dialogue, discussion and debate on suggesting & finding new direction for Bilateral trade development and creating a strong foundation for economic & commercial engagement between, India and Central Asia Republics.

Disclaimer: *The maps and the graphics are referred from many of the international secondary data, and it is inserted in the book to present a visual depiction of routes, etc. and not the actual national boundaries. The maps may be inaccurate and may not to the scale in terms of their international boundary demarcations. Any inconsistency, divergence or discrepancy in visual representation map is regrettable and unintentional.*

Map of Asia

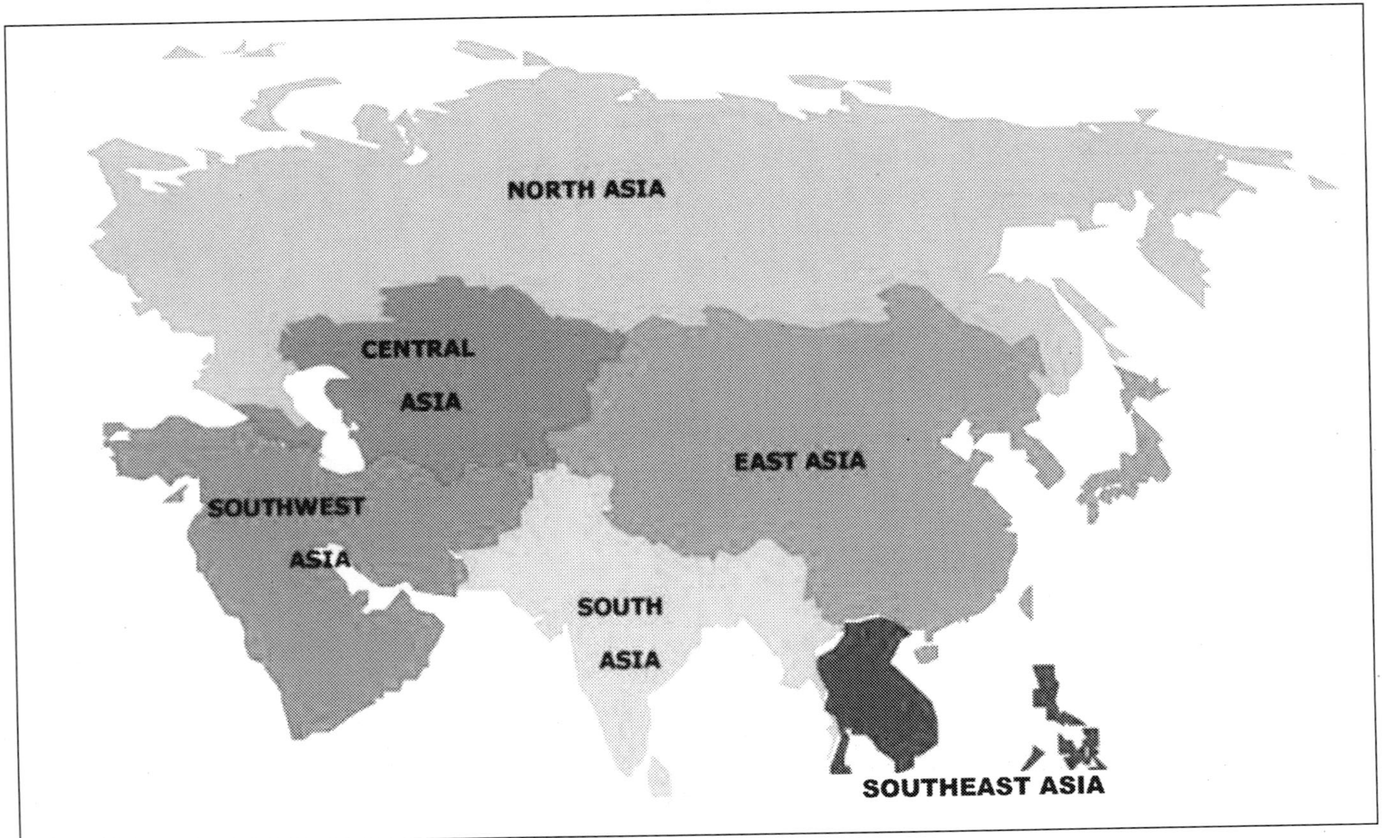
NORTH ASIA
CENTRAL
ASIA
EAST ASIA
SOUTHWEST
ASIA
SOUTH
ASIA
SOUTHEAST ASIA

Introduction

The Central Asia in its modern avatar came to life in 1991 with collapse of the USSR, until then the five Central Asian nations—Kazakhstan, Kyrgyzstan, Tajikistan, Turkmenistan, and Uzbekistan—were all part of the United Soviet Socialist Republic (USSR). The Central Asian Countries collectively cover a territory of approximately 4 million sq. km, with mixed population of around 53 million. It borders Iran and Afghanistan to the South, China to the East, Russia to the North and Caspian Sea to the West. The Central Asian region is the largest landlocked region, with no access to any of the major ocean and is dependent on Russia, China, Iran and other nations to provide it access to warm ports. The birth pangs were painful for these five Central Asian Republics (CARs), and they initially faced a severe economic downturn. The Central Asian countries were forced to create foreign trade ties with other countries since self-sufficiency in production of goods and services, which were established in the USSR, had collapsed. Coincidentally, India too initiated its economic liberalisation and globalisation policies in 1991. India was one of the first few countries to recognize these new nations and till date has an excellent political relationship and considers them as its valuable extended neighborhood.

Sharing their centuries-old historico-cultural, spiritual and civilisational linkages, India and Central Asia have experienced close interactions which have manifested through the movement of peoples, goods and ideas, cultural diffusion, exchange of language, literature and technology. Such interactions between the two regions can be traced back to the Kushana period until the end of the Mughal rule in India. During this long historical phase, the Silk Route connecting the two regions not only facilitated their trade links but also helped develop close relations and exchange of ideas among the various countries of Asia, Europe and Africa. Indian traders and travellers extensively used the Silk Route which also served as a channel for intercultural exchanges. Buddhism was transmitted along the

Silk Route by Buddhist missionaries from India who were a major force in spreading the religious ideas and beliefs across the vast Eurasian plains. Intellectual histories of the two regions too suggest that they evolved not in isolation, but through reciprocal cultural enrichment. However, the centuries-old relationship between India and Central Asia got disrupted in the modern period due to the development of European maritime trade as well as colonisation of the two regions by the two mighty empires viz., Russia and Britain, which also caused the eventual demise of the Silk Route. Yet, disruption did not bring an end to their relationship which continued even during the Soviet period.

With Central Asia today being treated as India's "extended neighborhood", the importance of Central Asia to India is now not merely civilisational and historical, but also geopolitical and economic. There are, however, debates among the scholars and experts on the concept of "extended neighborhood". While some of them have projected it as a relatively new addition to India's foreign policy practice and discourse, others have stressed that this concept has been shaping India's foreign policy ever since it got independence. Moreover, in philosophical terms, the concept of "extended neighborhood" is inextricably interwoven into the ancient Vedic ideal of "*vasudhaiva kutumbakam*", which signifies the whole world as one big family. The ethos of "*vasudhaiva kutumbakam*" was perhaps one of the earliest enunciations of the globalist view of foreign affairs and was a pithy condensation of the ideal of one world where developments in one part of the world invariably impact on the other, though obliquely. This sense of interconnectedness of the world and humanity, with its human-all-too-human aspirations is what animates India's engagement with the world, especially with its extended neighborhood.

Such importance of the Central Asian region as India's extended neighborhood came to the fore following the breakdown of the erstwhile Soviet Union and consequently the end of the Cold War which resulted in the emergence of the five Central Asian Republics (CARs) of Kazakhstan, Kyrgyzstan, Tajikistan, Turkmenistan and Uzbekistan as independent political entities with a common cultural heritage. Independence from the Soviet system led these five Central Asian Republics to confront a similar burden of economic problems which each of them have been trying to overcome by using their diverse economic resources. Though these republics have been acknowledged as being endowed with rich energy and other mineral resources, they require heavy investments and technical know-how to develop these resources. Above all, the CARs share common glitches of political instability, terrorism, mutual discord on border delineation, sharing of water resources and problems of landlockedness, etc. These issues have led the CARs to evolve models of developmental strategies suited to their national interests and at the same time, to advance common approaches towards finding such international partners as well as regional and international forums that could help preserve their national interests. The rationale behind carrying out this study on the economic dimensions of India-Central Asia relations emerges out of such changing contexts of post-Cold War international developments in which India till the collapse of the Soviet Union was seen merely as a country that enjoyed traditional, historical and civilisational ties with Central Asia.

The traditional historiography on the Indo-Central Asian studies have been dominated mostly by themes surrounding historical and cultural linkages or have been part of broader Soviet Studies during the Cold War period. In the post-Soviet period too, very few studies have been conducted to explore exclusively the geo-economics involving the two regions owing to their tenuous trade linkages. Such studies have been dedicated to a superficial analysis of India's economic interests in the Central Asian market, particularly the energy requirements, though the primary focus has been on themes involving common security challenges that India faces together with the Central Asian countries, which so far have kept India motivated for its involvement in the region. Nevertheless, these studies have helped in highlighting the existent mismatch between the intentions and rhetoric at the political level, marked by India's cordial political relations with each of the five Central Asian countries. The groundswell of friendly opinion that the people of the two regions cherish together has not been sufficient for India's striving to create a niche for itself in the economic space of the Central Asian region. Such studies have, however, overemphasised the transitional economic problems being faced by the Central Asian economies in the aftermath of the Soviet disintegration. Poor economic development has underrated the positive macroeconomic trends achieved since the early decades of the 20th century as the main structural constraint in working out worthwhile economic relations among the Central Asian countries. The landlocked geographical position, lack of road transportation and difficult market conditions are identified as constant factors that have hitherto acted as insurmountable physical constraints in eliciting Indian private investors' interest in the Central Asian market and vice versa.

Such studies further point to the failures of diverse Indian strategies to seek crucial breakthrough in the Central Asian space and has resulted in an all-round pessimism among the Indian policymakers with regard to the full realisation of the potential benefits of friendly political ties with each of the five Central Asian Republics. They have been critical of not only the tardy pace at which the economic and trade relations have progressed but that whatever its strategic presence in the region has been, it is steadily being squeezed by the presence of other regional and global players i.e., the U.S., China, Russia, Turkey, EU and Pakistan among others, leaving India as a mere fence-watcher. While there is a grain of truth in such arguments, it has unnecessarily hyped fears of the revival of the 19th century "Great Game" power struggle that had been played out by Russia and Britain in the region. Such a scenario wherein the regional players seem to be able to dominate the "weak" Central Asian Republics and may reduce countries like India, with little physical access to Central Asia, permanently to a fringe-player status, this is a hyper-exaggeration of the situation. Evidence shows that the last two decades have been a period of intense political engagement and a constant search for newer ways of economic engagement between India and Central Asia. Some recent academic literature describes India as playing a competitive "New Great Game" in Central Asia, and that it is in competition with the key regional and global powers for resources and influence.

While not sharing the above-mentioned pessimistic outlook, this study argues that India's relationship with Central Asia must be seen in terms of a unique model of political, economic, strategic, cultural and development partnership with a multilateral approach. India is not driven by an exclusive objective of access to resources, but has a more broad-based and balanced approach. The potential that India has points to its steadily rising engagement, not through any "game", but through meaningful political dialogue and economic cooperation with the Central Asian Republics. On the other side, the Central Asian Republics, now being sovereign entities in the new international order in their own right, are no longer facile political entities. These Republics have shown determination to insist upon their autonomy in foreign policy which is amply exemplified in their multi-vectored policy in which several regional and global powers have been given access to natural resources and preferential treatment. Similarly, they have also been quick to reap the benefits of competing interests among these regional and global powers to secure a better bargaining position. Since independence, the CARs have been part of several attempts by Russia to integrate the Central Asian region economically through regional economic and security blocs such as the Eurasian Economic Union (EAEU); previously known as Eurasian Economic Community (EurAsEC) and the Collective Security Treaty Organization (CSTO). Some of them, such as Turkmenistan and Uzbekistan, have maintained distance while asserting their autonomous political will. Likewise, all of them, except Turkmenistan, have preferred to join the Chinese-inspired regional organization, the Shanghai Cooperation Organization (SCO).

There has been an increasingly self-assertive stance among the CARs to pursue their own political and economic agendas. Since the 2000s, all of them have sought to attract investments from various powers that have shown a growing interest in the region. In the last two decades of their existence, the CARs have belied the widely shared pessimism that they would turn into failed states. In the past two decades, countries like Kazakhstan and Uzbekistan have held out and achieved a great degree of political stability and have made significant economic strides. The ever-growing regional economic integration of Central Asia in recent times is a manifestation of the larger global trend that allows it to be seen as a viable economic space in the new economic order. The large-scale strategies as outlined in the US and Chinese versions of the "New Silk Road" initiatives and the North-South Trade Corridor under the aegis of Russia to connect the Central Asian region with the wider world have underlined the growing geopolitical and geo-economic potential of the Central Asian Republics in recent times.

The past twenty years or so, which have seen India carry forward its cordial political relations with each of the five Central Asian Republics following the establishment of full diplomatic relations, have enabled the two sides to not only explore the new areas of economic, commercial, scientific, technological and cultural cooperation but also develop new systems of augmenting mutual prosperity. These have opened new horizons of bilateral and multilateral cooperation between India and the CARs in the 21st century. However, in the light of existing drawbacks in India's economic engagement with each of the five Central Asian Republics, this study makes an attempt to evaluate the extent and pattern of over two decades of their economic and trade ties in order to make a future projection of the ongoing relations. It seeks the Indian policymakers to be aware of the fact that an all-round economic engagement with Central Asia can be an answer to New Delhi's multiple objectives:

(a) To maintain India's positive political influence in the region
(b) To meet India's energy requirements
(c) To enhance and bring better efficiency in Indian manufacturing through strategic material sourcing
(d) To develop new markets for Indian products & services
(e) Mutual prosperity, promoting and strengthening people to people contact

Notwithstanding the above-mentioned objectives & benefits, India's trade with Central Asia has long been constrained by the absence of viable overland transit routes. It is well known that Central Asia lacks sea access. The nearest exit to the sea for the Central Asian Republics is provided by the Arabian Sea, providing a link to the Indian Ocean and from there to the South Asian countries and the western Pacific. In such a situation, Central Asia depends much on its land connectivity. Given the vast energy resources of the Central Asian region and its hunger for development and infrastructure, India, with its proven prowess in capacity-building and training, is uniquely equipped to play an important role in the transformation of the region. But this benevolent intent, as mentioned above, has been constrained by the lack of direct land connectivity to the Central Asian region. The instability in Afghanistan and the reluctance of Pakistan to grant overland access to India have come in the way of fructifying the potential of India's relationship with the region. Since the leaders of Central Asia are aware of the transit potential of their territories and at the same time of the need to secure the shortest and safest access to sea, they have developed a number of transit routes, including a network of oil and gas pipelines, not only to and from Russia but also to China, Europe and South Asia. It is widely believed that the Central Asian Republics can fulfill their dreams of access to warm-water ports if they can connect to India. It is for this reason that 'connectivity' was a key theme of India's "Connect Central Asia" policy launched in June 2012, which outlines New Delhi's re-energised engagement with Central Asia. This revitalised policy envisages cooperation on security issues, continued exchange of high-level visits, improvement of trade and economic engagement with the region and people-to-people contacts. In other words, this is India's connectivity strategy with short, medium and long-term objectives which have been elaborated as follows:

- Under the short-term objective, India is trying to reactivate a shorter, cheaper and quicker route to Central Asia. This is the International North-South Transport Corridor (INSTC) that runs through Iran and was agreed upon by India, Iran and Russia in 2002. The INSTC has been expanded to include several other members, such as Kazakhstan, Kyrgyzstan, Tajikistan, Ukraine and Belarus. The INSTC envisages a movement of goods to and from Mumbai to the Bandar Abbas port in Iran by sea, from Bandar Abbas to Bandar-e-Anzali (an Iranian port on the Caspian Sea) by rail and road, from Bandar-e-Anzali to Astrakhan, a Russian port, across the Caspian Sea by ship and from Astrakhan to other regions in Russia by rail. According to feasibility studies, this route could reduce the time and cost of container delivery by 30–40 percent. This route may provide not just Central Asia but also Russia and the South Caucasus with a viable access to the sea through the territory of Iran. India's bilateral trade with the Central Asian region was just around US$ 1 billion in 2012, which points to the fact that the economic and trade engagement with the region is not commensurate with the potential, mainly due to a lack of direct surface transportation routes. And herein lays the importance of developing the INSTC project, as also the Trans-Afghan Corridors. From India's point of view, the North-South Corridor will help India bypass Pakistan and yet reach out to Central Asia. There are other north–south routes coming up for Central Asia's access to the sea; like the Iran-Turkmenistan-Kazakhstan rail link provide an alternate rail connectivity from western Kazakhstan and Turkmenistan to Bandar Abbas through Gurgan in Iran. This transnational project will provide an impetus to regional cooperation and economic integration of countries in the Eurasian region with the Indian Ocean and Persian Gulf ports.
- A medium-term objective that India is working on focuses on connectivity through the Chabahar port in Iran. This would be beneficial to all those (particularly Uzbekistan), who need warm-water ports as they would get access to the Indian Ocean. A trilateral transit agreement with Iran and Afghanistan is in the pipeline for allowing transit rights of Indian goods through Iran to Afghanistan. During the Indian Prime Minister, Shri Narendra Modi's visit to Iran in May 2016, India signed a trilateral historic deal to develop the strategic port of Chabahar in Iran and agreed on a three-nation pact to build a transport-and-trade corridor

through Afghanistan that could help halve the time and cost of doing business with Central Asia and Europe.

- In the long term, the challenge is the creation of stable and competitive goods and energy supply networks for not just trade but also for the supply of oil from the Caspian Sea, gas from Turkmenistan and hydroelectricity from Tajikistan to India. The viability of such north–south energy supply networks will have to take into account factors of terrain, security and geopolitics. Energy cooperation thus forms an important component of India–Central Asia relations given the richness of the latter's hydrocarbon wealth and the vastness of India's appetite for energy. The Indian public sector companies are in active discussions with Kazakhstan, Turkmenistan and Uzbekistan in the oil and natural gas sector. The fact that the governments of the region have agreed to the construction of the TAPI (Turkmenistan-Afghanistan-Pakistan-India) gas pipeline project is a positive indication of the opportunities ahead, given the growing political will to enter into such cooperation between Central Asia and South Asia. The TAPI gas pipeline project is crucial particularly for India's energy security which, once completed, would provide access to the gas and oil resources of Central Asia. This will not only diversify our energy supply but also benefit Afghanistan and Pakistan and may bring in peace and prosperity to the region. India is also exploring uranium cooperation with the countries of the region and is also considering alternate dream projects, like oil pipelines from Kazakhstan and Russia to India.

As such, energy is an important focus of India's engagement with Central Asia. Indian companies are involved in active discussions with Kazakhstan, Turkmenistan and Uzbekistan for upstream, midstream and downstream activities in the hydrocarbon sector. Kazakhstan, Uzbekistan and Tajikistan are India's declared strategic partners in the region. The former Indian Prime Minister, Dr Manmohan Singh, visited Kazakhstan in April 2011. During the visit, many significant bilateral agreements were concluded, including acquiring a 25 percent stake in the Satpayev oil block, uranium, agriculture, health and IT. The President of Uzbekistan, Islam Karimov, visited India in May 2011 which resulted in the signing of as many as 34 agreements between the government and private entities, apart from issuing of a joint statement on a strategic partnership between India and Uzbekistan. The President of Tajikistan visited India in September 2012, when a strategic partnership was announced. A package of cooperation each on the defence and civilian side was also announced during this visit. India's Minister for External Affairs visited Kyrgyzstan and Uzbekistan in September 2013. However, the visit of the Indian Prime Minister, Shri Narendra Modi to all five Central Asian Republics in July 2015 has been most encouraging as far as the economic dimensions of the India–Central Asia relations are concerned. Significantly, Modi became the first Indian Prime Minister to have visited all five CARs—Uzbekistan, Kazakhstan, Turkmenistan, Kyrgyzstan and Tajikistan—during a single trip. His visit saw the signing of many important agreements and treaties which have further bolstered the India–Central Asia relations.

As regards to connectivity with Afghanistan, India has completed two major projects—the 218 km road project from Zaranj to Delaram in south-western Afghanistan to facilitate a movement of goods and services to the Iranian border and onwards to the Chabahar port; and the 202 km electricity transmission line bringing Uzbek electricity to Kabul. Hence, there is a lot of scope for creating new networks independent of the traditional land routes. In fact, with the entry of Afghanistan into SAARC in 2007, Central Asia is now contiguous to South Asia. This opens up possibilities of Afghanistan becoming a trade, transportation and energy hub linking together the countries of the region from Central to South Asia. The situation in Afghanistan post-2014 is of great concern and, therefore, it would be sensible if all stakeholders dwell upon common regional solutions through a dialogue on the issue of terrorism and present an integrated developmental economic paradigm as an alternative. The "Connect Central Asia" policy envisages building Afghanistan into an economic hub, connecting Central Asia and South Asia. While hydrocarbon resources form an important component of India's partnership with Central Asian countries, transcending from resource state–client relationships to a partnership for cooperative development would prove to be beneficial in the long run. This is signified by the India–Central Asia partnerships in bilateral investments; science and technology; high-tech sectors such as space application, nuclear energy, IT-related projects, Healthcare etc. along with India's constant endeavor to work towards viable land connectivity between the two regions.

India is engaged with Central Asia through multilateral forums as well. One of the forums through which the Central Asian Republics are tied together is the Shanghai Cooperation Organization (SCO). India was an observer at the SCO since 2005 and had contributed actively within the limited orbit as an observer. India, along with Pakistan, formalized its obligatory process to become a full member of the SCO in July 2015 and in June 2017 both the nations became full members of the SCO. India considers the SCO as an important body for regional economic development and cooperation, to tackle terrorism and drug-trafficking and to engage Afghanistan in a regional solution. India apart from SCO is participating actively in the still evolving Kazakhstan-promoted CICA (Conference on Interaction and Confidence Building Measures in Asia) which is now being pushed by Turkey as well. On the economic side, India has proposed a Comprehensive Economic Cooperation Agreement (CECA) with the Russia-Belarus-Kazakhstan Customs Union to further integrate into the region's multilateral processes like the Eurasian Economic Community (EEC) and the Eurasian Customs Union (EACU).

Trade and investment are not the only connections that India is seeking in Central Asia. Expanding the India–Central Asia development partnership programme in the region has allowed India to share its nation-building experience with its extended neighbors. Over the last two decades, India has completed projects in Central Asia on food processing, potato processing, renovation and up gradation of hydroelectric power plants, computerisation of post offices and setting up a machine tool making unit. It has also set up IT Centres for Excellence in Tajikistan, Turkmenistan, Kyrgyzstan, Uzbekistan and the latest is under way in Kazakhstan. Plans are also afoot for linking Central Asia through e-networking as was done in Africa in addition to delivering tele-medicine and tele-education projects. India contributes to capacity-building and human resource development of the region in a big way. From Central Asia, every year, around 500 mid and entry-level professionals and government officials attend various short-term courses in India under the ITEC programme. In addition, there are a number of Central Asian students studying in India on scholarships and self-financing basis. Also, under the framework of the Cultural Exchange Programme, a large number of cultural activities are organised in the region. In Kazakhstan, Tajikistan and Uzbekistan, the Indian Culture Centres are very active. Air connectivity between India and Central Asia is no less important. India has now permitted 14 weekly flights between the Indian cities and each of the Central Asian capitals and these are expected to become operational in a sustained way. Today, all five Central Asian capitals are connected to India by the Central Asian airlines. These flights may raise the volume of people-to-people contact and business opportunities. Besides, in order to remove all barriers to travel by tourists and businessmen of the two regions, India has been working to liberalise the visa regimes between the two sides.

In the current scenario, what one could find is that the salience of Central Asia basically flows from geopolitics. Today, the region is stable and has not been touched by the sort of turmoil as is being seen in the Middle East; hence, giving much credence to dire predictions of a "Central Asian Spring" might appear to be illogical. Both, the regimes and the people of Central Asia are strongly secular, though the forces of religious fundamentalism and terrorism now reside in the southern periphery of Central Asia thus posing a continuous threat to the stability of the regimes. The Central Asians have their own version of democracy with leaders and ruling elites being in place since 1991. The only exception perhaps is Kyrgyzstan which has chosen the path of a parliamentary democracy, apparently inspired by India. The absence of succession plans does threaten stability in other Republics, but the leadership seems to be capable of handling the situation. Each of the five Central Asian Republics has followed its own path of development in the last two decades. Kazakhstan has been served well by its Caspian oil and President Nazarbaev's vision of prosperity, while Turkmenistan has made good use of its gas reserves, sending pipelines in all directions. Uzbekistan has seen limited prosperity, while Tajikistan and Kyrgyzstan have been vulnerable due to the absence of hydrocarbon resources. India has been cooperating with Central Asia on security and counter-terrorism issues and has an interest in the development and stability of the region in order to make sure that fundamentalism and religious extremism do not find root in the region. India is also concerned about the use of the Central Asian region for transit by narco-traffickers and narco-terrorism, and has instituted Joint Working Group Mechanisms on Counter-Terrorism with Kazakhstan, Tajikistan and Uzbekistan, which meet regularly to share information, concerns and perceptions on this issue.

There are a number of Joint Commissions, Joint Consultative Groups, Inter-governmental Committees, Joint Working Groups that provide the necessary synergy and strength to the India–Central Asia relationship. The relationship has now been upgraded to a strategic level with at least three of the five Republics of Central Asia, i.e., Kazakhstan, Uzbekistan and Tajikistan. Essentially, New Delhi's discourse in the past twenty years or so has been to accord 'centrality' to India's relationship with Central Asia, which is its extended neighborhood. There has also been a commonality of views across the political spectrum. In 2002, the then Prime Minister, Shri Atal Behari Vajpayee, had stated at the CICA Summit in Almaty that it should not only work towards working of confidence building measures

(CBMs) to fight terrorism, but "should actively promote economic cooperation, cultural interaction and people-to-people contacts". In 2006, the then Prime Minister, Dr Manmohan Singh, during his visit to Uzbekistan said that it was "to build on our traditional ties in providing them with new meaning and substance in the political, economic, defence, energy, science and technology and cultural-fields". The ultimate aim was to transform the traditional friendly ties into a new relationship as present-day leaders seek "peace and prosperity" for the people of India and Central Asia. The same thoughts were again echoed in 2008 by the then External Affairs Minister, Shri Pranab Mukherjee, at an International Conference, when he stated that it was India's endeavor "to deepen and broaden India's engagement with the region and make it more purposeful, productive and mutually beneficial for both the sides". Several such statements by other dignitaries have followed suit in recent years. The common element that runs through these statements is that India is for a friendly and cooperative partnership with Central Asia, which is of a multifaceted nature encompassing all areas of mutual concern. In June 2016, Prime Minister Modi visited Uzbekistan and attended the SCO summit in Tashkent. At the summit, India signed the SCO's Memorandum of Obligations, thus kick-starting the process of its accession into the grouping as a full member. On June 24, 2016, during his speech at the SCO summit, Mr Modi said that India would significantly benefit from the grouping's strengths in energy and natural resources and in turn, India's strong economy and vast market could drive the economic growth in the SCO region. "India's membership of SCO would contribute to the region's prosperity. It would also strengthen its security. Our partnership will protect our societies from the threats of radical ideologies of hate, violence and terror," added Mr Modi.

In the backdrop of such developments taking place both in India and the Central Asian region, this study brings in the dilemma of India to pursue opportunities in Central Asia and work on its engagement with each of the CARs at the bilateral and multilateral levels. The study is based on the assumption that India's quest for establishing a strong foothold in the region is likely to depend on the consolidation of its presence until the political situation allows it to get a cheaper and more secure access to Central Asia through the Afghan, Chinese or Iranian territory. The process might take a long time and, hence, requires patience on the part of the Indian players involved. Such an approach may prove to be fruitful, keeping long-term stakes in mind so far as India's engagement with Central Asia is concerned. This assumption is grounded on the premise that by pursuing a "multi-vector" foreign policy, all the Central Asian Republics are seeking to avoid an overreliance on any one or a handful of foreign partners to ensure security in their political, economic and strategic fields. Since both Pakistan and India provide more convenient ports for sea-based imports and exports for Central Asia, it leaves ample opportunities for India regardless of China. The study examines some of India's diplomatic achievements in this context that not only showcase India's cordial political relations with each of the five Central Asian Republics but also help improve and open new areas of cooperation, particularly in the economic and trade fields in the 21st century.

This study argues that despite the centrality of the energy issue, the India–Central Asia economic relations now need to be seen through a wider prism that would involve important sectors of each of the CARs' economic development planning: uranium, electricity, hydroelectricity, infrastructure, construction, transport, banking, agribusiness, and above all, the other emerging service sectors, such as the Information and Communications Technology (ICT) sector, healthcare, hospitality, tourism etc. It explores various transportation networks which are likely to propel India into the Central Asian picture in the near future. In doing so, it seeks to arrive at a rationale to understand the new perspectives and orientations of the Indian policy towards the Central Asian Republics as enunciated in the "Connect Central Asia" policy unveiled in 2012.

With the growing profile of India at the regional and international levels, the Central Asian region now occupies a significant place in India's agenda of expanding its bilateral and multilateral ties with the outside world. In such a scenario, the hardest nut to crack is to overcome the crisis that is responsible for impeding the desired extent of economic relations between India and Central Asia, though geo-economics has essentially been playing a major role in comparison to geopolitics. It may further be added that apart from energy and uranium resources, Central Asia offers a relatively untapped market for the Indian consumer goods, especially as consumers in the region have little to choose from between the highly priced imported Western products and cheap but lower-quality Chinese manufactured goods that have flooded the region. Over the years, the Indian companies have acquired a foothold in some of the sectors of the Central Asian markets such as tea and pharmaceuticals, while the potential for Indian investment and expertise has been identified in the areas of IT, banking, construction and food processing. Besides, the potential for Indian assistance to the Central Asian Republics in developing their small and medium-scale enterprises is immense, in addition to the tremendous opportunity in joint ventures in different sectors especially service sectors. Limited assistance in some of these areas is, however, being provided by India as part of its long-running ITEC (Indian Technical and Economic Cooperation) Programme.

Despite the evident reality of the comparative invisibility of India in Central Asia in comparison to China and Russia, this study further argues that the goodwill and the contacts initiated between India and the Central Asian Republics during the past two decades can still serve as a foundation for fruitful cooperation in the near future by opening new vistas of economic and trade cooperation. Such optimism is also drawn from the fact that despite considerable difficulties in carrying out cooperation in India's trade and commerce with Central Asia, its slow but steady growth provides a basis for the argument that both the inventory and the scope of commodities exported to the region can further be expanded. Moreover, India's growing energy requirements and quest for diversifying its supply routes is bound to keep it looking for an area of cooperation with Central Asia. This study, therefore, debates on what should be done by India to engage itself more actively in the region's economic development.

To that end, this study also seeks to examine the benefits of New Delhi's growing reliance on a more "soft power" approach in recent times that is visible in India's engagement with its South Asian neighbors. India's involvement in Afghanistan and Iran is considered to be closely intertwined with the policy of promoting a cooperative framework in South Asia that is likely to influence its future relations with the Central Asian Republics. It underlines a new dimension to the burgeoning India–Central Asia relations. Enhanced interaction and collaboration between India and Central Asia will contribute to stability and development in the entire Central and South Asian region. The study further brings into focus the extent of India's involvement in major multilateral projects inspired by global powers such as Russia and the US in order to gain access in the region. However, the challenges India has been facing in Central Asia in competing with China on energy issues and Russia on matters of regional security need to be studied in the framework of a policy perspective, which this study has deliberated upon. Nevertheless, what is required today is to look at the possibility of the entire area stretching from Central Asia to South Asia becoming a prosperous economic corridor which would benefit all countries across the region.

The first chapter in this study deals with the evolution of the India–Central Asia relations over the past two millennia with a focus on economic and trade linkages that remained an integral dimension of the entire gamut of engagement even during the Soviet and post-Soviet periods. The main contours of their existing interests in each other have been brought out in the context of the end of the Cold War era following the Soviet collapse and the emergence of the five Central Asian Republics as independent and sovereign entities, the emergence of a new economic order the post-9/11 scenario and the world economic crisis. The shaping of India's strategies towards the CARs to promote economic and trade relations since the beginning of the 20th century has been discussed in the context of the "Extended Neighborhood Policy," the "Focus: CIS Programme" and the "Connect Central Asia Policy".

The second chapter examines the problem of transportation between India and Central Asia with a detailed discussion on the existing routes as well as the various projected routes, especially the North-South Corridor to which India is planning to connect through Iran and Afghanistan in order to gain physical access to the Central Asian Republics. India's engagement with Iran and Afghanistan has been highlighted in order to bring out the emerging scenario of the India–Central Asia relations. It also analyses the competing visions of the New Silk Route being envisioned by the US and China, and India's interest in it.

The third chapter contends with the issue of India's energy security pertaining to the availability of oil, gas and hydroelectric potential in the Central Asian Republics. It also discusses the status of various energy-related projects such as the TAPI project and other feasible options for India in this sector, besides highlighting the challenges being faced by India in harnessing energy resources in the region. In particular, the issues of landlockedness, distance factor, terrorism and the impact of the Chinese presence in the Central Asian countries have been discussed in detail.

The fourth chapter deals with economic cooperation between India and Kazakhstan, the foremost among the Central Asian countries due to its territorial size and abundance of resources. It presents the economic situation in Kazakhstan, highlighting its resource endowment as the emerging regional power. While dealing with the relations between India and Kazakhstan, it focuses on various sectors of economic cooperation between the two sides. Not only the extent and pattern of their growing and diversified interests but also the potential for cooperation in different sectors of their respective economies have been specified.

The fifth chapter depicts the various dimensions of the India–Uzbekistan economic cooperation in the light of the emergence of

Uzbekistan as a self-sufficient economy and as the second largest economy with a resource potential next only to Kazakhstan. Similarly, the sixth chapter provides various dimensions of the India–Turkmenistan economic cooperation with particular reference to the TAPI pipeline project. The viability of the TAPI pipeline vis-à-vis the Iranian gas pipeline has also been dealt with. Whereas, the seventh chapter deals with the India–Kyrgyzstan economic cooperation in the context of a relatively small size of the economy and open market policies adopted by the Kyrgyz government, the eighth chapter is all about the India–Tajikistan economic cooperation discussed in light of the poor economic development of the Tajik state that has primarily been seen as important due to its strategic location and being very close to India's borders.

The ninth chapter offers new perspective and recommends some key solutions for increasing trade between India and Central-Asian nations. It tries to reach out beyond the conventional hurdles that India is facing and suggests new means to come out of it. The final chapter concludes the entire gamut of the economic dimension of the India–Central Asia relations by making an assessment of the extent and pattern of their economic and trade relations in a comparative perspective with a long-term projection of their engagements in the context of India's ongoing "Connect Central Asia Policy". Besides, it also provides a perspective on New Delhi's growing attention to the region as a response to the changing dynamics of the major powers' relations with Central Asia, particularly the increased involvement of China.

1

Evolution of the India–Central Asia Relations

The evolution of the India–Central Asia relations owes much to their historical–cultural relations which have been forged over several millennia, witnessing various phases of vicissitudes since time immemorial. In this course, economic and trade linkages often remained an integral dimension of their entire gamut of relationship. It has been trade that has been the constant and motivating factor, so much so that it was essentially in the wake of trade that cultural interaction came to be established.[1] The underlying dynamism of their overall relations could be attributed to Central Asia's geostrategic location at the junction of two great civilisations—India and China—which proved to be a favorable factor in promoting cultural and economic linkages between the two regions.

Historical Background

The earliest evidence of the people of India and the Central Asian region being in close contact can be traced back to the late third millennium B.C. The archaeological evidence suggests that the Bronze Age people of Bactriana-Margiana Archaeological Complex (BMAC) covering parts of the Central Asian countries had had trade contacts with the people of the Indus Valley Civilisation. Such evidence has been derived from the site study of Altyn Depe, a Bronze Age culture of Turkmenistan, where artifacts of the late Harappan period have been found.[2]

During the second millennium BC, such interactions took the form of a large scale Aryan migration from Central Asia to the Indo-Iranian region.

As a result of this migration, a major development that took place in the Indian subcontinent was the introduction of horses which changed the whole perspective of life in South Asia including the political, social, economic and cultural aspects. Most importantly, the horse became an integral part of the South Asian war machinery.[3]

Since the early centuries BC, a major transformation in the economic relations between the two regions took shape with the emergence of the Great Silk Route[4] as a major international overland trade route. The Silk Route provided a powerful stimulus to trade in Asia by connecting the nomadic civilisation of Central Asia with the contemporary sedentary civilisations of China in the east, India in the south and the Parthian and the Roman Empires in the west. The Silk Route was essentially a web of routes linking Asia with Europe with three main branches: northern, southern and central. It was the southern branch of the Silk Route passing through Afghanistan near the Hindu Kush that connected India with Central Asia and China on the one side and Persia on the other.[5] the Strategically located Takshashila (now in Pakistan) and Purushpura (near Peshawar in Pakistan) on either side of the Sindhu (Indus) river were connected with the Indian trade routes on the Indian side and the Central Asian trade routes on the other. It was Takshashila, the capital of Gandhara, which was the terminus of several inland routes and the starting point of the great trade routes connecting India and Central Asia.[6]

In due course, many branches of the Silk Route emerged connecting Central Asia and India in diverse ways. The oases of Central Asia, Bukhara and Samarkand, were, however, the centres from which the feeder routes branched out. Historical evidence shows that the territory of present Kyrgyzstan existed in the ancient period with a territory in common with eastern Turkestan, and it was the place where the evidence of Buddhism and its roots were identified during the 2nd and 4th centuries AD. It is known from numerous sources that the earliest Central Asian tribes like the Sogdians, Juchis, Parthians, Khanguis, etc., settled along the route to the east. Indian merchants and traders traversed long distances along the Silk Route via Turkmenistan and the 'woollen silk' Caspii region (the Caspian region) to reach Kolkheti on the Black Sea (now in Georgia). Among the prized commodities in great demand by the nomadic tribes inhabiting Central Asia were the Chinese silk, Indian ivory, Syrian glass and Roman metal ware.

From the first BCE to second CE, a number of nomadic tribes such as the Sakas, the Parthians and the Kushanas migrated towards India leading

Figure 1.1: The Great Silk Route

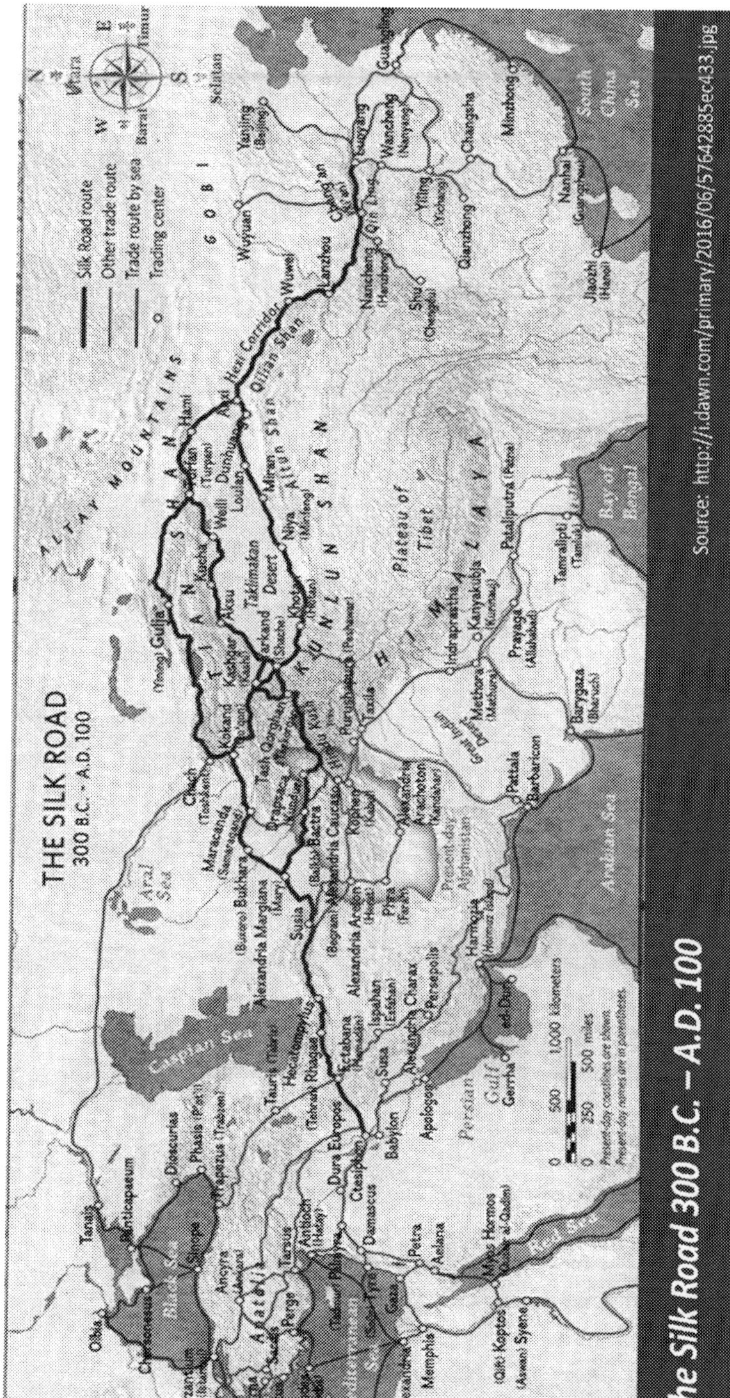

to the establishment of a number of polities in India. The establishment of the Kushana Empire over vast zones of Central Asia, Afghanistan, Pakistan and northern India was a landmark event since a unified political basis to the India–Central Asia relationship came into being for the first time. The political unification of the two regions was closely followed by an impetus to trade and cultural amalgamation between the two regions. The Silk Route not only stimulated commercial interactions but also acted as the conduit through which Buddhism was able to penetrate Central Asia and from there reached China. The process of synthesis is best exemplified in the artistic traditions of the Gandhara School of Art. The patronage to the Mahayana form of Buddhism by the Kushana rulers led to its immense popularity in Central Asia.

The development of the Gandhara School of Art resulted in the establishment of numerous monasteries in the region. They reveal the deep impact of Buddhism as well as the fine craftsmanship that existed in the ancient past. A twelve-meter-long sleeping statue of the Buddha in Tajikistan or the massive statues in Bamiyan in Central Afghanistan (destroyed by the Taliban in the year 2000) or the various historical sites discovered in the former North-West Frontier Province of Pakistan are part of the priceless heritage of humankind. Huien Tsang, a famous Chinese pilgrim, came to India in 631 CE via the Central Asian route and stayed in Kashmir for fifteen years, studying the scriptures and other Buddhist texts.

During the Early Medieval period, international trade remained disrupted between the East and the West due to the rise of the Sassanian Empire in Persia which had hostile relations with the Eastern Roman Empire. As a result, this period was marked by the diversion of the Silk Route towards the Indian subcontinent. While Buddhism was receding in the sub-continent, Central Asia too came under the influence of Islam which was introduced there by the Arabs.

The medieval period was an important phase in the historical ties between Central Asia and India that saw the Islamisation of Central Asia and launch of a series of Turkic invasions into India leading to the establishment of the Delhi Sultanate and a number of Muslim kingdoms in various parts of India. These political developments closely bounded India to the Islamic world of which Central Asia too was a part. Trade and economic relations were revived and strengthened between the two regions on a vigorous basis as a result of the different lifestyle and tastes of the new power elite that saw many Central Asian innovations finding their way to India such as the introduction of paper, treading wheel for weaving clothes, use of lime and mortar in construction activities, use of geared wheels in irrigation and so on. These innovations gave a fresh lease of life to the trade and urbanisation processes in the Indian subcontinent that reached their climax under the Mughals. During this period while the major items of Central Asian exports were horses, sheep, gold, silver, precious stones, metals and fruits, particularly dried fruits, the prominent items imported from India were sugar, cotton cloth, namda (woolen carpets), shawls and dyes. Many Central Asian rulers such as Timur brought masons and artisans from India to work in his own capital city, Samarkand. The expansion and diversification of the caravan trade and the Silk Route also gradually led to the emergence of a large Indian diaspora in the Central Asian region which kept on burgeoning till the advent of the British rule in India.

In 1526, Babur, hailing from Fergana, laid the foundations of the Mughal Empire in India. But, it was under his grandson Akbar that large parts of India were unified. By this time, the significance of the Silk Route trade had been realised by the rulers of Central Asia, as in the wake of the domination of maritime trade by the European countries, the Mughals of India, the Safavids of Iran and the rulers of Central Asia tried to dominate overland trade by encouraging a caravan trade across their borders and by giving favorable terms to the traders and merchants involved in inland trading.

During the Mughal period, the number of Central Asians living in the Indian subcontinent whose exact number is not known and is said to have greatly expanded to explore economic opportunities resulting from the prosperity of Mughal India. They lived in separate quarters, or *Mahallas*. Many of those who arrived were men of letters and came to occupy high positions in the royal courts. There were artisans and craftsmen whose most visible contribution lay in architecture. It was the Central Asians living in Kashmir who introduced the art of tailoring and embroidery, which changed the economic life of Kashmir. Finely embroidered shawls from Kashmir were in great demand among the Central Asian nobility.

Since the late 18th century, even as the mighty Mughal Empire in India was crumbling, paving the way for British colonialism in the subcontinent, the Central Asian region was similarly being brought under the Tsarist Russian Empire. Relations between the two regions henceforth, became more and more subject to strategic considerations of the two imperialist powers which vied with each other for a strategic leverage in the region which was famously known in the late 19th century history as the *"Great*

Game". The Great Game was essentially an imperialist political rivalry between Britain and Russia to control the resources and expand their influence in Central Asia and Afghanistan. These rivalries saw the Russians expand their control over Central Asia and orient their economies towards the north as the Central Asian cotton was essential for the textile factories of Moscow and St. Petersburg. Tashkent became the hub of transport routes going in the northern direction. The British in turn constructed the port cities of Bombay, Madras and Calcutta, thus orienting Indian trade by the sea route. Adding to this distancing was the changing language education in both the regions. While the British introduced English, the Tsarist Empire promoted education in Russian. In the process Persian, a common language, the root of centuries-old cultural links, was marginalised. These policies eventually led towards a complete dislocation of the Silk Route, severing to a large extent the centuries-old Central Asia and India's economic relations. A perceptive observer notes, "More important was the fundamental change they managed to mold into the minds of the people as a whole".

In spite of the caravan routes and camel traffic along the Silk Route that had begun to grow increasingly in operation, Bukhara, a commercial hub on the Silk Route, had 200 caravan-sarais and the Indians had been allotted one such sarai for their use. In 1832, Alexander Burnes noted that there were about 300 Hindus living in Bukhara. They were chiefly natives of Shikarpur in Sindh (Pakistan) and their number had increased over the period.[7] Besides the trading activity; the Indians were also engaged in moneylending and exchange. Apart from Bukhara, the Indian settlers were found all along the towns and cities on the Silk Route. Incidentally, in the ancient period, the ruling dynasty of Khotan (China) claimed an Indian origin. A large number of Indians were also found settled in Andijan, Fergana, Namangan as well as in small towns and villages of Central Asia. The Guide Book of Turkistan published in 1903 in St. Petersburg mentions the names of ten main trading firms of Andijan—two of which, Ramby Pasha and Ramsu Sufa—were Indian firms engaged in silk trading. According to archival materials, there were six Indians engaged in the bread and fruit business even in a small place like Khozhent (Tajikistan). Near Tashkent, there were nearly forty Indians actively engaged in trading activities who have left a valuable source of information. Many of the Indians were owners of land and horses.[8] In 1901, there were fifty-two Indians in Kokand while in Namangan and Osh there were twenty-eight and four Indians, respectively. Indian settlers also built viharas, and left behind texts, caravans and gardens. India's trading activity with the region suffered a setback with the opening of sea commerce and the rise of British colonialism in the subcontinent. Nevertheless, things changed during the first half of the 19th nineteenth century when the Silk Route trade got a "Modest renaissance" in Central Asia.[9] It is estimated that in the second half of the 19th century, there were approximately eight thousand Indian settlers in the region.

The Soviet period in the Central Asian history saw a revival of the Central Asia–India relations. During the Soviet period, the Central Asian region was organised into five autonomous Republics on the basis of its ethnic composition which gave a new identity to each of them. Under the Soviet system, each of these Republics theoretically had powers to secede from the Union, but practically these Republics were autonomous provinces under the tight control of Russia whose foreign policies were directed through Moscow. Central Asia, which bordered British India, was rendered apart from India since the time of its independence as the subcontinent was partitioned by the British into two nation states before they left. The creation of Pakistan in the north-western part of the subcontinent, having turbulent relations with India, greatly affected India's relations with the Central Asian countries. Even so after independence, due to its non-aligned foreign policy and leanings towards socialism, India had been among the few countries outside the socialist bloc to maintain close ties with the former Soviet Union which gave it a chance to interact with the five Central Asian Republics. However, these relations remained indirect, mediated through the Soviet government.

The Contemporary Period

As the five Central Asian Republics gained independence in 1991, a new opportunity opened up for them to forge relations with the wider world. After an initial period of economic crisis, the Central Asian Republics, in order to achieve economic stability, domestic democratisation and preservation of their newly acquired independence, adopted multi-vectored foreign policies to choose their international partners, while in the economic sphere they chose different degrees for opening of their economy. Within this framework the Central Asian Republics have attempted to forge diplomatic relations with India, in order to rejuvenate their age-old historical and cultural relations, which at the same time are tuned by a desire to meet the new contemporary imperatives.

The Regional Integration Process in the Central Asia–CIS Region

The mutual dependence and complementariness of the economies of the former Soviet Republics which form a part of some of the strong legacies of the Soviet system have been witnessing a revival since the beginning of the 21st century. This is so because since 1991, although most of the Central Asian Republics have strived to diversify, they still cannot find a demand for their products outside the former Soviet space except for its natural resources. In many cases, diversification has resulted in a trade deficit and huge indebtedness. These have forced them to restore to some extent the old Soviet division of labour to reach a level of competitiveness. The reason is that Russia continues to be a major trading partner for many of these Republics, and, therefore, removal of barriers for the movement of goods helps their products access to the Russian market. The process of a regional economic integration has been revived in the background of denial of the WTO membership to many CIS countries including Russia, as well as restrictions imposed by Kazakhstan to limit their access to the global markets.[10]

In October 2000, three countries of Central Asia, Kazakhstan, Kyrgyzstan and Tajikistan along with Russia and Belarus signed an agreement setting up the Eurasian Economic Community (EurAsEC) in Astana. A major aim of the exercise was to create a stronger economic bloc. The members of the Eurasian Economic Community pledged to form a common foreign trade border, create a unified foreign economic policy and collectively regulate export–import tariffs and prices. The new organisation will also work towards the establishment of common customs, fiscal, monetary and employment policies.

The EurAsEC was a regional organisation between 2000 and 2014 and was the first attempt to create a common economic space. It sought to create a free trade zone and help member countries during a crisis situation. The effort took a giant leap when eight CIS Prime Ministers—from Russia, Armenia, Belarus, Kazakhstan, Kyrgyzstan, Uzbekistan and Turkmenistan —agreed to be part of the EurAsEC after further consideration. Under the Agreement, import and export duties on most categories will be eliminated, although there would still be some exceptions. During the 14 years, the EurAsEC implemented a number of economic policies to unify the community. Uzbekistan joined the community on the 7 October 2005, however later withdrew on the 16 October 2008 without assigning any official reason for its withdrawal. On 10 October 2014, an agreement on the termination of the Eurasian Economic Community was signed in Minsk after a session of the Interstate Council of the EurAsEC. The Eurasian Economic Community was terminated from 1 January 2015 in connection with the launch of the Eurasian Economic Union.

Another regional integration effort was through the Common Economic Space or the Eurasian Custom Union that included Russia, Belarus and Kazakhstan. On January 1, 2010, the three countries launched the Custom Union, which finally came into existence in January 2012 after the three members fine-tuned their national custom legislations in accordance with the agreed document. As a second stage of the process, the Customs Code was signed in July 2010. The Customs Union foresees a single trade procedure in relation to the three countries. The objective was to create a Common Economic Space by 2012 with the freedom of movement of services, goods, labour and capital.

The Customs Union created a common market of 170 million people with a US$ 2 trillion economy, US$ 900 billion trade and 90 billion barrels of oil reserves. It created opportunities for all the participating countries. An easy access to technology and markets, a potential for diversification to manufacturing and infrastructure development were some of the general gains. For the Central Asian countries like Kazakhstan, this was likely to help benefit its agricultural and automobile sectors, and the nascent airline industry in Belarus and Kazakhstan can gain from the Union. In the short term, the Russian farmers could suffer due to competition from Belarus and Russian steel producers from Kazakhstan, but the single economic space will lead to better competitive sectors and diversification away from dependence on natural resources.

Kyrgyzstan and Tajikistan have shown willingness to join the Customs Union despite the fear of losing out on their main advantage, i.e., low import tariffs. Apart from the political and strategic attraction of joining the Union, both these countries also send a large number of labour migrants to Russia and Kazakhstan. Being part of the Union would facilitate labour movement, which will benefit Kyrgyzstan and Tajikistan immensely.[11]

Yet another regional integration process is the Eurasian Economic Union (EAEU) which is an economic union of the states of Armenia, Belarus, Kazakhstan, Kyrgyzstan and Russia which introduces a free movement of goods, capital, services and people and provides for common policies in the macroeconomic sphere, and in the spheres of transport, industry and agriculture, energy, foreign trade and investment, customs, technical regulation, competition and antitrust regulations. It was signed in May 2014 and came to force from January 2015. It is anticipated and predicted that the EAEU will have 25 percent growth for its member states GDP by 2030 and will be touching US$600 billion mark. The agreement will give member state citizens access to employment and education across the union.

India in the Central Asian Perception

For the Central Asian Republics, India constitutes an important direction to relate to in their respective multi-vectored foreign policies. India's dominant position in the South Asian region is clearly recognisable due to its sub continental size with land borders touching four out of the seven countries of South Asia viz. Nepal, Bhutan, Myanmar, Bangladesh and Pakistan and sea borders with two countries of the subcontinent viz. Sri Lanka and Maldives. All these countries are members of the South Asian Regional Organization (SAARC) to advance the common cause of their economic development.[12] In terms of the level of economic development and military power, India's position as compared to the rest of the regional states remains of great significance due to its vast population of more than 1.3 billion which makes it a huge export market for the Central Asian products. Due to their similar democratic structure which is buttressed by India's sub continental size and status as a large-sized economy, the new conditions and new correlation of forces in the international relationship has put the country towards a regional and probably a worldwide leadership, which has attracted the Central Asian countries to forge bilateral relations with India.[13] India's role in Central Asia is seen as being important from the point of view of meeting the common security threats arising from the changed geopolitical situation in the periphery of the two regions. Since most of the regional and global players' role is viewed with a degree of suspicion by the Central Asian countries for their national security due to their competitive political interests and prescriptive political approach, India's more peaceful, cooperative and understanding approach towards the Central Asian regimes has led them to view its engagement within the region more in terms of a balancing factor.[14]

While the Central Asian economies are still in the process of an economic and political transformation, which are moving forward at varying paces, the process of economic liberalisation was also initiated in India in 1991 coinciding with the start of the economic reforms in Central Asia that has yielded more positive results. As a result of these reforms, the Indian economy has grown at a stable rate without any drastic fluctuation, especially since the late 1990s. Apart from its expansion, the Indian economy had also diversified significantly during the last decade. Given its strong forex reserves, India is in a position to undertake huge investments.[15] From the perspective of the Central Asian countries, it constitutes not only a vast and growing market, but is also a competitive source of technology and knowledge-based services.[16] Countries across the globe are beginning to see India as an indispensable economic partner and seeking mutually rewarding economic and commercial links with its emerging economy. In recent years, its trade relation with the US and the European Union (EU) has increased in absolute terms. However, as a percentage of India's total trade, trade with the EU and the US has declined in the last decade. In comparison, there has been a rapid integration of the Indian economy with Asia, which has been reinforced by India's Look East policy that was initiated in the early 1990s. This is clearly evident from the figures of the India–China trade (with an average growth rate of 53 percent per year in 2004–2008), as well as the trade between India and the ASEAN (Association of South East Asian Nations) states, and the countries of the Middle East.[17]

Despite some serious challenges such as energy security, poverty, infrastructure, regional disparities and internal security, there are indications that a rapid growth of the Indian economy will continue in the near future. At the same time, it is also becoming quite clear that India, along with China and Japan, will be playing an important role in driving the Asian economy. However, India's economic moves will not be effective if its economic relations with the Central Asian region remain marginal.[18]

As a result, the diplomatic ties with India were restored by each of the CARs within a year of proclamation of their independence. Each of the five Central Asian States has developed different degrees of political, diplomatic, defence and security-related ties with India. However the economic relations between each of the five Central Asian countries and India, happens to be a weak link in the overall Central Asia–India relations.

India's Interests in Central Asia

Despite a distinct geographic disadvantage in Central Asia compared to the other regional players such as China and Pakistan, which have borders connecting them with the Central Asian countries, India has been able to establish political and diplomatic ties with each of the Central Asian state in a unique and specific way after their independence. The dynamics of these relationships remain influenced by some common concerns and challenges faced by the region as a whole, as well as in accordance with a proportionate strengthening of the Indian economy, which has allowed it to play a new role as a "stakeholder" in international politics.

From India's perspective, the post-1990s independence of Central Asia is a vastly different geopolitical space compared to the comfortable multifaceted relationship it enjoyed during the Soviet period. The sudden disintegration of the Soviet Union meant a huge loss for India which required a reorientation and restructuring of its policy towards Russia and its successor states and other socialist bloc countries, which came into being on the breakup of the Soviet Union. India felt a new responsibility on behalf of the cultural and historical ties it had had with the region, and also because of its non-aligned tradition that impelled it to renew its ties with the Central Asian states.[19]

Though India was quick to formally accord diplomatic recognition to all the states after the declaration of their independence, the establishment of meaningful ties with these countries was a difficult task. One reason was that during the Soviet era, India did not get much opportunity for direct interaction with the individual CAR republics. However, because of India's cordial relationship with the erstwhile Soviet Union, it was one of the only regional countries to have greater access to the Central Asian Republics and therefore, was expected to enjoy a lot of goodwill in these countries. Even then, this was not an easy task because apart from Russia, China and the United States, other countries of the region including Pakistan engaged themselves in trying to establish their stronghold in the Central Asian countries with some even trying to outmaneuver India.[20] Throughout the 1990s, India's stakes in Central Asia remained far from being projected and were largely confined to security interests.

India's strategies towards the Central Asian region during the 1990s were centred mainly on security issues in view of a number of important developments taking place in its neighborhood. In the post-11th September 2001 phase, Afghanistan emerged as a centre of activities for countering terrorism; the Central Asian Republics' geostrategic position was held to be of great significance. The religious revivalism witnessed in the Central Asian countries after the attainment of their independence got an impetus with the ascendency of the Taliban in Afghanistan which had a direct bearing on Uzbekistan, Tajikistan and Kyrgyzstan. It is widely assumed that the Islamic fundamentalist movement spearheaded by such radical organisations as the Islamic Movement of Uzbekistan (IMU) which threatens the stability of democratic regimes in Central Asian countries are mainly inspired by Taliban. Such groups are allegedly receiving clandestine support from across the border by Pakistan. The narcotics trade and the smuggling of small arms which can prove to be a destabilizing factor in Central Asia, is also a cause of concern.[21]

From India's point of view, Pakistan's search for depth had not ended with the victory of the Taliban in Afghanistan. Central Asia continues to be an important segment where Pakistan is attempting to establish its influence by playing the Islamic card and encouraging radical Islamic movement there and in Kashmir which inherently threatens the regional and national security. The scale of rivalry between the two has also entered a new phase since the nuclearisation of the two countries in 1998. By developing close relations with the Central Asian countries, India seeks to cut the depth of the Pakistani strategic defence and in checking Pakistan from behind.[22] These rivalries notwithstanding, the new geopolitical threat to its security was indeed complicated with the emergence of China as a new economic and military power at the beginning of the 21st century, which has created its huge profile in Central Asia through trade, energy deals, military agreements and SCO, which India is watching wearily.[23] In the post-9/11 phase, the United States has been granted an airbase in Uzbekistan and Kyrgyzstan, while Kazakhstan and Turkmenistan offered refueling and other facilities to the coalition forces. Such developments taking place in close proximity to India are bound to produce a spillover effect for India as well. Therefore, India could ill-afford to ignore these developments in Central Asia.[24]

The security-centric approach of India towards the Central Asia Republics was basically a consequence of its own economic troubles which hampered the growth of a significant level of bilateral economic relations. During the same period, like the Central Asian states, the Soviet disintegration led to a loss of economic support for India which had the former Soviet Union as the largest external trading partner. Consequently, the Indian economy underwent a period of economic crisis during the mid-1990s which was a period full of domestic transformation. Privatisation disrupted trade mechanisms, reduced the role and resources of the state, and altered politics to a new merchant class that wanted a vastly reduced role for the state in decision-making, while the capacity for foreign investment remained low.[25] As recognised by most Indian scholars on Central Asia, New Delhi wanted to "lead the way" for the Central Asian states, but could not help the governments and societies through the worst of the economic collapse that followed the loss of links between the Soviet Republics.[26] Thus, since the early 1990s, India lost the course in Central Asia as the Western multinationals were able to find a way to the Central Asian markets and have still been making frantic efforts for exploiting energy resources of the Central Asian countries.[27]

Since the closing years of the 20th century which saw a resurgence of the Indian economy and India emerging as a nuclear power, apart from security issues, economic diplomacy has gradually become an integral component in the Indian perspective towards Central Asia. The success of India's economic liberalisation and a further expansion of India's economic profile necessitate it to find access to the Central Asian market which in addition to territorial proximity also wields strategic importance in terms of trade routes and connectivity with a wider Eurasia. At a time when a fast-growing economy is fuelling India's energy needs, the country needs to expand and diversify its present sources of supply which are bound to prove insufficient as well as unreliable in the future. In this context, supplies from the oil and gas-rich Central Asia become crucial for 'energy security'. As a source, this area is "the most attractive oil domain outside the Persian Gulf". The region has added geographical proximity to South Asia. There is therefore, "an immense potential for upstream oil and gas companies to invest in exploration and production in the region and to develop it as an alternative to indigenous resources".[28]

Also in this phase of transition, when the Central Asian states' external relations remain focused on trying to strengthen and develop various sectors of their economy, it creates a scope for enhancing bilateral trade and cooperation because of liberalised, growing economies and streamlining of banking operations; the Central Asian countries now need up gradation/modification and are looking for foreign investment and the international organisations are making available funds for revitalising the economy of this region under various schemes. These states are also viewed as an untapped market for Indian investments and export in other core areas such as agriculture, small scale industrial and commercial goods, pharmaceuticals, education and training, IT software, banking, healthcare and hotels.[29] India can be a significant partner through joint ventures in banking, insurance, agriculture, information technology and the pharmaceutical industry.[30] The Central Asian Republics are also extremely rich in mineral resources that need to be tapped, exploited and converted into value-added products. There is a great scope for cooperation in the tourism sector. It is only natural then that India is "trying to befriend the regions' leaders and, if possible, gain a foothold. To support energy security interests in Central Asia, India has already stationed troops in Tajikistan, provided it with a $40 million aid package and has undertaken to refurbish the air base".[31]

Development of India's Central Asian Strategy

In view of some vital issues at stake, India's foreign policy towards the five countries of the Central Asian region has seen considerable recasting over the last two decades. It has been widely acknowledged that such recasting has been concomitant with a degree of pragmatism that the Indian foreign policy has acquired in the post-Cold War era which allows it to give more priority to its national interest over and above the idealistic positioning that was embedded under the Nehruvian socialistic and internationalist position.

In the post-1990 period, India's foreign relations have been envisioned more in terms of widening circles around historical and cultural commonalities across the globe into categories viz. the immediate neighborhood, the extended neighborhood and the global powers.[32] In this framework Central Asia has come to be described as India's "extended" and "strategic neighborhood", underlying India's strong historical and cultural affinity with the region.

Despite India's assertion that Central Asia is part of its strategic neighborhood, its policies were initially not as robust as they ought to have been. India has perhaps been unable to match the expectations in economic terms, but nonetheless, the Central Asian states' stability was of prime concern from the point of view of India's interests in the region. Since the beginning of the 21st century, therefore, following the Look East policy and Look West policy which took care of India's interests in the East Asian countries covered by the ASEAN and West Asia respectively, the Look North policy was envisaged to underline its national interests in Central Asia.[33] Within this framework the declared policy objectives of India in the Central Asian region are: maintaining peace and stability; preventing terrorism; securing energy security; making the region an integral part of the expanded trade network; establishing mutually beneficial economic ties; working for greater regional cooperation and controlling drug trafficking.[34] These goals and objectives of the Indian foreign policy have remained almost constant since the end of the 1990s.[35] The Indian policy, henceforth, has been more consistent and focused with respect to its opportunities, concerns and challenges in Central Asia.

Another significant attitudinal change in the conduct of the Indian foreign policy post-1990s has been a shift from the unilateralism of previous eras to a multilateral approach which has begun to result in a perceptible shift in India's new proactive approach towards Central Asia.[36] This has allowed India to leverage multilateral solutions with regard to conflict resolutions in both India and the Central Asian countries. Such flexibility in India's approach helped it to enhance its footprints across various Central Asian Republics in the beginning of the 20th century. These are reflected in an increased profile of bilateral exchanges between India and its regional partners—Tajikistan, Turkmenistan, Kazakhstan, Kyrgyzstan and Uzbekistan—and which manifest in the progress taking place towards the establishment of a meaningful and mutually beneficial ties. National leaders from the five Republics have been invited on state visits to India and over a period of time there has been a regular flow of high-level visits. There have been wide-ranging bilateral agreements and MoUs on economic, commercial, educational and other issues between India and the five Republics. There are bilateral programmes to promote Defence Cooperation and the training of defence personnel in India. There are inter-governmental commissions which meet regularly; ministerial and official visits are encouraged.[37]

Focus CIS (Commonwealth of Independent States) Programme

Considering the opportunities that the Central Asian region offers and India's insignificant presence in that market, the Focus CIS Programme was launched by the Ministry of Commerce & Industry of the Government of India in 2003 at the time of the announcement of the Exim Policy on March 31, 2003. The programme focused on the countries of the CIS region with emphasis in the first phase on seven countries, namely, Azerbaijan, Kazakhstan, Kyrgyzstan, Tajikistan, Turkmenistan, Ukraine and Uzbekistan. With a view to enhancing India's trade with the countries of the CIS region, including Central Asia, the scope of the Focus CIS Programme was extended further till the financial year 2007–2008.[38] Subsequently, with a view to further enhance India's trade with countries of the CIS region, the scope of the Focus CIS Programme was extended w.e.f. April 2004 to the rest of the CIS region, namely to the Russian Federation, Armenia, Belarus, Georgia and Moldova as well.[39]

Under this programme, the government of India extends assistance to exporters, business chambers, etc., to visit these countries, organise trade fairs, invite trade delegations to visit India and undertake various other market promotional activities. The initiative taken under this Programme received an encouraging response from the Indian trading community to boost bilateral trade with each of the five Republics.

Comprehensive Economic Partnership Agreement (CEPA)

In view of the ongoing regional economic integration processes going on in Eurasia, India attempts to position itself to take advantage of the Eurasian Integration process by working out a Comprehensive Economic Partnership Agreement (CEPA) with each of the Central Asian Republics. CEPA is an omnibus free trade agreement with the Eurasian Customs Union under which both sides cut a large percentage of tariffs on goods from each other. During former Prime Minister Dr Manmohan Singh's visit to Russia in December 2011, talks on this were taken forward. According to press reports in India, the government sources indicated that most of the issues relating to CEPA had been sorted out with Russia. For India, tailoring the CEPA to fit in with Russia's Customs Union with Kazakhstan, by far the largest Central Asian country, and Belarus, will help enlarge the market for Indian entrepreneurs.[40]

At the same time, the Eurasian Union is an opportunity for expanding trade with a much larger region. The Indian goods entering a member country would easily and freely access the markets of other member states. The first step to access the member states has been taken with the transportation links being created. The next step for a special arrangement is being worked out through a Comprehensive Economic Partnership Agreement. If all these materialise in the future, India is surely poised to play a much larger economic role in the Eurasian region.[41]

India-EAEU FTA

It has been proposed to have an FTA between India and EAEU (Eurasian Economic Union). The EAEU's GDP amounted to US$ 2.18 trillion in 2015, whereas India's GDP amounted to US$ 2 trillion with an annual GDP growth of 6 percent to 7 percent in recent years. The total trade basket of EAEU has reduced by 18.7 percent in the last six years. Russia has the largest share, occupying 82.5 percent in the total trade, followed by Kazakhstan with a share of only 10 percent. The exports from EAEU contribute to nearly two-thirds of the trade basket of the EAEU. Comparatively India's export of goods and services worldwide has increased by 46.9 percent since 2010 till 2013, despite the slowdown in global demand. On the other hand, imports also increased by 32 percent.

India's trade with the rest of the world stopped growing in 2013 due to adverse global economic conditions. In the course of the year, imports decreased by 14.9 percent and exports by 15.4 percent.

The bilateral trade between India and the EAEU has improved in the recent years but has remained low. The total trade increased from US$ 9.3 Billion in 2010 to US$ 11.3 Billion in 2014. Though when compared overall, in terms of India's exports to EAEU as a proportion of India's total exports to world or India's imports from EAEU as a proportion of India's imports from the world, the mutual importance between India and EAEU turnout to be low suggesting weak trade linkages. Within the EAEU, the Russian Federation accounts for the highest share of bilateral trade with India followed by the Republic of Kazakhstan. Conversely, the level of trade between India and Republic of Armenia and India and Republic of Kyrgyzstan is low reflected in terms of the trade turnover which doesn't exceed 0.001 percent of total EAEU's trade turnover. India's total exports to the Member States of EAEU stood at US$ 1.8 billion (2016), which is too meager as it constitutes only 0.69 percent of the total export basket of India and has been declining over the last five years. The majority of exports are accounted for by Russia (US$ 1.5 billion) followed by Kazakhstan (US$ 151 million), Belarus, Kyrgyzstan and Armenia. The total imports, however, from the EAEU by India, are higher at US$ 5.1 billion (2016). It also has Russia accounting for the maximum imports (US$ 4.5 billion) followed by Kazakhstan (US$ 352 million), Belarus, Armenia and Kyrgyzstan. It, therefore, appears that the bilateral trade linkages between India and the EAEU are very weak except for Russia and Kazakhstan. Barring Armenia and Kyrgyzstan, India has a trade deficit with the rest of the countries of the EAEU.

The EAEU Member States are the top producers of sugar beet, sunflower, rye, barley, buckwheat and oats. They are also large producers of wheat, potatoes, grain and legumes. Machine, equipment and transport, together with chemicals, are the most buoyant import categories of the EAEU. These two categories along with agricultural products account for almost 80 percent of the EAEU imports. Over the last 5 years, the share of machinery, equipments and transport in the EAEU's exports was declining, similar to its share of fuel and mining products. However, mineral fuels, mineral oil, mineral waxes along with natural or cultured pearls, precious or semiprecious stones, pre-metals, clad with pre-metals, jewelry, coins, etc., are the most buoyant import categories of India. The top four major categories account for more than 80 percent of India's total imports. Natural or cultured pearls, precious or semiprecious stones, premetals, clad with premetals, jewelry, coins along with mineral fuels, mineral oil, mineral waxes, etc. were the most buoyant export categories.

Interestingly, the EAEU member states have immense potential as a market for the Indian seafood. Looking at the bilateral commodity analysis, the major areas of interest for India at present are pharmaceutical products, tobacco, coffee, meat, fish and crustaceans. Although all these products have a majority share in the trade basket of the various member states, pharmaceutical products, especially medicaments, figure in the most traded baskets across all the member states. Hence, to gain a greater market access in the current situation, pharmaceutical products appears to be a good option followed by tobacco, coffee and meat/bovine meat. Nevertheless, there are unexplored markets in this Economic Union which India can take advantage of as a first mover by fully utilising the opportunity provided under the current FTA negotiations.

Expectedly the goods trade within India-Eurasia is anticipated to grow as a direct result of the FTA, which would directly benefit bilateral services trade growth, due to the essentiality of "trade-enabling" services such as logistics, insurance banking & other financial services, telecommunication & IT services, hospitality and other professional services like legal, engineering & architectural services etc. Additionally Indo-EAEU FTA could provide the basis for increasing trade in other areas of mutual interest where strong complementarities exist, such as hi-tech research and development, satellite and space exploration, healthcare & pharmaceuticals, tourism, engineering services, environmental and agricultural services, energy, academic studies, etc. Till now the majority of the bilateral trade in services was conducted between India and Russia, for instance in 2014, accounting for approximately 80 percent of the EAEU exports to India, and almost 89 percent of its services imports from it.

Indian Technical and Economic Cooperation (ITEC)

Since the 1990s, students and professionals from all the five Central Asian Republics have been receiving training through the Indian Technical and Economic Cooperation (ITEC) programme. The success of the ITEC programme can be judged from the fact that more than 3,000 people in the region have taken advantage of the programme since its commencement.[42] Over the years, a positive response to the programme has led India to increase the number of training slots offered to the individual Republics of Central Asia (Table 1.1). Programmes like information technology, management, journalism, diplomacy, entrepreneurial programmes, banking and the service sector programmes have been attracting students and professionals from the CARs. Such engagements with the region through an inflow of Central Asian students and professionals into India can help strengthen ties between the two regions.

Table 1.1: Training Slots offered to Central Asia under the ITEC Programme, 1996–2016

Country	*1996*	*2000*	*2004*	*2012*	*2016*
Kazakhstan	14	80	60	55	40
Kyrgyzstan	9	50	65	60	90
Tajikistan	10	1	100	150	125
Turkmenistan	14	20	32	35	40
Uzbekistan	18	80	109	150	130

Source: Hemant Shivakumar, Persis Taraporevala, Kailash K. Prasad, and Rani D. Mullen (2014), "India-Central Asia Relations: Moving towards Broader Development Partnerships," India Development Cooperation Research (IDCR) Project, Background Paper no. 4, 6 January, URL: http://idcr.cprindia.org/blog/india-central-asia-backgrounder and Embassies Websites for the year 2016.

India's Trade with the Central Asian Republics

Although India's engagement with Central Asia through the ITEC programmes and other scholarships has been a successful story, this has been a futile attempt as far as substantive trade and commercial relations between the two sides are concerned. Trade between India and Central Asia remained lower than US$ 800 million in 2012–13,[43] much below the potential of the two sides , however, in 2013–14, the total trade between the two sides had risen to US$ 1,238 million but it is only with Kazakhstan that the bilateral trade increased sharply (US$ 914.5 million); with the other Republics the trade figures remained more or less the same (Table 1.2). Hence, what one may find is that India's lack of a direct overland access to the region due to Pakistan's unwillingness in letting the Indian goods move across its territory has limited India's trade interests in the Central Asian region as a whole. The trade with the CARs has indeed grown sluggishly from US$ 115 million to US$ 738 million, between 1996 and 2012.[44] However, as shown in Figure 1.2, India maintains a positive trade balance with the CARs and over half of India's trade to the region is with Kazakhstan (55 percent), followed by Uzbekistan (20 percent), Turkmenistan (10 percent), Kyrgyzstan (9 percent) and Tajikistan (6 percent).[45]

Table 1.2: Trade between India and Central Asian Republics (in million US$)

Year	*Kazakhstan*	*Kyrgyzstan*	*Tajikistan*	*Turkmenistan*	*Uzbekistan*
1996-97	16.96	NA	1.53	1.65	10.74
1997-98	51.16	10.80	NA	1.70	20.30
1998-99	50.43	8.80	3.04	2.04	14.50
1999-00	40.64	15.62	4.71	6.02	22.91
2000-01	64.12	22.02	4.09	3.83	19.97
2001-02	53.09	11.53	2.56	6.30	23.80
2002-03	59.61	15.14	8.73	15.69	25.62
2003-04	84.07	38.74	8.42	28.55	42.84
2004-05	96.81	15.20	10.68	26.13	52.81
2005-06	117.16	29.56	12.13	31.18	50.57
2006-07	171.48	37.84	15.41	45.94	63.60
2007-08	188.77	32.43	22.21	45.64	56.52
2008-09	290.71	23.95	34.18	53.50	116.27
2009-10	291.45	27.48	32.56	46.15	84.40
2010-11	310.58	26.99	41.33	35.89	81.05
2011-12	436.25	31.44	30.14	63.41	126.43
2012-13	426.22	37.08	48.02	78.25	156.75
2013-14	914.50	35.13	55.13	87.73	145.57
2014-15	952.35	38.53	58.09	105-03	226.31
2015-16	504.84	26.90	32.24	115.50	139.89

Source: Based on Export-Import Data (1997-98 to 2015-16) collected from Directorate General of Foreign Trade (DGFT), Department of Commerce, Ministry of Commerce & Industry, Government of India.

Figure 1.2: India's Trade with the Central Asian Republics, 1996-2012

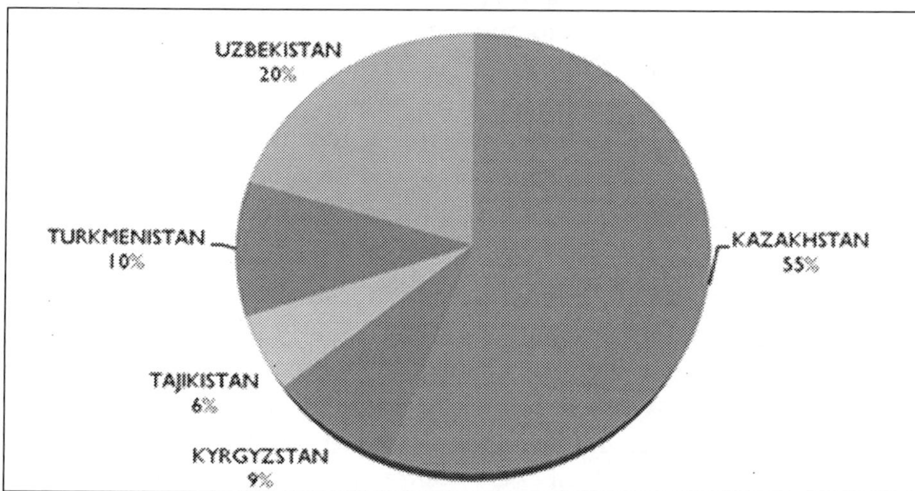

Source: Based on data collected from EXIM Bank 1996-2012, Ministry of Trade and Commerce, Government of India. Data collated and calculated by Indian Development Cooperation Research. See Hemant Shivakumar, Persis Taraporevala, Kailash K. Prasad, and Rani D. Mullen (2014), "India-Central Asia Relations: Moving towards Broader Development Partnerships," India Development Cooperation Research (IDCR) Project, Background Paper no. 4, 6 January, URL: http://idcr.cprindia.org/blog/india-central-asia-backgrounder.

Despite the fact that the volume of the overall Indian trade with the Central Asian region remains low, the evolving tendency between 2008 and 2013 has been that of a sharp rise in the export of Indian pharmaceuticals to the region. Rising at 16 percent annually in the CARs,[46] pharmaceutical products now remain as India's main exports to the region. Retailed mostly as over-the-counter drugs, India fulfills more than 30 percent of the pharmaceutical needs of Central Asia. Indian imports from Central Asia principally include minerals such as zinc, sulphur and limestone. Moreover, India has started importing uranium for its civil nuclear reactors from Kazakhstan under an agreement on Cooperation in Peaceful Uses of Nuclear Energy that was signed in 2011. Until 2013, India was preparing to import uranium from Uzbekistan as well.[47] Undoubtedly, as Figure 1.3 shows, there has been a fall in the Indian imports from Central Asia but exports to the region have been increasing.

Indian Investment in Central Asia

During 2008–2013, not only a low trade volume but also the Indian investments, particularly from the private sector in Central Asia, have remained inadequate—to the tune of just US$ 29 million.[48] So far, the Indian investments in the region have included recreation, automotive manufacturing, pharmaceuticals and power projects. For example, the Indian company Minda Industries LLC has a joint venture with an Uzbek company to manufacture automotive products.[49] In 2011, an amusement theme park "Fun and Food Village" in Tashkent was established by the Polo Group, an Indian enterprise. JPM, an iron and steel manufacturing firm, has been planning to establish a ferrosilicon manufacturing plant in Kyrgyzstan. Similarly, IOT Infrastructure and Services has been negotiating to acquire a majority stake in a Kazakhstan-based company, Kazakhstan Caspi Shelf.[50]

Nevertheless, due to limited private investments, India's trade with the Central Asian region remains low, particularly when compared with the other major regional power, China. China's geographical proximity to the CARs and its aggressive economic clout has helped it emerge as the largest trading partner in four of the five countries in CARs.[51] China has registered an annual trade of US$ 29 billion with the CARs in 2012, ahead of US's trade of US$ 26 billion and Russia's trade of US$ 27 billion with the region.[52] Besides, as already mentioned, India's trade with Central Asia has also been troubled by Pakistan's reluctance to allow the Indian goods to transit through its territory, thereby forcing India to reroute its goods

Figure 1.3: Evolution of India's Trade with Central Asia (Imports and Exports), 1996-2012 (in million US$)

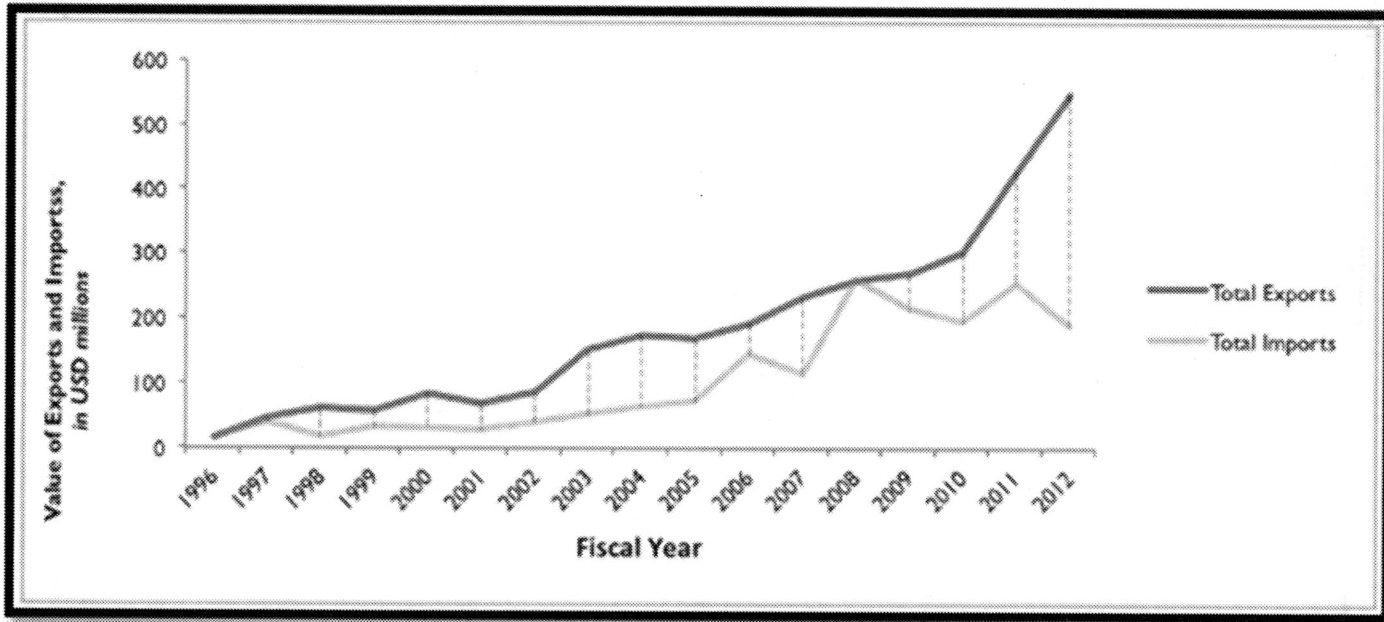

Source: Based on trade data collected from EXIM Bank, Ministry of Trade and Commerce, Govt. of India. Data collated and calculated by Indian Development Cooperation Research. See Hemant Shivakumar, Persis Taraporevala, Kailash K. Prasad, and Rani D. Mullen (2014), "India-Central Asia Relations: Moving towards Broader Development Partnerships," India Development Cooperation Research (IDCR) Project, Background Paper no. 4, 6 January, URL: http://idcr.cprindia.org/blog/india-central-asia-backgrounder.

through Iran and Afghanistan. With a continuous lower volume of India's trade with the CARs, New Delhi needs to chalk out proper plans to have its weight in the region.

Investment in Energy and Pipeline Projects

The intensive economic growth of India in the last two decades is the cause for its growing need for energy resources. This has led India, since the early years of the 21st century that coincides with its rise as an economic power, to take on the political and financial risks inherent in overseas investments. By improving ties with resource-rich countries, India hopes to enhance its energy security. Indian oil and gas companies are thus encouraged to invest overseas and to build strong relations with strategically important countries. A detailed discussion on the above issue in the context of bilateral relations with each of the Central Asian Republics has been taken up in the next chapter.

Reaching out to Central Asia through Transport Linkages

In order to establish a physical connectivity with each of the Central Asian Republics, India has been making a slow but steady investment in infrastructure development projects in Iran and Afghanistan, especially since the beginning of the 21st century and is using various multilateral forums to reach out to Central Asia (Discussed in detail in Chapter 3).

India's "Connect Central Asia" Policy

2012 was a landmark year for India's relations with the Central Asian countries as it marked the twentieth year of the establishment of diplomatic relations with these Republics. It was occasioned by the initiation of a series of policy measures to strengthen India's ties with the Central Asian countries. The then Indian Foreign Minister, Shri S.M. Krishna, formally unveiled the "Connect Central Asia Policy" in June 2012 at Bishkek, Kyrgyzstan. A month later in July 2012, the then Minister of State for External Affairs of India, Shri E. Ahmad, outlined some of the main objectives of the "Connect Central Asia" policy, which are as follows:[53]

- To continue to build on our strong political relations through the exchange of high-level visits on a regular basis at bilateral and multilateral forums.
- To strengthen the strategic and security cooperation with the Central Asian states by forging strategic partnerships with each of them. These strategic partnerships would focus on military

training, joint research, counter-terrorism coordination and close consultations on Afghanistan.

- Step up multilateral engagement with Central Asian partners using the synergy of joint efforts through existing forums like the SCO, Eurasian Economic Community (EEC) and the Customs Union. In the above context, India has already proposed a Comprehensive Economic Cooperation Agreement to integrate its markets with the unifying Eurasian space.
- India also looks to Central Asia as a long term partner in energy, and natural resources. In the agricultural sector, India sees immense potential for cooperation in the production of profitable crops with a value addition.
- The medical field is another area that offers huge potential for cooperation. India intends to extend cooperation by setting up civil hospitals/clinics in Central Asia.
- To help assist in establishing a higher education system in the Central Asian countries that delivers at a fraction of the fees charged by Western universities. In this context, India would assist in the setting up of a Central Asian University in Bishkek that could come up as a centre of excellence to impart world-class education in areas like IT, management, philosophy and languages.
- To set up a Central Asian e-network with its hub in India, to deliver tele-education and tele-medicine connectivity, linking all the five Central Asian States.
- To showcase the Indian companies' capability in the construction sector and build world-class structures at competitive rates. The Central Asian countries, especially Kazakhstan, have almost limitless reserves of iron ore and coal, as well as abundant and cheap electricity. India can help set up several medium-size steel rolling mills, producing its requirement of specific products.
- To reactivate land connectivity, join in the laying of the International North-South Transport Corridor (INSTC). India intends to join efforts to discuss ways to bridge the missing links in the Corridor at the earliest and also work on other connecting spurs along the route.
- To help expand the presence of Indian banks to help create a viable banking infrastructure in the region has proved to be a major barrier to trade and investment.
- To jointly work with the Central Asian countries to improve air connectivity with them. India is one of the biggest markets for outbound travellers estimated at US$ 21 billion in 2011. Many

countries have opened tourist offices in India to woo Indian tourists. The Central Asian countries could emerge as attractive holiday destinations for tourists and even for the Indian film industry which likes to depict exotic foreign locales in its films.

- To help improve cultural relations between the people of India and the Central Asian countries through regular exchanges of scholars, academics, civil society and youth delegations to gain deeper insights into each other's cultures.

Prime Minister Shri Narendra Modi's visit in July 2015 to all the five CARs was a decisive shift from the clichéd iterations of deep historical connections and friendship to a new economic and strategic engagement of India with the region. This was the first comprehensive visit by an Indian Prime Minister since P.V. Narasimha Rao had gone on a goodwill tour of the CARs in 1993 and 1995.

Modi's six-day tour, followed by a visit to Ufa in Russia to attend the SCO-BRICS summit, which confirmed India and Pakistan as full members from 2016, was a fresh unveiling of India as a regional and global power, and was noted by the international media. The visit scripted a new chapter in India's relations with the region, and it was designed to challenge China's dominance. Its key outcome was upgrading the India–Central Asia relations to a new level by expanding cooperation in the trade, infrastructure and energy sectors, making India visible as a neutral third vector, poised to deploy its soft power in a regional geopolitical and economic terrain dominated respectively by Russia and China.[54]

Thus, despite India's weak presence in Central Asia at the end of the first decade of the 21st century, the Indian viewpoint has undergone a reformulation as underlined in the Connect Central Asia policy. The unveiling of the policy is "a grand strategy of engaging with Central Asia. This policy is based on a proactive political, economic and people-to-people engagement with all the five Central Asian countries, both individually and collectively".[55] The policy is hailed to be India's latest broad-based approach that aims to include political, security, economic and cultural connections to expand its level of engagement with the Central Asian Republics. It is in consonance with its overall policy of deepening engagement in Eurasia that would also include measures that would help strengthen relations with China and Pakistan and build upon the traditional relationship with Russia. By launching its broad-based policy of engagement with the Central Asian Republics, New Delhi attempts to demonstrate its readiness for a deep, meaningful and sustained engagement with the Central Asian countries in the immediate context. At the collective level, India also strives to help create a cooperative security structure for maintaining peace in Asia. Through its policy of peaceful coexistence and of playing a constructive and meaningful role in the United Nations (now also as a non-permanent member of the UN Security Council), India also hopes to work with a deep sense of responsibility along with the Central Asian Republics on all global issues. India's engagement in Central Asia, therefore, must be seen in the context of a quest for a world order which is multipolar.

REFERENCES

1. Joshi, N., *Reconnecting India and Central Asia: Emerging Security and Economic Dimensions*, New Delhi: Pentagon Press, 2011, p. 3.
2. Ibid.
3. Ibid.
4. "Great Silk Road" is an agreed name for a trans-continental land road of the ancient period and the Middle Ages.
5. Sarma, A.S., *India and Central Asia: Redefining Energy and Trade Links*, New Delhi: Pentagon Press, 2010, p. 11.
6. Kumar, B.B., 'India and Central Asia: Links and Interactions' in *India and Central Asia: Classical to Contemporary Periods*, New Delhi: Concept Publishing Company, J.N. Roy and B.B. Kumar (eds), 2011, p. 9.
7. Burnes A., *Travels into Bokhara: Being an Account of a Journey from India to Cabool, Tartary and Persia. Also, Narrative of a Voyage on the Indus from the Sea to Lahore*, London: John Murray, 1934, p. 286.
8 Joshi, N., 'Introduction' in *Reconnecting India and Central Asia*, Nirmala Joshi (ed.), 2011. http://www.silkroadstudies.org/new/docs/publications/1004Joshi-IV-Intro.pdf
9. Levi, Scott 'India, Russia and the Eighteenth-Century Transformation of the Central Asian Caravan Trade', in *India and Central Asia: Commerce and Culture 1500-1800*, Scott Levi (ed.), New Delhi: Oxford University Press, 2007, p. 103.
10. Patnaik, A. 'Customs Union: Implications for India', in *Perspectives on Bilateral and Regional Cooperation: South and Central Asia*, R. Malhotra, et al. (eds), Chandigarh: CRRID, 2013, pp. 80-1.
11. Ibid.
12. Mavlanov, I. R., 'Central Asia and South Asia: Diplomatic Potential of Uzbekistan and India for Sustainable Inter-Regional Economic Cooperation', in *India's Engagement with Central Asia with Focus on India-Uzbekistan Relations*, Jyotsna Bakshi (ed.), Tashkent: University of World Economy and Diplomacy, 2007, p. 145.
13. Kasymova, Valentina and Batyrkul Baetoy, 'The Kyrgyz Republic: The Present and Future of Interstate Cooperation in the Energy Sphere', *Central Asia and the Caucasus*, 6(48), 2006, p. 141.
14. Wikipedia, 'India's 'Connect Central Asia' Policy'. URL: http://en.wikipedia.org/wiki/IndiapercentE2percent80percent99s_percentE2percent80percent98Connect_Central_ AsiapercentE2percent80percent99_Policy

15. Mavlanov, op. cit., p. 145.
16. Ibid.
17. Sachdeva, G., 'India's Objectives in Central Asia', School of International Relations, Jawaharlal Nehru University, 2012. URL: *http://uschinacenter.as.nyu.edu/docs/IO/23889/Sachdeva_Abs.pdf* (accessed: 22 February 2013).
18. Mavlanov, op. cit., p. 156.
19. Peyrouse, S., 'Domestic and International Articulation of the Indian Involvement in Central Asia' in *Mapping Central Asia: Indian Perception and Strategies*, M. Larulle and S. Peyrouse, (eds), Surrey and Burlington: Ashgate, 2011, p. 76.
20. Singh, Kuldip, 'Introduction', in *South-Central Asia: Emerging Issues*, Amritsar: Guru Nanak Dev University, 2004, pp. 2-4.
21. Ibid., pp. 2-4.
22. Jiali, Ma, 'Central Asia: Geostrategic Situation and Big Power Policies', in *Contemporary Central Asia*, New Delhi, Vol. iii (i), 1999, p. 45.
23. Sachdeva, G., op. cit.
24. Singh, op. cit.
25. Peyrouse, op. cit., p. 76.
26. Ibid., p. 76.
27. Khaydarov, A., 'Afghan Factor in India-Central Asia Relations', in *India's Engagement with Central Asia with Focus on India-Uzbekistan Relations*, Jyotsna Bakshi (ed.), LBSCIC, CPS, Tashkent: University World Economy and Diplomacy, 2007, p. 34.
28. Brar, B., 'Images in the Mirror: India and 'Central Asia in Transition" in *South-Central Asia: Emerging Issues*, Kuldeeep Singh (ed.), Amritsar: Guru Nanak Dev University, 2004, p. 28.
29. Mavlanov, op. cit., p. 143.
30. Singh, op. cit., pp. 2-4.
31. Brar, op. cit., p. 28.
32. Sengupta, A., 'Perceptions and Strategies: India's Relations with the Central Asian Region' in *Mapping Central Asia: Indian Perception and Strategies*, M. Larulle and S. Peyrouse (eds), Ashgate Publishing Limited, p. 54.
33. Peyrouse, op. cit., p. 78.
34. Singh, op. cit., pp. 2-4.
35. Peyrouse, op. cit., p. 78.
36. Sengupta, op. cit., p. 54.
37. Tayal, S.R., 'Indian Foreign Policy: Engagement with Central Asia', *India's Engagement with Central Asia with Focus on India-Uzbekistan Relations*, Jyotsna Bakshi (ed.), LBSCIC, CPS, Tashkent: University of World Economy and Diplomacy, 2007, p. 6.
38. Mavlanov, op. cit., p. 149.
39. Trade Promotion Programme - Focus: CIS. URL: http://commerce.nic.in/trade/international_tpp_cis_2.asp.
40. A. Patnaik (2013), "Customs Union: Implications for India", in Malhotra, R. et a. (eds), *Perspectives on Bilateral and Regional Cooperation: South and Central Asia*, CRRID: Chandigarh, India, p. 87.
41. Ibid, p. 86.

42. Shivakumar, Hemant, Persis Taraporevala, Kailash K. Prasad, and Rani D. Mullen, 'India-Central Asia Relations: Moving Towards Broader Development Partnerships', India Development Cooperation Research (IDCR) Project, Background Paper no. 4, 6 January, 2014. URL: http://idcr.cprindia.org/blog/india-central-asia-backgrounder
43. Ibid.
44. Ibid.
45. Ibid.
46. Ibid.
47. 'India looking to Import Uranium from Uzbekistan', *Business Standard*, 5 July 2014. URL: http://www.business-standard.com/article/current-affairs/india-looking-to-import-uranium-from-uzbekistan-113100600248_1.html
48. Shivakumar et al., op. cit.
49. 'Overview of UZ Minda LLC', URL: http://www.minda.co.in/UzMinda/forms/overview. aspx
50. IOT, 'Seismic Services'. URL: http://www.iotinfraenergy.com/business/seismic_services. htm
51. 'Rising China, Sinking Russia', *The Economist*, 14 September 2013. URL: http://www. economist.com/news/asia/21586304-vast-region-chinas-economic-clout-more-match-russias-rising-china-sinking.
52. Malhotra, Jyoti, 'Second Chance in Asia's Cockpit', *The Hindu*, 20 July, 2012.
53. 'Keynote Address delivered by E. Ahamed at the First India-Central Asia Dialogue', July 12, 2012. URL: http://www.mea.gov.in/Speeches-Statements.htm?dtl/19791/Keynote+address+by+MOS+Shri+E+Ahamed+at+First+IndiaCentral+Asia+ Dialogue.
54. Bhavna Dave (2016), 'Resetting India's Engagement in Central Asia: From Symbols to Substance', Policy Report, URL: https://www.rsis.edu.sg/wp-content/uploads/2016/02/PR160202_Resetting-Indias-Engagment.pdf.
55. Soni, Sharad K., 'Book Review: *Mapping Central Asia: Indian Perceptions and Strategies*, edited by Laruelle, Marlène and Peyrouse, Sébastien', *India Quarterly*, 69(1), 2011, p. 90.

2

Energy Cooperation

The evolving pattern of global economic development has influenced the whole world so much so that energy security has emerged as one of the major development goals of any nation, whether it is in the economic take-off stage or has reached the stage of high mass consumption. Without having sufficient energy resources "nations can neither initiate the process of economic growth and development nor sustain it for long".[1] It is because of this realisation of the importance of energy security that nations all over the world are now developing sophisticated and appropriate technology to harness both the renewable and non-renewable sources of energy. While doing so, these nations are not only involved domestically but also externally through bilateral and multilateral ties in their immediate and extended neighbourhoods as well as in the far-off regions and continents. However, one cannot deny the fact that the nearer the source of energy to a country, the greater is the comparative advantage in actualising that resource potential.[2]

In recent years, as the list of countries among the emerging economies category get increasingly characterised by high rates of economic growth, it has also led to difficulties in achieving a sound balance between demand and supply of energy resources necessary to maintain their national economic development. Although they are trying hard to arrive at an appropriate energy mix, increase their energy efficiency and diversify their sources of supply, the question of maintaining a stable supply of fossil fuels continues to pose several security challenges: one is to boost one's own production, another to diversify one's sources of import, and a third to secure the transportation of oil and gas on vulnerable sea routes or over land through pipelines that depend on long-term strategic relationships with the producing countries. This has resulted in the formation of a system of mutual relations in the world such that the totality of its volume and scope may most effectively serve the interests of both the manufacturers of energy resources as well as their consumers.[3] In this context, West Asia has so far remained the traditional major source of supply of oil and natural gas for the rest of the world. Traditionally, India has been dependent for most of its oil and gas supplies on the West Asian countries from which it receives more than 50 percent of its imported oil. But West Asia has, in recent years, been faced with an increasing political instability leading to fluctuation in the energy supply from this region that poses a serious challenge to the energy security for nations around the world including India, just as it does for Japan, China, the US and many European countries.

India's Energy Demand

The intensive economic growth of India in the last two decades has been the cause of its growing needs for energy resources. During the past decade, the Indian economy has been growing on an average of 8 percent annually, and it is predicted that if the current rates of development are maintained, in 10–15 years, India will move from the fourth place on volume of gross national product (GNP) to the third place in the world. The fast rate of the country's economic development along with its enormous demographic potential has provided the basis for its recognition as a new "stakeholder" in the post-Cold War international politics. Today, India is recognised as one of the four fastest developing states in the world, i.e., the BRIC countries (Brazil, Russia, India and China), which in the mid-term future will be transformed from the economic globalisation's active participants into world political actors, capable of having not only a "visible" but a real influence on the formation of world political processes and their development.[4] The achievement and maintenance of the above-mentioned role by India gives rise to the necessity of guaranteeing its energy security. In this connection, the former Prime Minister of India, Dr Manmohan Singh had once underlined that "the issue of energy security is already on second place after food security".[5] The current Indian government has decided to come up with a new national energy policy, which bears Prime Minister Modi's stamp as it focuses on renewable energy and making India energy independent. In the words of Mr Modi: "Energy security based on clean & reliable sources is essential for India's future. Nuclear energy has a key role in India's energy strategy".

At the end of 2010, India was the world's fifth largest net importer of oil, importing more than 2.2 million barrels per day (bbl/d), or about 70 percent of its consumption. Most of India's crude oil imports came from Saudi Arabia (18 percent), Iran (11 percent) and other West Asian countries (34 percent) as well as Africa (22 percent).[6] However, in 2015, India became the fourth-largest consumer and fourth-largest net importer of crude oil and petroleum products in the world after the United States, China and Japan. The gap between India's oil demand and supply is widening due to the growing demand that reached almost 4.1 million bbl/d in 2015, while compared to less than 1 million bbl/d of the total liquids production.[7] In June 2016, the US Energy Information Administration (EIA) released the *India Country Analysis Brief* on domestic energy usage and activity. While highlighting the estimates given by *the Oil & Gas Journal* (*OGJ*), it states that India held almost 5.7 billion barrels of proven oil reserves at the end of 2015.[8] Whereas, 48 percent of the reserves are part of onshore resources, 52 percent are offshore and most of the reserves are found in the western part of India, particularly the western offshore region near Gujarat and Rajasthan. The Assam–Arakan basin in north-eastern India is also a key oil-producing region holding more than 22 percent of the country's reserves.[9]

As regards natural gas, it mainly serves as a substitute for coal for electricity generation and as an alternative for LPG and other petroleum products in the fertiliser and other sectors. According to the EIA, India was self-sufficient in natural gas until 2004, when it began to import LNG from the West Asian country of Qatar. Since it has not been able to create a sufficient natural gas infrastructure or produce adequate natural gas to meet the domestic demand, it remains dependent on imported LNG. India was the world's fourth-largest LNG importer in 2015, following Japan, South Korea, and China and consumed almost 7 percent of the global market.[10]

As of December 2015, according to the *OGJ*, India possessed approximately 53 trillion cubic feet (tcf) of proven natural gas resources. The EIA estimates that India produced approximately 1.8 tcf of natural gas in 2010—a 63 percent increase over the 2008 production level. The total natural gas production in India declined from a record high of 1.8 tcf in 2010 to 1.1 tcf in 2014 as a result of some technical issues including unexpected declines and reservoir performance problems apart from high development costs. The bulk of India's natural gas production comes from the western offshore regions, especially the Mumbai High Complex. The fields in the Krishna–Godavari (KG) belt are also increasingly important.[11]

The natural gas consumption grew at an annual rate of 6 percent from 2000 and 2014, although supply disruptions starting in 2011 resulted in a declining consumption. The natural gas consumption in India was tied closely to the domestic production until imports became available in 2004. In 2014, India consumed 1.8 trillion cubic feet (tcf) of natural gas. The LNG imports accounted for about 37 percent of the 2014 demand and are expected to account for an increasing portion of demand at least in the next several years. Higher LNG imports will depend on the pace of expansion in the regasification terminal capacity and the pipeline infrastructure connecting natural gas supplies to markets that currently lack access. The government's recently revised natural gas pricing system that provides a premium for production from India's more technically-challenging fields acts as an economic incentive for the producers to invest upstream and raise domestic output. India's demand will rely on both LNG imports and production to supply for the country's growing fuel needs.[12]

Most of the natural gas demand in 2014 came from the power sector (23 percent), the fertiliser industry (32 percent) and the replacement of LPG for cooking oil and other uses in the residential sector (14 percent), according to India's MOPNG. The government has labelled these as priority sectors for receiving new natural gas supplies. The fertiliser sector, which is highly price-sensitive, has been able to maintain low fuel costs by using natural gas. The recent unexpected dry natural gas production decline since 2011 has forced the electric generators to seek fuel alternatives, primarily coal, and this sector has seen the largest decline in natural gas use. The government is promoting the use of natural gas in the residential sector as an alternative to LPG and biomass as cooking fuels.[13]

Overview of Various Sources of India's Energy Supply

Conventional thermal-generated power accounted for more than 80 percent of the electricity in India in 2008. Of all the sources of India's energy resources, coal predominates, generating 70 percent of India's power. India is both the third largest consumer as well as the third largest producer of coal in the world. India's domestic coal is low in quality which renders the coal fired power generation relatively inefficient and necessitates the imports of metallurgical coal. Natural gas, which is primarily to offset the seasonality of the hydroelectricity mix, is expected to expand from 11 percent in 2008 to 16 percent in 2035.[14] According to the International

Energy Statistics published in 2010, coal was the major source of energy in India during the year 2009 as it accounted for 42 percent of the total energy consumed in the country. It was followed by oil that formed the second important source of energy as it constituted 24 percent of all energy and fuel resources of the country. Natural gas constituted only 7 percent of the total energy consumption of the country.[15]

Thus, quite clearly, keeping in view India's fast growing population, the expansion of its economy and a steep rise in the demand for energy resources, there is an internal compulsion to diversify the country's energy sector and to seek for the economically more viable sources of oil, natural gas and hydroelectricity. As part of India's goal of diversifying its sources of electric power generation, the government plans to increase the use of electricity. International organisations such as the World Bank are providing funding for a variety of hydroelectric projects in the country. However, the lack of reliability, environmental and land-use concerns surrounding construction may make it difficult to utilise fully this domestic energy resource.[16] In the International Energy Outlook (IEO) 2011, electricity consumption in India has been projected to grow at an average rate of 3.3 percent per year through 2035. In order to meet this growth projection, India will have to expand the current generation capacity by 234 GW.

Given the problems posed by issues such as the unrest in West Asia as well as the perennial threats to India's oil refineries by potential terrorist attacks, other sources of energy such as sand tar from Canada which are very difficult to access, has led it to explore the alternate sources of energy such as natural gas, hydropower and nuclear power projects. Even though India plans to ramp up 15,000 megawatts over the next 20 years, nuclear power appears to be the least realistic, not only because of safety concerns but also due to economic realities. Under the given scenario, oil and natural gas continue to remain central to India's energy requirements. The energy-resource-rich Central Asian region owing to the geographical proximity and friendly relations with India offers enormous opportunities for New Delhi to meet its energy demand.[17] The pressures of maintaining a fast growing national economy and an increasing population too motivate India to embark on vigorous efforts to ensure its energy security.

The Energy Resources of Central Asia

The Energy Resources of Central Asia were developed and controlled by the former Soviet Union for many decades in the past but soon after the Soviet disintegration, the Central Asia has emerged as a new energy frontier for the world. Almost 4 percent of the world's oil and 7 percent of natural gas are estimated to be located in Central Asia.[18] As already pointed out, of the five Republics of post-Soviet Central Asia, three—namely, Kazakhstan, Uzbekistan and Turkmenistan, are rich in hydrocarbon resources; the other two—namely, Tajikistan and Kyrgyzstan—though poor in hydrocarbon resources have a huge potential for the development of hydroelectricity. Kazakhstan is rich in oil, while Turkmenistan is the fourth largest producer of the natural gas and though Uzbekistan's energy reserves are modest in comparison to the two, its potential for the unexplored finds is very high. The region as a whole has a very high potential of conventional energy resources but only 10 percent of this potential has been utilised so far which conversely implies that a large part of these energy resources can be exported by these Republics to achieve economic stability.

In the current discourse of energy security, the Central Asian Republics have assumed a prominent place since their independence as a new channel of energy supply in both the eastern and western directions—a fact that has been accentuated in the backdrop of the global financial crisis, international crisis, international food price hike and turbulence in the West Asian and North African countries.[19] This has naturally manifested in the form of a tough competition among the major energy-consuming economies of the world like the United States, China, Russia, India and the European Union to compete for the Central Asian energy resources with a view to achieve their respective national energy security.

Table 2.1 reveals that in the year 2000 the Central Asian Republics had 3261.9 million tonnes of proven and recoverable oil resources, 6716.74 billion cubic metres of proven and recoverable natural gas and 38.11 billion tonnes of proven and recoverable coal. In the same year, the region had an economically viable hydropower potential of 413 billion Kwh/year. The uranium resources as estimated by the World Energy Council with mining costs at below US$ 130/kg for Kazakhstan and Uzbekistan were put at 6,01,000 and 8,37,000 tonnes respectively.

Table 2.2 shows that during the year 2007, Kazakhstan produced energy resources worth 136 million tonnes of oil equivalent (Mtoe) out of which it consumed only 66.5 Mtoe, whereas Uzbekistan produced 60 Mtoe out of which it consumed 48.7 Mtoe but Turkmenistan produced 66.1 Mtoe out of which it consumed only 18.1 Mtoe.

Table 2.1: Energy Resource Base of Central Asia in 2000 and 2020

	Kazakhstan		*Kyrgybstan*		*Tajikistan*		*Turkmenistan*		*Uzbekistan*		*Central Asia*	
Energy Resources	2000	2020	2000	2020	2000	2020	2000	2020	2000	2020	2000	2020
Coal* billion tonnes	34.1	34.1	1.34	1.27	0.67	1.0	Insig.	Insig.	2.0	2.0	38.11	38.11
Oil*, Million tonnes	2760	2760	11.5	10.2	5.4	10.0	75.0	75.0	350.0	350.0	3261.9	3261.9
Gas*, billion Cu.m.	1841	1841	6.54	6.2	9.2	Insig.	2860	2860	2000	2000	6716.74	6716.74
Uranium**, thousand tons	601	601	Insig.	Insig.	Insig.	317.0	Insig.	Insig.	83.7	83.7	684.7	684.7
Hydropower,*** billion kWh/Year	27.0	27.0	52.0	99,0	317.0	18.4	2.0	2.0	15.0	15.0	413.0	413.0
Renewable Energy Sources, including small hydro billion kWh/year	66.0	66.0	Insig.	lnsig.	18.4	17.4	n/a n/a	n/a	n/a	64.4	64.4	

* Figures for coal, oil and natural gas refer to proven recoverable resources.
** Uranium resources estimated by the World Energy Council, with mining costs at below US $ 130/kg.
*** Economically viable potential (for Uzbekistan-Technological hydroelectric capacity).
Source: Analytical Reports, Statistics and Forecast submitted by national experts from Kazakhstan, Kyrgyzstan, Tajikistan and Uzbekislan: 2, Survey of Energy Resources, WEC, 1998.

Table 2.2: Production and Consumption of Primary Energy in 2007

Resource	*Kazakhstan*	*Turkmenistan*	*Uzbekistan*
Production in Mtoe			
Coal	43.01	0.00	1.15
Crude Oil	53.54	9.30	3.21
Natural Gas	24.79	56.08	52.94
Natural Gas Liquids	11.87	0.7	2.20
Hydro Power	0.7	0.0003	0.6
Biomass and Wastes	0.07	0.00	0.0002
Total	136.0	66.1	60.0
Gross Inland Consumption in Mtoe			
Coal	31.00	0.00	1.12
Crude Oil	11.90	7.39	3.21
Natural Gas	23.63	13.40	41.90
Natural Gas Liquids	0.9	0.7	2.20
Hydro Power	0.7	0.0003	0.6
Biomass and Wastes	0.07	0.00	0.0003
Petroleum products	-1.59	-3.30	-0.3
Electricity	-003	-0.1	-0.007
Total	66.5	18.1	48.7
Final Energy Consumption in Mtoe			
Industry	16.79	0.27	7.97
Transport	4.40	0.91	3.30
Residential	2.70	0.16	15.06
Other	19,49	9.40	8.01
Tolal	43.4	10.7	34.3

Source: International Energy Agency, *Market Observatory for Energy*, issued by the European Commission, March, 2010.

During the year 2008, out of a total installed capacity of 10,616 MW of hydroelectricity, Tajikistan produced 4,037 MW followed by Kyrgyzstan and Kazakhstan which produced 2,910 MW and 2,248 MW respectively, while Uzbekistan produced 1,420 MW, whereas Turkmenistan produced just 1 MW of hydroelectricity. According to the Eurasian Development Bank's Industry Report for the year 2008, Tajikistan has 69 percent of the hydropower potential of Central Asia, followed by Kyrgyzstan with 22 percent (Table 2.5).

As revealed in Table 2.3, natural gas constituted 48 percent of the primary fuel and energy produced in the Central Asian region in the year 2004. The next important fuel and energy resources are oil and coal which accounted for 33 percent and 17 percent respectively of the primary fuel and energy, while hydro-power constituted just two percent of the energy resources of Central Asia.

Table 2.3: Structure of the Production of Primary Fuel and Energy in Central Asia, 2004 (Percent)

Country	*Gas*	*Oil*	*Coal*	*Hydro*	*Total*
Kazakhstan	16	50	33	1	100
Kyrgyzstan	2	5	11	82	100
Tajikistan	2	1	1	96	100
Tukmenistan	83	17	0	0	100
Uzbekistan	84	13	2	1	100
Central Asian Region	45	33	17	2	100

Source: International Energy Agency, 2004.

Table 2.4 displays the total production of fuel in the Central Asian region at 236.6 million tonnes during the year 2004. The internal consumption was only 130.5 million tonnes in that year and the remaining 106.1 million tonnes were exported to other countries outside the region. The same year the highest proportion of energy resource production was shared by Kazakhstan (118.6 million tonnes). Today, Turkmenistan is extracting oil and gas reserves in its six oil and gas deposits on land and in two regions in the shelf of the Caspian Sea. The most promising regions in this sense are the eastern regions of Turkmenistan, especially in the Amu with the total area of 17 thousand square kilometres. Turkmenistan is rich in oil and gas resources. According to their official figures, Turkmenistan's resource base is approximately 71.64 billion tons of oil equivalent, including 53 billion tons located in onshore fields and 18.21 billion tons in the Caspian Sea. In November 2015, the China National Petroleum Corporation (CNPC) reported that the accumulated volume of natural gas exported from Turkmenistan to China reached 121bcm. The State Committee of Statistics of Turkmenistan reported a total production of 76.2bcm in 2014. The British

Table 2.4: Annual Production and Consumptions of Primary Fuel and Energy in Central Asia in 2004

Country	*Production, Million Tonnes Fuel*	*Internal Consumption Million Tonnes Fuel*	*Production to Consumption Ratio*
Turkmenistan	58.1	15.6	3.74
Kazakhstan	118.6	54.8	2.16
Uzbekistan	56.0	54.0	1.05
Kyrgyzstan	1.5	2.8	0.55
Tajikistan	1,5	3.3	0.45
Central Asian	236.6	13D.5	LSI

Source: Fuel and Energy Balance Statements, International Energy Agency, 2004.

firm Gaffney, Cline, and Associates conducted an audit of the country's Galkynysh gas field and concluded that it holds 28.2 trillion cubic meters of natural gas, making it the second-largest natural gas field in the world. According to Turkmenistan's State Statistics Committee, Turkmenistan produced about 11,589 million tons of oil, including gas condensate, in 2014. According to official figures, the Turkmenbashy Complex of Oil Refineries produced 270 thousand tons of liquefied petroleum gas (LPG) in 2014.

The average production-to-consumption ratio of primary fuel and energy for the Central Asian region as a whole has been 1.81, but in absolute terms it varies from 3.74 for Turkmenistan to just 0.45 for Tajikistan, which is an indication of the fact that Turkmenistan produced about four times the primary fuel and energy than its domestic consumption, whereas Tajikistan produced less than half of its domestic consumption. Uzbekistan is self-sufficient as its production-to-consumption ratio is 1.05 (Table 2.4).

During the year 2008, out of a total installed capacity of 10,616 MW of hydroelectricity, Tajikistan produced 4,037 MW followed by Kyrgyzstan and Kazakhstan which produced 2,910 MW and 2,248 MW respectively. In the same year, as Table 5 shows, Uzbekistan produced 1,420 MW, whereas Turkmenistan produced just 1 MW of hydroelectricity. According to the Eurasian Development Bank's Industry report for the year 2008, Tajikistan had 69 percent of the hydroelectricity potential of Central Asia, followed by Kyrgyzstan with 22 percent (Table 2.5).[20]

Table 2.5: Hydro Energy Potential of the Central Asian Rivers

Country	*HPP Installed Capacity MW*	*Electricity Production and HPP 2005 billion*	*Economic Hydro Potential billion*	*Utilisation of Hydro Potential (Percent)*	*Hydro Potential of the CA Region (Percent)*
Tajikistan	4037	17.1	317	5	69
Kyrgyzstan	2910	14.0	99	14	22
Kazakhstan	2248	7.9	27	29	6
Uzbekistan	1420	6.0	15	49	3
Turkmenistan	1	0	2	0	0
CA Region	10,616	45.0	460	10	100

Source: Ghulam M. Shah (2013), "Energy Cooperation between Central Asia and South Asia: Prospects and Challenges", p. 102, 104-6)

Table 2.6 demonstrates that Rogun, Nurek and Dashtijum are the three major hydropower plants of Tajikistan which have an aggregate generation capacity of 10,600 MW. The Toktogul hydropower plant in Kyrgyzstan has a power generation capacity of 3,000 MW. The other important hydropower projects of Kyrgyzstan are Kombarata 1 and 2 and Sary Djaz (5 series) with an aggregate power generation potential of 3,760 MW.[21]

Table 2.6: The Largest Hydro Power Plants in Tajikistan and Kyrgyzstan

Country	*Location*	*Status*	*Capacity of MW*	*Average Annual Performance Billion, kWh*	*Estimated Cost, billion US Dollars*
Region HPP	River Vaksh (Tajikistan)	Project	3600	13.1	2.2
Nurek HPP	River Vaksh (Tajikistan)	Operational	3000	11.2	
Dashtijum HPP	River Pyanj (Tajikistan)	Project	4000	15.6	3.5
Kambarata 1 and 2 HPP's	River Naryn (Kyrgyzstan)	Project	1900+360	7.0	2.0
Toktogul HPP	River Naryn (Kyrgyzstan)	Operational	1200	4.4	
Series of 5 HPP's on Sary-Djaz	River Sary-Djaz (Kyrgyzstan)	Project	1500	5.0	2.5

Source: Eurasian Development Bank, Industry Report, 2008.

Problems and Prospects of Energy Cooperation

In spite of India's geographical proximity to the Central Asian Republics and the economic advantages in importing energy resources such as hydrocarbons and hydroelectricity from Central Asia, exploring the viability of energy cooperation in the recent years is beset with a host of problems. Although various estimates are available on the untapped Central Asian energy reserves, the exact figures need to be thoroughly evaluated. The competition for energy security among the major powers of the world and the regional powers which is commonly referred to as the "New Great Game" and is often compared with the 19th century British–Russian imperial rivalry nicknamed as the "Great Game" is currently being played. The prominent global and regional powers involved in the "New Great Game" include the United States, China, Russia, the European Union, Turkey and Iran, in which India is constantly trying to find a toehold.[22]

The US interests in Central Asia stem out of security, energy and democracy promotion reasons. The security concerns in the Central Asian region have acquired new dimensions in the post-9/11 world. The threat of the al-Qaida and Taliban-inspired radical Islam has not only brought the US into this region but also provided opportunities to ensure the frequent supply of hydrocarbons from West Asia. However, the Central Asian production of primary fuel and energy is much smaller than the total output of the Organisation of Petroleum Exporting Countries (OPEC).[23]

Given that the Central Asian region is important geopolitically and economically, Russia controls the majority of oil export routes from the reserves in the Central Asian and the Caspian region. Though Russia wants to oust the United States from its traditional sphere of influence, it is also worried that the investment in the Caspian Sea oilfields will divert the Western financial backing and interests from its oilfields in Siberia and the Far East and captures some of its market. In the competition over Caspian oil, therefore, Russia sees both the erosion of its geopolitical position and the loss of key economic resources and their potential revenues.[24] The earlier and continuing efforts by major Western oil companies, particularly the Baku-Tbilisi-Ceybran (BTC) pipeline as well as the current and planned investments in the Central Asian oil sector by India and China, have yielded more options for the non-Russian export routes and the diversification of Central Asian energy exports.[25]

China is steadily increasing its involvement in Central Asia's energy sector as demonstrated by the purchase of the Pedro Kazakhstan Oil Company apart from the acquisition of the Canada-based Nations Energy as well as the International Trust and Investment Cooperation in 2006, and the signing of several significant pipeline agreements. Both Russia and China have been cooperating to reduce the US influence in the region and to prevent its encroachment into their sphere of influence.[26] From Kazakhstan, 2,00,000 barrels of oil are now being pumped everyday across the border into the western Chinese province of Xinjiang, and there are plans to double this pipeline's capacity. From Turkmenistan, a pipeline carrying gas to China via Uzbekistan was opened in December 2009 by the along with the Presidents of Turkmenistan Gurbanguly Berdimuhamedov, the President of Uzbekistan Islam Karimov and the President of Kazakhstan Nursultan Nazarbayev. It was projected that it could satisfy around half of China's demand by the time it reaches its full capacity in 2013. Turkmenistan's President called the deal "political" as well as commercial and praised China's "wise policy", saying it had become "one of the key guarantors of global security".[27]

Significantly, the Europeans want to break free from their growing dependence on Russian energy supplies from the region to make the Nabucco pipeline viable. In January 2006, due to clashes with Ukraine over gas pricing, Russia cut off all gas supplies to many EU countries. This incident alarmed the EU about its growing dependence on Russian gas at that point, consisting of 40 percent of the EU gas imports, and urged the EU to accelerate its alternative pipeline projects. One of the most promising EU suppliers for Europe, Nabucco, at once circumvented Russia's hold of the transit routes, while Russia has been doing everything to prevent Nabucco from being realised, including announcing the Southern Stream pipeline project in 2007, which is being seen as a strong rival to the Nabucco project.[28]

Since the Central Asian Republics are on the path of sustainable development in their energy and socio-economic sectors and this process promises to be irreversible, all these Republics need to refurbish their energy infrastructure through foreign direct investments, profit-sharing agreements as well as a consolidation and concentration of the domestic resources. The current state of the Central Asian oil and gas industry demands more concrete measures to be taken in order to further attract major oil and gas transnational corporations to invest in innovative technology, international know-how and introduce top-notch and world class conditions, improve policy mechanisms to efficiently utilise the resources and help set up joint ventures to produce chemical products. Generally speaking, almost all the Central Asian Republics have survived the world financial crisis and in most cases they are doing well, particularly Kazakhstan and Uzbekistan have stabilised well partly due to their inadequate exposure to the major world financial systems. For a further improvement of the hydrocarbon industry, it is essential for the Central Asian Republics to have a comprehensive and reliable picture of the trends of the global market in the foreseeable future in order to be able to provide their competitive advantage to the consumer states.[29]

Further, the Central Asian Republics have always been cautious and alert in terms of maintaining their state sovereignty and territorial integrity while they are pursuing varied bilateral and multilateral relations with outside powers such as China, Russia and the US. The current status quo shows that these Central Asian countries have so far offered cooperative frameworks at bilateral and multilateral levels. However, these CARs are highly reluctant to find themselves at the behest of an external power on unbeneficial terms and, therefore, they have the right to cease the operation of any deal, provided it impinges upon their freedom of action in international relations.

The list of dilemmas that the Central Asian Republics are perennially faced with regard to decisions to be confronted with in the utilisation of their respective energy resources can be summed up as follows:

1. Whether to extract the energy resource as quickly as technically possible or to keep it in the ground for the future? In terms of economic efficiency, the answer depends on the expected rate of increase in the energy prices as against the expected rate of return on extraction, as of now. However, the government may be pushed by many political and commercial interests to extract the resources more quickly rather than efficiently.
2. Whether to run the energy sector as a state monopoly or to open access to international and national private investors? The rational answer to this question depends on the government's capacity to manage the national energy state enterprise as against its ability to regulate and tax private companies in a way that generates optimal national returns. But again, the decision in fact may hinge on how hard and with what licit or illicit means the key players push for one particular set-up against another.
3. Whether to spend or save the national earnings from the energy resources? If the money is spent, it can be used for investment or consumption, including for subsidies. But if the money is spent in the public sector or is channelled to the private sector, the question arises as to how best to do that.
4. Finally, who is the best to sell the energy to? In landlocked Central Asia, much of the energy has traditionally been sold to or through Russia, but increasingly the Central Asian governments want to widen their export market opportunities. This requires negotiations with many national and international parties and international investments in pipeline infrastructure.[30]

The landlocked geopolitical position and their urgent necessity to keep their economy afloat has, however, seen these Central Asian Republics in the recent years to shed their hesitation and seek for diversifying their supply routes into various markets and regions to avert any unexpected downturns as well as to reduce the risk of overdependence and guarantee predictability. After an exposure to the peculiar practice of the political and economic statecraft of a number of regional players, now Kazakhstan, Turkmenistan and Uzbekistan seem to be inclined to no longer rely on and be dependent on a single pipeline route. These are the most pressing issues that confront the CARs currently, including the expansion of the resource base of the Central Asian exporters and their transportation capacity, especially in the context of competition for the key consumer market, investment flows and routes of supply.[31]

The unequal and uncompromising terms set by the regional states have triggered the Central Asian Republics to search for alternative ways of reaching regional and global markets. This has enhanced the level of competition in the oil and gas segments among the importer states. This is explained by the growing demand for energy resources to develop their economies. The major global and regional actors engage and compete in the processes of Central Asian petroleum and gas industry exploration, infrastructure development and management, as well as technology transfer to maximise their standing in the existing and projected transport corridors. The Central Asians, after being exposed to the "rules of the game" of the energy market are striving to influence or change the end result in a new context. They are wary that an efficient and commercial use of the energy resources of Central Asia should not turn into a scramble for the Central Asia, i.e., a fierce battle or competition between the regional and global powers. By playing on the differences of external actors active in the region, the CARs are trying to learn from the best practices of the international partners who mostly express readiness to share their know-how. However, as the global and regional powers keep on aspiring to meet their increasing energy demands by using the Central Asian energy resources, all stakeholders, including importers, exporters and transit countries, are poised to take into account not only the commercial benefits but also their political implications.

Finally, while the Central Asian countries are actively engaging themselves in integrating into inter-regional and subsequently global markets with their diversified oil and gas pipeline industries, they lack the common intra-regional integration involving all the five countries. In this regard, an efficient regional mechanism should be put into place to address the challenges of a political and economic nature. In the absence of a viable regional mechanism, some irritants may trigger conflict, especially in yet to be resolved areas in the hydropower industry. However, there is a mechanism called the Central Asian Regional Economic Cooperation (CAREC) supported by the Asian Development Bank with its Secretariat at Manila, Philippines that is helping finance the Central Asian Republics' efforts towards laying various infrastructural projects.

The CAREC programme has focused to date on financing infrastructure projects and improving the region's policy environment in the priority areas of transport (especially road transport), energy (including the water-energy nexus), trade policy, and trade facilitation (especially customs cooperation). CAREC is also an alliance of multilateral institutions comprising Asian Development Bank, European Bank for Reconstruction and Development, International Monetary Fund, Islamic Development Bank, United Nations Development Programme, and World Bank. CAREC operates in partnership with other key regional cooperation programs and institutions, including the Shanghai Cooperation Organization (SCO) and the Eurasian Economic Community. As of 2016, 176 CAREC-related projects worth around US$ 29.4 billion have been implemented and it is one of the key financing mechanism for the silk road passing through the CARs.

Central Asia in India's Energy Strategy

As mentioned earlier, since the early years of the 21st century, India has been willing to take on political and financial risks inherent in the overseas investments. Observers have remarked that India is emulating China in its overseas energy security strategies. By improving ties with resource-rich countries, India hopes to enhance its energy security. The Indian oil and gas companies are thus encouraged to invest overseas and to build strong relations with the strategically important countries. In addition to upstream investments, India has entered into agreements on energy cooperation with several countries, including a 'strategic energy partnership' with Saudi Arabia. India apparently seeks 'niche markets' that have remained off-limits to the more politically sensitive multinational oil companies.[32]

India's major state-owned oil company is ONGC (Oil and Natural Gas Corporation), which has an international subsidiary, ONGC Videsh Ltd. (OVL). ONGC stands for 77 percent of India's crude oil and 81 percent of its natural gas production, and is currently the most profit-making corporation in the country. During the past few years, India's public sector oil companies such as the ONGC and IOC have made successful bids in oil exploration and production deals in a number of countries, including Australia, Egypt, Iraq, Iran, Ivory Coast, Libya, Burma, Syria and Central Asia. Since it started looking abroad in 2001, the ONGC has acquired interests in at least 14 oil and gas projects in 11 countries around the world. The largest stakes so far are the company's 25 percent share of the Greater Nile Oil Project in Sudan in which the CNPC is the majority stakeholder, and a 20 percent share of the Sakhalin 1 project in Russia led by ExxonMobil. In December 2005, the OVL completed a 741 km multi-product pipeline linking the Khartoum Refinery to Port Sudan. Among the OVL's exploration assets are a 100 percent share of the Iraqi Block 8, a 100 percent share of Qatar's Najwat Najem, a 70 percent share of the Egyptian North Ramadan and a 49 percent share of the Libyan NC 188 and 189. This record seems impressive, yet according to a *Reuters* report, in spite of that, the ONGC has acquired minority shares in projects like Sakhalin 1, Iran's Yadavaran oilfield and Sudanese properties abandoned by Western investors, and hence the company has yet to take a lead role in any concession. The ONGC must boost its reserve-to-production ratio or the number of years its reserves will last with the current level of output by improving its drilling technology and management practices will reduce. ONGC's ratio is currently at 22 years.[33]

In order to help meet its growing demand for gas imports, India has also acquired overseas gas production assets in Vietnam and Burma. The OVL currently holds a 45 percent share in the Vietnamese Block 6.1 (where Statoil used to have a share), which produces 7.5 million standard cubic metres of gas per day. Together with the Korean companies, Daewoo International and KOGAS, the Indian companies OVL and GAIL (Gas Authority of India Limited) are also stakeholders in the Burmese offshore Shwe gas field. OVL has further been negotiating with Russia's Gazprom over a string of major oil and gas deals, involving the production and shipping of gas, as well as petrochemicals and oil. The two companies have signed a memorandum of understanding to jointly develop energy projects in India, Russia and other countries. One of the planned projects involves gas production in the Russian Sakhalin and building LNG facilities on the Pacific coast.[34]

In the contemporary scenario, India is optimistic about a strong cooperation with the Central Asian Republics in the energy sector. This optimism stems from the fact that India has an enormous potential for improving its energy efficiency which is a promising area for technological cooperation with the CARs. Some analysts have suggested that steps should also be taken to slow the rise in energy consumption in India, especially the growth of electricity demand. This is ethically and politically difficult since the per capita energy consumption is, in fact, much higher in the mature market economies of North America, Europe and Japan than in India. However, in recent years, the growing concern for energy security and rising oil prices has led to a much increased awareness of the importance of energy efficiency among Indians. Improving energy efficiency hence is regarded as a key measure for enhancing energy security and developing cooperation in this field with the outside world.

It is obvious that only giving access to Indian energy companies in exploration and development of oil and gas deposits in the Central Asian Republics cannot provide regular deliveries of hydrocarbon raw material to India unless there is a proper transit corridor within the regional cooperation framework. To this extent, the Central Asian Republics are increasingly showing greater interest in the diversification of its energy routes. Taking into account this fact, the Central Asian energy strategy of India has made a shift from forging ties in business-to-business relations by the respective oil companies, sharing technical know-how in exploration of oil and gas fields and entering into joint production mechanisms. The efforts now have come to be directed more towards the creation of an energy corridor between Central Asia and South Asia. In the prevailing scenario, energy cooperation between Central Asia and India can be a feasible reality in the context of linking the two regions of Central Asia and South Asia. This entails regional cooperation between the Central Asian Republics on the one hand and involving Afghanistan, Pakistan, Iran together with India within the regional cooperation framework on the other. Most importantly, this would mean that the transmission of energy from one region to the other requires such a scenario where old adversaries need to join hands for the sake of shared prosperity. In the case of hydropower and export of electricity from the upper riparian countries, i.e. Tajikistan and Kyrgyzstan which have enormous hydropower potential, they can export it to Afghanistan, Pakistan and India. The lower riparian countries such as Turkmenistan, Uzbekistan and Kazakhstan can sell hydrocarbon energy resources to these South Asian countries. There are many hydrocarbon and hydropower projects under consideration by various governments of Central Asia to develop energy cooperation for energy security in Central Asia and South Asia.

In view of the growing internal energy demand and unstable situation in the world energy sector caused by "the Iranian crisis" and high prices for hydrocarbons, India expresses keen interest in close cooperation with the largest Asian consumers and suppliers of hydrocarbon resources. In this direction, India has initiated a number of large-scale projects aimed at promoting a coordinated action by the above-mentioned states in the oil and gas sphere. As regards the oil and gas sector, the construction of two proposed variants of pipelines, i.e. the Turkmenistan-Afghanistan-Pakistan-

India (TAPI) and Iran-Pakistan-India (IPI) are under consideration. However, the complexity of the problem of the long-term Afghan crisis settlement remains an obstacle till date for the realisation of the TAPI project. The 1,814 Kilometer long pipeline from Galkynysh gas fields in Turkmenistan will run alongside Kandahar-Herat highway in Western Afganistan, pass through Quetta & Multan in Pakistan and reach Fazilka a border town in India. The pipeline will be 56 inch in diameter with a working pressure of 100 standard atmospheres (10,000 kPa). Its capacity will be 33 billion cubic metres of natural gas per year of which 5 billion cubic metres will be provided to Afghanistan and 14 billion cubic metres to each Pakistan and India. The much delayed pipeline is now expected to be operational by 2022. The standing committee on petroleum and natural gas said in a report submitted to Parliament in July 2017, that a consortium for Turkmenistan-Afghanistan-Pakistan-India pipeline—TAPI Pipeline Company Ltd (TPCL)—was incorporated in Isle of Man, and shareholders' agreement signed in December 2015. Turkmenistan will own 85 percent of TPCL while India, Pakistan and Afghanistan will each have 5 percent stake. "The construction of pipeline has commenced in December 2015 and is likely to be completed in about 7 years," it said.

The second project, the Iran-Pakistan-India (IPI) pipeline, also creates an opportunity of energy resource transportation from Central Asia through Iran and Pakistan. According to some Indian experts, this project is more favourable from the economic point of view. India had almost abandoned the IPI pipeline in 2008 following the US sanctions against Iran over its suspected nuclear programme India should consider reviving the long-delayed IPI gas pipeline following easing of sanctions on Tehran. The standing committee on petroleum and natural gas said in a report submitted to Parliament in July 2017, that "The government should examine the idea of reviving the IPI project as international conditions have become favourable following lifting of sanctions against Iran." Still due to the unpredictability of the Iranian crisis, with the newly sworn President of the USA, Donald Trump, stating that he will review and repeal the agreement signed by Obama and his hawkish stand on Iran has generated great concerns with regard to the materialisation of this project in the near future, the TAPI project remains a more realistic goal to be pursued.

Turkmenistan-Afghanistan-Pakistan-India (TAPI) Pipeline

The TAPI project has been in making for last 22 years and it will see another 5-8 years before it accomplish its objective. The TAPI project was initially mooted by the Argentinian company Bridas Corporation in March 1995 that was meant to include Turkmenistan, Afghanistan and Pakistan. However, the US Company Unocal, in conjunction with the Saudi Oil Company Delta, promoted an alternative project without Bridas' involvement and signed separate agreements with the Turkmen President Niyazov. Later, a consortium for the construction of the pipeline led by Unocal called the Central Asian Gas Pipeline Ltd. (CentGas) was formed in August 1996 to implement the project.[35] However, the project was shelved following the bombing of American embassies at Nairobi and Dar-es-Salaam and launching of the American war on terror.[36]

The new deal on the pipeline involving the three earlier stakeholders and India evolved under the aegis of the Asian Development Bank's project feasibility report. Consequently, on April 25, 2008, Turkmenistan, Afghanistan, Pakistan and India signed a framework agreement to buy natural gas from Turkmenistan. The intergovernmental agreement on pipelines was signed on December 11, 2010 in Ashgabat. They announced that a 1,814 Kilometer route would follow the ancient trading route from Central to South Asia, extending from the Galkynysh gas field in Turkmenistan, this field is world's second largest field holding gas reserves of 28.5 trillion cubic meters, the pipeline will be laid along the highway through Herat, Helmand and Kandahar in Afghanistan to Quetta and Multan in Pakistan and on to Fazilka (Punjab) in India.[37]

The pipeline will reopen a historic route that reconnects South Asia to Central Asia, in the way it was, before the British Empire sealed it off. It will also bring India and its neighbours the much-needed energy at competitive pricing, and could easily supply a quarter of Pakistan's gas needs, about 15 percent of India's projected needs, as well as Afghanistan's requirements, by the time it is completed in the 2020s. This is a growing need, and even if India is able to source energy from other countries like Iran and further afield, both the proximity and abundance of Turkmenistan's reserves that rank sixth (as reported in ADB report) in the world will make it an attractive proposition. At a time when China has already secured nearly half of its energy requirements from the region, and is working on the US$ 400 billion Russia–China gas pipeline, India has no time to lose in securing its interest in Central Asia. Finally, the TAPI pipeline gives this fractured region a reason to work on a project together as well, and it is hoped that the shared stakes in TAPI's success will ensure that India, Pakistan and Afghanistan find ways of cooperating on other issues as well.[38]

The ADB updated the feasibility study in 2008 which estimated the capital cost upto US$ 7.6 billion, and said that it would consider financing the project. It also concluded and projected 2016-2017 as a possible time frame for its operation, but it still remains unoperational and is now expected to become operational in 2022. The main factors that have led to delays, according to various reports, include lack of consensus on pricing, gas certification, financing and security issues,[39] even though the TAPI offers benefits to all the four participating countries and has the potential to enhance regional cooperation.[40] The consensus between all stake holders has been reached just recently, and an intergovernmental agreement is signed amongst them.

Further, on July 11, 2015, during his talks with Turkmenistan President Gurbanguly Berdimuhamedov in Ashgabat, Prime Minister Narendra Modi pitched for an early implementation of the US$ 10 billion TAPI gas pipeline project. Describing the TAPI project as a significant initiative in the relationship between India and Turkmenistan, Modi stressed on exploring the possibility of the land–sea route through Iran for the pipeline. The project has been envisaged to take gas from Turkmenistan, which holds the world's fourth-largest natural gas reserves, to India and Pakistan through Afghanistan.[41] The multi-billion dollars Turkmenistan-Afghanistan-Pakistan-India (TAPI) gas pipeline project entered its practical phase in Pakistan after the process of initiating front-end-engineering-and-design (FEED) route survey was formally inaugurated by the Pakistani Prime Minister in March 2017.

Inevitable Competition with China

India's energy needs as well as its continued reliance on oil have inevitably put the country in a direct collision and competition with China. India is at a competitive disadvantage in several ways. The overseas oil acquisition is a stated policy for both the countries, though the Chinese companies are granted more autonomy while receiving greater government support than their Indian counterparts. The Chinese banks make energy-backed loans, which help secure oil for the Chinese companies, all the while profiting them financially. For several reasons including the government regulations, the Indian oil companies do not receive such benefits. With its proactive policies and sustained efforts, China has gained access to more oil-producing assets in more countries than India has. Beijing has also developed a mutually beneficial economic relationship with these countries through the provision of funding for infrastructure and other development projects.[42]

India's stated policy to maintain its strategic autonomy from Moscow and Washington has also hampered its major initiatives to counter the Chinese and Pakistani influence in Central Asia while it has also hurt its economic interests. At present, Moscow has essentially shut India out from Kyrgyzstan after sending the first instalments of a new US$ 1 billion military aid package to that country. This follows the strategic setback that India suffered in 2010 when it lost use of Tajikistan's Ayni airbase to Russia. The situation has allowed China to outmanoeuvre India in the energy-rich nations of Kazakhstan and Turkmenistan.

In early September 2013, India's loss of 8.4 percent stake in Kazakhstan's Kashagan oilfield to the Chinese National Petroleum Company (CNPC) was a major blow to its goal of developing long-term partnerships in energy development with the Central Asian Republics. Earlier, India's Oil and Natural Gas Corporation (ONGC) had concluded an agreement to purchase an 8.4 percent interest in the Kashgan oilfield in November 2012. It had been viewed by New Delhi as a significant foothold in the Kazakh oil industry.

India has been sidelined by China's energy and trade diplomacy in Turkmenistan as well. Despite the fact that the two countries have concluded an agreement to expedite the project, it is still to see the light of day. Meanwhile, China has inaugurated its operations of Turkmenistan's Galkynysh gas field, the world's second-largest gas field. A highly symbolic accomplishment for China, the Galkynysh field was developed by a CNPC-led consortium without the participation of any major Western gas companies.[43] Japan is leading in one of the phases in Galkynysh, which will be ready by the time of commissioning of TAPI and it is devoted to TAPI, as well as Turkmenistan started construction of its own section from Galkynysh to the Afghan border with length of 240 km.

It can, thus, be observed that the increase in the role of the energy component in the Indian strategy towards Central Asia reflects its adequate recognition of a tough competition for Central Asian Energy resources, creating the necessity to play a more active role in this process. It is obvious that in future the energy routes will significantly determine the regional unions and the geopolitical situation not only in Central Asia but also in the world as a whole. The conclusion of the TAPI project, in future, undoubtedly will result in the strengthening of the value and priority of the southern direction pipeline routes. Moreover, in this connection, the route of the future pipeline from Central Asia to India is extremely important in India's evolving relationship with the Central Asian Republics.[44]

REFERENCES

1. Shah, G.M. , 'Economic Cooperation between Central Asia and South Asia: Prospects and Challenges' in , *Perspectives on Bilateral and Regional Cooperation: South and Central Asia*, in, R. Malhotra et al. (eds),Chandigarh: CRRID, 2013, p. 100.
2. Ibid.
3. Urazdoboeva Sojida, 'Some Aspects of Indian Energy Interests in Central Asia, in *India's Engagement with Central Asia with Focus on India-Uzbekistan Relations*, Jyotsana Bakshi (ed.) Tashkent: University of World Economy and Diplomacy, 2007, p. 178.
4. Ibid.
5. Ibid., p. 188.
6. Shah, op. cit., p. 107.
7. Country Analysis Brief: India, http://www.eia.gov/beta/international/analysis_includes/countries_long/India/india.pdf.
8. Ibid.
9. Government of India, Ministry of Petroleum and Natural Gas Economics and Statistics Division, Indian Petroleum and Natural Gas Statistics 2014-15, page 23.
10. Country Analysis Brief: India, http://www.eia.gov/beta/international/analysis_includes/countries_long/India/india.pdf.
11. Ibid.
12. Ibid.
13. Ibid.
14 Shah, op. cit., p. 107.
15. Ibid., p. 108.
16 Ibid.
17. Ibid.
18. Mahalingam Sudha, 'India-Central Asia Energy Cooperation', in *India and Central Asia: Advancing Common Interest*, K. Santhanam, and R. Dwiwedi (eds), New Delhi: Anamaya Publishers, p. 111.
19. Saipov, Zabilkulla, 'Energy Diplomacy in Strategic Calculations of Central Asia', in R. Malhotra, et al (eds),op. cit., p. 96.
20. Shah, op. cit., pp. 101-106.
21. Ibid., p. 107.
22. Saipov (2013), op. cit., p. 95.
23. Shah (2013), op. cit., p. 109.
24. Ibid., p. 109.
25. Ibid., p. 110.
26. Ibid., p. 109.

27. Ibid., p. 110.
28. Ibid., p. 109.
29. Saipov (2013), op. cit., p. 96.
30. Linn, Johannes F., 'Central Asia's Energy Challenge: Overcoming the Natural Resource Curse', 11 August, 2008. URL: http://www.brookings.edu/research/opinions/2008/08/11-central-asia-linn
31. Saipov (2013) op. cit., p. 96.
32. Tonnesson, Stein and Ashlid Kolas, 'Energy Security in Asia: China, India, Oil and Peace', Report to the Norwegian Ministry of Foreign Affairs, Oslo (PRIO): International Peace Research Institute, 2006, pp. 44-45.
33. Ibid., p. 46.
34. Ibid.
35. Ghazali, Abdus Sattar Ghazali, 'The Politics of Gas Pipelines in Asia', 21 November, 2011. URL: http://www.countercurrents.org/ghazali211111.htm
36. Shah (2013), op. cit., p. 111.
37. Ibid., p. 112.
38. 'Peace in the Pipeline'. URL: http://www.thehindu.com/opinion/editorial/tapi-project-peace-in-the-pipeline/article7992806.ece.
39. Ibid.
40. Ibid.
41. 'India, Turkmenistan ink 7 Pacts; Agree to Combat Terrorism Together'. URL: http://indianexpress.com/article/india/india-others/indiaturkmenistan-ink-7-pacts-pm-modi-for-early-operation-of-tapi/.
42. 'India's Energy Security Challenges: An Insider's View', *Sigur Centre Asia Report*, Issue No. 13, 2012. URL: http://www.gwu.edu/~sigur/assets/docs/publications/asiareports/asiareport13.pdf
43. Tanchum, Michael, 'India's Central Asia Ambitions outfoxed by China and Russia', *East Asia Forum*, 12 October, 2012. URL: http://www.eastasiaforum.org/2013/10/12/indias-central-asia-ambitions-outfoxed-by-china-and-russia/
44. Urazdoboeva, op. cit., p. 188.

3

Transportation Routes

Among the most significant factors that is hampering a full realisation of the historical and friendly bonds and promoting the contemporary national economic interests of India and the Central Asian Republics is the lack of physical connectivity between them. The landlocked condition of the Central Asian Republics makes it difficult for them to sell their products in the international market. Further, the lack of inter-state connectivity among the Central Asian Republics due to strained relations with the bordering states has hitherto rendered them as a relatively small market.[1] Despite new trading opportunities emerging after the independence of the CARs, economic recovery in these Republics has not always been accompanied by increased foreign trade. Therefore, the need to overcome their landlocked position and be land-linked as a way of integrating their respective markets to the rest of the world is a common challenge.[2] Due to their peculiar regional history and landlocked geography, each of the CARs have to rely on border crossings and transit through neigh-bouring states. Such a possibility can be achieved by expanding regional cooperation amongst themselves and with other regional powers. Similarly, for India to fulfil its energy requirements and sell goods in the Central Asian markets on any significant scale, it requires a definite transportation system in place connecting the two regions.

The easiest and shortest route between India and Central Asia since the olden days has been the "Great Silk Road" that passed through the Indian subcontinent, particularly the north-western part of India where Pakistan and Afghanistan are now located. The feeder routes branched out from there to connect India. Another trade route connecting India and Central Asia via Kashmir now lies under the Chinese territory. These traditional routes have for long been held hostage to the twists and turns of the India–Pakistan and India–China relations which have hampered the effective long-term solution to India's quest for improving trade and commercial exchanges with the Central Asian region. However, in the beginning of the 21st century, India's substantial economic growth as well as the identification of its interests beyond the confines of its immediate neighbourhood have encouraged it to find pragmatic solutions to problems in reaching out to Central Asia in terms of viable economic and trade linkages.

Improving its economic profile in Central Asia remains India's primary concern and, therefore, it has constantly been exploring ways and means to transport goods to and from Central Asia as well as regional integration avenues such as the cooperation with Iran and Afghanistan to bring about a greater interaction among them. It is in this backdrop that this chapter seeks to examine the various transportation routes being explored among India, Central Asia and Iran, i.e., the North-South Transport Corridor and the routes such as Mumbai-Chabahar-Zaranj-Dilaram-Herat-Naibabad-Khairaton-Termez as well as Mumbai-Bandar Abbas-Mashhed-Turkmenabad-Bukhara. It is to be noted that the establishment of transportation routes among these three regions would result in massive transnational trade and business opportunities.

Inter-Regional Transportation Infrastructure in Central Asia

The efforts made by the Central Asian Republics to overcome their small population and small market and emerge as viable economies are praiseworthy. They have, in fact, tried to achieve infrastructural development in the transportation sector by forging regional cooperation, i.e., establishing not only regional-level organisations but also cooperating in international efforts led by the EU and the United States to link the landlocked countries of Eurasia with the wider world. One such regional effort is promoted by the Central Asian Regional Economic Cooperation (CAREC), which is an association 11 countries; Afghanistan (2005), Azerbaijan (2003), People's Republic of China (1997), Georgia (2016), Kazakhstan (1997), Kyrgyzstan (1997), Mongolia (2003), Pakistan (2010), Tajikistan (1998), Turkmenistan (2010) and Uzbekistan (1997).[3] The CAREC has been instrumental in creating not only the infrastructure and putting it in place but also addressing issues on cross-border agreements and trade facilitation. A number of international organisations such as the ADB (Asian Development Bank), the European Bank for Reconstruction and

Development, the Islamic Development Bank, the World Bank, the IMF and the United Nations Development Programme have been active in financing different infrastructure projects in these countries in essentially three areas of activity: transportation, energy integration and trade facilitation. CAREC, project-based program funding has grown from 6 projects worth US$ 247 million in 2001, to 176 projects worth more than US$ 29.4 billion in 2016.

Transportation projects as illustrated in Figures 3.1 and 3.2 have largely been approved or in the process of being sanctioned; Turkmenistan established Afghanistan-Turkmenistan-Azerbaijan-Georgia, Oman-Iran-Turkmenistan-Uzbekistan, Iran-Turkmenistan-Kazakhstan transport and transit corridors. After the completion of the projects, the Central Asian countries are expected to have a sizeable transport infrastructure in place by 2017. In December 2010, cross-border transport agreements were signed by Kyrgyzstan and Tajikistan, while Afghanistan joined in November 2011. This has set a platform for many other countries to join the cross-border agreements.[4]

The New Silk Road

Since the early 1990s, there have been several ideas proposed by regional organisations as well as individual countries to revive the old Silk Road, which connected Europe with Central Asia and China over a distance of around 7,000 km. When these ideas failed to materialise substantially, the US came to the forefront with its own vision of a New Silk Road that got a push under the then Secretary of State, Hillary Rodham Clinton in 2010, which was supposed to revitalise Afghanistan as the link between Central Asia and South Asia. During her visits to Central Asia and India in 2011, Clinton spoke in favour of the New Silk Road, while making India one of the pivots of this project.[5] Two years after the American proposal to launch the New Silk Road project, Chinese President Xi Jinping too advanced his vision of two new "Silk Roads" to connect China with the West and secure its energy supplies—one by land and another by sea.[6] The Chinese President spoke of the two new "Silk Roads" during his visit to Kazakhstan in September 2013.

In his call for a New Silk Road, Xi was underlining the importance of China securing its energy supplies, overland to the gas fields of Central Asia and beyond, and by sea through Asia's contested waters and via the busy Strait of Malacca. Pursuing such a vision, Xi travelled to Kazakhstan,

Figure 3.1

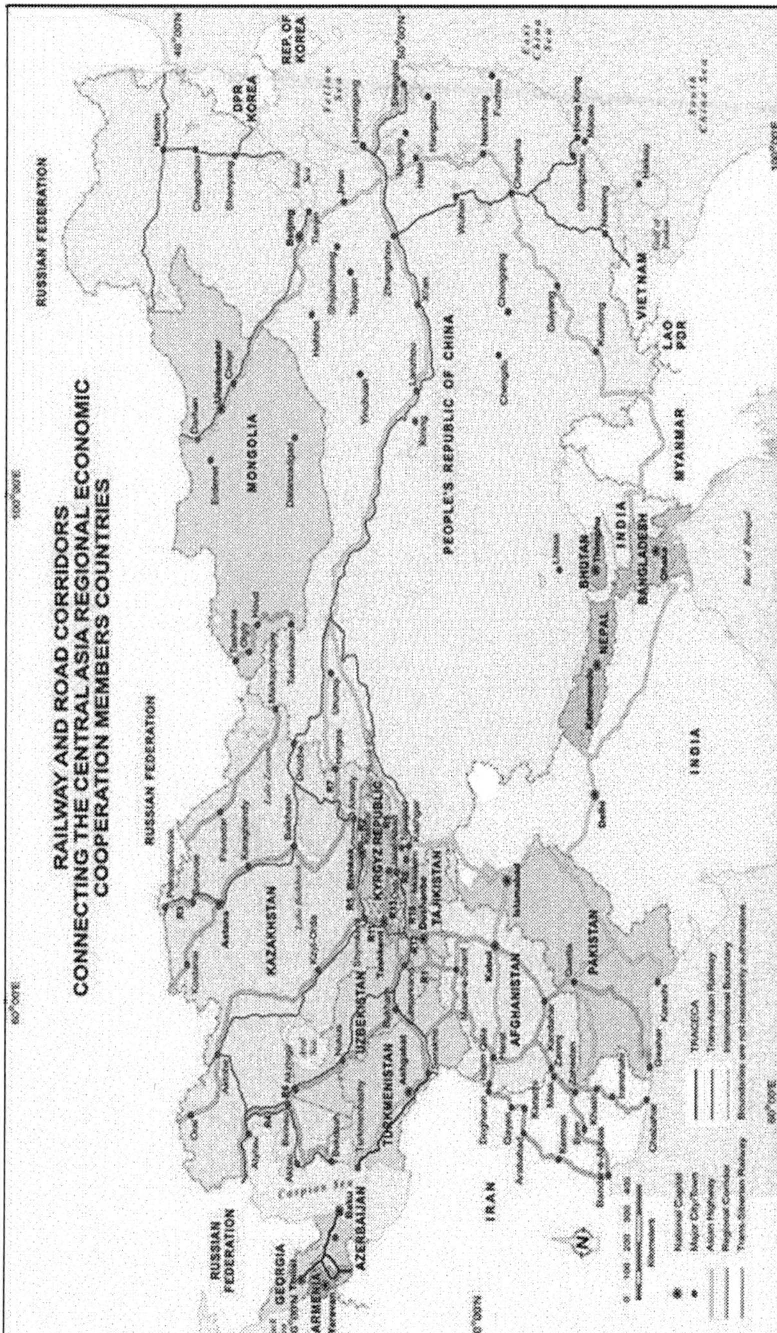

Source: M Prakash (2006), "Connecting Central Asia: A Road Map for Regional Cooperation". ADB, Manila, p.9, URL: http://unohrlls.org/UserFiles/File/LLDC%20Documents/MTR/ADB%20connecting-CA-roadmap.pdf

Figure 3.2

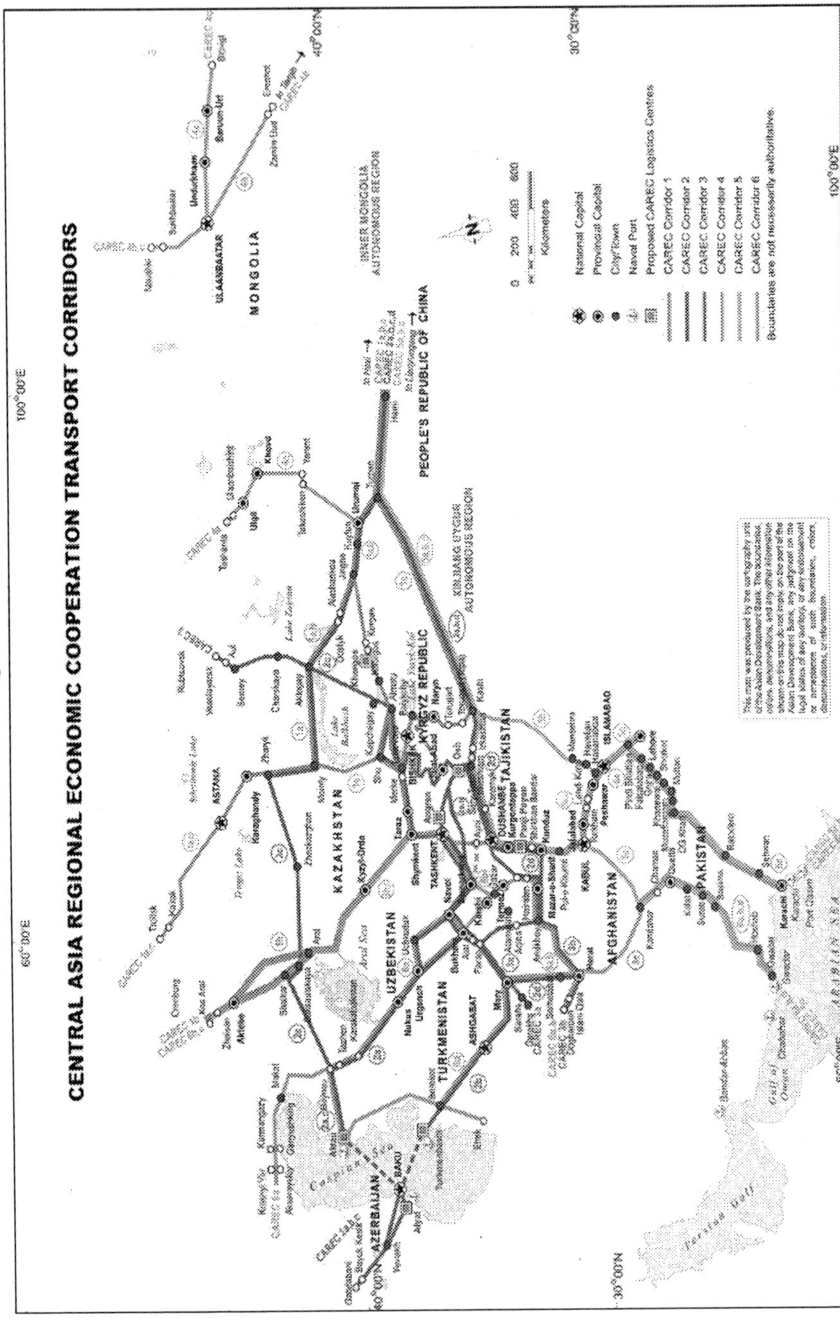

Source: CAREC , http://www.carecprogram.org/uploads/pages/corridor-map-1024x640.gif

Figure 3.3

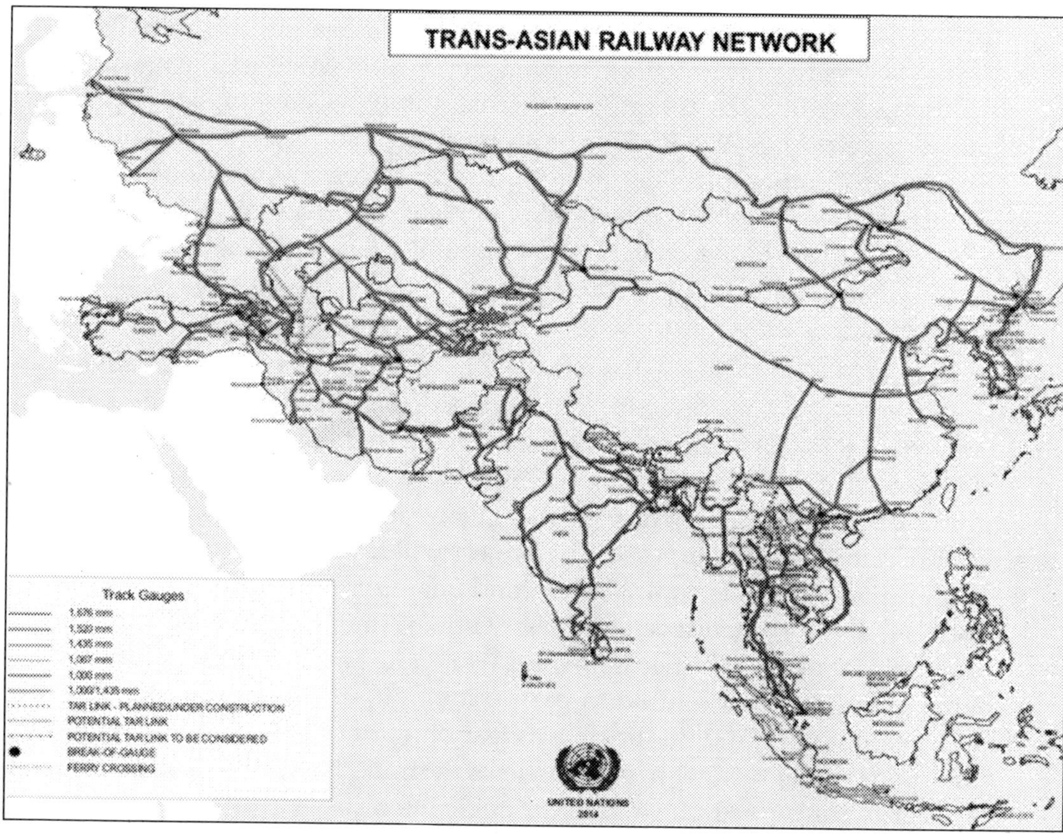

Source: Trans-Asian Railway Network-2014, http://www.railroad.net/forums/viewtopic.php?t=31943
https://www.google.co.in/imgres?imgurl=http%3A%2F%2Fwww.un.org%2FDepts%2Frcnyo%2Fnewsletter% 2FNL20%2Fasian% 2520railway% 2520 ESCAP.bmp&imgrefurl=http%3A%2F%2Fwww.railroad.net%2Fforums %2Fviewtopic.php%3Ft%3D31943&docid=J1PtSCOUi0tjxM&tbnid=h9Pmx58sp5FYqM%3A&vet=10ahUKEwjz3p-VvLPVAhXEsI8KHV1ZAWwQMwhDKAEwAQ..i&w=1328&h=977 &bih=490&biw=1024&q=trans%20asian%20railway%20network&ved=0ahUKEwjz3p-VvLPVAhXEsI8KHV1ZAWwQMwhDKAEwAQ&iact=mrc&uact=8

Kyrgyzstan, Turkmenistan and Uzbekistan and signed tens of billions of dollars worth of investment deals, taking a share in major Kazakh oilfields and expanding gas imports piped from Turkmenistan. He also proposed the establishment of a "Silk Road Economic Belt" as well as the "Maritime Silk Road"to boost trade and transport links and strengthen the regional policy coordination from the Pacific to the Baltic Sea. By this initiative, Beijing sees economic benefits in moving goods from western China, which has lagged behind the booming east coast, through Central Asia. Beijing also expects the new Silk Road to be much bigger and better than the older one as the "proposed routes are meant to transform bi-directional east-west exchange into multi-directional networking."[7] Through this vision, China's courting of the Central Asian Republics has drawn comparisions to the Great Game, the 19th-century rivalry between Russia and Britain in the region.[8]

On 14 May 2017, Beijing launched the so-called "Belt & Road" initiative, better known as the New Silk Road project or also known as "One Belt One Road (OBOR)", during a summit of global leaders. Chinese President Xi Jinping, who led the opening ceremony as the keynote speaker, hosted the leaders of 28 nations, who were more than eager to benefit from Beijing's grand ambitions and largesse. The project will involve 65 countries with a total population reach 4.4 billion and share of global economy of 30 percent. It's more than seven times larger than America's Marshall Plan to rebuild Europe after the Second World War. India has till date stayed away from the project and refused to participate in it, unless India's concerns are not addressed and till the time a clear blueprint of the initiative is not discussed and agreed with it. India views the initiative with suspicion and a security threat for India and its strategic interests.

Nevertheless, India supports the US-initiated New Silk Road project as the lack of connectivity and common borders remain a major challenge for transporting Central Asian oil, gas and other resources to India. This concern was highlighted by India's Minister for External Affairs, S.M. Krishna, during his address at the Institute of South Asian Studies, Singapore, on March 9, 2012. He said that "the lack of appropriate communications, especially transportation linkages with this region has acted as a major challenge to us. The proposal for a New Silk Road Initiative, which would enable the countries and more importantly the peoples of Central and South Asia ... is therefore, of paramount importance for us".[9] India may hopefully get benefit from at least reasonable ties with most

Figure 3.4: Silk Road

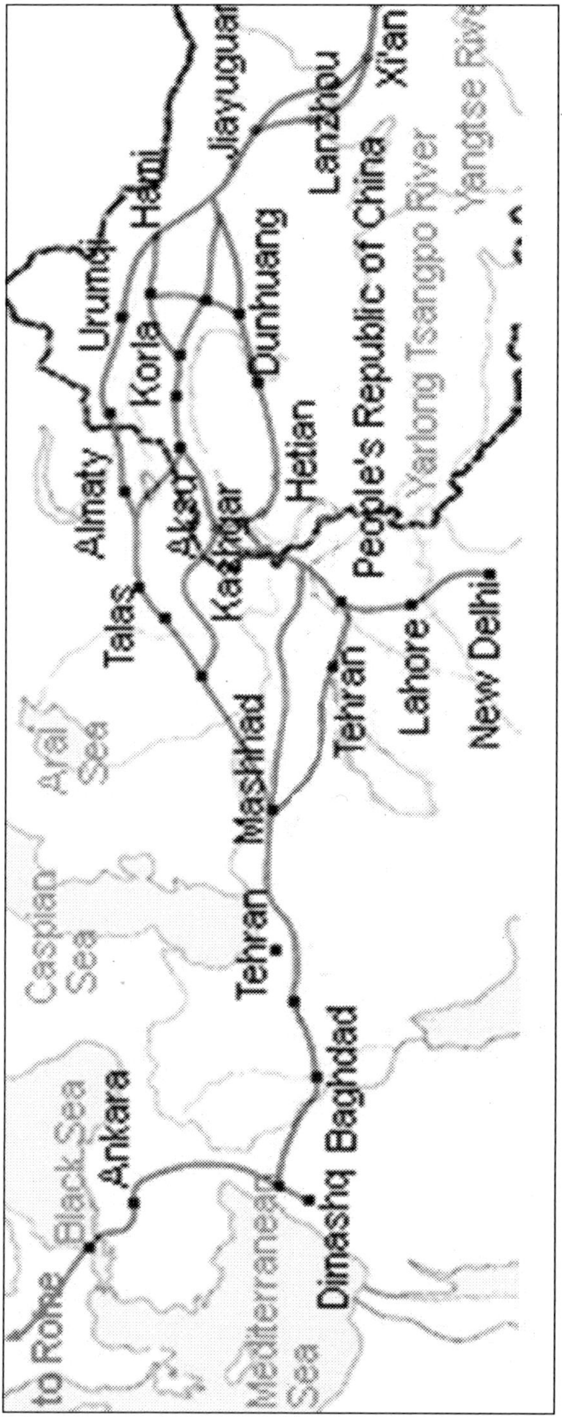

Source: Silk Road Map, URL: https://www.travelchinaguide.com/images/map/silkroad/silkroad-s.gif

stakeholders in the New Silk Road, including Iran, where India has invested heavily in the Chabahar Port.[10] In addition, the "New Silk Road" project will also help materialise the TAPI gas pipeline that would not only link the four countries involved but also enable India to have access to Central Asia. However, India needs to modify its approach towards the border regions, and not allow security to cloud its primary concern as one of the key bases of China's New Silk Road vision, which "has been its emphasis on utilizing border regions, while also making use of their strategic location."[11]

Existing Transport Connectivity between India and Central Asia

Currently, India's trade and commercial linkages with the Central Asian Republics and other members of the CIS countries is largely conducted through the sea route. The goods are transported from Mumbai (Nhava Sheva) through the seaport Bandar Abbas in Iran. From there, the goods are transported via roadways to Afghanistan and then to the Central Asian Republics of Tajikistan, Turkmenistan and Kyrgyzstan. Another alternative route takes the Red Sea route to travel around the Gibraltar and the Baltic Sea to finally reach Russia and the CIS countries. The third route is through the seaport of Qingdao in China that starts from Mumbai in the Arabian Sea, moving along the Indian Ocean and on to the Pacific port of Qingdao in China.[12]

In the landlocked Central Asian Republics of Kazakhstan, Kyrgyzstan, Tajikistan, Turkmenistan and Uzbekistan as well as in Azerbaijan and Armenia, the movement of goods are taking place via Bandar Abbas and alternatively via Qingdao. As per the India–CIS Chamber Study Report, even though the transit time from Bandar Abbas is much less compared to Qingdao, the Indian companies route their shipments via China which is 35 percent cheaper than the other route. From the seaport in Iran, the goods are transported by rail or road, while from the Chinese seaport, the only movement of goods is by rail.[13] Though Turkmenistan and Uzbekistan have bilateral arrangement for transit of Uzbek goods via Turkmenistan and Iran to the Gulf, the train connectivity is lacking between Uzbekistan and Tajikistan and between Kyrgyzstan and Uzbekistan.

Figure 3.5 shows a map depicting the above-mentioned existing sea routes of access to Russia and other CIS countries.

Figure 3.5: Existing Sea Routes

Source: A Strategy Paper for CIS Countries: India-CIS Roadmap 2020, FT (CIS) Division, July 2012, URL: http://www.epch.in/projects/IndiaCISRoadmap.pdf

The other mode of India's connectivity with the Central Asian Republics is through airways, though it is limited at present. Under the 'Connect Central Asia Policy', India has outlined a number of e-connectivity projects to establish communication with the Central Asian countries. As per the provisions laid down in the 'Connect Central Asia Policy', New Delhi now plans to launch 14 flight connections with the five Central Asian Republics to promote regional development.[14]

New Transport Links and Transit Routes

Despite the fact that on the map the Central Asian region is barely separated by a strip of the Wakhan corridor from greater Kashmir, the Indian goods have to undergo transit on circuitous routes before they reach Central Asia. It is, therefore, India's need to reconnect with Central Asia through a new viable transportation system. In this context, Indian efforts have mainly been to search for cost-effective alternative routes to Central Asia that could at the same time bypass both Pakistan and China. The new geopolitics since post-9/11 has been especially helpful as it has seen other friendly West Asian powers like Iran getting oriented towards a greater regional cooperation with Afghanistan and the Central Asian states. It is to be noted that the establishment of transportation routes among Iran, Afghanistan and Central Asia is likely to emerge as a new dimension in the 21st century geopolitics that may result in massive transnational trade and business opportunities between the three regions, besides the fulfilment of energy requirements. The transportation routes in these regions have thus been receiving wide attention in recent years.

The emerging geopolitical scenario in the Central Asian region provided an opportune time for India also to put in its stakes due to its long friendly relations with all the countries of the region since the heydays of the Cold War period. A significant factor driving it towards cooperation in the new regional formation has been its connectivity to the Iranian ports with which it is connected directly via the sea route. On November 10–11, 1992, the issue of using the transit facilities in Iran for India's trade with the Central Asian Republics came up for discussions at a meeting of the Indo-Iranian Joint Ministerial Commission held in New Delhi.[15] This resulted in sending two expert delegations to Iran (July 7–19, 1993) as well as to the Central Asian Republics (November 13–27, 1994) by India's Ministry of Commerce for conducting studies on the transport infrastructure and transit facilities.[16] Both the studies recommended that the best option in terms of practical, feasible and a cost-effective way would be the transit route through Iran.

There were two reasons for this option: firstly, the roads and other transport infrastructure were found to be in good condition for the movement of both container and break-bulk cargo, and secondly, the law and order situation was normal and stable.[17]

Overall, the studies indicated that the transit trade through Iran was not only logistically sound and commercially cost-effective but also held the potential of being fast, smooth and safe. Analysts like Puri (1997) commented that the wide-ranging Iranian network of well-maintained roadways, which allow heavy-haul traffic to ply at 80 to 100 km/hour, offers faster and cheaper transportation due to the availability of a large quantity of cheap fuel and other low-cost logistics there.[18] This is supplemented with an equally efficient railway system capable of carrying the load of bulk and heavy cargo. The recommendations of the two studies resulted in concluding a trilateral MoU between India, Iran and Turkmenistan on April 18, 1995 to give road and rail access for Indian goods to Central Asia through Iran and vice versa. It meant that the movement of the Indian goods was to take place from Mumbai and other ports in western India to the Iranian port of Bandar Abbas by sea and onwards by surface transport to Sarakhs on the Iran–Turkmenistan border. In addition, the MoU also permitted Indian registered vehicles to ply in both the countries and vice versa.[19] These two networks of sea and surface transport have been considered to be a reliable, cheap and less time-taking transit route from India to Central Asia via Iran.

The International North–South Transport Corridor

The origin of the International North–South Transport Corridor (INSTC) lies in the fact that in August 2000, Russia, India and Iran took a decision to develop a strategic transport corridor connecting the countries of the Persian Gulf, India and Pakistan to Iranian and Russian ports on the Caspian Sea. The corridor was proposed to stretch through Russian water routes, railways and highways to east and central Europe and to Scandinavia, thus covering areas of Northern Europe, the Russian Federation, Central Asia, the Caucasus and the Persian Gulf.[20] Further, on September 12, 2000 at the second Eurasian Transport Conference held in St. Petersburg, the transport authorities of the three countries as well as Oman signed an intergovernmental agreement to proceed with this North–South Transport Corridor project.[21] India ratified the agreement in April 2001, followed by Iran and Oman in October 2001, while Russia endorsed it in February 2002.

Figure 3.6

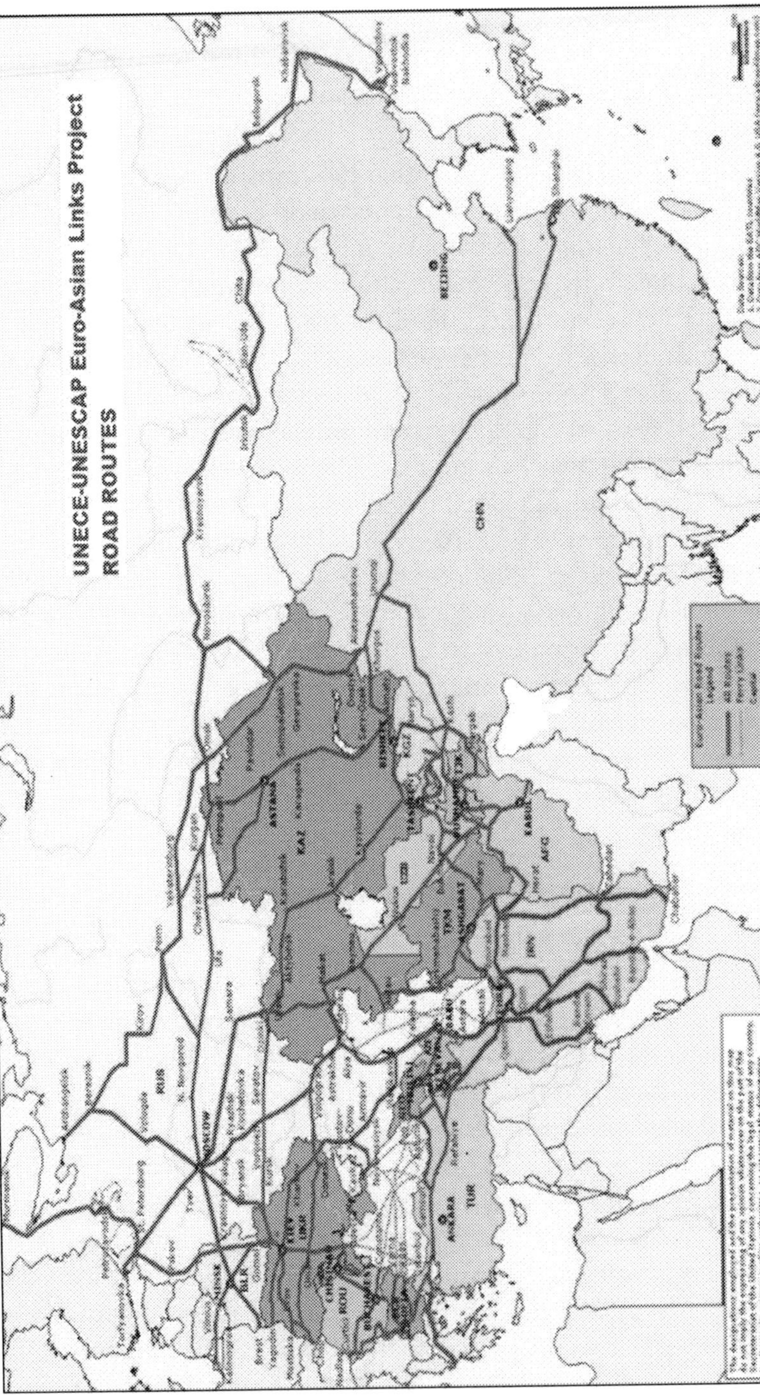

Source: *United Nations Economic Commission for Europe*
http://www.unece.org/fileadmin/DAM/trans/main/eatl/maps/Eatl_road_A3_schematically_one_color.pdf

Figure 3.7

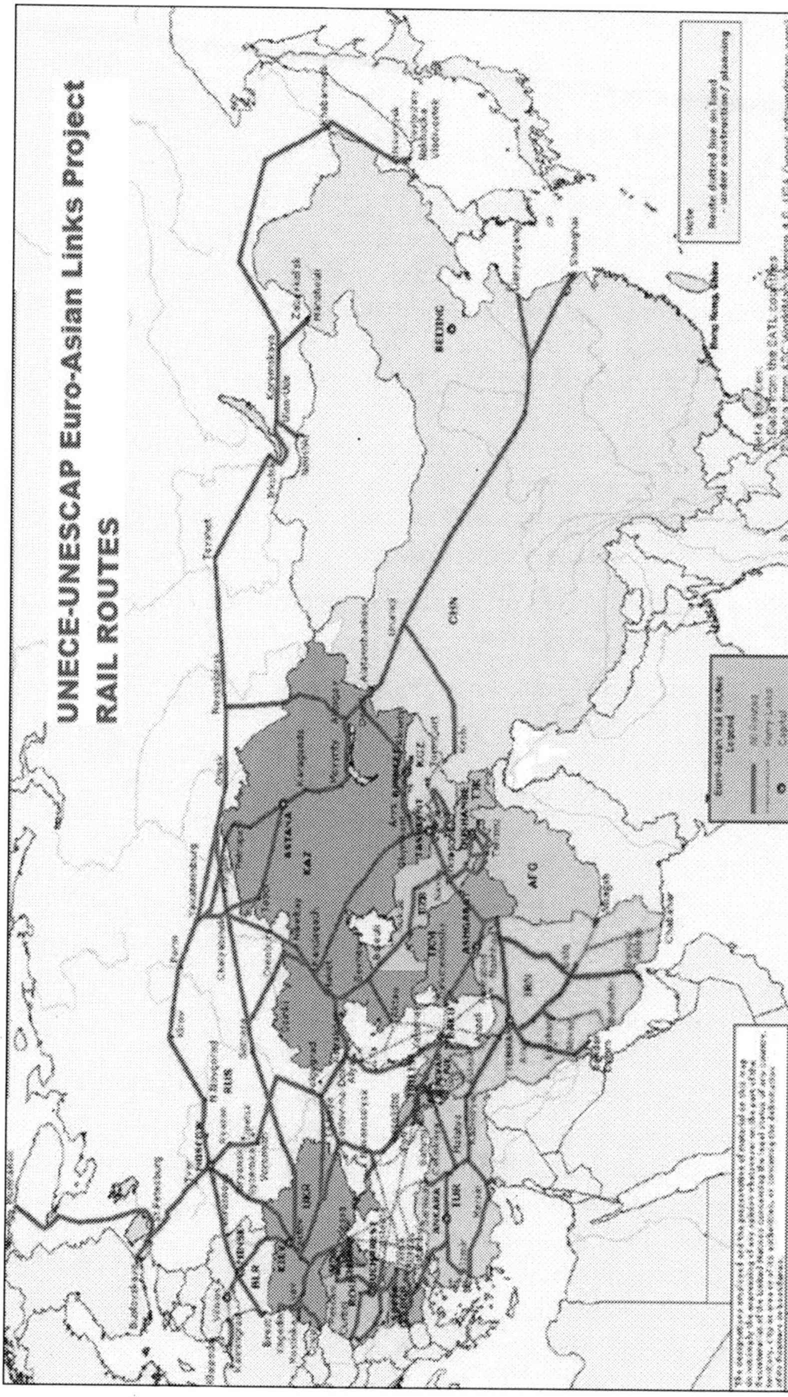

Source: *United Nations Economic Commission for Europe*
http://www.unece.org/fileadmin/DAM/trans/main/eatl/maps/EATL_rail_A3_schematically_one_color.pdf

The key objectives of the agreement include the following:[22]

(a) Increasing effectiveness of transport ties in order to organise passengers and goods transport along the international North–South Transport Corridor
(b) Promoting access to the international market through rail, road, sea, river and air transport
(c) Assisting the international transport of goods
(d) Providing security of travel, safety of goods as well as environmental protection according to international standards
(e) Harmonisation of transport policies as well as laws and legislative basis in the field of transport for the purpose of implementing this agreement
(f) Setting up equal non-discriminative conditions for all types of transport service providers from all parties in the transport of passengers and goods within the framework of the international North–South Transport Corridor

While adhering to the above-mentioned objectives, the countries involved decided to focus on the following:[23]

(a) Reducing transit time for passenger and goods transport in their respective territories
(b) Minimising transit and transport costs to 30 percent cost
(c) Simplifying and unifying all administrative documentation and procedures (including customs) applicable to goods and passengers.

However, the idea of this International North–South Transport Corridor has gone through many ups and downs. The rapidly changing dynamics of the Eurasian region, the volatility in the post-Soviet space, and the crisis in Afghanistan and the Iraq quagmire affected the contours of the whole project. Even though, not only India, Russia, Iran and the five Central Asian Republics but also Armenia, Azerbaijan, Belarus and Bulgaria, have accepted the project. Azerbaijan is heavily involved in the project currently building new train lines and roads to complete missing links in the INSTC. Turkmenistan currently is not a formal member but has road connectivity to the corridor. Indian Prime Minister Modi during a state visit to Turkmenistan formally invited it to become a member state on the project. As such, the project envisages a multimodal transportation network that connects ports on India's west coast to Bandar Abbas in Iran, then to Rasht and Astara on the Azerbaijan border onwards to Kazakhstan and further towards Russia, and through the Mediterranean to reach the Ukrainian ports of Odessa and Kiev, and then onwards to Russia and Central Asia.[24] A dry run of container movement via the corridor is scheduled to be conducted during 2017 to test and verify the smooth customs facilitation, connecting India with Russia and Europe via Iran.

The transit routes between Northern Europe and the Persian Gulf under the International North–South Transport Corridor can be categorised in the following manner:

- Route I (The Caucasus Route)
- Route II (The Central Asian Route)
- Route III (The Caspian Sea Route)
- Route IV (The South Asian Route)

Table 3.1 shows all the main routes and their transit regions as well as the status of a possible corridor continuation in South Asia. In addition, it shows various route lengths, number of border crossings, number of break-of-gauge points, status of electrification, double and single track routes as well as the major players involved, i.e. Iran and Russia.

Route I: The Caucasus Route

The Caucasus Route connects Finland with Iran through the territories of Armenia, Azerbaijan and the Russian Federation. Table 3.2 gives an idea of the transit route through the Caucasus Republics. The Caucasus part of the length of the North–South Transport Corridor route has a major thrust in Russia (50 percent) and in Iran (36 percent), though Azerbaijan plays a dominant role.

Route II: The Central Asian Route

The Central Asian route originates in Finland to connect Iran through the territories of Kazakhstan, Russia, Turkmenistan and Uzbekistan. As shown in Table 3.3, there are two alternative routes passing through the Central Asian Republics: one is through Taxiatash (Uzbekistan) and Station-449 in Turkmenistan and the other is through Nukuss in Uzbekistan. Lengthwise, both the routes are roughly the same.

A study conducted by the UNESCAP on the Development of the Trans-Asian Railway in the North-South Corridor that was published in 2001 gives a detailed description of various routes under the North-South Transport Corridor.[25] As per this study, the origin and destination of different routes and their alignments have been outlined in the following paragraphs:

Table 3.1: The North-South Transport Corridor

The North-South Corridor	*Helsinki (Finland) - Bandar Abbas (Iran) Caucasus Route (Route I)*	*Helsinki (Finland) - Bandar Abbas (Iran) Central Asian Route (Route II)*		*Helsinki (Finland) - Bandar Abbas (Iran) Caspian Sea Route (Route III)*		*Corridor continuation in South Asia South Asian Route (Route IV)*	
		Through Taxiatash	*Through Nukuss*			*Pakistan*	*India*
						Railways	
Total length	6,501 km	7,549 km	7,885 km	5,842 km through Bandar-E-Anzali	5,938 km through Noshahr	7,718 km / 445 km	62,809 km
				With 1200 kms (Through Caspian Sea)	With 1400 kms (Through Caspian Sea)		
Major Players	Russia, Iran	Russia, Iran	Russia, Iran	Russia, Iran	Russia, Iran	Iran, Pakistan	Iran, India
Number of Border Crossings	5	7	5				
Number of Break-of-gauge **points:**	1	1	1				
Double-track	3,046 km (47%)	2,438 km (32%)	2,438 km (31%)	2,812 km	2,812 km		
Single-track	3,455 km (53%)	5,111 km (68%)	5,447 km (69%)	1,587 km	1,443 km		
Electrification	2,360 km(36.3%)	1,598 km (21.1%)	1,598 km (20%)	1,563 km	1,563 km		

Source: UNESCAP (2001), *Development of the Trans-Asian Railway: Trans-Asian Railway in the North-South Corridor - Northern Europe to the Persian Gulf*, ST/ESCAP/2182, p.15.

Table 3.2: The Caucasus Route

Origin	Helsinki (Finland)		
Destination	Bandar Abbas (Iran)		
			%
Total length	6,501 km	• 283 km in Finland (1,524 mm track gauge)	4
		• 3,221 km in Russia (1,520 mm track gauge)	50
		• 622 km in Azerbaijan (1,520 mm track gauge)	10
		• 50 km in Armenia (1,520 mm track gauge)	.1
		• 2,325 km in Iran (1,435 mm track gauge)	36
No. of Border Crossings	5	• Finland – Russia	
		• Russia – Azerbaijan	
		• Azerbaijan – Armenia	
		• Armenia – Azerbaijan (AR of Nakhchivan)	
		• Azerbaijan (AR of Nakhchivan) – Iran	

Source: UNESCAP (2001), *Development of the Trans-Asian Railway: Trans-Asian Railway in the North-South Corridor—Northern Europe to the Persian Gulf*, ST/ESCAP/2182, p.15.

The Central Asian Route in Finland

The Central Asian route in Finland starts from the port of Helsinki and goes to Vainikkala (283 km)—the border station between the Finnish Rail Administration (RHK) and Russian Railways (RZhD). The Helsinki–Vainikkala link is a double-track covering 250 km distance to reach Luumäki and thereafter, it is a single track covering 33 km to finally reach Vainikkala. The entire link is electrified.

The Central Asian Route in Russia

From Finland, the route connects with the Russian railways (RZhD) at Buslovskaya, and from there it covers a distance of 2,513 km to reach Aksarayskaya through St. Petersburg, Bologoye, Moscow, Kochetkovka, Rtishevo, Saratov and Volgograd. With the exception of the Volgograd–Verhny Baskunchak section (214 km) and some portions of the Saratov to Petrov Val and Verhny Baskunchak to Aksarayskaya sections, the Buslovskaya–Aksarayskaya section is a double-track. Over 52 percent of the distance has been electrified. At Aksarayskaya, the route takes a turn eastwards and covers around 85 km to join the railways of Kazakhstan at Ganushkino.

The Central Asian Route in Kazakhstan

The Central Asian route in Kazakhstan covers a comparatively short section of 815 km from the border between Kazakhstan and Russia to the border between Kazakhstan and Uzbekistan.[26] From Ganushkino near the

Table 3.3: The Central Asian Route

	Through Taxiatas (Turkmenistan)		*Through Nukuss (Uzbekistan)*	
Total Length	7549 kms	• 4% Finland (1,524 mm track gauge) • 34% Russia (1,520 mm track gauge) • 10% Kazakhstan (1,520 mm track gauge) • 7% Uzbekistan (1,520 mm track gauge) • 12% Turkmenistan (1,520 mm track gauge) • 33% Iran (1,435 mm track gauge)	7885 kms	• 4% Finland (1,524 mm track gauge) • 32% Russia (1,520 mm track gauge) • 10% Kazakhstan (1,520 mm track gauge) • 16% Uzbekistan (1,520 mm track gauge) • 6% Turkmenistan (1,520 mm track gauge) • 32% Iran (1,435 mm track gauge)
No. of Border Crossings	7		5	
No. of Break-of-gauge points			1	1
Double-track	2438 (32%)		2,438 km (31%)	
Single-track	5,111 km (68%)		5,447 km (69%)	
Electrification	1,598 km (21.1%)		1,598 km (20%)	

Source: UNESCAP (2001), *Development of the Trans-Asian Railway: Trans-Asian Railway in the North-South Corridor - Northern Europe to the Persian Gulf*, ST/ESCAP/2182, pp.21-23.

Table 3.4: Specific Border Crossings

Through Taxiatas (Turkmenistan)	7	• Finland – Russia • Russia – Kazakhstan • Kazakhstan – Uzbekistan • Uzbekistan – Turkmenistan • Turkmenistan – Uzbekistan • Uzbekistan – Turkmenistan • Turkmenistan – Iran
Through Nukuss (Uzbekistan)	5	• Finland – Russia • Russia – Kazakhstan • Kazakhstan – Uzbekistan • Uzbekistan – Turkmenistan • Turkmenistan – Iran

Source: UNESCAP (2001), *Development of the Trans-Asian Railway: Trans-Asian Railway in the North-South Corridor - Northern Europe to the Persian Gulf*, ST/ESCAP/2182, pp.21-23.

border between Kazakhstan and Russia, the route travels through Makat and Beyneu covering a distance of 368 km and 668 kms respectively, and goes further south to the Kazakh–Uzbek border for over 90 km. The connection is completely single-track and operated under diesel traction. At Beyneu (Kazakhstan) a single-track, diesel-operated line section goes westwards to Eralievo (Kazakhstan) over a distance of around 480 km. From there, according to the UNESCAP study, a possibility could exist in the future to connect with the railways of Turkmenistan.[27]

The Central Asian Route in Uzbekistan

Departing from the territory of Kazakhstan, the Central Asian route connects with Uzbekistan Railway at Karakalpakia (100 km south of the Beyneu station in Kazakhstan). From there, the route further continues south to Pitnyak over a distance of 593 km. It is, however, to be noted that only 521 km of this distance is on Uzbekistan Railways, i.e. the 409 kms-long section between Karakalpakia and Taxiatash, and the 112 km-long section between Station '449-km' and Pitnyak. The 72 km-long section between Taxiatash and Station '449-km' is located in Turkmenistan.

The UNESCAP study argues that "after the break-up of the former Soviet Union, it is understood that the joint inter-operability of the line section from Karakalpakia (Uzbekistan) to Türkmenabat (Turkmenistan) could pose some operational problems between the two countries due to the number of new border crossings along the line resulting from their new status as independent states".[28] This line was then the only rail section linking the Uzbek capital city of Tashkent to the country's north-western region. In 1993, Uzbekistan began constructing a 342-km long section linking Uchkuduk and Nukuss in order to be able to reach Karakalpakia by rail without transiting through the territory of Turkmenistan. The inauguration of the Uchkuduk–Nukuss section in February 2001 created another possibility of routing cargo through the Central Asian Republics. This new line section now makes it possible to route cargo from Karakalpakia to Khodchadavlet, the border point between Uzbekistan and Turkmenistan, through Nukuss, Uchkuduk, Navoi and Bukhara.

The Central Asian Route in Turkmenistan

Leaving the territory of Uzbekistan, the Central Asian route connects with Turkmenistan State Railway at Taxiatash in Uzbekistan, from where the route continues further south to reach Türkmenabat, Mary and Sarakhs at the border with Iran over a distance of 1,002 km. But, only 890 km of this distance is on the Turkmenistan State Railway, i.e. the 72 km-long section between Taxiatash in Uzbekistan and Station '449-km' and the 818 km-long section between Gazodjak and Sarakhs. The 112 km-long section between Station '449-km' and Pitnyak is located in Uzbekistan. The Sarakhs railway station in the Turkmen territory has both swop body and transshipment facilities but it is preferable to transfer the containers from one guage to another rather than resorting to swop bodies.[29]

The Central Asian Route in Iran

After crossing Sarakhs, the Central Asian route leaves Turkmenistan and connects with the Iranian Islamic Republic Railways (RAI) through the 120-km long Sarakhs–Mashad section that was commissioned way back in May 1996. After the commissioning of this section, the movement by rail between the Central Asian Republics and the port city of Bandar Abbas on the Persian Gulf became possible, notwithstanding a break-of-gauge between the rail systems of the Central Asian Republics (track gauge of 1,520 mm) and the rail system of the Islamic Republic of Iran (track gauge of 1,435 mm). From Mashad, the route further continues over 926 km to reach Tehran through Azadvar, Sharood and Garmsar. From Tehran, the route continues towards south to reach Bandar Abbas through Qom, Meybod and Bafq covering a distance of over 1,443 km. Late 2004 saw Iran completing a 756-km long, double-track section between Mashad and Bafq. This has reduced the shipment costs and transit times for the traffic originating from Central Asia to Bandar Abbas.[30] This route is beneficial as it bypasses Tehran, thereby reducing the overall distance to Bandar Abbas, i.e. it is 1,000 km shorter than the route through Tehran. If all these links come into reality, the Central Asian route would be around 7,000 km as compared to the 7,593-km-long existing route through Turkmenistan and Uzbekistan.

Iran, however, has given a higher priority to the Astara–Qazvin link, and hence constructing simply the 230-km-long line section between Eralievo (Kazakhstan) and Bekdash (Turkmenistan) and the 240-km-long section between Bekdash and Turkmenbashi would still allow connection with the Iranian Islamic Republic Railways through Sarakhs. From Turkmenbashi, the route would then continue for 894 km to reach Sarakhs via Ashgabat and Tedjen on a single track, diesel-operated section. This would, however, be the longest possible route with a total distance of about 7,900 km.

Route III: The Caspian Sea Route

The Caspian Sea route connects Finland with Iran through Russia and the Caspian Sea. Shipping services across the Caspian Sea which are of relevance to the route are between the Russian port of Astrakhan and the Iranian ports of Bandar-e-Anzali and Noshahr. In 1998, the two Caspian Sea ports of Bandar-e-Anzali and Noshahr handled 1.6 and 0.83 million tonnes of cargo, respectively.

Container traffic is also predominantly routed through Bandar-e-Anzali which in 1998 handled cargo of 1,121 TEU (twenty-foot equivalent unit) against 485 TEU handled in Noshahr. On the other side, given the unmanageable process of using icebreakers to secure port operation at Astrakhan during winter, Russia has started a year-round-operation port at Olya. Ferry services are already regularly operated between Olya, Turkmenbashi and Bandar-e-Anzali. From Astrakhan, shipping distances across the Caspian Sea are 1,200 km to Bandar-e-Anzali and 1,400 kms to Noshahr. Russia further planned to develop a port-hub with a freight turnover of almost 8 million tonnes a year on the base of port Olya under the "Russian transport infrastructure modernization" programme.[31]

Route IV: The South Asian Route

The North-South Transport Corridor can also serve for the transportation of goods destined for South Asian countries, particularly India and Pakistan and even beyond. The links to countries in South Asia could be by rail or shipping.[32]

India and Pakistan are the two main countries in South Asia with a realistic chance of being served directly by rail through the North-South corridor, though this has been visualised as a long term prospect. However, with the completion of the construction of a single-track 545-km-long Kerman-Bam-Zahedan section of 1,435 mm gauge in conformity with the rest of the Iranian rail system, transshipment facilities are being provided at Zahedan. Once the standard gauge extends from Zahedan to Mirjaveh in Iran, the break-of-gauge point will be at the border between Iran and Pakistan. At present, the gap existing between the railheads at Zahedan and Kerman is bridged by road transport, although there is comparatively little traffic to the west of Zahedan.

From Kerman, a line runs in a north-western direction to Bafq, which is the junction station for the trunk line running south to the port of Bandar Abbas. As Bafq is also expected to become the junction station for the new line under construction, it will provide a direct link with Central Asia. Moreover, the Kerman–Zahedan line also permits direct movements by rail between places in Central Asia with its final destination in Pakistan or India.

The North–South Transport Corridor Continuance in Pakistan

Two main lines on the Pakistan Railways would continue the North–South Transport Corridor. The first one would be the 1,730 km line which follows a west-to-east alignment connecting Koh-i-Taftan at the border with Iran to Wagah at the border with India through Rohri and Lahore.[33] At Lahore, the line continues either northwards or eastwards. The northwards connection goes to Pakistan's capital city of Islamabad and its twin city, Rawalpindi (around 290 km from Lahore) and Peshawar, the capital city of the former North-West Frontier Province (462 km from Lahore). The eastward connection goes to Wagah at the border with India. The other line branches off at Rohri to travel south to Pakistan's main ports at Karachi and Qasim over a distance of 480 km. The overall line between Koh-i-Taftan and Wagah comprises 1,021 km of non-electrified single-track line, 245 km of electrified single-track line, 423 km of non-electrified double-track line and 41 km of electrified double-track line. Its 462 km extension to Islamabad and Peshawar is a non-electrified single-track with the exception of short double-track sections between Lahore and Shahdara (7 km) and between Chaklala and Golra Sharif (19 kms). Meanwhile, the 480 km line from Rohri to Karachi and Qasim is non-electrified and double-tracked over its entire length.

The North–South Transport Corridor Continuance in India

With its impressive 63,000 km route (44,000 of which is on broad gauge), the Indian Railway network goes in all directions from New Delhi to serve India's major cities and towns. Since starting its operation in November 1989, the Container Corporation of India Limited (CONCOR) has extensively developed rail container transport across India. There are two alternatives to the continuance of the North–South Transport Corridor in India.[34] The first-and existing-alternative is to use shipping services between Bandar Abbas and the two main ports serving Mumbai, i.e. Mumbai Port or Jawaharlal Nehru Port, which handles over 60 percent of India's container traffic, and from there continue by rail to inland destinations in India. The Mumbai–New Delhi line covers a distance of 1,510 km of 1,676 mm gauge and is multiple tracked and electrified throughout. It passes through important commercial centres such as Mathura, Kota, Ratlam, Baroda and Mumbai.

The other alternative is dependent on the Kerman–Zahedan line which directs cargo to Mirjaveh and then pushes ahead through Pakistan Railways to connect with India's rail system at Attari at the border between India and Pakistan. From Attari, the line goes in a southerly direction to New Delhi through Amritsar, Jalandhar, Ludhiana and Ambala. It covers a distance of 470 km on the 1,676 mm broad gauge. This line is important in the sense that it provides the lone effective land transport connection with Pakistan despite the fact that at the moment, there is only a limited exchange of freight and passenger traffic between the Indian border station of Attari and the Pakistani border station of Wagah.

Implications for Central Asia–South Asia Linkages

The International North–South Transport Corridor offers a platform for improvement in the Central Asia–South Asia linkages by reducing barriers and developing communications that allow each country of the two regions to grow independently, achieve national economic objectives and enhance its economic growth and development so that multiple countries could be benefitted without compromising their own national interests or sovereignty. Since the corridor envisions the opening of vast markets in India, Russia, Central Asia and Europe, the idea of Eurasia has started assuming significance. In this context, the Customs Union of Russia, Ukraine and Belarus can further be extended to involve other countries of Eurasia in order to have a wider economic unity, which can use this transportation corridor to their advantage.[35]

The Central Asian leaders are keen to see the network of transportation routes open. Uzbek President Islam Karimov and the Kazakh President Nazarbaev have already stressed on the need of increasing cooperation between regional countries.[36] The North–South Transport Corridor Project must be seen in the light of a broader attempt by regional Central Asian countries to create as many trade and transport opportunities as possible.[37] Current developments in the Corridor Project reflect the constantly evolving system of diverse routes and relationships of the historic Silk Road. However, despite offering much trade and transport opportunities in the landlocked regions of Central Asia and South Asia, the strategic and political dangers, such as the potential for militarisation of the Caspian, could pose a significant threat to the Corridor Project. Even though, it is considered as the most important link between Europe and Asia for transit goods, the important section of this route is passing through the Iranian territory and is much faster and cheaper than the other routes (Suez Canal). This route, at present, commences from the Indian Ocean sphere (Mumbai port) and links to Bandar Abbas in southern Iran through maritime transport. The goods are shipped from Bandar Abbas to northern Iranian ports on the Caspian Sea (Bandar Anzali and Bandar Amirabad) through roads and railway and then dispatched to the Astrakhan and Lagan ports in Russia. This route also connects India to the CIS countries and Afghanistan by road and railway.

India gets the benefits of being the entrepôt and final port for these goods by securing a reliable access to Russian, Iranian and Central Asian goods including energy. Pakistan has very great ambitions for its own trade routes through Central Asia, which would eventually end up at its Indian Ocean port of Gwadar (Pakistan). Iran has been instrumental in bringing the Central Asian Republics into this North-South corridor.[38] The importance of this corridor was realised when trade routes through Afghanistan and Pakistan came under the grip of Pakistan-backed terrorism. The North-South corridor bypasses Afghanistan and Pakistan and is a lynchpin of India's political closeness with Iran, Russia and Central Asia.

India's links to Iran are perhaps the most remarkable aspect of New Delhi's attempt to connect with Central Asia economically. Whereas India's ties with Russia are long-standing and visibly saturated with strategic implications, the Indo-Iranian relations have never been so prominent or important. While this relationship substantiates India's own claims to be a rising power and reflects Iran's awareness that cooperation with India is essentially beneficial to it in and around Central Asia, it also represents the broader trend of India's relations with the key actors there. Indeed, back in the beginning of the first decade of the new millennium, some analysts considered this relationship as opening the way to a new structure of regional relations including an Iran–US rapprochement.[39] The powerful linkages that India has created thereby enable it to project itself for the development of the North-South Transport Corridor with Russia and Iran, which could take shape only on the basis of common political goals. The relationship with Iran is not exclusively based on this fact or on the fact that India's main supplier of oil will continue to be the Gulf countries; Iran among them.[40] Iran has sought assistance in building an overland gas pipeline through Pakistan to India. Other options include a pipeline along Pakistan's shallow water coastline, or on the seabed from the Persian Gulf to India's west coast, or an already existing fourth option, the Liquefied Natural Gas (LNG), which is most expensive.

Still it is believed that this Transport Corridor is primarily an attempt to restore the historic trade of conventional commodities between South Asia and Europe.[41] The idea of the North–South Transport Corridor is a bold initiative to bring Central Asia on to the global trade map. There are various reasons behind India being so keen in pushing the North–South Transport Corridor. India is fast developing into an industrial powerhouse apart from being a major consumer of energy and so its dependence on outside markets is increasing day by day. Significantly, India became the fourth-largest consumer of energy in the world in 2011 itself. Eager to skirt its arch-rival Pakistan, India had earlier supported a controversial 890-mile, two-billion dollar "energy highway" that would run from Russia via Uzbekistan, Turkmenistan and Kazakhstan and on to Kashmir through the Line of Control between India and China.[42] Moreover, a decade ago, at the India–Central Asia Conference in Tashkent on November 6–8 2003, the then Indian External Affairs Minister Yashwant Sinha had already confirmed the addition of a Tajik leg to the planned Russia-Iran-India trade corridor that would reduce the distance between India and Central Asia by 1,500 km (932 miles).[43]

Yet, in order to sustain its present level of growth, India needs to emerge as a big exporter and its export items must become competitive in the world market (the current share in the global trade is merely one percent). Industry sources maintain that a boost can be given to the Indian exports if the North–South Transport Corridor becomes fully operational.[44] This is a project that has a massive potential, but neither Russia nor India has enough cash flow to invest rapidly and Iran has its own problems. Over the years, Russia and Iran have invested in road, rail and port infrastructure, but the expenditure hardly matches the required need for a vastly improved infrastructure.[45] Nonetheless, due to the usual hold up of ships/traffic at the Black Sea ports and the relative insecurity of goods in transit through Ukraine and Russia, the Iran route has good prospects of developing as the trade highway between India and the Central Asian Republics.[46] In essence, the Iran route will not only save 15 to 20 days of transit time on each shipment but will also be cheaper.

Recent Progress in the North–South Transport Corridor Project

So far as the development of the Iranian sector of the North–South Transport Corridor which has been of crucial importance to India for re-linking with Central Asia is concerned, the long unsatisfactory progress in the Iranian sector of the North–South Transport Corridor project has been a cause of concern. Some progress has been noticed recently with the beginning of the Iran-Kazakhstan railway project and the construction of the Qazvin-Rasht-Astara in northern Iran in order to complete the North-South Corridor which are considered to be positive developments. A three-day meeting of experts from 16 countries on May 30, 2012 in New Delhi discussed ways to smoothen the way for the International North–South Transport Corridor and at least six supplementary issues.[47] Experts also proposed the setting up of two four-nation groups to resolve many of the issues. Iran along with Russia and India (all three initiators of the project) will be in both the groups.[48]

Iran certainly plays a crucial role in the multi-modal North–South Corridor as its port Bandar Abbas will be the hub of all activities. Already on November 25, 2011, Iran and Russia signed an agreement to make efforts for developing bilateral and multilateral cooperation in road, rail, air and marine transportation. In 2012, the Russian FZE was awarded the Armenia–Iran railway project and the southern section of the North–South Road Corridor in order to complete the key missing link in the International North–South Transport Corridor. Another development took place in Iran when Tehran inaugurated the Astara port located in the south -west of the Caspian Sea on March 10, 2013. The port will allow Russian goods to reach the inland provinces of Iran faster and at cheaper costs. Products from Russia, Azerbaijan, Kazakhstan and Turkmenistan can be sent to India through Iran's Bandar Abbas port which is the fastest way to reach India.

Earlier, the New Delhi meeting on the International North–South Transport Corridor, which took place on May 30, 2012, proposed a joint venture between Iran, India, Russia and Azerbaijan for infrastructure and funding.[49] It also suggested a core group on customs—India, Russia, Iran and Turkey—consisting of experts from these countries, based in New Delhi, to sort out issues. The meeting aimed at achieving progress on four fronts including identifying the residual construction on the main North–South Corridor and the time frame for the harmonisation of customs and insurance documents. Discussions were also held on procedures and identification of complementary routes and their status as well as actionable points for member countries, which may prove to be fruitful in the times to come.

The 7th Meeting of Expert Groups and the 6th Meeting of the Coordination Council on the International North–South Transport Corridor (INSTC) was held from August, 19–21, 2015, in New Delhi, hosted by the Indian Ministry of External Affairs to review the INSTC Project. All INSTC member states excluding Armenia, Belarus, Oman, Syria and Bulgaria, participated. It was agreed that India with the assistance of the Federation of Freight Forwarders Association in India (FFFAI) would devise a template highlighting various parameters including tariff, details of ports, railways, freight forwarders, shipping agents, banking, insurance and logistics support by December 2015 for its circulation among the member countries for comments/suggestions. Member countries agreed to provide periodical updates of this data for uploading on the website. The meeting concluded that the requests for accession to the INSTC received from Afghanistan and Kuwait would be shared with the members.[50]

Meanwhile, the Foreign Trade Policy of India, 2015–20, has highlighted the importance of the INSTC in expanding India's trade and investment links with Central Asia.[51] Prime Minister Narendra Modi, who issued a joint statement with Turkmenistan on July 11, 2015, proposed that Turkmenistan become a member of the INSTC.[52]

Other Routes

Chabahar Port

The Chabahar Port in Iran is meant to give India access to Afghanistan and Central Asia bypassing Pakistan and also to give Afghanistan access to warm waters without going through Pakistan. Traditionally, India's relationship with Iran has revolved around trade. In 2010, the two countries conducted US$ 14 billion worth of business, mostly in oil and gas. India's decision to invest US$ 100 million in Chabahar, a port in the Sistan-o-Balochistan province on the south-eastern tip of Iran, is part of this relationship.[53] The Chabahar port acquired urgency in view of the potential Indian investment in the mining sector of Afghanistan. In the recent years, India has invested heavily on roads connecting the Kandahar–Herat highway to Iran in order to get goods and services into Afghanistan using this alternate route. India is being driven by a desire for increased trade with Central Asia and for a direct access to Afghanistan's mineral market, worth an estimated US$ 1 trillion to US$ 3 trillion. Analysts argue that "investing a relatively small sum of money would, in theory, yield a very nice return: at least 60-90 years of operating Chabahar."[54]

A viable alternative route could be a railway line from Afghanistan's Hajigak running westwards to Iran along the Zaranj–Delaram highway to the Iranian port of Chabahar. In order to secure the Iran route, India and Afghanistan are now looking to build a 600-mile railway line connecting Chabahar to Hajigak, which contains the country's largest iron ore deposits. India is of the view that the evacuation of iron ore from the Hajigak region will have to be mainly through the Chabahar port. While Iran is looking to use Chabahar to develop its infrastructure and levy substantial duties, India's investment serves as a critical lifeline for Iran in the face of international sanctions.[55] However, there is slow progress with regards to Chabahar due to fluctuating India–Iran relations. With a target of 12 million tonnes per year, the present two harbours at Chabahar have a capacity of only 2.5 million. In a significant trilateral meeting held in Tehran on August 30, 2012, India, Iran and Afghanistan discussed the regional security and economic situation, including ways to commercially exploit the Chabahar port.[56]

At the same time, all the three parties agreed to establish a working group to explore the trade and transit potential of the Chabahar port in an effort to boost economic development and inter-regional connections.[57] India views it as a success to have moved so close to finalising the decade-long project. Iran has already invested approximately US$ 340 million in the port, while India, as already mentioned, is expected to invest US$ 100 million. India reportedly spent US$ 136 million to connect Chabahar to Afghanistan's ring-road highway, a logical extension of the deal concluded by Iran, India and Russia in 2000 to develop the INSTC linking the Indian subcontinent and Central Asia. The coming into reality of almost two transportation links will undoubtedly position India to take advantage of the Eurasian integration process.

India signed a historic deal on May 24, 2016 to develop the strategic port of Chabahar in Iran and agreed on a three-nation pact to build a transport-and-trade corridor through Afghanistan that could help halve the time and cost of doing business with Central Asia and Europe. Developing the Chabahar port was seen as crucial for India because it will not only allow New Delhi to bypass Pakistan and access global markets but also counter China's expanding influence in the Indian Ocean region. But the project's land route through Afghanistan remains a security headache.

"We want to link with the world. (The) agreement ...can alter the course of history of the region," said Prime Minister Narendra Modi after the deal was signed in the presence of the Afghan President Ashraf Ghani and Iranian President Hassan Rouhani. Studies show that the corridor could bring down the cost and time of cargo trade to Europe by about 50percent. India has watched with unease the Chinese funding for the strategic port in Gwadar, Pakistan, which New Delhi believes will give Beijing access to the Indian Ocean region. In response, New Delhi began negotiations with Tehran more than a decade ago to develop the Chabahar port to counter the Chinese moves in what is seen as part of India's sphere of influence.

India's bilateral deal with Tehran will see India spend about US$ 500 million (Rs 3,400 crore) to develop the port in south-eastern Iran's Sistan-Baluchistan province as a regional trade hub. This will allow it to open up an alternative land–sea route for trade with Afghanistan. "The bilateral agreement to develop the Chabahar port and related infrastructure, and availability of about $500 million from India is an important milestone," said Modi. On his part, Rouhani said, "Chabahar can become a very big symbol of co-operation between Iran and India."

From the Chabahar port, the existing Iranian road network can link up to Zaranj in Afghanistan. This road can then connect to the 218-km Zaranj–Delaram road—constructed by India in 2009 at a cost of Rs 680 crore – and finally to Afghanistan's Garland Highway. This will give India road access to four major cities in Afghanistan—Herat, Kandahar, Kabul and Mazar-e-Sharif—but Kabul has already warned New Delhi to be ready for possible attacks by Pakistan-backed elements to delay the project. Future plan include an INSTC through Iran to Russia and Europe. Indian will invest US$ 500 million (Rs 1,000 crore) in phase-1, including a US$ 150 million line of credit from the Exim Bank to Iran's Maritime and Ports Organisation for making jetties and berths at Chabahar. The State-owned construction firm Ircon signed an agreement to lay a rail line from the Chabahar port to Zahedan and Nalco signed a deal to look at the possibility of setting up a 0.5 million-tonne aluminium smelter at Chabahar free-trade zone, provided Iran gives cheap natural gas.[58]

Zaranj–Delaram Road

India has built a 213 km-road from Zaranj on the Iran–Afghanistan border to Delaram on the Garland Highway that connects all major cities in Afghanistan. After completion, the Zaranj–Delaram road was handed over to the Afghan government on January 22, 2009. The road links the

Garland Highway to the Iran border through the Milak Bridge and onwards to Chabahar.[59] This road also links further north to the Central Asian Republics. Iran facilitated the entry of Indian equipment and the purchase of material. However, due to the worsening security situation in south-western Afghanistan, the execution of the Zaranj–Delaram road project has cost India US$ 152 million, instead of the earlier estimated US$ 84 million. In fact, the Zaranj–Delaram road, on the main Herat–Kandahar Highway, constructed by thousands of Indian nationals in the face of stiff resistance from the Taliban, was meant to be one of the most long-lasting and visible symbols of India's commitment to Afghanistan's reconstruction and rebuilding of its nationhood.[60] The second project involves the linking of the Chabahar port to the Iranian rail network which is connected to Central Asia and Europe. For Iran, the Chabahar complex could become the main entrepot for energy and commercial trade with Afghanistan, Central Asia and the Caspian region. Islamabad, too, has been pursuing a similar objective and has plans to develop the Gwadar port not too far away from Chabahar on the Makaran coast of Pakistan. The third project is building the marine oil tanking terminal in Iran.

An Indian consortium was engaged by the Iranian Ports and Shipping Company to undertake development work at the Chabahar port and on the Chabahar-Fahraj-Bam railway link. Following an agreement concluded in February 1997 between India, Iran and Turkmenistan, the three parties are now involved in the transit of goods from the Iranian port of Bandar Abbas to Central Asia via Turkmenistan. The agreement provides for Mumbai-Bandar Abbas-Sarakhs route for the carriage of freight onwards to the Central Asian Republics.[61] Goods are then transferred either by road or rail as the Iranian and the Central Asian railway systems have been interconnected since the mid-nineties. With the opening of the Bandar Abbas route after the completion of the rail link between Meshed and Sarakhs on Turkmenistan's border with Iran, India's difficult access to Central Asia has completely been changed. The new route connecting India to Central Asia via Mumbai-Chabahar-Zaranj-Delaram-Herat-Naibabad-Khairaton-Termez and further, has great potential. It reduces the distance by 1,500 kilometres when compared to the existing operational route, i.e. Mumbai-Bandar Abbas-Mashhed-Turkmenabad (earlier Chahar Su)-Bukhara.[62]

In addition to these transportation routes, there is hope on the trans-Afghan Transport Corridor, which can be extended to India. This corridor could be a new bridge between India and the Central Asian Republics via

Afghanistan, and will break the dependence on the existing systems by connecting Uzbekistan and other Central Asian markets with India. The corridor from Uzbekistan and Mazar-e-Sharif will connect Herat, Dogarun, Delaram or Milak in Afghanistan to Iranian ports and further on to Ahmedabad and Mumbai in India.

In accordance with a MoU on the "Development and Construction of Transit and Transport Infrastructure in Chabahar-Milak-Zaranj-Delaram route", which was signed in Tehran on January 4–5, 2003, India, Iran and Afghanistan have been trying to upgrade the infrastructure at Chabahar besides improving the route from Chabahar to the Afghan cities of Zaranj and Delaram.[63] The development of this route will have major implications for Afghanistan, Iran and India as Afghanistan has so far been highly dependent on Pakistani ports for its trade. But access to Chabahar will give it more options to govern its overseas trade and lessen Islamabad's political leverage on it.[64]

To conclude, these transport routes are very important for India, Iran and Central Asia. In particular, the idea of the North–South Transport Corridor has multiple purposes.[65] While it is an opportunity for Russia to bypass the Silk Road, Iran gains political and economic benefits from trade with Russia, Central Asia and India. And India gets access to Russian, Central Asian and East European markets for its goods, and links to a variety of energy import sources. Similarly, other routes too have tremendous importance in terms of an overall development. These routes provide opportunities for an increased transnational trade not only among the nations involved, but also among other countries of the Asian and the European region. Such trade and transit routes also provide a platform to ameliorate relationships and partnerships, reduce barriers and hurdles, and improve communications. Keeping in view the importance of these trade and transportation routes, the policymakers of these countries should make all-out efforts to realise these goals for the greater benefit of the individual countries as well as the entire region. However, the flip sides of the coin are the various risk factors and the lack of classical trading and business norms.[66] Indian trade has a history of adapting itself to the unique opportunities of non-traditional trading practices. The opening of the transit trade and transportation route through Iran will help in providing the competitive edge required for the Central Asian markets.

REFERENCES

1. Prakash, Mohan, 'Connecting Central Asia: A Roadmap for Regional Cooperation', Asian Development Bank, 2006. URL: http://www.unohrlls.org/UserFiles/File/LLDCpercent20 Documents/MTR/ADBpercent20connecting-CA-roadmap.pdf
2. Conference Report, 'Central Asia, Afghanistan and the New Silk Road: Political, Economic and Security Challenges', University Club of Washington, D.C., Jamestown Foundation, November 14, 2011, p. 56.
3. http://www.carecprogram.org/index.php?page=carec-countries
4. Conference Report, 'Central Asia, Afghanistan and the New Silk Road: Political, Economic and Security Challenges', University Club of Washington, D.C., Jamestown Foundation, November 14, 2011
5. Maini, Tridivesh Singh, 'China's New Silk Road Vision: Lessons for India', *The Diplomat*, 17 May, 2014. URL: http://thediplomat.com/2014/05/chinas-new-silk-road-vision-lessons-for-india/
6. Ma, Haiyun and Chang, I-wei Jennifer, 'China's New Silk Road Strategy', *Middle East Research and Information Project*, 20 May, 2014. URL: http://www.merip.org/chinas-new-silk-road-strategy
7. Ibid.
8. Denyer, Simon, 'China bypasses America's 'New Silk Road' with two of its Own', *The Washington Post*, 14 October, 2013. URL: http://www.washingtonpost.com/world/asia_pacific/china-bypasses-american-new-silk-road-with-two-if-its-own/2013/10/14/49f9f60c-3284-11e3-ad00-ec4c6b31cbed_story.html
9. Krishna, S.M., 'Address by External Affairs Minister on "India's External Environment and Current Foreign Policy Challenges" at the Institute of South Asian Studies, Singapore', 9 March 2012. http://www.mea.gov.in/mystart.php?id=530119102.
10. Maini, op. cit.
11. Ibid.
12. Denyer, op. cit. .
13. *A Strategy Paper for CIS Countries: India-CIS Roadmap 2020*, FT (CIS) Division, July 2012, pp. 28-32. URL: http://www.epch.in/projects/IndiaCISRoadmap.pdf
14. Ibid., pp. 28-29.
15. Puri, M.M., 'Central Asian Geopolitics: The Indian View', *Central Asian Survey*, 16 (2), 1997, p. 243.
16. *India's Trade with Central Asian Republics: Transport Infrastructure and Logistics for Transit through Iran*, Ministry of Commerce, Government of India, January 1995.
17. Pandey, S.K. , 'India and Central Asia: Alternative Trade Routes and Transit Options, in *Geopolitics and Energy Resources in Central Asia and Caspian Sea Region*, Shams-ud-din (ed.), New Delhi: Lancer Books, 2003, p. 193.
18. Puri, op. cit., p. 243.
19. Pandey, op. cit., pp. 195-96.
20. Kushkumbayev, Sanat, 'Kazakhstan', in *The New Silk Roads: Transport and Trade in Greater Central Asia*, S. Frederick Starr (ed.), Stolkholm: Central Asia-Caucasus Institute & Silk Road Studies Program, 2007, p. 288.
21. *Inter-Governmental Agreement on International North-South Transport Corridor*, 12 September 2000. URL: http://www.unescap.org/sites/default/files/tarns_annex2.pdf

22. Ibid.
23. Ibid.
24. Mahapatra D.A., 'North-South Corridor: Prospects of Multilateral Trade in Eurasia', 14 March, 2012. URL: http://indrus.in/articles/2012/03/14/the_north-south_corridor_prospects_ of_multilateral_trade_in_eurasia_15134.html
25. UNESCAP, *Development of the Trans-Asian Railway: Trans-Asian Railway in the North-South Corridor - Northern Europe to the Persian Gulf*, ST/ESCAP/2182, 2001, pp. 7-36.
26. Molnar, Eva and Lauri Ojala, 'Transport and Trade Facilitation Issues in the CIS-7 Countries, Kazakhstan, and Turkmenistan', 2003. URL: http://www.cis7.orgl
27. UNESCAP, op. cit.,p. 16.
28. Ibid., p. 18.
29. Chandra, Amiya, 'Turkmen-India Cooperation for Peace and Development', *Strategic Analysis*, 19 (9), 1996, p. 1248.
30. RAI, "Railways of Islamic Republic of Iran (RAI) Opens Bafq-Mashad Line", *Japan Railway & Transport Review*, no. 41, October, 2005, p. 34.
31. 'The Sea Port-Hub will be developed on Base of the Port Olya (Astrakhan district)', 26 November 2009. URL: http://global-port.ru/en/info/20.html
32. UNESCAP, op. cit. , pp. 27-28.
33. Ibid., pp. 29-30.
34. Ibid., p. 30.
35. Mahapatra, op. cit..
36. Ibid.
37. Spector, Regine A., 'The North-South Transport Corridor', 7 March, 2002. URL: http://www.cacianalyst.org/publications/analytical-articles/item/7062-analytical-articles-caci-analyst-2002-7-3-art-7062.html
38. Calabrese, John, 'Indo-Iranian Relations in Transition', *Journal of South Asian and Middle Eastern Studies*, 25 (5), 2002, pp. 60-82.
39. Ibid.
40. Pattanayak, Satyanarayan, 'Oil as a Factor in Indo-Gulf Relations', *Strategic Analysis*, 25 (3), June, 2001, pp. 465-480.
41. Roy, Meena Singh, 'Geopolitics of Central Asia's Search for New Transport Corridors', 5 February, 2005. URL: http://www.idsa.in/node/3235
42. Alibekov, Ibrahim, 'India Set to Expand Presence in Central Asia', 2 September, 2003. URL: http://www.eurasianet.org/departments/business/articles/eav120303.shtml
43. Ibid.
44. Roy, op. cit.
45. Ibid.
46. Chandra, op. cit., p. 1250.
47. 'Despite U.S. Opposition, Iran to be Transport Hub for North-South Corridor', *The Hindu*, 31 May 2012.
48. Patnaik, A., 'Customs Union: Implications for India', in *Post-Soviet State: Two Decades of Transition and Transformation*, New Delhi: Oscar Publications, 2012, pp. 84-85.
49. "Despite U.S. opposition...",op. cit.

50. URL: http://www.instc-org.ir/Pages/News.aspx.
51. 'An Opportunity for India in Central Asia'. URL: http://thediplomat.com/2015/05/an-opportunity-for-india-in-central-asia/.
52. 'PM Modi Proposes Membership in International North South Transport Corridor for Turkmenistan'. URL: http://www.newindianexpress.com/business/2015/jul/11/PM-Modi-Proposes-Membership-in-International-North-South-Transport-Corridor-for-Turkmenistan-782501.html.
53. Jorisch, Avi, 'Port of Damaged Goods: India's Dangerous Investment in Iran's Chabahar', *Forbes*, 16 September, 2013. URL: http://www.forbes.com/sites/realspin/2013/09/16/port-of-damaged-goods-indias-dangerous-investment-in-irans-chahabar/
54. Ibid.
55. Ibid.
56. Patnaik, op. cit., p. 84.
57. Ibid., p. 85.
58. 'India, Iran and Afghanistan sign Chabahar Port Agreement'. URL: http://www.hindustantimes.com/india/india-iran-afghanistan-sign-chabahar-port-agreement/story-2EytbKZeo6zeCIpR8WSuAO.html.
59. Chandra, Amiya, 'India and Afghanistan: Renewing Economic Relations', in *Afghanistan: The Challenge*, K. Warikoo (ed.), New Delhi: Pentagon Press, 2007, p. 184.
60. 'Indian built Zaranj-Delaram Highway under Taliban Control', 31 March 2011. URL: http://defence.pk/threads/indian-built-zaranj-delaram-highway-under-taliban-control.101103/
61. 'Transport Corridor to Afghanistan through Iran', Priority-VI Starred Question No 46, Parliament Q & A, Rajya Sabha (Answered on 20 February 2003).
62. Dwivedi, Ramakant, 'President Romanov's Visit to India', 25 April, 2006. URL: www.idsa.in/publications/stratcomments/RamakantDwivedi170806.htm.
63. 'Transport Corridor to Afghanistan through Iran', op. cit.
64. 'India, Iran, Afghanistan discuss New Transit Routes', 7 January, 2003. URL: http://hindu.com/2003/01/07/stories/2003010704161200.htm
65. Blank, S., *Rethinking Asymmetric Threats*, Carlisle Barracks, PA: Strategic Studies Institute, U.S. Army War College, 2003, p. 149.
66. Chandra, op. cit., p. 1252.

4

India and Kazakhstan

Kazakhstan is the largest landlocked country in the world and the largest country in Central Eurasia. Area-wise, it is almost 86 percent of India and is the second most populous country among the CARs. Due to its long boundary with Russia, territorial size and coastline with the Caspian Sea, Kazakhstan enjoys a central position in Eurasia. The emergence of Kazakhstan as an independent nation-state in the Central Eurasian region in the body-politics of the former Soviet Union has been a significant event in international affairs since it is the largest, the most resource-abundant and industrialised among the CIS countries after Russia. In more than two decades of its independence and the collapse of its command system of economy, Kazakhstan under the leadership of President Nursultan Nazarbayev has been able to successfully oversee the process of a painful economic transition and has achieved great strides of development in the political, economic and other areas to earn recognition internationally as the regional powerhouse. Apart from geostrategic considerations, Kazakhstan's aspiration to remain a democracy with moderate Islamic values, in a multicultural framework and shared oriental values, culture and traditions, have all been significant factors contributing to its international image.

Economic Situation of Kazakhstan

Kazakhstan is highly rich in natural resources. More than 74 percent of Kazakhstan's territory is suitable for agricultural production such as wheat, rye, barley, cotton, sugar beets and other vegetables and livestock production.[1] The mountains in the south are important for apples and walnuts both of which grow there.[2] Almost the entire periodic table of Mendeleyev can be found beneath the surface of the country. The country ranks seventh in terms of oil deposits and sixth in terms of gas reserves in the world.[3] It contains almost a quarter of the world uranium deposits, ranks sixth in gold reserves, eighth in iron ore and coal, third in copper, lead and zinc and second in chromite and phosphate rock. Its industrial sector rests on the extraction and processing of these natural resources and also on a relatively large machine-building sector specialising in construction equipment, tractors, agricultural machinery and some military items and it has also developed space infrastucture. It, therefore, has set its goals to be among the top ten oil producing countries and be among the 30 most competitive economies of the world.

Economic Geography of Kazakhstan

Kazakhstan consists of five large economic regions:

- **North Kazakhstan:** efficient grain economy, extraction of iron ore and coal, mechanical engineering, production of oil products and ferroalloys and energy.
- **East Kazakhstan:** efficient nonferrous industry, energy, mechanical engineering and forestry products.
- **West Kazakhstan:** one of the largest oil and gas extraction regions
- **Central Kazakhstan:** efficient ferrous and nonferrous industries, mechanical engineering and cattle-breeding.
- **South Kazakhstan:** cotton, rice, wool, grain, fruits, vegetables, grapes, an efficient non-ferrous industry, instrument manufacturing, light manufacturing, food production, fish farming and forestry products.

In the backdrop of its resource potential, Kazakhstan was able to recover soon from the economic crisisfollowing the Soviet collapse in 1991. The resource potential of the country allowed the Kazakh government under President Nazarbaev to follow a technocratic model of economic development strategy. The success of the above policy allowed the country to recover its economy since the mid-1990s. Since the first decade of the 21st century, Kazakhstan has emerged as the largest economy in the Central Asian region accounting for 70 percent of the combined GDP and stands second-largest after the Russian Federation amongst the Commonwealth of Independent States (CIS). During the period 2000–2007, Kazakhstan registered an impressive growth rate of about 11.6 percent. In 2008, it was around 9.5 percent. During the global financial crisis, Kazakhstan's growth rate fell to 3.3 percent in 2008 and 1.2 percent in 2009. However, global recovery helped growth rebound to 7.3 percent in 2010 and 7.5 percent in 2011.[4] In the last six years, it has maintained its growth rate of more than 9 percent. As such in recent times, Kazakhstan has seen a surge from 13th ranking in the former USSR to the top five most dynamic economies in Asia.[5] It has also achieved significant results in the Human Development Index (HDI), ranking 56th among 188 countries, according to the United Nations 2015 Human Development Report.[6]

Since mid-1996, Kazakhstan has followed a liberal trade policy when export duties were removed and the average tariffs on imports were brought down sharply. As a result, on the basis of its current 2.1 percent MFN Tariff Trade Reflective Index (TTRI), Kazakhstan's economy is viewed as a more open economy—more open than Europe and other Central Asian countries. On the basis of the low TTRI, Kazakhstan's trade regime stands as the seventh most liberal out of 125 countries.[7] In recent years, trade in goods and service has shown an impressive performance as is obvious by the trade to GDP ratio (81.6 in 2009–2010). In 2016, the country was ranked 41th amongst 189 countries in terms of doing business, registering a significantly better rank amongst the CIS countries with Russia placed at 51.[8] In 2012, the country was ranked 47th amongst 183 countries in terms of doing business, registering a significantly better rank amongst the CIS countries with Russia placed at 120th. The improvement in rank came just within a year or so as it was at 58th rank in 2011 receiving 80 percent of the total Foreign Direct Investment that has come to the Central Asian region.[9]

Kazakhstan's major concern has been to work for the diversification of its economy since under the Soviet System its economic resources were not meant for national development; rather they were geared to strengthen the Soviet system.[10] Going towards the direction of a national development agenda, a programme for cluster development in oil and gas, tourism, machine-building, food and textile industry, transport, metallurgy and construction has been adopted by the government. The strategy for industrial and innovative development upto the year 2015 is under execution to speed up the industrialisation process. The government has gone about creating the legal and normative base required for further reforms in the processing industry and for stimulating enterprises for appropriation of new types of high-tech and innovative products with a gradual access to the world market.

Innovative ideas have been given importance like the establishment of techno-parks in different parts of the country. The Scientific Production Association has set up the Progress Techno-Park and the Park of Nuclear Technology in Kurchatov. Ambitious education initiatives have brought the latest young Kazakh generation as among the most highly skilled in the world. Every year 3,000 young Kazakhs are sponsored by the government to study at the world's most prestigious educational institutions before returning home.[11]

Economic Indicators of Kazakhstan

(a) Foreign Exchange Reserve: US$ 29.31 billion (31 December 2015 est.)
(b) Exchange Rate of Local Currency (Tenge): 215.1 per US$ (2015).
(c) Inflation Rate (2012): 6.5 percent (2015 est.)
(d) External Debt: US$ 157.1 billion (31 December 2014)
(e) GDP: US$ 464.2 billion (2015 est.)
(f) GDP per Capita: US$ 24,300 (2015 est.)
(g) Real GDP Growth: 1.2 percent (2015 est.)
(h) Sector-wise Distribution of GDP (2015 est.): agriculture (4.8 percent), industry (35.3 percent), services (59.9 percent)
(i) Population: 18, 157,122 (July 2015 est.)
(j) Population below poverty line: 5.3 percent (2011 est.)
(k) Unemployment: 5 percent (2015 est.)
(l) Main industries: oil, coal, iron ore, manganese, lead, zinc, copper, titanium, bauxite, gold, silver, phosphates, sulphur, iron and steel, tractors, other agricultural machinery, electric motors, construction materials
(m) Exports: US$ 82.28 billion (2014 est.)
(n) Export goods: oil and oil products (59 percent), ferrous metals (19 percent), chemicals (5 percent), machinery (3 percent), grain, wool, meat, coal
(o) Main export partners: China (15.1 percent), Russia (12.3 percent), France (9.2 percent), Germany (7.9 percent), Italy (6.7 percent), Greece (4.1 percent) (2015 est.)
(p) Imports: US$ 43.58 billion (2014 est.)
(q) Import goods: machinery and equipment, metal products, foodstuffs
(r) Import partners: Russia (32.9 percent), China (25.9 percent), Germany (4.2 percent), (2015 est.)

Development of India–Kazakhstan Relations

Since the very beginning of Kazakhstan's independence, India has held an important place in its international relations due to the fact that India has not only for a long time been a resilient multi-ethnic, multicultural society with a vast experience of managing delicate intra-ethnic relations, but has also been a secular and stable democratic polity. From India's perspective, Kazakhstan has been an area of vital importance to India due to its geostrategic importance in the Central Asian region as well as India's geographical proximity and historical and cultural links with the region. In the post-Cold War era, Kazakhstan's centrality in the regional geopolitics of Central Asia as the most prominent country similar to its own position in South Asia has led India to accord a special place to Kazakhstan in its foreign policy priorities. India was one of the first countries to recognise Kazakhstan's Independence. Both the nations established formal diplomatic relations in February 1992 during the Kazakh President, Nazarbayev's visit to India which was followed by the visit of the then Indian Prime Minister, Narasimha Rao to Kazakhstan in 1993.

The bonds of friendship between India and Kazakhstan as prominent members of their respective regions as well as their presence in the comity of nations worldwide has given them a boost to come closer in recent times. Kazakhstan's role in the region in terms of promotion of regional forums such as the Conference of International and Confidence Building Measures in Asia (CICA) makes it important for India. In 2010, it chaired the 56-nation Organization for Security and Cooperation in Europe (OSCE) and the OIC (Organization of Islamic Countries) in 2011.[12] Kazakhstan in association with Russia and Belarus has launched the Customs Union as a first step towards forming a broader economic alliance of the former Soviet states which has come into effect on July 6, 2010. Adjudged in the traditional frame of relations, during the last two decades, the two countries have accorded great emphasis on the mutuality of their concerns on various political issues such as expansion of the United Nations Security Council, terrorism, etc.

Both the countries aspire to play a much greater role beyond their respective regional spheres to mark their presence in global politics and therefore, aspire for a permanent seat in the United Nations Security Council (UNSC). They hold that the present asymmetry in international relations gets reflected in the structure of the Security Council which stands out as out of sync with post-Cold War realities. The two sides, therefore, hope that the expansion of the UNSC would go a long way in bringing about equitable relations among the members of the international community and would ensure stability and security in the world. Therefore, on this issue, both the countries support each other's candidature as and when the expansion of membership of these organisations is considered by the member states. Both the countries also support each other at various other international forums. In this context, Kazakhstan supports India's greater participation in Central Asian regional organisations such as the Shanghai Cooperation Organization (SCO) by advocating an enhanced role for Observers while India supports Kazakhstan joining the ASEAN Regional Forum of which it is a member state. Kazakhstan has also backed India's NSG's waiver at Vienna and persuaded India to be a member of CICA which is the only Central Asian Forum of which India is a full member. Such a shared approach has come a long way in consolidating their bilateral ties giving it new directions particularly since the beginning of the 21st century. India has supported the initiatives of Kazakhstan aimed at reinforcing peace, stability and mutual understanding in Central Eurasia.[13]

High-Level Bilateral Visits

Positive trends on different fronts of the Kazakh economy can only be sustained if Kazakhstan diversifies its relations with the countries within or outside the region including the emerging powers of the world. This realisation has led Kazakhstan to seek a fruitful economic cooperation with India which is one of the emerging powers in the world and the largest among the South Asian countries. Also, India's growing economic, commercial and technological performance has paved the way for Kazakhstan to establish close relations with India.

India is recognised as a huge market of 1.2 billion people, and its economy is the ninth largest in the world by nominal GDP and the fourth largest by purchasing power parity (PPP). India has a per capita GDP (PPP) of US$ 3,586 as per 2010 figures and its GDP (Official Exchange Rate) is US$ 1.538 trillion (2010 est.). However, for its developmental needs, India requires most of the minerals and raw materials produced by Kazakhstan through bilateral trade. The bilateral trade between the two countries has currently shown a growth but it is much below the potential and there is an immense scope for its expansion. There are significant opportunities for expanding bilateral cooperation not only for meeting India's own needs but also for meeting the requirements of other Central Asian and neighbouring countries.

The political relations between the two countries have gained an impetus with high-level visits by the leaders of the respective countries. President Nazarbayev is the first and only leader from Central Asia to have been invited by India in the capacity of the Chief Guest on the occasion of the 60th anniversary of India's Republic Day celebrations. This invitation also effectively underscores the importance India attached to Kazakhstan and the Central Asian region and the bright prospects for further strengthening and diversifying ties between the two countries. The visit by President Nazarbayev in January 2009 was his fourth visit to India. Prior to this, Nazarbayev had visited India in 1992, 1996 and 2002. During the 2009 visit, a joint declaration on strategic partnership was adopted which has become the guiding document for consolidation of the bilateral cooperation between Kazakhstan and India. The Kazakh President's visit provided a significant impetus to the relationship at all levels and has led to an intensive exchange of delegations between the two countries for exploring possibilities to enhance cooperation. In this regard, the Kazakh President's statement holds importance: "I came here to confirm and reaffirm our full respect and recognition of India's global and regional standing. India is one of the key players in political and economic global affairs and regional affairs. We respect India as the country who was one among the first to recognize and support our Independence 21 years ago. We see the growth of India and we have full appreciation for the opportunities the growth of India presents to the world and to our part of the world".[14]

From the Indian side, an impetus for the bilateral relationship was provided during the visit of Prime Minister Narasimha Rao in 1993 and later during Prime Minister Atal Behari Vajpayee's June 2002 visit to participate in the first CICA Summit. The Vice President of India, Mohammad Hamid Ansari visited Kazakhstan in April 2008. Productive discussions to provide greater economic and commercial content to bilateral relations were held with President Nazarbayev. Several areas including IT, space, agriculture, food processing and others were identified as key to bilateral ties. The visit of Indian Prime Minister Dr Manmohan Singh to Kazakhstan in 2011 needs to be viewed in the context of regional developments in and around Central Asia, India's growing energy needs and Kazakhstan's desire to expand its trade and commerce.[15] The Indian Prime Minister's visit to Kazakhstan in 2011 further strengthened the evolving strategic partnership between the two countries. Prime Minister Modi, visited Kazakhstan in July 2015. During his visit, the Indian and the

Kazakh governments signed five agreements that included sectors such as defence, railways and uranium supplies.

"Kazakhstan is our biggest economic partner in the region. We will work together to take economic ties to a new level," Modi said. The two nations signed an agreement for Kazakhstan's nuclear company NAC Kazatomprom to deliver 5,000 tonnes of Uranium between 2015 and 2019. The Indian Prime Minister's visit to Kazakhstan in 2015 has further strengthened the evolving strategic partnership between the two countries.[16]

As a result of these visits the strategic partnership between the two countries based on the principles of sovereignty and equality has been established. The strategic partnership foresees comprehensive cooperation in all spheres, including political, economic, science and technology, military and technical, counter-terrorism mechanism, education and human resources development. This got reflected in the Joint Action Plan signed by the two sides during the 2011 visit of the Indian Prime Minister to Kazakhstan which definedthe roadmap till 2014 covering a large number of strategic sectors including defence, civil nuclear energy and hydrocarbons as well as cooperation in the fields of health and medicine, science and technology, space activities, information technology and education.[17]

India–Kazakhstan Inter-Governmental Commission

In order to enhance the area and degree of cooperation between both the countries, an India-Kazakhstan Inter-Governmental Commission on Trade, Economic, Scientific, Technological, Industrial and Cultural Cooperation to explore avenues for expansion of bilateral cooperation for mutual benefit was established in 1992. Later, a Joint Working Group under the India–Kazakh Inter-Governmental Commission was established in February 2005, which is currently working to identify areas wherein specific Indian investments could take place. The first meeting of the Joint Working Group on Trade and Economy was held in New Delhi on January 13–14, 2011,[18] while the second meeting was held in Astana on July, 19–20, 2012. The third meeting of the Joint Working Group on Trade and Economic Cooperation was held in New Delhi from 20–21 February, 2014.

The functioning of the institutional mechanism has steered bilateral cooperation between the two countries to a new phase and to a qualitatively higher level. During the last two decades, there have been 12 meetings of the India–Kazakhstan Inter-Governmental Commission on Trade, Economic, Scientific, Technological, Industrial and Cultural Cooperation (IKIGC), the latest of which took place in 2015. At the 9th meeting of the IKIGC which was held in Astana on October 11–12, 2011, the Kazakh delegation was led by Minister of Oil and Gas, Sauat Mynbayev and the Indian side was led by Minister of State, Petroleum and Natural Gas, R.P.N. Singh. The two sides reviewed the progress of the last Inter-Governmental Commission and agreed to expand the scope of mutual cooperation under the forum.

The 10th meeting of the India–Kazakhstan Inter-Governmental Commission was held on January, 8–9 2013 in New Delhi.[19] The discussions took place in 20 sectors of cooperation like Energy, Trade, Agriculture, IT, Science & Technology, Mines etc. Both sides agreed that the current level of bilateral trade is not commensurate with the potential existing between the two countries and called for conscious efforts to increase the Indo-Kazakh trade through the Joint Working Group on Trade and Economic Cooperation and the India–Kazakhstan Joint Business Council. Both sides also agreed that tourism provides an opportunity to strengthen links between the two countries at human and cultural levels. The latest 11th meeting of the India–Kazakhstan Inter-Governmental Commission took place in Astana on 24–25 April 2014, where both countries discussed economic, scientific, technological, industrial and cultural cooperation.[20] The meeting was significant in the sense that India has received an offer from the Kazakhstan Government to explore the Abai oil block in the Caspian Sea.[21] It is to be noted that the Abai offshore block that is located in the northern part of the Caspian Sea, 65 km from the shore at a depth of 8m–10m, has estimated reserves of 387 million tonnes (2.8 billion barrels) of oil equivalent. India planned to finish the exploration of the block by March 2015 but OVL, the overseas arm of state explorer Oil and Natural Gas Corporation (ONGC), after one year of studying the field data found it not attractive enough, and hence the exploration did not take place. Meanwhile, the 12th meeting of the India–Kazakhstan Inter-Governmental Commission on Trade, Economic, Scientific, Technical, Industrial and Cultural Cooperation was held in New Delhi on June 16–17, 2015. There were substantive and productive discussions covering all aspects of bilateral relations between India and Kazakhstan. Both countries reviewed developments since the last meeting of the IGC in Astana in April 2014 and also discussed various ideas and proposals to further strengthen their bilateral relationship. A new Joint Working Group on Connectivity was established during the 12th meeting of IGC in New Delhi. The 4th meeting of the India-Kazakhstan Joint Working Group on Trade & Economic Cooperation was held in Astana in November 2015.[22] During the meeting both sides reviewed the status of bilateral economic cooperation and discussed wide range of issues to boost bilateral trade and investment. The identified areas of cooperation included power, energy, telecommunication, IT, transport and connectivity, healthcare, leather, textiles, mining, chemicals and fertilizers, agriculture, and gems and jewellery. The two sides agreed to discuss simplification of visa regime to promote bilateral trade in the next bilateral consular consultations. Both sides also agreed to identify future opportunities for investments in each other's countries and implement the roadmap for trade and investment signed during the visit of Prime Minister Modi to Kazakhstan in July 2015. Besides, the future action on conclusion of Free Trade Area between Eurasian Economic Union (EAEU) and India was also discussed during the meeting.

Both India and Kazakhstan have shown a positive response and agreed to cooperate in the production and development of oil and gas fields in Kazakhstan. The Indian side expressed its willingness to participate in the exploration and production of hydrocarbons in Kazakhstan, both as a sole developer and as consortium partner, besides offering its cooperation in the field of renewable energy as well as atomic energy for peaceful purposes. Leading the Indian side at the IKIGC the Petroleum Secretary Saurabh Chandra also highlighted that "Indian oil and gas explorer ONGC Videsh is currently working on Satpayev offshore field in the northern Caspian Sea, where the potential reserves are estimated at 1.8 billion barrels and first oil is expected in 2020".[23]

India–Kazakhstan Trade Relations

The bilateral trade including exports and imports between India and Kazakhstan from 1996 to 2016 can be seen in Table 4.1. The figures show that the bilateral trade increased from US$ 16.96 million in 1996 to US$ 64.12 million in 2000–01 representing a growth of about 38.98 percent. It further grew to register a three-digit figure in 2005–06 and crossed the figure of 300 to reach US$ 310.68 million in 2010–11 which represents a seven-fold increase. Since then it has been showing a continued growth to touch the figure of US$ 410.74 million in 2012–13 which in the following year (2014–15) increased sharply to reach US$ 952.35 million.

Table 4.1: India-Kazakhstan Bilateral Trade, 1996-2016 (in US$ million)

Year	*Export from India*	*Growth Percentage*	*Percent share in total Exports from India*	*Imports from Kazakhstan*	*Growth Percentage*	*Percent share in Total Imports to India*	*Total Bilateral Trade*
1996-97	4.39	0.0131	NA	12.57	NA	0.0321	16.96
1997-98	15.13	244.61	0.0435	36.03	186.72	0.0869	51.16
1998-99	38	151.12	0.1144	12.43	-65.50	0.0293	50.43
1999-00	27.19	-28.44	0.0738	13.45	8.24	0.0271	40.64
2000-01	50.08	84.18	0.1124	14.04	4.33	0.0278	64.12
2001-02	45.70	-8.74	0.1043	7.39	-47.33	0.0144	53.09
2002-03	46.88	2.58	0.0889	12.73	72.14	0.0207	59.61
2003-04	74.81	59.58	0.1172	9.26	-27.23	0.0119	84.07
2004-05	81.42	8.83	0.0975	15.39	66.18	0.0138	96.81
2005-06	90.86	11.60	0.0881	26.30	70.87	0.0176	117.16
2006-07	83.18	-8.46	0.0658	88.30	235.76	0.0475	171.48
2007-08	111.99	34.63	0.0686	76.78	-13.04	0.0305	188.77
2008-09	131.68	17.58	0.0711	159.03	107.11	0.0524	290.71
2009-10	136.54	3.69	0.0764	154.91	-2.59	0.0537	291.45
2010-11	172.16	26.09	0.0686	138.42	-10.64	0.0374	310.58
2011-12	244.39	41.95	0.0799	191.86	38.60	0.0392	436.25
2012-13	286.23	17.12	0.0953	139.99	-27.04	0.0285	426.22
2013-14	261.51	-8.64	0.0832	656.33	368.85	0.1458	917.84
2014-15	250.68	-4.14	0.0808	701.67	6.91	0.1566	952.35
2015-16	151.91	-39.40	0.0579	352.93	-49.70	0.0926	504.84

Source: Based on Export-Import Data (1997-98 to 2015-16) collected from Directorate General of Foreign Trade (DGFT), Department of Commerce, Ministry of Commerce & Industry, Government of India.

Pharmaceuticals, coffee, tea, spices, textiles and apparels are the main categories of India's exports to Kazakhstan (Table 4.2). However, except for pharmaceutical products, among the top 15 merchandise imports to Kazakhstan, Indian exports accounted for less than one percent. Even in the case of Indian pharmaceutical exports to Kazakhstan, the percentage share of this item as a percentage of total Indian export of pharmaceutical products is less than one percent. The Indian export of services to Kazakhstan is negligible. Other than personal travel, financial services accounted for 3.94 percent of India's total export in that category and architectural, engineering and other technical consultancy accounted for 1.95 percent.

In addition to tea and pharmaceuticals, engineering goods represent the largest components of India's export basket to Kazakhstan. The Indian tea has been gradually losing market in Kazakhstan on account of a variety

Table 4.2: Main Indian Exports to Kazakhstan, 2015-16 (In US$ million)

S.No.	*Commodity*	*Value*	*Percent Share of India's Total Exports to Kazakhstan*
1	Pharmaceutical products	46.38	30.53
2	Coffee, tea, mate and spices.	31.18	20.53
3	Nuclear reactors, boilers, machinery and mechanical appliances; parts thereof.	17.52	11.53
4	Articles of apparel and clothing accessories, knitted or corcheted.	13.39	8.81
5	Optical, photographic cinematographic measuring, checking precision, medical or surgical inst. and apparatus parts and accessories thereof;	12.6	8.29
6	Ceramic products.	4.33	2.85
7	Articles of apparel and clothing accessories, not knitted or crocheted.	4.29	2.82
8	Rubber and articles thereof.	3.7	2.44
9	Ships, boats and floating structures.	2.86	1.88
10	Electrical machinery and equipment and parts thereof; sound recorders and reproducers, television image and sound recorders and reproducers,and parts.	2.35	1.55
	Total Export of top 10 items	138.6	
	Total Export to Kazakhstan	**151.91**	
	India's Global Export	**262,290.13**	

of reasons including quality, packaging, marketing, etc. The Indian Embassy in collaboration with the Tea Board regularly organises Tea Festivals in Almaty and Astana. Several other initiatives have been undertaken by the Government of India to retain and further enhance India's position in this sector. In the area of pharmaceuticals, most large Indian companies are represented in the market. However, given India's strong position in this sector, both in terms of quality as well as pricing, Indian companies can expand their share in the Central Asian market in general and Kazakhstan in particular with a little focused and aggressive marketing skill.

Since Kazakhstan is a major source of metals and minerals including iron and steel, these items accounted for about 50 percent of India's imports from that country (Table 4.3). Zinc and its compounds constituted another 27.7 percent of India's imports and about 16 percent included salt, sulphur, lime and other minerals. Thus, more than 90 percent of India's imports from Kazakhstan are accounted for by these commodities. Significantly, oil and natural gas do not feature in this list of major import items.

Table 4.3: Main Indian Imports from Kazakhstan, 2015-16 (US$ million)

S.No.	*Commodity*	*Value*	*Percent Share of India's Total Imports from Kazakhstan*
1	Mineral fuels, mineral oils and products of their distillation; bituminous substances; mineral waxes.	261.49	74.09
2	Salt; sulphur; earths and stone; plastering materials, lime and cement.	61.12	17.32
3	Iron and steel	11.43	3.24
4	Zinc and articles thereof.	9.98	2.83
5	Inorganic chemicals; organic or inorganic compounds of precious metals, of rare-earth metals, or radi. Elem. Or of isotopes.	5.25	1.49
6	Edible vegetables and certain roots and tubers.	1.92	0.54
7	Ores, slag and ash.	0.55	0.16
8	Copper and articles thereof.	0.5	0.14
9	Raw hides and skins (other than furskins) and leather.	0.35	0.10
10	Optical, photographic cinematographic measuring, checking precision, medical or surgical inst. and apparatus parts and accessories thereof.	0.12	0.03
	Total import of top 10 items	352.71	
	Total Import from Kazakhstan	352.93	

Joint Ventures

The India–Kazakhstan Business Forum was established in 1995 during the visit of the then Indian Finance Minister, P. Chidambaram to Kazakhstan. The Forum is meant to provide business organisations and corporate houses of the two countries a place to discuss opportunities for trade and investment as also the implementation of joint projects in Kazakhstan under the aegis of the Innovative-Industrial Development Program. Under the programme of industrial innovation launched by the Kazakh Government meant for a rapid industrialization of its economy, the Kazakh and Indian companies both participate and share their technical capabilities for mutual benefit.

Of late, a number of Indian companies such as Tata International Limited, Sun Group, Apollo Hospitals, Punj Lloyd, Tata Motors, BHEL,

ONGC, etc. have registered their presence in Kazakhstan. The experience of Indian companies is used in the IT parks which are functioning as special economic zones in Kazakhstan. The regional IT parks are functioning at Ural, Karaganda and Almaty. The IT park is a pre-economic zone with various customs and tax preferences such as tax exemption on land and property from VAT on services and goods.[24] In 2010, the Indian Foreign Minister S.M. Krishna participated in a meeting of the India-Kazakhstan Business Forum along with the Kazakh First Vice Minister of Industry and New–Technologies Albert Rau in Kazakhstan. They were accompanied by Indian business leaders representing leading organisations and business houses like Tata International Limited, Sun Group, Apollo Hospitals, Punj Lloyd, Tata Motors, BHEL, ONGC, etc.

ONGC Videsh Limited has already acquired a 25 percent stake in the Satpayev oil block in the Caspian Sea based on agreements that were reached when the Indian Prime Minister visited Kazakhstan. The signing of the package of documents relating to the Satpayev Exploration Block between the National Oil Company of Kazakhstan, KazMunaiGas and ONGC Videsh Limited on April 16, 2011 was a landmark development in the flourishing bilateral economic relations of the two countries. India had invested US$ 60 million in oil exploration by ONGC in the Satpayev oil block of Kazakhstan.

India has also requested the support of the Government of Kazakhstan for an important bid that OVL is making for a stake in the Kashagan oilfield. Another project between NPCIL and Kazatomprom envisaging cooperation including a supply of uranium to India is also in the agenda.[25] Lakshmi Mittal acquired the Karmet steel plant in Kazakhstan in 1995, now known as Ispat Karmet, which is contributing to the Kazakh economy. Mittal has been the largest producer of steel in that country. Besides, Larson and Toubro, India's largest engineering and construction conglomerate, has its office at Astana.

The Indian company Punj Lloyd has set up joint ventures in large and small-bore pipelines and in a sulphur processing plant in Kazakhstan. Punj Lloyd has built a crude KAM pipeline for PetroKazakhstan, large and small-bore pipelines for Tengizchevoil and oil and gas export pipelines for AGIP in Kashgan. The Company has gained goodwill for its work in Kazakhstan. The PFD International LLC, Kazakhstan, describes Punj Lloyd as a "model employer among the many international companies working at Tengiz" and for its "outstanding performance in Industrial Relations for projects in Kazakhstan".[26] Two new joint ventures in the engineering sector were also signed between M/s. Rakesh & Associates and M/s. Sharp Power & Communication of India and M/s. Kainar and M/s. AVYL of Kazakhstan (industrial batteries and concrete).

Earlier, as many as 50 delegations from India mostly in the business sector visited Kazakhstan during 2009 including CII and FICII-led delegations. The 4th Joint Business Council between the Indian Chamber of Commerce and Industry (FICII) and the Kazakh Chamber of Commerce and Industry (KCCI) was held in Almaty in October 2009. Week-long Indian Food Festivals were also held in Astana and Almaty in September 2009. An official-cum-business delegation comprising of officials from the Department of Commerce, CII representatives and executives of select 12 Indian companies visited Kazakhstan for the Ministry of Commerce flagship trade exhibition "INDIA SHOW-2014".[27] The India Show was held in Almaty from March 27–30,2014, where over 140 Indian companies and PSUs representing diverse sectors such as manufacturing, engineering products, mechanical equipment, chemicals, pharmaceutical products, oil sector, food-processing industry, textiles, garments, handicrafts and mining participated.

Scientific and Technological Cooperation

The cooperation between India and Kazakhstan in high technology areas holds immense promise. India has a pool of highly trained manpower in the scientific field and is also in the forefront of advanced technologies like biotechnology, nano-technologies and space. To materialise cooperation in the field of science and technology, during the Third Session of the Indo-Kazakh Joint S&T Committee held in New Delhi in August 2001, the two sides concluded a Programme of Cooperation (POC) in Science and Technology and a separate Letter of Intent for cooperation in Biotechnology and a MoU on Agricultural Research were signed.

This was followed by visits of Kazakh specialists in the areas of mining and metallurgy; Catalysis and Solar Energy during 2000–2001 on exploratory and projects-based visits to discuss and formulate joint research projects of mutual interest. A bio-sensor based earthquake prediction equipment from Kazakhstan has been installed in New Delhi.[28] In addition, a new programme on India–Kazakhstan cooperation in S&T for the period 2009–2011 including the fields of nano-technology, biotechnology and chemical catalysis was signed in September 2009.[29]

Information Technology

As far as Kazakhstan's development strategy is concerned, it realises the vital importance that information technology has come to play in the development of industries. India's comparative advantage in the information technology (IT) sector is seen as a positive factor in developing the bilateral economic cooperation. The contribution of the IT sector in India's total exports is comparatively higher than that of other commodities and attracts huge foreign direct investment. Presently, relations in this sector between India and Kazakhstan are very poor. If Kazakhstan is able to provide a better infrastructure for the Indian IT firms, then it would be beneficial for both the countries. India has its own interest in providing technical help to Kazakhstan for building up IT parks.[30]

Nonetheless, a significant cooperation in the IT sector was underway when the first India–Kazakhstan Joint Working Group on Information Technology was held in 2006 in Almaty. During the session, a Joint Protocol on Cooperation in the IT Sector was signed. It included the training of Kazakh programmees in IT parks, establishment of the IT University and assistance in e-governance. One such IT Park has already been established in Alatau.[31]

India–Kazakhstan Nuclear Cooperation

After the Indo-US nuclear deal (2005), which was finally ratified in August 2008, the same year the 45-nation Nuclear Suppliers Group (NSG) also lifted a 34-year old ban on New Delhi that paved the way for it to join the international nuclear trade. During these international negotiations, Kazakhstan actively supported India's position for the unconditional waiver for international commerce in civil nuclear energy at the International Atomic Energy Agency (IAEA) and the Nuclear Suppliers Group (NSG). Peaceful nuclear energy cooperation is a new important area of Kazakhstan–India partnership and agreements in this field were materialised between Kazakhstan and India during the high-level visits of Kazakh President Nursultan Nazarbaev in 2009 and Indian Prime Minister Dr Singh to Kazakhstan in 2011.

As a result of the initiatives of the Kazakh President, a MoU between the National Company Kazatomprom and the Nuclear Power Cooperation of India Limited was signed in which Kazakhstan agreed to supply uranium to India. An Inter-Governmental Committee on Cooperation in the area of civil nuclear energy was achieved, covering diverse areas such as fuel supply, nuclear medicine, use of radiation technologies for healthcare including isotopes, reactor safety mechanism, exchange of scientific and research information, exploration and joint mining of uranium, design, construction and operation of nuclear power plants.[32]

During Prime Minister Modi's visit to Kazakhstan, India and Kazakhstan inked a deal for a renewed long-term supply of natural uranium, and a wide-ranging defence cooperation pact besides a railway cooperation agreement to boost connectivity to realise the full economic potential. The Kazakh uranium mining company Kaz Atom Prom signed a contract with India's Department of Atomic Energy (DAE) to supply 5,000 tonnes of uranium over the next four years (2015-19).[33]

However, the agreement between India and Kazakhstan in the field of nuclear cooperation needs to be viewed in the background of India's energy security vision as laid down in its 12th five-year plan (2012–2017) which seeks to generate an additional 1,00,000 MW of power to meet its energy needs.[34] Undoubtedly, the hydrocarbon deficit leads India to fall upon nuclear energy as an important component in its energy mix in its national strategy to meet the future energy needs. Being the largest producer of uranium ore, overtaking Canada and Australia, and the second largest country in terms of uranium deposits (1.5 million tonnes), which constitute approximately 16 percent of the world total—Kazakhstan has a great prospect to help India in fulfilling its energy needs and in turn enhance its energy security.[35] Now India is forming civil nuclear deals with other countries also, namely—Argentina, France, Kazakhstan, Mongolia, Namibia and Russia apart from the United States and in this way it is bridging the 33-year gap of nuclear isolation. Recently, Canada and Australia have joined the group of seven countries already having civil nuclear deals with India. Now, there are no significant stumbling blocks before India and Kazakhstan that could hinder a further collaboration on the nuclear issue.

India–Kazakhstan Cooperation in Space Research

Kazakhstan hosts the famous Baikonur Cosmodrome and is a major centre for space research. However, Kazakhstan has more or less remained a passive partner of Russia. The Indian space programme is also recognised as highly advanced. It has built and launched its own satellites for communications and remote-sensing purposes and has been utilising these satellites successfully. Recognising the complementary needs and demands of Kazakhstan and India's expertise in space research has created a platform for both the countries to collaborate together in space research.

The agreement on cooperation in space research was signed between the two countries during Foreign Affairs Minister Krishna's visit to Kazakhstan on June 14–15, June 2011. Following this an MoU was also signed between ISRO and the Kazakh National Space Agency to explore the possibilities of expanding cooperation in this area. This agreement is expected to assist the Kazakh space programme in a big way since the agreement provides for technology transfer from India in the space arena.[36] The manufacture of satellites as well as utilisation of remote-sensing technology for improving the living conditions of the people through uses like telemedicine, geo-prospecting, etc., can be harnessed to a mutual advantage.[37]

India–Kazakhstan Cooperation in the Field of Solar Energy

The impact of conventional sources of energy on the environment and their finite quantities has stimulated both the countries to explore alternative sources of energy as an urgent imperative. India being one of the largest global consumers of energy has also been exploring alternative sources of energy, including solar and wind power. In 2011 during a meeting between Farooq Abdullah, India's Minister of New and Renewable Energy and the Kazakh Ambassador to India, Dulat Kuanyshev, both sides expressed an interest in establishing cooperation in the field of new and renewable energy sources, including solar energy.[38] More recently, during the 11th meeting of the India–Kazakhstan Inter-Governmental Commission that took place in Astana on April 24–25, 2014, the Indian experts proposed to consider the possibility of cooperation in the field of renewable energy.

India–Kazakhstan Cooperation in the Field of Healthcare

Several major Indian pharmaceutical companies have their operations in Kazakhstan and are increasing their market share every year. For example, a joint venture between the State Trading Corporation (STC) of India Ltd. and M/s Eke Pharma, a Kazakh pharma company, has already been established.[39] During the visit of President Nazarbayev, the pharmaceutical sector was identified as an important segment of the market where the Indian companies could make a dent. Indian pharmaceutical companies can consider possibilities of starting manufacturing of pharmaceutical drugs and products in Kazakhstan because Kazakhstan imports more than US$ 500 million worth of medicines and drugs annually from other countries. In addition to the population of Kazakhstan, these products could also be supplied to neighbouring countries in Central Asia as well as in southern republics of Russia.

Following the Agreement between the two countries in the field of healthcare, some medical institutions have visited Kazakhstan for exchange of experts and joint research. Efforts are being made to encourage Indian pharmaceutical companies to set up joint ventures in Kazakhstan. The proposed Agreement between the two countries in the field of pharmaceuticals is still pending.[40]

Cooperation in the Field of Agri-Business

Agriculture has become a growing field of cooperation between Kazakhstan and India. To feed its vast population, India needs huge quantities of fertilisers to increase agricultural productivity and food security. On the other hand, agriculture in Kazakhstan is one of the most promising sectors of the economy with Kazakhstan being among the top ten world exporters of grain. Grain production makes up 65 percent of Kazakhstan's agricultural enterprises and dominates 75 percent of the total cultivated area. On the other hand, wheat accounts for over 80 percent of total grain production. It has to be noted that Kazakhstan has the lowest wheat production cost (US$ 105 per tonne) when compared to Ukraine, France, Russia, UK and the US (US$ 248 per tonne).[41]

It also mainly exports primary products such as wheat, rye, barley, flour and rice. On the other hand, Kazakhstan experiences an annual shortage of milk for internal consumption due to a low-level pedigree livestock. The Kazakh government has naturally accorded priority sector status to agriculture, and a further development of the sector was set out in the Program of the Agricultural Sector for 2010–2014.[42]

During the visit of the Vice President of India Hamid Ansari to Kazakhstan in April 2008, agriculture was identified as a promising area of cooperation that led the relevant Ministries of the two sides to sign an Agreement on Cooperation in Agriculture and Allied Sectors which was an important step to facilitate cooperation in this field. Several Indian companies (both in the public and private sector) are trying to set up joint ventures for the manufacture of fertilisers in Kazakhstan.

The Indian side has also proposed setting up a gas-based fertiliser plant like urea, potash-based fertilisers and phosphate fertilisers and establishment of an Entrepreneurship Development Centre in Kazakhstan. It was recommended that feasibility studies on the two projects by Indian agencies should be undertaken immediately and considered by the two sides for implementation. The two sides have also explored the possibility of collaboration in research and development activities and the setting up of a Regional Research and Training facility in Kazakhstan catering to the Central Asian region under the framework of the proposed Agreement.[43] In this regard, a 17-member delegation led by the Minister of Agriculture, Government of Punjab, visited Kazakhstan from October 10–13, 2011 to explore the possibilities of investment in the agriculture sector.

Cooperation in the Field of Education

The 21st century has been remarkable for the growing recognition of India as a leader in software technologies. In April 2005, the leading Indian IT Company, NIIT, jointly opened the first India–Kazakh Centre for IT education in collaboration with the prestigious Al-Farabi University in Almaty.

As a part of the Connect Central Asia Policy of India, India will set up a Central Asia E-Network which would bring tele-education and telemedicine to the people of Kazakhstan.[44]

Recently, bilateral cooperation between the Indian and Kazakh higher education institutions has taken one more step forward with a student exchange agreement being inked between Amity University, Noida, and the Almaty-based Al-Farabi Kazakh National University (KazNu).[45]

Cooperation under the ITEC Programme

An extremely important and useful role is being played by the Indian Technical and Economic Cooperation (ITEC) Programme which is an excellent initiative to enhance knowledge and upgrade skills of the Kazakh officials and business entrepreneurs through training programmes in India. Under this programme, India offers around 60 scholarships to Kazakh specialists, entrepreneurs and officials, both in the public and private sectors, to receive training in areas and sectors including Information Technology, English-Speaking, Mass Communication, Environment, Educational Planning, Bank Management, Remote Sensing, Textiles, Pharmaceuticals, etc. These programmes are conducted in some of the best and most reputed institutions in India. Similarly, there are around 3,000 Indian students in Kazakhstan studying medicine at Almaty and other cities of Kazakhstan.

Cooperation in the Field of Tourism

Tourism has of late emerged as a significant area of focus in improving bilateral economic relations between the two countries. The Tourism Ministry has been regularly participating in the Kazakhstan International

Tourism and Travel Fair. Mutual visits of major Tour and Travel Operators from India and Kazakhstan have received an impetus since 2009. A 10-member delegation from the Leather Export Promotion Council visited Kazakhstan from May 26–29, 2010, and had a fruitful interaction with Kazakh leather exporters. A "Great India Bazaar" was organized by M/s Spacesence Designs, New Delhi with the support of the Indian Embassy and Chambers of Commerce and the Industry of Kazakhstan at the Atakent International Exhibition Centre in Almaty from August 14–22, 2010. Around 70 companies representing different fields from India participated in the Bazaar. A 14-member business delegation representing various sectors visited Almaty from September 1–4, 2010, under the aegis of the Associated Chambers of Commerce and Industry of India (ASSOCHAM) with an aim to develop trade relations and to promote economic cooperation with Kazakhstan. A road show was organised by India Tourism, Frankfurt, on September 27, 2010 in Almaty. Three Indian tour operators from India along with tour operators of Kazakhstan participated in this event. A 25-member Chemexcil delegation visited Almaty whereby a Buyer–Seller Meet was organized on July 7, 2011.[46]

India was one of the first countries to confirm its participation in the Astana EXPO 2017.

This was reaffirmed by PM Modi during his visit to Kazakhstan. The India Trade Promotion Organisation (ITPO), a government of India enterprise, has been assigned the responsibility to coordinate India's participation in the expo. India signed an official participation contract last month. One of the largest service sector segments of the Indian economy is tourism and hospitality—a sector where the two countries could improve cooperation.[47]

There are about 3,500 NRIs in the whole of Kazakhstan. This includes students studying medicine in Kazakhstan. Most of the NRIs are in the private sector (oil exploration, downstream industries, steel and IT) and business (tea, pharmaceuticals, etc.). An Indian Association is in place with headquarters in Almaty and with branches in the major cities of Kazakhstan.[48]

Energy Cooperation

The impact of conventional sources of energy on the environment and their finite quantities has stimulated countries all over the world to explore the alternative sources of energy as an urgent imperative. India being one of the largest global consumers of energy has also been exploring alternative sources of energy, including solar and wind power.

The hydrocarbon sector is another strategic sector for the India–Kazakhstan cooperation. Kazakhstan is among the top ten countries in the world in terms of oil reserves with an estimated 39.8 billion barrels.[49] Being an energy-deficient country, India depends on the import of oil, mainly from the Persian Gulf region. But to enhance its energy security, India looks at alternative sources. In terms of oil, Kazakhstan has been recognised as the "second Kuwait" and the next "petro-state", whereas in the production of uranium, Kazakhstan emerged as the largest country in December 2009.[50]

The extraction of gas in Kazakhstan is carried on in three of the largest deposits: Karachaganak (gas condensate), Kashagan (with oil extraction) and Tengiz. Also, Kazakhstan is realising the project in the south of the country by developing the Amangeldi group of deposits, with the extraction of about 0.7 trillion cubic metres of gas annually.[51] Kazakhstan signed several agreements including cooperation on nuclear energy with India during a visit by the Kazakh Foreign Minister Erlan Idrissov to New Delhi in March 2013.[52] India has also urged Kazakhstan to make a decision on the Indian energy firm ONGC Videsh's purchase of ConocoPhillips's stake in the Kashagan oilfield. It may be noted that ConocoPhillips sold its 8.4 percent share in the oilfield in 2012, though the Kazakh national energy firm, KazMunaiGas (KMG), had the right to refuse the transaction.

Major Oil and Gas Deposits in Kazakhstan

Kashagan is the largest sea deposit in Kazakhstan. It is situated 80 km to the south-west from the port of Atirau. It was opened in July 2001. The potential geological stock estimate is around 38 billion barrels of oil. It is operated by a consortium of seven international companies led by "AgipKazkhstan North Operating Company B.V.".[53]

Tengiz is the world's largest sea deposit. It was opened in 1979. Since 1993, the Government of Kazakhstan in cooperation with "Ceveron" has founded a joint venture "Tengizshevroil". Now it has four partner companies: KazMunaiGas, Chevron Overseas, Exon Mobil and LukArko.

Karachaganak is one of the largest gas, gas condensate and oil deposits in the world whose stocks are estimated at more than 1.3 trillion cubic metres of gas. It is situated in Aksay in Kazakhstan's Ural region, 130 km from Orenburg. It was discovered in 1979 but the development of the deposit started in 1984. Its annual extraction of gas was predicted to increase to 25 billion cubic metres in 2012. The Karachaganak project is being realised in the framework of the final Agreement on Separation of Production, which was signed between the Government of Kazakhstan and an alliance of foreign companies like BG, ENI and Lukoil. The agreement was signed in November 1998 for a period of 40 years which came into force on January 27, 1998.[54]

During his visit to Kazakhstan in May 2002, the former Prime Minister of India, Atal Behari Vajpayee, declared that India was ready "to make big investments" in Kazakhstan's oil and gas sector. This intention found a practical realisation during subsequent visits of the delegations of ONGC-Videsh Ltd. in Kazakhstan when the Indian company became an owner of 15 percent of the share holdings in project Alibekmola and 10 percent of the share holdings in project Kurmangazy.

Bilateral cooperation in the field of investigation and development on a shelf of the Caspian Sea between two big energy companies of Kazakhstan and India, KazMunaiGas and ONGC Videsh Ltd, was fixed by the Report of the Fifth Session of the Kazakh-India Inter-Governmental Commission on Trade and Economic Ties, Scientific, Technical, Industrial and Cultural Cooperation and was signed on February 18, 2005.[55]

The intense Chinese competition in this sector initially aborted the Indian companies' acquisition of oil and gas fields in Kazakhstan. However, the cooperation in the energy sector between the two countries saw a turning point during PM Singh's visit to Kazakhstan which resulted in a package of three agreements—a participating share assignment, carry agreement and joint operation agreement—on the Satpayev oil block. The Satpayev block is in the Caspian Sea covering an area of 1482 sq. km. The block contains two prospective structures—the Satpayev and the Satpayev Vostochni (East) with estimated hydrocarbon reserves of 256 million metric tonnes (MMT). On the basis of the above agreement, the Indian company ONGC Videsh Limited has now already acquired a 25 percent stake in the Satpayev oil block together with the National Company KMG. The ONGC has invested US$ 60 million in oil exploration in this joint collaboration. The implementation of the Satpayev deal was significant, given the past experience of China outbidding India to acquire the Petrokazakh deal in 2005. If the Kazakh government considers India's request for supporting an important bid that OVL is making for a stake in the Kashagan oilfield, it will be a major achievement for New Delhi as far as cooperation in the oil and gas sector is concerned.

Cooperation in the Defence Sector

India is buying some spare parts from Kazakh companies and is getting its torpedoes upgraded in Kazakhstan. The Joint Working Group meeting was held on November, 26, 2012 and several new areas of cooperation were identified which included India's assistance in the development of the Kazakh Navy in the Caspian Sea, cooperation in the manufacture of arms and ammunition, upgradation of Indian torpedoes in India itself and joint military exercises. Several new projects related to defence surveillance equipments are under consideration. Most of the equipment being used by the Indian armed forces has been of Soviet origin and both sides could explore the possibility of setting up joint ventures in the field of defence production and equipment upgradation.

Opportunities for Indian Investors

For India, access to the wheat, cotton and hydrocarbon sectors of Kazakhstan constitutes a strategic priority. Although, currently, India is self-sufficient in wheat, it does at times need to import grains to meet its domestic requirements. Wheat as well as other agricultural products can be obtained from these republics of Central Asia at favourable rates, as they have a lower cost of grain production. They can also take advantage of the fact that Kazakhstan accords agriculture as its priority sector and hence provides various incentives and benefits to attract investors. Kuanyshev has mentioned that his country was the second largest importer of tea and India exported around US$ 40 million of tea to Kazakhstan. He informed that consumption of premium tea was becoming a trend in Kazakhstan.[56]

Construction Industry

The construction industry provides a favourable investment climate for foreign investors in Kazakhstan. Several regions of Kazakhstan are considered as having a great potential for this sector. Construction in Kazakhstan is in a robust shape and the sector has shown a strong growth potential. The construction sector accounted for 25 percent of the country's GDP and employed more than 5,00,000 people in 2008.[57] In real terms, Kazakhstan's construction industry registered positive growth during 2011–2015, driven by public and private sector investments in construction projects. The latest figures released by Astana reveal that the total spending on building work has grown by 6.8 percent from January to May 2016. Construction spending has totalled 733 billion tenge (over US$ 2 billion) during this period. All areas of construction across Kazakhstan have contributed to this record growth. Spending on housebuilding rose by 9.9 percent and renovation and maintenance grew by 25 percent while a further 11 percent more has been spent on building new facilities. A huge amount of US$ 1 billion was allocated for housing construction by President Nursultan Nazarbayev. In addition, a little over US$ 1 billion has been set aside for the building of affordable housing across the country following a Presidential announcement in February 2016. A surge in housing construction is expected across the next five years as Kazakhstan is heavily investing in its "Affordable Housing 2020" programme.

An important aspect of this industry is the high level of its material import. India can take advantage of the fact that Kazakhstan has a sufficient raw material base for industrial development. Also at present, there is no flat glass production in Kazakhstan. Thus, Indian investors can invest in the unexplored sub-sectors of the construction industry.[58] The main markets remain in Almaty and Astana, where many construction projects, such as roads and bridges, need to be built to improve the transport system leading to the cities.

Future Prospects of the India–Kazakhstan Economic Relations

For India, Kazakhstan offers the best possible opportunity as a gateway to the Central Asian region. Following are certain suggestions that may serve these goals:

- Keeping in mind the overall pattern and indices of Kazakh imports, key products and services sectors that are of importance for the diversification of India's export basket to Kazakhstan are: machine tools, construction and building materials, processed food and spices, edible oils, engineering and construction services, business management and consultancy, agro-business services, public relations and advertising, travel services.
- India can also take advantage of the fact that Kazakhstan is trying to overcome its predominant reliance on natural resources so as to diversify into sectors such as food processing, construction, telecommunications, financial services, transport, construction and pharmaceuticals. With the possibility of developing many key industrial sectors and modernisation in the services sectors, Kazakhstan offers an enormous amount of opportunities for trade and investment for India.

Moreover, given the current state of affairs and the high rating of Kazakhstan's FDI potential, looking beyond energy and mineral sectors in Kazakhstan is important for India. In order to ensure a better stake in Kazakhstan's energy resources, a larger presence of India in the other sectors is necessary. The expansion of business ties in sectors like banking and infrastructure will help India to enhance the ease of doing business not only in Kazakhstan but also in other fast-growing and resource-rich countries in Central Asia.

There should be target-oriented promotional policies for increasing investment in Kazakhstan's mineral sector. The investment risk assessment in Kazakhstan should be conducted on a regular basis with a view to dynamically review the effectiveness of the provisions of the India–Kazakhstan BIPA.

It is also important to allocate specific funds in the annual supplements of India's Foreign Trade Policy for regular business delegation meetings in different cities in both the countries. There should be Business Consular Service Centres in Astana, Almaty, New Delhi and Mumbai and such institutions should be set up as public–private partnerships with business associations and other civil society groups.

Economic diplomacy with Kazakhstan must take into account the larger goal of increasing better trade and investment ties with the CIS region. Increased bilateral ties would help leverage the larger market potential of Belarus-Russia-Kazakhstan Customs Union as well as the combined market potential of the CIS countries.[59]

REFERENCES

1. Jafarova, Aynur, 'Leasing Kazakhstan's Farmlands to Foreign Firms needs Legal Elaboration: Minister", 21 January, 2014. URL: http://www.azernews.az/region/63589.html; Republic of Kazakhstan, CII, p.113.
2. 'Economy of Kazakhstan', 17 May 2014. URL: http://en.wikipedia.org/wiki/Economy_of_Kazakhstan
3. Mohanty, A. and S. Swain (eds), *Contemporary Kazakhstan: The Way Ahead*, New Delhi: Axis Publications, 2009, p. vii.
4. Mir, M.A., 'India-Kazakhstan Relations: Special Reference to Trade and Investment', in *Perspectives on Bilateral and Regional Cooperation: South and Central Asia*, R. Malhotra, S. S. Gill and N. Gaur (eds), Chandigarh: CRRID, 2013, p. 147.
5. Ibid.
6. 'Human Development Report 2015: Work For Human Development'. URL: http://hdr.undp.org/sites/default/files/2015_human_development_report.pdf.
7. Mir, op. cit., p. 147.

8. Embassy of the Republic of Kazakhstan, 'Economy and Business Overview'. URL: http://www.kazakhembus.com/content/economy-business-overview.
9. Mir, op. cit. , p. 145.
10. Embassy of the Republic of Kazakhstan, Washington DC, 'Economy', URL: http://www.kazakhembus.com/page/economy
11. Ibid.
12. Soni, Sharad K., 'Kazakhstan OSCE Chairmanship and Regional Security', in *Materials of International Scientific-Theoretic Conference on World Politics and Kazakhstan: Problems and Perspectives*, Almaty, 2011, pp. 51-58.
13. Srivastava, Deepti, 'Nuclear Fuel and Emerging Dynamics of Indo-Kazakh Relations, *Mainstream*, 48 (33), August 7, 2010. URL: http://www.mainstream weekly.net/article2219.html
14. Ministry of External Affairs, Government of India, 'Transcript of the Joint Media Interaction of External Affairs Minister and Foreign Minister of Kazakhstan', 5 March 2013. URL: http://www.mea.gov.in/media-briefings.htm?dtl/21268
15. Ibid.
16. Ibid.
17. 'Narendra Modi's Visit brings Central Asia Back in Focus', URL: http://www.livemint.com/Politics/7iJD1gvVb9VWUoIiPLHjQK/Narendra-Modis-visit-brings-Central-Asia-back-in-focus.html
18. Ministry of External Affairs, Government of India, 'Transcript of the Joint Media Interaction of External Affairs Minister and Foreign Minister of Kazakhstan', 5 March 2013. URL: http://www.mea.gov.in/media-briefings.htm?dtl/21268
19. Embassy of India, Astana, 'India–Kazakhstan: 20 Years of Diplomatic Relations'. URL: http://indembastana.in/ieb.php?id=Bilateralpercent20Relations
20. Ministry of Petroleum & Natural Gas, Government of India, 'Oil Ministers of India and Kazakhstan Sign Inter-Government Protocol for enhancing Mutual Corporation', 9 January 2013. URL: http://pib.nic.in/newsite/erelease.aspx?relid=91433
21. 'India receives Offer to undertake Development of Kazakh Abay Oil Block', 29 April 2014. URL: http://www.offshore-technology.com/news/newsindia-receives-offer-to-undertake-development-of-kazakh-abay-oil-block-4254886
22. Ibid.
23. 'India-Kazakhstan Relations'. URL: http://www.mea.gov.in/Portal/ForeignRelation/Kazakhstan1__July_2016.pdf.
24. 'India receives offer...' op. cit.24. Bek-Ali, 'Kazakhstan-India Trade and Economic Relations', *Contemporary Kazakhstan: The Way Ahead*, A. Mohanty and S. Swain (eds), New Delhi: Axis Publications, 2009, p. 145.
25. Warikoo, K., 'India and Central Asia: Political Implication for Power Rivalries in Eurasia', in *India and Central Asia: Two Decades of Transition*, P.L. Das (ed.), New Delhi: OUP, 2011, p. 107.
26. Sarma, A.S., *India and Central Asia: Redefining Energy and Trade Links*, New Delhi: Pentagon Press, 2010, p. 38.
27. Embassy of India, Astana, 'India-Kazakhstan Relations', July 2014. URL: http://www.mea.gov.in/Portal/ForeignRelation/Kazakhstan_July_2014.pdf
28. Department of Science and Technology, Government of India, *Annual Report 2001-*

2002: *International S&T Programmes*. URL: http://www.dst.gov.in/about_us/ar01-02-international.htm

29. Embasssy of India, Astana, 'India-Kazakhstan: 20 Years of Diplomatic Relations' op. cit.
30. Malik, Ishfaq and M.A. Mir, 'India's Trade Relations with Kazakhstan: Problems and Prospects', *Abhinav*, 1 (12), 2012, pp. 67-81. URL: http://www.abhinavjournal.com/images/Commerce_&_Management/Dec12/8.pdf
31. Sarma, op. cit.,p. 36.
32. Sajjanhar, 'Perspectives on India-Kazakhstan Relations: Challenges and Opportunities', 2013, p. 41.
33. 'PM Modi's Visit to Central Asia: India and Kazakhstan ink Deals on Uranium Supply, Defence'. URL: http://economictimes.indiatimes.com/news/defence/pm-modis-visit-to-central-asia-india-and-kazakhstan-ink-deals-on-uranium-supply-defence/articleshow/47996585.cms.
34. Sajjanhar, op. cit .
35. Ibid.
36. Ibid.
37. Ibid.
38. "India Interested in Renewable Energy Cooperation with Kazakhstan', 31 October 2011. URL: http://www.chinaeurasia.org/news-digest/962-india-interested-in-renewable-energy-cooperation-with-kazakhstan.html
39. Sarma, op. cit., p. 36.
40. Ibid.
41. *A Strategy Paper for CIS Countries: India-CIS Roadmap 2020*, FT (CIS) Division, July 2012, p. 256.
42. Ibid.
43. Ministry of External Affairs, Government of India, 'Transcript of the Joint Media Interaction of External Affairs Minister and Foreign Minister of Kazakhstan', 5 March 2013.
44. Ibid.
45. 'Potential for Indo-Kazakh Higher Education Cooperation Huge, says Academic'. URL: http://www.business-standard.com/article/news-ani/potential-for-indo-kazakh-higher-education-cooperation-huge-says-academic-115032200047_1.html
46. Embasssy of India, Astana, 'India-Kazakhstan 20 Years of Diplomatic Relations', op. cit.
47. 'India, Kazakhstan Nurture Millennia-Long Trade Relationship'. URL: http://astanatimes.com/2016/03/india-kazakhstan-nurture-millennia-long-trade-relationship/.
48. 'India-Kazakhstan 20 Years of Diplomatic Relations', op. cit.
49. Srivastava, op. cit ".
50. Sajjanhar, op. cit p.42.
51. Ibid.
52. 'India, Kazakhstan agree on Nuclear Energy Cooperation', March 5, 2013. URL: http://www.universalnewswires.com/centralasia/kazakhstan/security/viewstory.aspx?id=13739
53. Sajjanhar, op. cit., p. 42.

54. Ibid., p.185.
55. Urazdoboeva, Sojida, 'Some Aspects of Indian Energy Interests in Central Asia', in *India's Engagement with Central Asia with Focus on India-Uzbekistan Relations*, Jyotsna Bakshi (ed.), Tashkent: University of World Economy and Diplomacy, 2007, p. 187.
56. *A Strategy Paper for CIS Countries: India-CIS Roadmap 2020*, p. 286.
57. CII: 115.
58. Ibid.
59. 'A Note on India-Kazakhstan Trade and Investment Relations', CUTS International. http://www.cuts-citee.org/pdf/briefing_paper-india-kazakhstan_trade_and_investment_ relations.pdf

5

India and Kyrgyzstan

Kyrgyzstan which until recently has been a low-income country is the second smallest country in Central Asia with a population of about 5.7 million people. According to the 2016 Income Classifications released by the World Bank, Kyrgyzstan has been re-classified from a low income country to a lower-middle income country.[1] Its Gross National Income (GNI) per capita in 2013 was estimated at US$ 1,200, increasing from US$ 1,040 in 2012. Moreover, compared with other Central Asian Republics, Kyrgyzstan is generally perceived as the most progressive country in the region. In a period of more than twenty years of independence, Kyrgyzstan appears to be going well along the path of democratisation and economic reforms despite intermittent violent uprisings such as the one that took place in April 2010.

In the post-independence period, a new leadership under Askar Akaev moved swiftly to create a new political culture in Kyrgyzstan by adopting the Western liberal democratic ideology and leaving aside the old socialist ideology as a form of state establishment. A major political change occurred in 2005 when a popular revolution, called the '*Tulip* Revolution', overthrew the regime of Akaev and replaced it by the Kurmanbek Bakiev regime which aimed at bringing greater transparency in the administration. However, in 2010, large-scale ethnic violence gripped Kyrgyzstan, which ousted the Bakiev government and a caretaker government under Roza Otunbayeva was formed.[2] Peace finally prevailed on Kyrgyz soil once a new government headed by Otunbayeva was democratically elected in the first-ever parliamentary elections under a revised constitution. Otunbayeva set a good example in terms of opening the possibility for

Kyrgyzstan to have the first peaceful transfer of power in Central Asia. After the October 30, 2011 Presidential election, Almazbek Atambayev became the fourth President of Kyrgyzstan.[3]

Meanwhile, like other countries emerging from the former USSR, the Kyrgyz economy too was characterised by heavy subsidisation during the Soviet period as it was oriented to contribute to the USSR economy mainly as a supplier of raw materials, and hence became the source of instability.[4] With no substantial industrial base in order to lift the country out of the severe economic crisis that engulfed it soon after breaking from the Soviet system, the Kyrgyz governments during the Akaev, Bakiev, Otunbayeva and Atambayev era continue to recognise a need for opening up the state economy to private sector entrepreneurship and seek external players' role in developing the economy in a quicker manner.

Economic Situation of Kyrgyzstan

Kyrgystan is a relatively less developed mountainous country with a dominant agricultural sector. Cotton, tobacco, wool and meat are the main agricultural products, although only tobacco and cotton are exported in some quantity. Industrial exports include gold, mercury, uranium, natural gas and electricity. The economy depends heavily on gold exports, mainly from the output at the Kumtor gold mine.[5] Apart from gold, there is also a huge potential for the mining sector in specialised metals like antimony, mercury, molybdenum, uranium oxide, tin and rare metals. The Kyrgyz Republic is the world's third largest producer of mercury after Spain and China.[6]

The sudden occurrence of independence from the Soviet Union led the political leaders to handle the country's economy virually unprepared. Therefore, an economic decline in the first decade of independence impacted the economic growth of Kyrgyzstan. This is evident from the fact that the Gross Domestic Product declined by about –5 to –20 percent per annum in the 1990s with an equally sharp decline in industrial production. Hyperinflation was ranging between 800 and 2,000 per annum in the first half of the 1990s, and unemployment was ranging between 20 and 30 percent. As a result, over 40 to 50 percent of the population went below the poverty line, and the country experienced a huge external debt.[7]

Notwithstanding the above challenges at the economic front, the Kyrgyz leaders took progressive policy measures in carrying out economic reforms in which they were guided by neo-liberal economic reform measures such as an improved regulatory system in economic management and land reforms in agriculture. These also include some aspects of a controversial "shock therapy". In fact, Kyrgyzstan was first among the Central Asian Republics to launch a programme to privatise state industries. In order to implement economic liberalisation policies it reduced tariffs and subsidies; privatised state-owned enterprises and liberalised investment policies. Kyrgyzstan also set up Free Economic Zones (FEZs) in Bishkek, Naryn, Karakul, etc., to attract foreign investment, joint ventures and so on. The government provided incentives for investment, simplified customs and registration procedures. Apart from these reform policy measures, Kyrgyzstan has also been the first country to implement a full current account convertibility, which helped the country become a member of the World Trade Organization (WTO). Infact, Kyrgyzstan was the first Commonwealth of Independent States (CIS) country to be accepted into the WTO. Even before this, it had acquired membership of the Asian Development Bank (ADB) in 1994.[8] These post-1998 reforms have resulted in a growing business and investment climate with the economy growing at an average of about 4 percent per annum.[9]

After overcoming the crisis period of the 1990s, Kyrgyzstan registered a 5 to 6 percent annual average GDP growth during 2000–08. In fact in 2005, the Bakaev government and financial institutions initiated a comprehensive medium-term poverty reduction and economic growth strategy. Moreover, Bakaev agreed to pursue the much-needed tax reforms, and in 2006, the country became eligible for support under the scheme of Heavily Indebted Poor Countries (HIPC). As a result, the government made steady strides in controlling its substantial fiscal deficit, nearly closing the gap between revenues and expenditures in 2007–08. The GDP grew at about 8 percent annually in 2007–08, partly due to higher gold prices globally, but slowed down to 2.3 percent in 2009. The overthrow of President Bakaev and subsequent violent ethnic clashes damaged the country's infrastructure. Dwindling trade and agricultural production as well as political instability caused the GDP to contract to about 3.5 percent in 2010. The fiscal deficit widened to 11 percent of the GDP, reflecting a significant increase in crisis-related spending, including both rehabilitation of the damaged infrastructure and bank recapitalisation. Hence, progress in reconstruction, in fighting corruption, restructuring the domestic industry and attracting foreign aid and investments remained key to future growth.

During the last two decades, there has been a major change in the composition of the GDP. In the Soviet times, the industry accounted for the largest share while the services sector was the lowest. But as Table 5.1 shows, in 2011–12, there was a substantial growth in the service sector mainly due to the fact that Kyrgyzstan had emerged as the largest service provider in the Central Asian region. This is a new development with high potential. A major problem that is persisting is the underdevelopment of the country which is evident from the fact that even at present about one-third of the population is below the poverty line in the country having about 2.5 million labour force. Agriculture accounts for about 40 percent of the population, service sector about 40 percent and industry a mere 13 percent. Officially, the unemployment rate is about 18 to 20 percent of the working age group of population.[10]

Table 5.1: Sectoral Contribution to GDP in Kyrgyzstan during 2014-15

Sector	*Percent Contribution*
Agriculture	18 percent
Industry	25.5 percent
Services	56.4 percent

Key Economic Indicators

(a) Foreign Exchange Reserve: US$ 1.916 billion (2015 est.)
(b) Exchange Rate of Local Currency (Som): 60.58 per US$ (December 2015).
(c) Inflation Rate (2012): 6.5 percent (2015est.)
(d) External Debt: US$ 7.101 billion (31 December 2014)
(e) GDP (2015): US$ 20.1 billion
(f) GDP per Capita (2015): US$ 3,400 (PPP)
(g) Real GDP Growth (2015): 3.5 percent
(h) Sector-Wise Distribution of GDP (2015): Agriculture (18 percent), Industry (25.5 percent), Services (56.4 percent)
(i) Population below poverty line: 33.7 percent (2011 est.)
(j) Unemployment: 8 percent (2013 est.)
(k) Main industries: small machinery, textiles, food processing, cement, shoes, sawn logs, refrigerators, furniture, electric motors, gold, rare earth metals.
(l) Exports: US$ 1.933 billion (2015 est.)
(m) Export goods: gold, cotton, wool garments, meat, tobacco, mercury, uranium, electricity, machinery, shoes
(n) Main export partners: Switzerland (26 percent), Uzbekistan (22.5 percent), Kazakhstan (20.08 percent), Russia (4.2 percent), UAE (4.9 percent), Afghanistan (4.5 percent) (2015 est.)

(o) Imports: US$ 4.268 billion (2015 est.)
(p) Import goods: Oil and gas, machinery and equipment, chemicals, foodstuffs
(q) Import partners: China (56.4 percent), Russia (17.1 percent), Kazakhstan (9.9 percent) (2015 est.)

The Government of Kyrgyzstan considers the complete integration of the country into the world trading system as a key to the long-term success of the economic reforms and development. The first steps towards this goal were made in 1995 when experts of the relevant ministries and organizations of the country were sent to participate in the training seminars of the WTO. Being a small country and lacking sufficient natural resources, Kyrgyzstan recognises the necessity and importance of foreign supplies of particular raw materials and products. Access to new foreign markets is indispensable for both the balance of payment stabilisation and for attracting foreign and domestic investors to those industries where Kyrgyzstan has comparative advantages in the international market. For these reasons, Kyrgyzstan has accorded great importance to membership in the WTO.

Earlier in May 2001, Kyrgyzstan adopted a Comprehensive Development Framework (CDF) to year 2010, which contained broad policy measures to be realised in economic, social and political spheres in a decade.[11] The CDF strategy primarily relied upon a major shift from ongoing dependence on state investments based on official borrowing abroad to reliance on the private sector investment, supported by domestic saving and Foreign Direct Investment (FDI). The Kyrgyz economy is generally acknowledged as having one of the most open trade policies among the former Soviet Republics. In the process of macro-economic stabilisation, a unified exchange rate system has also been adopted resulting in the reduction of inflation. Small scale privatisation has been completed and reforms in the telecommunications and energy sectors are underway. Kysrgyzstan had no foreign exchange controls before it acceded to the WTO (United Nations 2001: 26-28). However, FDI in Kyrgyzstan is still low and half of the foreign investment goes to a single project, the Kumtor gold mining, which is a joint venture set up by the Kyrgyz government and Cameco Gold Co. of Canada. This company was established in 1992 to develop the Kumtor mine, which has estimated reserves of 9.3 million ounces of gold.[12]

Development of India–Kyrgyzstan Relations

Political ties between India and Kyrgyzstan have traditionally been warm and friendly. After Kyrgyzstan gained independence on August 31, 1991, India not only accorded recognition to its independent status but also initiated the process of establishing diplomatic relations at the highest political level. While Kyrgyzstan opened its Resident Mission in 1993, India established its embassy in Kyrgyzstan in 1994. Since then, both Bishkek and New Delhi have taken various initiatives in order to strengthen their bilateral cooperation which includes bilateral exchanges of high-level visits and signing of important agreements in the fields of culture, trade and economic cooperation, civil aviation, investment promotion, avoidance of double taxation, consular conventions, etc.

Bilateral Visits and Agreements

Close India–Kyrgyzstan relations have been reinforced by several high-level visits. President Akaev visited India four times in March 1992, April 1999, August 2002 and November 2003. Other important visits from Kyrgyzstan to India include those of Vice Prime Minister, Mira Jangavacheva (March 1997), State Secretary I.A. Abdurrazakhov (April 1997), Prime Minister Apas Jumagulov (May 1997), Defence Minister, Lt. Gen. I. Isakov (November 2005), Foreign Minister Ednan Karabaev Oskonovich (February 2008); Defence Minister Kudaiberdiev Abibilla Alymovich (September 2011), Defence Minister, Maj. Gen. Talaibek Omuraliyev (September 2013) and Foreign Minister Erlan Abdyldaev (February 2014).

The first Ministerial level visit from India since the independence of Kyrgyzstan took place on October 13, 1992 which marked the beginning of cooperation in the economic sphere. The then Minister of State for External Affairs R.L. Bhatia paid a goodwill visit to Bishkek on October 13–14, 1992. This was followed by the visit of Prime Minister P.V. Narsimha Rao in September 1995. The other important visits to Kyrgyzstan from the Indian side were of the former Vice Presidents, the late K.R. Narayanan and the late Krishna Kant in September 1996 and August 1997 respectively; Minister of External Affairs Yashwant Sinha (January 2003); Defence Minister George Fernandes (November 2003); Defence Minister A.K. Antony (July 2011); Minister of State for External Affairs E. Ahmed (June 2012); Minister of State for Commerce Dr D. Purandeswari (July 2013) and Minister of External Affairs, Salman Khurshid (September 2013). In addition, recently a 16-member NDC delegation led by Major General Anurag Gupta also visited Kyrgyzstan from 11 to 16 May 2014.

The diplomatic relations between the two countries reached their 20th year in 2012, which is also marked by India announcing its Connect Central Asia Policy at the first India–Central Asia Track-II Dialogue held in Bishkek during the visit of the Minister of State for External Affairs, E. Ahmed, on June 10–13, 2012. The visiting dignitary called on the Kyrgyz Prime Minister and held discussions on bilateral cooperation with the Kyrgyz Foreign Minister. The Kyrgyz Foreign Minister, Elan Abdyldaev paid a return visit to India from February 13–15, 2014, during which the two sides exchanged documents operationalising a bilateral treaty on mutual legal assistance and an agreement on visa -free travel for diplomatic, official and service passport holders.[13] They also expressed satisfaction with the progress in the implementation of the protocol of the 6th India–Kyrgyz Republic Inter-Governmental Commission on Trade, Economic, Scientific, Technological and Cultural Cooperation held in Bishkek in July 2013. Not only did they observe the below-potential trade levels between the two countries but also agreed to take steps to stimulate bilateral trade.

Prime Minister Modi visited Kyrgyzstan on July, 11–12 2015. The visit by an Indian Prime Minister took place after a gap of 20 years. During his visit, the PM laid a wreath at the Victory Square; gifted medical equipment to the Field Hospital; visited the Kyrgyz–India Mountain Bio Medical Research Center; inaugurated tele-medicine links between hospitals in Kyrgyzstan with super-specialty hospitals in India and unveiled Mahatma Gandhi's statue. Four MOUs/Agreements in the field of Defence Cooperation, Culture, Election and Standardisation were signed. A joint statement by the Prime Minister and President Atambayev was issued.[14]

Injecting fresh momentum in the ties, President Atambayev also paid a visit to India in December 2016. In their comprehensive talks, Prime Minister Modi and President Atambayev also decided to strengthen ties in the areas of defence, security, mining, IT, agriculture and energy. The two sides also reviewed progress in the work of the Joint Study Group that has been considering the feasibility of a Free Trade Agreement between India and the Eurasian Economic Union.[15]

By and large, high-level visits have enhanced the scope of cooperation in sectors like mining, pharmaceuticals, textiles and garment industries, transport and communication, education, health and tourism which are being treated as priority sectors for promoting bilateral investment. Both countries also share common concerns on the issue of terrorism, extremism and drug trafficking. Kyrgyzstan has largely been supportive of India's stand on Kashmir, India's bid for a permanent seat at the United Nations Security Council (UNSC) and India's role in the Shanghai Cooperation Organization (SCO).

India–Kyrgyzstan Economic Cooperation

In the post-1991 period, in addition to the commonalities in tradition, culture and custom, the similarity in political and economic structures provided a new basis for both India and Kyrgyzstan to forge mutually beneficial bilateral relationships as well as reinvigorate the process of multilateral cooperation. While geostrategic importance and security perception as represented by the two geographical entities remain central in developing their bilateral cooperation, Kyrgyzstan's proximity to India is of great significance due to India's size and potential as a big market. The success of India's economic reforms and development in several areas like science and technology, human resource development, service sector, etc. as well as its growing profile at the regional and international levels has been welcomed by Kyrgyzstan. The overall development and fast pace of technological advancements taking place especially in information and communication technology, space, etc. have opened the door for both India and Kyrgyzstan to establish and conduct their economic relations by pursuing a pragmatic approach.

On the other hand, inspite of lacking hydrocarbon fuels like Kazakhstan, Uzbekistan and Tajikistan, Kyrgyzstan has abundant natural resources in terms of hydropower potential and the presence of many minerals which more or less compensate for the economic potential of this small county. Kyrgyzstan is rich in several mineral products like mercury, iron, copper, lead, antimony, tin, wolfram, zinc, rare-earth, molybdenum, bismuth, arsenic, cobalt, gold, etc. The mining industry is one of the major sources for the Kyrgyz economy and accounts for over 48 percent of the cost of all industrial products and 10.1 percent of the GDP, 41 percent of the total export volume and 11 percent of the tax revenues. This mining industry also provides employment to over 15,000 workers. It has substantial gold deposits explored from several parts of the country, especially from the Kumtor (gold) exploration area. According to Kyrgyz government statistics, Kumtor accounts for up to a quarter of the country's GDP besides being responsible for more than 50 percent of Kyrgyzstan's exports thereby remaining the country's main resource of tax revenue.[16] India has shown interest in jointly managing the Kumtor gold mine so that its output could be increased further.[17]

About 25,000 gold deposits have been explored with total reserves of 2,500 to 3,000 tonnes of which 560 tonnes of reserve have been surveyed. There are 430 tonnes of potentially recoverable gold, worth more than US$ 105 billion at the current prices, and hence Kyrgyzstan ranks third among the CIS in the production of gold. The "Kyrgyzaltyn" Open-End Joint Stock Company (JSC) is the largest company of the Kyrgyz Republic specializing in the development of gold deposits. "Kyrgyzaltyn" JSC was created in 1992 as a Kyrgyzaltyn State Concern in order to combine the enterprises of the mining industry of the Kyrgyz Republic for maintaining production of existing enterprises and realisation of new gold mining projects. Together with its joint venture partners, Kyrgyzaltyn JSC produces more than 97 percent of gold in Kyrgyzstan. Nearly 10 percent of the GDP, 40 percent of the industrial output and 60 percent of the exports of Kyrgyzstan fall on gold mining.[18] From the beginning of industrial production in May 1997 to September 30, 2013, the Kumtor gold mine has produced about 8.9 million ounces, or 277.7 tonnes of gold (kumtor.kg/).[19] Apart from gold, other mineral deposits are found in places like Khaidarkan (mercury), Kadamzhai (antimony) and Kara-Korum (vollastonite) basins.[20] Table 5.2 shows the major mineral deposits in Kyrgyzstan.

Table 5.2: Mineral Deposits in Kyrgyzstan

Type of Minerals	*Number of Deposits*	*Type of Minerals*	*Number of Deposits*
Oil	11	Beryllium	1
Gas	11	Fluorite	4
Coal	49	Gypsum	9
Gold ore	24	Stony salt	8
Placer gold	24	Facing stone	11
Silver	12	Ceramic raw material	2
Mercury	4	Vollastonite	1
Antimony	7	Bentonite clay	1
Tin	2	Mica	1
Wolfram	2	Sulphuric pyrite	1
Copper	7	Clay	65
Lead	3	Gravel	86
Zinc	2	Limestone	8
Rare earth	1	Building stone	25
Molybdenum	1	Sand	6
Bismuth	3	Haydite and agloporite	6
Arsenic	2	Basalt	2
Cobalt	1	Potter clay	1

Source: UNDP in Kyrgyz Republic (2007), *Kyrgyzstan: Environment and Natural Resources for Sustainable Development*, State Agency on Environment Protection and Forestry under the Government of the Kyrgyz Republic, Bishkek, p. 26.

Coal is another useful mining asset in Kyrgyzstan. Since a number of coal mines, which were once operated under the former Soviet Union, are now non-functional, it needs foreign investments. Whereas between 1992 and 2003, coal production dropped from about 2.4 million tonnes to 411,000 tonness per year, it increased substantially in 2006 to meet the target of 607,000 tonnes in 2009. However, despite the increased coal production, imports still continue to cover between half and two-thirds of Kyrgyzstan's coal needs. As of January 2008, the proven reserves at Kyrgyzstan's 70 main coal deposits were reported as 1.3 billion tonnes, while prospective reserves were assessed as 2.2 billion tonnes, thus making Kyrgyzstan one of the potential leaders of Central Asia's coal sector.[21] Deposits are concentrated in four coal basins (Southern Fergana, Northern Fergana, Uzgen, and Kavak) and three smaller coal-bearing areas (Alai, Alabuka-Chatyr-Kol and Southern Issyk-Kul). The biggest coal deposit Kara-Keche in northern Kyrgyzstan is very promising with a capacity of producing 5,00,000 to 1 million tonnes per year.[22]

Some of the mining assets like mercury, iron, titanium, vanadium, aluminium, copper, molybdenum and beryllium are available in the form of reserves and resources which are shown in Table 5.3.

Table 5.3: Mineral Assets in Kyrgyzstan

Minerals	*Size*
Mercury	79,200 tons of metal
Wolfram	386,000 tons (including those ready for exploitation - 125,200 tons)
Tin	318,800 tons (including those ready for exploitation - 214,700 tons)
Beryllium Oxide	104,000 tons,
Uranium	11,000 tons
Cole	1.345 billion tons
Aluminium	400 million tons
Copper	3.5 million tons
Iron	2.8 billion tons

Source: Tabulated on the basis of data obtained from UNDP in Kyrgyz Republic (2007), *Kyrgyzstan: Environment and Natural Resources for Sustainable Development*, State Agency on Environment Protection and Forestry under the Government of the Kyrgyz Republic, p. 27.

Looking at the above data, Kyrgyzstan appears to be blessed with various types of rare mineral deposits except hydrocarbons, but due to technological and capital shortage these natural resources have remained untapped. Hence Kyrgyzstan needs massive foreign investment, despite having an abundance of water which can be used for hydroelectricity purposes. Unfortunately for Kyrgyzstan, its post-Soviet hydroelectric facilities are not geared towards the post-Soviet economy. Furthermore, Bishkek has been forced to release water from its reservoirs during autumn and winter to generate electricity to compensate for energy import shortfalls, subsequently flooding downstream areas in Uzbekistan and Kazakhstan while causing summer irrigation droughts. Both Uzbekistan and Kazakhstan are craving for Kyrgyzstan's waters. If these two downstream states successfully develop their hydroelectric potential, they might achieve an equitable energy arrangement with their more prosperous neighbours to the east.

From India's economic and trade perspective, Kyrgyzstan holds immense opportunities in sectors such as food processing, textiles, construction, tourism, logistics and mining. Besides, the country is extremely promising for mid-sized Indian firms in the hydroelectric energy and IT sectors. What one could argue is that doing business in Kyrgyzstan is comparatively cheap in comparison to other Central Asian Republics.[23] Kyrgyzstan possesses a skilled and educated workforce, its economy is stable and the national currency is easily convertible. Moreover, the leadership has been committed to free market economic reforms with a liberal foreign investment regime and a stable macro-economic environment. Inflation is low and most importantly there is a direct access to CIS and Chinese consumer markets. Apart from this, a wider opportunity for investment is also available in areas like agriculture, manufacturing, electronics, energy and transport.[24]

In order to strengthen bilateral trade and economic cooperation, the first Kyrgyz President Akaev, who visited India in 1992, invited Indian investment in the Kyrgyz banking and mineral exploration sector. Since Kyrgyzstan has rich deposits of a wide range of minerals, Akaev stressed that his government was willing to avail Indian technology to explore those mineral resources which were mutually beneficial.[25] But the main foundation of the India–Kyrgyzstan economic cooperation was laid down only after the Indian Minister of State for External Affairs R.L. Bhatia's official visit to Bishkek from 13 to 14 October 1993. During this visit, the two sides signed an agreement on the establishment of Inter-Governmental Commission on Trade and Economics besides Indian assistance of over eight tonnes of medicines for the earthquake victims of Kyrgyzstan.[26] Since then, both the countries have been involved in mutual economic cooperation in various sectors.

Institutional Level Cooperation

At the institutional level, to facilitate more flexibility at the foreign office level, both countries involved themselves in a Foreign Office Consultation Framework which provides a useful framework for the exchange of views on bilateral and international issues, thereby facilitating greater understanding. The establishment of the Indo-Kyrgyz Inter-Governmental Commission (IKIGC) on Trade, Economic, Scientific and Technological Cooperation was established in 1992. The fourth session of the IKIGC was held in Bishkek on September 5, 2007 under the Co-Chairmanship of O.P. Arya, Additional Secretary, Department of Commerce, Ministry of Commerce and Industry from the Indian side and Japarov Akylbek Usenbekovich, Minister of Finance of the Republic of Kyrgyzstan from the Kyrgyz side. The Fifth Session of the IKIGC was held in New Delhi in March 2010 in which the delegation from Kyrgyzstan was led by Kapar Kurmanaliev, the Minister of Natural Resources and the Indian side was headed by Jyotiraditya Scindia, the Minister of State for Commerce & Industry. The Sixth Session of the IKIGC was held in Bishkek during July 17–19, 2013 in which a protocol was signed between the two countries for the promotion of mutual investments in mineral exploration and development, food processing, chemicals and petrochemicals, information technology, healthcare, science and technology, tourism, education, sports and culture.[27] The Seventh Session of the Indo-Kyrgyz Inter-Governmental Commission on Trade, Economic, Scientific and Technological Cooperation was held in New Delhi on March, 17–18, 2015 and a protocol was signed between the two countries. An MOU on cooperation in the field of Textiles and Hydropower between the two countries was also signed.[28]

Business and Joint Ventures

In May 1997, following the signing of a Bilateral Investment Promotion and Protection Agreement (BIPA), the first Indo-Kyrgyz joint venture, the Kyrgyz Ajanta Pharma Ltd. for the production of pharmaceuticals, was established in Bishkek. Another joint venture that has been formed was between a Kyrgyz company Krivyh Anastasia Vladimirovna and an Indian company Gateway of Goa Holiday Resorts Pvt. Ltd. in the tourism and hospitality sector. Since 2002, India has been organising industrial exhibitions in Bishkek to promote relations with Kyrgyzstan.[26] The Sixth Session of the the Indo-Kyrgyz Inter-governmental Commission on Trade, Economic, Scientific and Technological Cooperation, held in Bishkek in 2013, discussed the creation of joint ventures in the textile sector.[30] India expressed its interest in strengthening cooperation with Kyrgyzstan in the textile sector including the manu-fac-turing of ready-made garments, artificial fibres and silk. While India also agreed to cooperate in the supply of cashmere strands for Kyrgyz knitting industries, Kyrgyzstan proposed technological cooperation in the processing of cotton fibre, cotton yarn and fabrics as well as processing them into semi-finished and finished products. At present, textile exports from India to Kyrgyzstan contribute 50 percent of the total exports from India. The Indian side also noted the possibility of increasing imports from Kyrgyzstan to India of hides and skins, the supply of which are made in small quantities.

Cooperation in Agriculture and Food Processing

The agriculture sector of Kyrgyzstan possesses a gap in terms of its potential and actual achievements. The slow growth of the sector can be attributed to the antiquated machinery, inadequate market orientation, management skills of the producer, improper marketing of products and inadequate finance. Various sub-sectors of agriculture have still not achieved their full potential. The sub-sectors that offer potential for Indian investments include cotton, tobacco, barley, sugar beet, seed potatoes, berries, fresh beans, medicinal herbs, cattle meat, milk, hides, yak, pig, silk and wool. Indian investors with their rich expertise in agriculture can exploit these investment areas of Kyrgyzstan.[31]

The two countries signed an MoU in May 2009 for setting up a potato processing plant for the production of potato chips and potato flakes at Talas in Kyrgyzstan. The project was undertaken under India's aid to Central Asia. The equipment for potato processing worth US$ 0.05 million was given by India in 2010 in the form of a grant. The plant will be producing 100 kg of chips and 95 kg of bran per hour and provide jobs for 50 people. The plant became operational on June 12, 2012 after it was inaugurated by the then India's Minister of State for Foreign Affairs, E. Ahmed.[32]

Indian Line of Credit and Investment in Kyrgyzstan

Under a Credit Agreement signed on June 1, 1995, India disbursed a credit line of US$ 5 million to Kyrgyzstan, which was used for various projects—for example, US$ 2.78 million for establishing four plants to manufacture polythene bags, toothbrushes, toothpastes and pharmaceuticals.[33] Out of the US$ 2.78 million disbursed, the Kyrgyz government paid back US$ 1.66 million, while a rescheduling agreement for US$ 1.15 million of unpaid dues was concluded in 2004.[34] The types of projects that were to be financed under the Credit Agreement included the modernisation and reconstruction of existing industrial units, the setting up of Indo-Kyrgyz joint ventures in industries and the setting up of small scale industrial enterprises. The agreement was an important step in further strengthening economic cooperation between India and Kyrgyzstan. It underlined a relationship of partnership between the two democratic countries involved in serious economic reforms.

In 2003, India announced another grant of US$ 2 million for setting up a mini-hydel station in Kyrgyzstan. The matter was further discussed during the Indo-Kyrgyz Foreign Office Consultation held in New Delhi in August 2006 and the Indian side requested a specific project proposal.[35] As for the credit line, India had extended US$ 1 million for setting up four oil and diesel filling stations in the Osh province.[36] Outside the line of credit, India has gifted a mini-dairy plant to Kyrgyzstan under the ITEC. Following an MoU signed between the two governments in May 2009, India agreed to set up a potato processing plant unit in the Talas Province of Kyrgyzstan under India's Central Asia Aid at a total cost of Rs. 10,80,4400.[37] In 2010, New Delhi provided 60 tonnes of humanitarian aid worth about US$ 1 million comprising medicines, food items and tents to Kyrgyzstan that had witnessed bloody ethnic violence in its southern parts (Osh and Jalalabad).[38]

Cooperation in the IT Sector

During President Akaev's visit to India in August 2002, India offered to set up an IT development centre following which an MoU was signed in Bishkek on March 20, 2006. The Indo-Kyrgyz Centre for Information Technology in Bishkek which was formally inaugurated on August 15, 2007 by the then Indian Petroleum Minister, Murli Deora, had been set up by HMT (I), the Indian implementing agency.[39] The project has already been completed.

Though Indian IT companies have extensive experience in software development which is recognised worldwide, they have failed to make a breakthrough in the Kyrgyz market. On the other hand, since Kyrgyzstan aspires to emerge as a regional hub in the IT sector, it seeks to develop High-Tech Parks (HTP) in the southern province of Osh which remains inconveniently connected to northern Kyrgyzstan.

One of the successful examples of the India–Kyrgyzstan cooperation in the IT sector is the cooperation between India's Nucleus Software Company and Kyrgyzstan's Bai-Tushum & Partners Microfinance

Company. The Nucleus Software Company launched its FinnOne software programme in Bai-Tushum activities, which has now been implemented successfully. This is the only cooperation of the Nucleus Software Company with an institution located in any of the CIS countries and can undoubtedly be called as the beginning of a new fruitful cooperation of India and Kyrgyzstan in the IT sphere.[40]

During the visit of the First Deputy Prime Minister of Kyrgyzstan Joomart Otorbaev to India on July 18, 2012, it was proposed to open an information centre in Kyrgyzstan with Indian help.

Cooperation under the ITEC Programme

Technical assistance under the Indian Technical and Economic Cooperation (ITEC) programme, particularly in terms of human resources development, is the cornerstone of India's economic involvement in Kyrgyzstan. Every year, Kyrgyzstan is allotted slots for civilian training under the ITEC programme. For the years 2014–2016, Kyrgyzstan was allotted 90 slots. Since 1992, more than 800 professionals from Kyrgyzstan have received training in India.[41]

Cooperation in Medicine

As of January 2014, almost 1,900 Indian students were studying medicine in various medical institutions in Kyrgyzstan.[42] During the visit of India's Defence Minister, A.K. Antony to Kyrgyzstan, the Kyrgyz President Roza Otunbaeva inaugurated the Indian government-assisted Kyrgyz–India Mountain Bio-Medical Research Centre at Too Ashu Pass at a cost of nearly US$ 1.5 million (Rs. 6.5 crore) on July 5, 2011.[43] The Centre was established by the Defence Research and Development Organization (DRDO) under a project sanctioned by the Indian Defence Ministry for a joint collaborative R&D study with the National Centre for Cardiology and Internal Medicine (NCCIM). At the inauguration ceremony of the Centre, the DRDO Chief, V.K. Saraswat emphasised on "the significant contributions of Life Sciences group of laboratories under DRDO for improving health and operational efficiency of the troops and offered to provide all necessary support to the Kyrgyz Defence Forces and to the people to extend the benefit of this research".[44]

The Indo-Kyrgyz collaboration in the area of mountain medicine was developed by signing the Memorandum of Intentions (MoI) on Biomedical Research Programme with the National Centre of Cardiology and Internal Medicine (NCCIM), Ministry of Health of the Kyrgyz Republic, Bishkek.

Following the MoI, an Indian team involving 7 scientists and 10 volunteers visited Kyrgyzstan during July–August 1999, for a collaborative Indo-Kyrgyz Research Project entitled "Study of Physiological Mechanism of Human Adaptation to High Altitude in Population to Evaluate and Increase their Acclimatization at High Altitude" undertaken by the DIPAS (DRDO) in collaboration with the NCCIM, Bishkek.[45] Detailed studies of physiological mechanism of acclimatisation on ten soldiers each from the Indian and Kyrgyz armies were carried out at Bishkek and the Tuya-Aashu Field Station for High Altitude Medical Research. It brought about important findings including a few physiological and genetic markers associated with better performance while acclimatising at high altitude. Later, in November 2003, during the visit of the then Kyrgyz President A. Akaev in November 2003 and his meeting with the then President of India, A.P.J. Abdul Kalam, it was decided that the two countries would collaborate in areas of Biomedicine, Herbal Medicine and a proposal for a Research Centre in mountain medicine to be established in Kyrgyzstan was put forward.

The objectives of the Kyrgyzstan–India Mountain Bio-Medical Research Centre are to "study short term and long term high altitude acclimatization; methods for facilitating acclimatization; study the mechanism of development of mountain maladies; experiment on improving physical endurance; explore therapeutic application of moderate altitude in treatment of specific patho-physiological conditions like asthma, HAPO bag, NO delivery system, Aloe vera cream, heating gloves and biodigestor in facilitating anaemia etc., and to evaluate potential of products such as HAPO performance at high altitude".[46] Under India's Connect Central Asia Policy, it has been decided to set up a super-speciality hospital and a diagnostic centre in Kyrgyzstan.

Cooperation in Tourism

With its unique natural resources and original culture of nomadic people, Kyrgyzstan has a large unused potential for tourism. Some of the distinguishing features of the country's tourism are recreational resources and the historical and cultural heritage as well as the originality and uniqueness of customs and traditions of the Kyrgyz people and the artisans' work. Kyrgyzstan has also been integrated with the international tourism market.

The tourism sector in Kyrgyzstan has been recognised as one of the priority sectors of the economy at the state level as it ensures a steady growth of employment and sources of income for the population. It encourages development of the different sectors of the economy involved with tourism, and increases investment inflows into the national economy. The direct contribution of Travel & Tourism to GDP was 1.8 percent of GDP in 2010 and 2 percent of GDP in 2011. The Issyk Kul region attracted most of this investment capital. The direct contribution of tourism is expected to rise by 6.2 percent per annum to US$ 0.18 billion in 2021 (at constant 2011 prices).

On February 6, 2008, India and Kyrgyzstan agreed to enhance levels of cooperation in the tourism and culture sectors.[47] While visiting India, the Kyrgyz Foreign Minister Ednan Karabaev met the then India's Tourism and Culture Minister Ambika Soni and both agreed on the need for promoting further cooperation in these two sectors. Karabaev was of the opinion that India could offer training to Kyrgyz students in the tourism and hospitality sector and both the countries could sign a document for strengthening bilateral cooperation in the tourism sector. While he expressed his country's desire to organise "Days of India in Kyrgyzstan", Soni suggested that the people of Kyrgyzstan take advantage of beach tourism, wellness tourism and shopping festivals in India. Soni said that both governments could also exchange information on ways to increase the tourist traffic. Earlier, on March 19, 1997, a Memorandum of Understanding was signed between the two countries in New Delhi to organise "Days of India in Kyrgyzstan" and "Days of Kyrgyzstan in India". In recent years, both sides have shown a serious interest in enhancing their cooperation in the tourism sector.

During the February 2014 visit of Kyrgyz Foreign Minister Erlan Abdyldaev to India, while discussing cooperation in filmmaking the Kyrgyz side proposed a joint theatrical production of the epic *Manas*. India, on its part, expressed appreciation at the visit of a Kyrgyz cultural troupe to the Suraj Kund Mela in 2014 and emphasised the importance of bilateral tourism and cultural exchanges.

India–Kyrgyzstan Trade Relations

Indo-Kyrgyz bilateral trade stood at US$ 10.8 million in 1997–98 which increased to US$ 22.02 million in 2000–01. At the beginning of the first decade of the 21st century, i.e., 2001–02, the total trade turnover between the two countries stood at US$ 11.53 million which at the end of the decade, i.e., 2010–11, stood at US$ 26.99 million, representing over a two-fold increase. The bilateral trade between the two countries continued to maintain an upward trend until 2012–13 when it reached US$ 37.08 million but in the very next year, i.e., 2013–14, it saw a little slowdown to register a figure of US$ 35.13 (Table 5.4). From 2008 to 2013, bilateral trade thus increased by 85 percent though the trade is carried out by small businessmen and the trade structure is not focussed. As Table 5.4 shows, all these years, the trade figures remained imbalanced as India's exports have always been much more than its imports from Kyrgyzstan. Besides, India's imports from Kyrgyzstan never crossed US$ 2 million except in 2000–01 when it was US$ 4.43 million, and most of the time, it has even remained less than US$ 1 million. Moreover, the bilateral trade relations are much lower in comparison to India's trade relations with the other Central Asian Republics.

Table 5.4: India-Kyrgyzstan Bilateral Trade, 1996-2016 (In US$ million)

Year	*Export from India*	*Growth Percentage*	*Percent Share in Total Exports by India*	*Imports from Kyrgyzstan*	*Growth Percentage*	*Percent Share in Total Imports by India*	*Total Bilateral Trade*
1996-97	0.98	NA	0.0029	NA	NA	NA	NA
1997-98	10.79	1,005.98	0.0310	0.01	NA	0.0000	10.80
1998-99	8.70	-19.29	0.0262	0.10	1,197.44	0.0002	8.80
1999-00	13.80	58.50	0.0375	1.82	1,695.65	0.0037	15.62
2000-01	17.59	27.50	0.0395	4.43	143.78	0.0088	22.02
2001-02	10.97	-37.66	0.0250	0.56	-87.44	0.0011	11.53
2002-03	14.67	33.72	0.0278	0.47	-16.15	0.0008	15.14
2003-04	38.20	160.49	0.0598	0.54	16.48	0.0007	38.74
2004-05	49.57	29.76	0.0593	0.63	15.03	0.0006	15.20
2005-06	28.09	-43.32	0.0273	1.47	135.83	0.001	29.56
2006-07	37.08	31.97	0.0293	0.76	-48.39	0.0004	37.84
2007-08	31.52	-14.98	0.0193	0.91	19.83	0.0004	32.43
2008-09	22.92	-27.29	0.0124	1.03	13.26	0.0003	23.95
2009-10	26.84	17.11	0.015	0.64	-38.34	0.0002	27.48
2010-11	25.79	-3.93	0.0103	1.20	88.02	0.0003	26.99
2011-12	30.55	18.46	0.0100	0.89	-25.64	0.0002	31.44
2012-13	34.99	14.53	0.0116	2.09	134.28	0.0004	37.08
2013-14	34.49	-1.42	0.0110	0.64	-69.29	0.0001	35.13
2014-15	37.76	9.32	0.0122	0.77	20.14	0.0002	38.53
2015-16	25.11	-33.49	0.0096	1.79	132.17	0.0005	26.90

Source: Based on Export-Import Data (1997-98 to 2015-16) collected from Directorate General of Foreign Trade (DGFT), Department of Commerce, Ministry of Commerce & Industry, Government of India.

India's total bilateral trade with Kyrgyzstan is less than 1 percent but it has a positive growth in both the import and export sectors. Kyrgyzstan's major trading partners are Russia, Kazakhstan, Canada, Turkey, China, Iran, Afghanistan, Switzerland, Uzbekistan, UAE and the USA.[48] But in

Table 5.5: Main Indian Exports to Kyrgyzstan during 2015-16 (In US$ million)

S.No.	Commodity	Value	Percent Share of India's Total Export to Kyrgyzstan
1	Pharmaceutical products	6.88	27.40
2	Articles of apparel and clothing accessories, not knitted or crocheted.	6.76	26.92
3	Articles of apparel and clothing accessories, knitted or corcheted.	6.4	25.49
4	Articles of leather, saddlery and harness; travel goods, handbags and similar cont. articles of animal gut(othr than silk-worm) gut.	0.74	2.95
5	Electrical machinery and equipment and parts thereof; sound recorders and reproducers, television image and sound recorders and reproducers, and parts.	0.6	2.39
6	Coffee, tea, mate and spices.	0.51	2.03
7	Manmade filaments.	0.48	1.91
8	Nuclear reactors, boilers, machinery and mechanical appliances; parts thereof.	0.42	1.67
9	Footwear, gaiters and the like; parts of such articles.	0.34	1.35
10	Essential oils and resinoids; perfumery, cosmetic or toilet preparations.	0.33	1.31
	Total Export of top 10 items	23.46	
	Total Export to Kyrgyzstan	25.11	
	India's Global Export	262,290.13	

Table 5.6: Main Indian Imports from Kyrgyzstan during 2015-16 (In US$ million)

S.No.	Commodity	Value	Percent Share of India's Total Imports from Kyrgyzstan
1	Edible vegetables and certain roots and tubers.	1.31	73.18
2	Aluminium and articles thereof.	0.25	13.97
3	Edible fruit and nuts; peel or citrus fruit or melons.	0.16	8.94
4	nuclear reactors, boilers, machinery and mechanical appliances; parts thereof.	0.04	2.23
5	Raw hides and skins (other than furskins) and leather	0.02	1.12
	Total import of top 5 items	1.78	

recent years, it has been noticed that there is a considerable increase of the Indian share in the Kyrgyz trade basket, even though India's share is only 0.4 percent of the total trade turnover of Kyrgyzstan.[49]

The major items of Kyrgyz exports to India include raw wool, metal manufactures, raw silk, crude minerals and metal scrap while the Kyrgyz imports from India include wool, cotton, leather goods, handicrafts, machinery and instruments, cosmetics and toiletries.[50] Kyrgyzstan imports from India pharmaceutical products, light industry products, food, and jewellery while India imports from Kyrgyzstan tanned leather and canned meat.

Potential Areas of Economic Cooperation

On March 19, 2014, Kyrgyzstan hosted a Kyrgyz–Indian Business Forum organized by the Chamber of Commerce and Industry of Kyrgyzstan (CCI) with the support from the Embassy of India in Kyrgyzstan and the Federation of Chambers of Commerce of India (FICCI).[51] The forum was organised with the aim of developing trade and economic cooperation between the two countries through direct contacts between the businessmen of the two sides. The Indian delegation headed by FICCI discussed possible cooperation with Kyrgyz entrepreneurs in healthcare, logistics, information technologies, engineering, production and advisory services. At the forum, about 50 companies from Kyrgyzstan showed their interest in establishing contacts with Indian businessmen, which is an encouraging sign for economic cooperation between the two countries, though the state of bilateral trade and economic relations does not meet the existing potential. The forum provided a good opportunity for direct negotiations between the entrepreneurs of the two countries. In particular, the Kyrgyz pharmaceutical companies were interested in cooperation with the Indian pharmacists.

A pharmaceutical delegation of 50 companies from India under the aegis of Pharmexcil visited Bishkek on March 12–13, 2015, to promote exports of pharmaceutical products. Six members of the Agrarian Platform from Kyrgyzstan took part in the 30th Aahar International Fair 2015, an annual agricultural event organised by the Indian Trade Promotion Organization (ITPO) from 10 to 14 March 2015. 'Days of India' were celebrated on June 19–21, 2015, at the biggest mall 'Bishkek Park'. Indian companies representing textiles, handicrafts, artificial jewellery and footwear participated in it. A Round Table on Agricultural Cooperation was held in Bishkek on July 15, 2015. Around 110 Kyrgyz representatives of agricultural associations, media houses and individual farmers participated in the Round Table.[52]

Kyrgyzstan is rich in unexplored natural resources like coal, gold ore, placer gold, rare earth material and is keen on India investing in them. Water is one of the major resources that Kyrgyzstan has but unfortunately hydropower production is very low though its potentiality is very high. Total production of hydropower was recorded at 15.853 billion kWh in 2005 with a total potential of 26,000 MWh. The present energy system has 20 power stations with a total capacity of 3372 MW.[53] This is a major area for bilateral cooperation between the two countries as India with its huge technology and expertise can tap the untapped Kyrgyz hydropower sector.

Another potential area of cooperation is the mining sector which remains untapped. The Kyrgyz Republic offers abundant resources for gold extraction to Indian investors. Only two gold mines operating in the Kyrgyz Republic (Kumtor and Makmal) are producing a majority of the gold, and hence there is a huge potential for further exploration and development of existing and unexplored deposits. Indian investors can also explore the sub-sector of industries that manufacture mining and ore-processing equipment for this sector.

Tourism is another area for bilateral economic cooperation. Kyrgyzstan's climate is most conducive for being a world-class tourist destination and is often referred to as the 'Switzerland of the East'. Its sky-touching mountains have a great potential for mountain tourism and trekking. Lake Issyk Kul is one of the major tourist attractions not only in Kyrgyzstan but in the whole of the Central Asian region and possesses great potential. The Indian experience in tourism sector particularly in hotels, travelling facility, and mountain tourism like mountain expeditions can be used in Kyrgyzstan for better economic returns. In March 2014, during the Kyrgyz–Indian Business Forum the two sides held detailed discussions on cooperation in the tourism industry, particularly in mountain tourism and ecotourism.[54]

But the major problem with the Indian economic activity in Central Asia is the geographical constraint. The lack of a direct land route and sea route is the major hindrance for bilateral economic cooperation. The only accessible route is the airways. At present, some of the key Indian export items, including apparel and clothing as well as drugs and pharmaceuticals, are mainly exported by air through special charted flights. The necessitating fact for this is that the surface route includes transport by ship up to Iran's port of Bandar Abbas and Chabahar and onwards, the rail/road corridors through Iran and then by surface through Turkmenistan.[55] This is a long route which results in considerable cost overheads on account of transportation, thereby significantly eroding the competitiveness of Indian exports in comparison to those exports coming into Kyrgyzstan from neighbouring countries like Russia, China, Kazakhstan, Turkey, Iran, etc.

The banking system in Kyrgyzstan is not fully developed. It is at a nascent stage of reform, the eventual goal of which is a sound, competitive and market-oriented banking system. Today, the country badly needs domestic investment, but citizens do not trust the local banks. There has been a demand that the banking reforms must include improvement of banking policy and the regulatory environment.[56] At present there are 22 commercial banks operating in Kyrgyzstan, including banks with foreign participation and one branch of a foreign bank. According to the law of the Kyrgyz Republic, banks are not allowed to establish direct correspondent relations with offshore banks, their affiliates and envelope banks. Offshore companies cannot act as founders or shareholders of resident banks of the Kyrgyz Republic.[57] The absence of an Indian bank in Kyrgyzstan seems to be a setback in providing a requisite back-up to promote Indian exports to this country. Moreover, corruption remains a major obstacle in materialising the benefits of economic reforms. During the Akaev period, high-level corruption is said to have been particularly severe under Vladimir Nosov, the Head of the State Department for Completion of Punishments (GUIN) under the Kyrgyz Republic's Ministry of Justice.[58]

In addition, the major non-tariff barriers, rigid norms and stringent visa regimes happen to be disastrous for investment in Kyrgyzstan. At present, visas and that too single entry ones, to Indian nationals, are given by the Kyrgyz missions abroad on the basis of sponsorship of specific Kyrgyz concerns or individuals. Even if such sponsors are located, obtaining visas from the concerned Kyrgyz missions often tend to be time-consuming and difficult. Moreover, language stands as a prominent barrier in establishing relations between the two countries. The lack of proficiency in Russian, the official language of Kyrgyzstan, could hardly add to the comfort levels of Indian entrepreneurs desirous of doing business in this country. However, both sides have recently expressed their concerns over problems in the smooth sailing of their economic cooperation. Once the problems are overcome, the two countries would be able to explore the potential areas of their economic cooperation to realise the actual benefit.

Both the countries are also engaged in developing favourable sectors like tourism, training of specialists, small and medium-sized businesses, the processing and mining industries and information technology.[59]

In a nutshell, for both India and Kyrgyzstan, there are opportunities for cooperation in agriculture, tourism and textile industries as well as in energy and renewable energy development. India could share its experience in information technology and call-services. Further expansion of economic and trade relations, including the establishment of direct air links, are now the focus of the India–Kyrgyzstan bilateral relationship. However, the lack of direct transport links should not be an obstacle to business cooperation, as there are many possibilities of indirect connections and modern means of communication. In order to improve the business environment between the two countries, Kyrgyzstan is developing an ambitious programme that includes liberal legislation, the lowest tax rates in the region, cheap labour as well as special preferences granted under the Free Economic Zones. For creating attractive conditions for doing business in the country, Kyrgyzstan plans to simplify visa requirements for the citizens of India.[60] Recently, Indian companies have shown interest in non-ferrous metal processing in Kyrgyzstan, besides participating in the development of major infrastructure projects in the metal industry and the dairy sector through public–private partnerships.

REFERENCES

1. '2014 World Bank Income Classifications: Kyrgyz Republic becomes Lower Middle Income Country', July 24, 2014. URL: http://www.worldbank.org/en/news/press-release/2014/07/24/kyrgyz-republic-becomes-lower-middle-income-country
2. Schwirtz, Michael, 'Ethnic Rioting Ravages Kyrgyzstan', *The New York Times*, 14 June 2010. URL: http://www.nytimes.com/2010/06/14/world/asia/14kyrgyz.html.
3. Akcali, P., 'Kyrgystan: Back to Being "The Island Democracy', in *The State in Eurasia: Local and Global Arenas*, A. Sengupta and S, Chatterjee (eds), 2012, Maulana Abul Kalam Azad Institute of Asian Studies/KW Publishers Pvt Ltd., 2012, p.94
4. Makara, Peter and Anna Ritsatakis, *Gaining Health: Analysis of Policy Development in European Countries for Tackling Non-communicable Diseases*, Denmark: WHO Regional Office for Europe, 2009, p. 179.
5. Gidadhubli, R.G., 'Kyrgyzstan: Achievements and Problems', in Sengupta and Chatterjee (eds), op. cit., p. 119.
6. *A Strategy Paper for CIS Countries: India-CIS Roadmap 2020*, FT (CIS) Division, July, 2012, p. 288.
7. Ibid.
8. ADB Report, 'Key Indicators of Developing Asian and Pacific Countries (2007)',

2007, URL: http://www.adb.org/Documents/Books/Key_Indicators/2007/pdf/kgz.pdf: p.1.

9. Usui, Norio and Arnelyn May A. Abdon, 'Structural Transformation in the Kyrgyz Republic: Engineering Future Paths of Capability Accumulation', *ADB Economics Working Paper Series No. 200*, 2010, p. 3. URL: http://www.adb.org/publications/structural-transformation-kyrgyz-republic-engineering-future-paths-capability-accumulat., p.3.
10. Gidadhubli, op. cit.
11. Yadab, T.G.K.Y., "Kyrgyzstan's Foreign Policy and its Relations with India, 1991-2009", PhD Thesis submitted to Jawaharlal Nehru University, New Delhi, 2012, p. 51.
12. Ibid., p. 52.
13. Ministry of External Affairs, Government of India, 'Official Visit of the Foreign Minister of the Kyrgyz Republic to India', 14 February, 2014. http://mea.gov.in/press-releases.htm?dtl/22925/Official+Visit+of+the+Foreign+Minister+of+the+Kyrgyz+Republic+ to+India
14. Embassy of India Bishkek, 'India-Kyrgyz Republic Bilateral Relations'. URL: https://www.embassyofindia.kg/relationpages.php?id=174
15. India, Kyrgyzstan to step up eco, defence, anti-terror cooperation, URL: http://indianexpress.com/article/india/india-kyrgyzstan-to-step-up-eco-defence-anti-terror-cooperation-4437231/
16. Daly, John C.K., 'Kyrgyzstan's Kumtor Mine Becomes Political Football', 14 June, 2013. URL: http://www.cacianalyst.org/publications/analytical-articles/item/12757-kyrgyzstans-kumtor-mine-becomes-political-football.html
17. Das, Jyoti Prasad, 'India's 'Connect Central Asia' Policy', *Foreign Policy Journal*, October 29, 2012. URL: http://www.foreignpolicyjournal.com/2012/10/29/indias-connect-central-asia-policy/
18. Yadab, op. cit.
19. Daly, John C.K., 'Kumtor Gold Mine Nationalism Issue Roils Kyrgyz Politics', *Eurasia Daily Monitor*, 11 (1), January 6, 2014. URL: http://www.jamestown.org/regions/centralasia/single/?tx_ttnewspercent5Btt_ news percent5D=41779&tx_ttnewspercent5BbackPidpercent5 D=658&cHash=288196de78c1b4a7d90e931dadfab671
20. Yadab (2012), op. cit.,p. 46.
21. Hasanov, Rafkat and Kemal Izmailov, 'Kyrgyzstan's Energy Sector: A Poverty and Social Impact Assessment', Commissioned by UNDP's Regional Bureau for Europe and CIS, 2011. URL: http://km.undp.sk/uploads/public1/files/vulnerability/Seniorpercent20Economistpercent 20Webpercent20site/PSIA_Energy_Kyrgyzstan.pdf
22. Zozulinsky Artyom, 'Kyrgyzstan: Mining Industry Overview', *BISNIS*, 2007. URL: http://bishkek.usembassy.gov/uploads/images/3wmFOoklg0fRzbRWAUjnhg/KG_07_Mining_ Report.pdf
23. Pandey, Sanjay Kumar, 'Indo-Kyrgyz Relations: The Search for New Horizon', in *India-Kyrgyzstan Relations: Perspectives and Prospects*, K. Santhanam and Ramakant Dwivedi (eds), New Delhi: Anamaya Publishers, 2008, p. 8.
24. Yadab, op. cit., p. 48.
25. Ministry of External Affairs, *Foreign Affairs Record*, 1992, pp. 127-128.

26. Ibid, p. 289.
27. 'India-Kyrgyzstan Relations', July 2013. URL: http://mea.gov.in/Portal/ForeignRelation/India-Kyrgyzstan_Relations_EN.pdf
28. 'India – Kyrgyz Republic Relations'. URL: https://www.mea.gov.in/Portal/ForeignRelation/Kyrgyzstan_09_02_2016.pdf
29. Roy, Meena Singh, 'India-Central Asia Relations: Changing Dynamics and Future Prospects', *South-Central Asia: Emerging Issues*, Kuldip Singh (ed.).
30. 'Kyrgyz-Indian Commission discusses Textile Joint Ventures', July 20, 2013. URL: http://www.fibre2fashion.com/news/announcement/newsdetails.aspx?news_id=148973
31. *A Strategy Paper for CIS Countries: India-CIS Roadmap 2020*, FT (CIS) Division, July, 2012, p. 288.
32. 'India-Kyrgyz Republic Bilateral Relations', Embassy of India, Bishkek, January 2014. URL: http://www.embassyofindia.kg/relationpages.php?id=114
33. Ministry of External Affairs, *Foreign Affairs Record*, 1995, p. 149.
34. Pandey, op. cit.p. 8.
35. Ibid.
36. Musaeva. Indira, 'Prospects of Kyrgyz-India Economic Cooperation', in K. Santhanam and Ramakant Dwivedi (eds), op. cit., p. 39.
37. 'India-Kyrgyzstan Relations', July 2013. URL: http://mea.gov.in/Portal/ForeignRelation/India-Kyrgyzstan_Relations_EN.pdf
38. Ministry of External Affairs, Government of India, *Annual Report: 2011-2012*, New Delhi, 2012, p. 37.
39. 'India-Kyrgyzstan Relations, op. cit.
40. Nazarov, Nazizhon, 'Perspectives of Kyrgyz-Indian Partnership in IT Industry', in *Post-Soviet States: Two Decades of Transition and Transformation*, A. Patnaik and Tulsiram (eds),New Delhi: KW Publishers, 2012.
41. Ibid.
42. 'India-Kyrgyz Republic Bilateral Relations', Embassy of India, Bishkek, January 2014. URL: http://www.embassyofindia.kg/relationpages.php?id=114
43. Ministry of External Affairs op. cit., p. 3.
44. Chacko, Joseph P., 'DRDO's Kyrgyz India Mountain Biomedical Research Centre inaugurated, 8 July, Frontier India, 2011. URL: http://frontierindia.net/drdos-kyrgyz-india-mountain-biomedical-research-centre-inaugurated
45. Ibid.
46. Ibid.
47. 'India, Kyrgyzstan to Enhance Cooperation in Tourism and Culture', 6 February 2008. URL: http://news.oneindia.in/2008/02/06/india-kyrgyzstan-enhance-cooperation-tourism-culture-1202307300.html
48. Sen Sarma, Angira, *India and Central Asia: Redefining Energy and Trade Links*, New Delhi: Pentagon Press, 2010, p. 3.
49. Levina, Maria, 'Kyrgyzstan-India Business Forum held in Bishkek', *Times of Central Asia*, 2014. http://www.timesca.com/index.php?option=com_content& view= article&id= 13568:kyrgyzstan-india-business-forum-held-in-bishkek&catid=79: economy-a-finances&Itemid=567

50. Daly, John C.K., 'The Aftermath of the Kyrgyz Revolution - The Lesser Players', 2010. URL: http://oilprice.com/Geopolitics/Europe/The-Aftermath-Of-The-Kyrgyz-Revolution-The-Lesser-Players.html.
51. Levina, op. cit.
52. 'India-Kyrgyz Republic Bilateral Relations', op. cit. URL: https://www.embassyofindia.kg/relationpages.php?id=174
53. Musaeva, op. cit., p. 41.
54. Levina, op. cit.
55. Kak, Kapil, 'Security Interests in Central Asia", in *Central Asia: Present Challenges and Future Prospects*, V. Nagendra Rao (eds.), New Delhi: Knowledge World, 2005, p. 216.
56. Lutfu, Sagbansu, 'Banking System in Kyrgyz Republic', *IBSU Scientific Journal*, 1(1), 2006, p. 45.
57. Kalikova, 'Banking Systems in the Kyrgyz Republic', *Global Legal Resources*, 27 November, 2007. URL: http://www.hg.org/article.asp?id=4923.
58. International Crisis Group, 'Kyrgyzstan's Prison System Nightmare', 16 August, 2006, p. 11. URL: http://www.crisisgroup.org/~/media/Files/asia/central-aia/kyrgyzstan/118_kyrgyzstans_prison_system_nightmare.pdf
59. Mavlonov, I.R., 'Central Asia and South Asia: Potential of Indian's Multilateral Economic Diplomacy in Inter-Regional Cooperation', *Strategic Analysis*, 30 (2), 2006, p. 431.
60. Levina, op. cit.

6

India and Tajikistan

Tajikistan is the smallest and the least developed of the five Central Asian Republics. It is, however, strategically located on the borders of Afghanistan in the south, Uzbekistan in the West, Kyrgyzstan in the north and China in the east. It is separated from Pakistan-occupied Kashmir (PoK) by a small strip of land in eastern Afghanistan called the Wakhan Corridor. Tajikistan's strategic location along the borders of Afghanistan has led it to emerge as an important actor in the war in Afghanistan against the Islamist Taliban and the al-Qaida. Its strategic location has also led it to be viewed in the calculus of a big power rivalry in the region as an important geopolitical space. In particular, since post-2001, it has become a playground for major powers—Russia, United States and China. Having a military base in Tajikistan, Russia continues to enhance its engagement, while China's economic engagement in the country has witnessed a steady rise. Despite being an economically poor country, Tajikistan is also endowed with a rich variety of mineral resources which have led to external powers seeking their presence by participating in the economic development of Tajikistan.

Economic Situation of Tajikistan

Tajikistan continues to remain the poorest among the five Central Asian Republics even after over two decades of independence from the former Soviet Union. Tajikistan remained embroiled in a civil war which affected its economic progress. With the recognition of the Islamic Political Party in 1997 it was able to achieve a great deal of political stability which has allowed it to deal with the agenda of national economic development based on an open market economy.

The current economic situation of Tajikistan, however, still remains fragile. In 2007, about 41 percent of the population lived below the poverty line at US$ 41 per month and 17 percent below the extreme poverty line at US$ 26 per month. Poverty is fuelling the drugs trade, with some reports estimating that between 30 and 50 percent of the country's economic activity is linked to narcotics trafficking. HIV rates are rising rapidly due to migrant workers and growing drug use. Child labour is widespread, in particular in the cotton-growing regions and girls in rural areas often stay without even basic education, being forced into early marriage.[1]

One of the primary reasons for the low economic development has been that almost 90 percent of Tajik territory is mountainous, creating problems of availability of arable land. Further, Tajikistan's agricultural production is largely oriented to produce cotton which was derived from the Soviet legacy, as such creating problems for diversified agricultural production. On the other hand, in spite of the presence of precious mineral resources such as gold, uranium and aluminium, economic development during the post-Soviet era has remained hampered by dislocation of the Soviet system and a prolonged civil war which continued upto 1997 that severely damaged its economy. It was only after the signing of the peace agreement between the government and the opposition that the slump in production was arrested.[2] The economic development of Tajikistan is further hampered by corruption, uneven economic reforms, and economic mismanagement.

Tajikistan, like Kyrgyzstan, lacks in carbon fuels. However, according to the Tajik President Emomali Rahmon the country has 14 percent of the world's uranium reserves and some natural gas fields in the southern part of the country,[3] though no one can say exactly how much uranium is there in Tajikistan. It is also richly endowed with hydropower potential. But Tajikistan lacks technical expertise and an investment potential in the area to undertake the development of the resource potential on its own. Tajikistan currently uses 5 percent of water energy resources and only 20 percent of the cotton fibre produced in the country is currently processed.[4] In order to utilise its resources efficiently, Tajikistan has adopted a market-oriented economy to seek external assistance in the economic development strategy, particularly since the turn of the 21st century.

Several Western countries have intervened to help Tajikistan since the very beginning of its independence. With foreign revenue precariously dependent on exports of cotton and aluminium, the Tajik economy has been highly vulnerable to external shocks. In 2000, international assistance remained an essential source of support for rehabilitation programmes that reintegrated former civil war combatants into the civilian economy, thus helping to maintain peace.[5] Such assistance was also necessary to address the second year of a severe drought that resulted in a continued shortfall of food production. China not only provided a preferential loan of US$ 608 million since 2005 but it is also the main partner of Tajikistan in developing its hydropower sector. With almost 80 Chinese companies operating in Tajikistan as of 2008, there are plans to build a number of hydro and thermal power plants with Chinese participation. A Chinese company TBEA in December 2016 has already built and commissioned a thermal power plant in the capital Dushanbe purported to cost $350 million. The project is expected to contribute 60 percent of local power and heating services for Dushanbe.

In recent years, Tajikistan has sought to establish greater economic ties with Afghanistan, which has been facilitated by the construction of a bridge across the Panj river in 2004. Afghanistan and Tajikistan agreed to create free economic zones on both sides of the bridge and ease customs and visa regimes to promote trade. The bridge has increased the flow of Tajik goods into Afghanistan and has enhanced commercial opportunities on both sides of the river. In addition, Tajikistan, Afghanistan and Iran agreed to form the Economic Council of the Persian-Speaking Union in 2008, and work is underway to improve transportation links, both road and rail, in order to facilitate trade among the three countries.[6]

The Gross National Income of Tajikistan was less than US$ 2 billion in 2004. Its per capita income in Central Asia (about US$ 280 in 2004) remains the lowest. In 2006, agriculture and manufacturing goods (mainly aluminum) contributed 22 percent and 45.4 percent of the GDP, respectively. According to the IMF, the overall GDP grew by 6 percent in 2011 to a total of US$ 6.54 billion. The FDI inflow to Tajikistan was only US$ 9 million in 2001 which in 2015 increased to total US$ 470.8 million. The major sources of FDI are the UK, Russia, the USA, Cyprus, Pakistan and Canada. However, Tajikistan has experienced significant economic growth over the past decade, which can be attributed to the strong commitment of the Tajikistan Government to maintain macro-economic stability and implement structural reforms.[7] Such an economic growth is driven mainly by foreign remittances which support domestic trade and services as well as exports. Whereas the FDI in Tajikistan reached $209 million in the third quarter of 2013, the Tajik Ministry of Economic Development and Trade had anticipated that in 2014, 2015 and 2016 the FDI stocks would be maintained around US$ 400 million a year.[8] According to World Bank data, the Tajik economy has been growing at a rate of 9 percent per annum over the last decade.[9] Yet, there still remain challenges of tackling corruption and economic mismanagement which pose a serious threat to the benefits of legislative and market reforms.

Key Economic Indicators

Major indicators of the Tajik economy are given below.

(a) Foreign Exchange Reserves: US$ 430.2 million (2015 est.)
(b) Exchange Rate of Local Currency (Somoni): 6.20 per US$ (2015 est.)
(c) Inflation Rate (2012): 5.8 percent(2015 est.)
(d) External Debt: US$ 3.612 billion (31 December 2014)
(e) GDP (2015): US$ 23.31 billion
(f) GDP per Capita (2015): US$ 2,700 (PPP)
(g) Real GDP Growth (2012): 3 percent
(h) Sector-wise Distribution of GDP (2015 est.): agriculture (25.7 percent), industry (17.3 percent), services (57 percent)
(i) Population below poverty line: 35.6 percent (2013 est.)
(j) Unemployment: 2.5 percent (2013 est.)
(k) Main industries: aluminium, cement, vegetable oil
(l) Exports: US$ 555.6 million (2015 est.)
(m) Export goods: aluminium, electricity, cotton, fruits, vegetable oil, textiles
(n) Main export partners: Turkey (19.7 percent), Kazakhstan (17.6 percent), Switzerland (13.7 percent), Iran (8.7 percent), Afghanistan (7.5 percent), Russia (5.1 percent), China (4.9 percent), Italy (4.8 percent) (2015 est.)
(o) Imports: US$ 3.162 billion (2015 est.)
(p) Import goods: petroleum products, aluminium oxide, machinery and equipment, foodstuffs.
(q) Import partners: China (42.3 percent), Russia (17.9 percent), Kazakhstan (13.1 percent), Iran (4.7 percent) (2015 est.)

Development of India–Tajikistan Relations

The strategic importance of Tajikistan, which is the closest of all the five Central Asian countries to India, has been the key factor in developing the India–Tajikistan relations. Tajikistan's 1,400-km long border with Afghanistan in terms of geopolitics motivated India to develop closer ties with it, especially as the Taliban came to power in Afghanistan. It was in the late 1990s that both countries supported the anti-Taliban resistance forces, the Northern Alliance, in Afghanistan.[10] Tajikistan provided Indian military advisers with access to the ethnic Tajik leader of the Northern Alliance, Ahmad Shah Massoud. Until 2002, Dushanbe hosted a medical facility set up by the Indian Army to treat injured anti-Taliban resistance fighters at the Farkhor airfield on Tajikistan's southern border with Afghanistan. India also used the airfield to supply the Northern Alliance with military equipment, munitions and intelligence, and to repair its combat helicopters.

Tajikistan is not only an important country for India in its Afghan policy but also continues to have a long-term geopolitical relevance for New Delhi in the wake of the announcement of the 2014 withdrawal of the US and NATO forces fighting the Taliban.[11] A military presence in Tajikistan, therefore, is sought-after by major powers such as the US, Russia, China, and even India. Tajikistan thus remains to be an important country in India's strategic vision in Central Asia. It may be noted that security ties between India and Tajikistan received a push when a bilateral defence agreement was signed in 2002. In accordance with the agreement, India renovated a Soviet-built airfield at Ayni, 25 km west of Dushanbe. The renovation, which cost India over US$ 70 million, included upgrading the runway, construction of the traffic control tower, hangars and administrative buildings. Despite widespread speculation that India intended to use the facility as its first-ever foreign military base, Indian specialists handed over the renovated facility to the Tajik Defence ministry in 2010.[12]

India also hopes to establish its influence in Tajikistan to curtail Chinese and Pakistani influence in the Central Asian region. With this objective, it is trying to make its presence in Tajikistan to acquire access to the Central Asian market. Recent Indian interests in Tajikistan also stem from the reported presence of substantial quantities of uranium and natural gas. Similarly, Tajikistan hopes to strengthen its relations with India in order to avert threats of Uzbek invasion in its territory in case of its conflict with the neighbouring country. It also faces a threat from the Taliban-linked terror groups like the Islamic Movement of Uzbekistan (IMU). The bilateral cooperation on security and defence-related issues has acquired preponderance since post-September 2001 that still loom large in the light of the USA's declaration of exit from Afghanistan in 2014.[13]

Bilateral Visits and Agreements

India and Tajikistan have shared common perspectives on several international and regional issues that have been reiterated formally at the highest political level. In May 1994, India opened its diplomatic mission in Dushanbe and Tajikistan opened its embassy in New Delhi in June 2003. Since then, regular exchanges of the highest level visits that have taken place have been reflecting the growing mutual trust between the two countries. PresidentRahmon has so far visited India six times, the latest of which was on December 14–18, 2016 (his earlier visits took place in 1995, 1999, 2001, 2006 and 2012). It was during his 2016 visit that both the countries elevated their bilateral relationship to the level of a strategic partnership.

From the Indian side, eminent visitors include Prime Minister Vajpayee who visited Dushanbe in November 2003. An important landmark of this visit was Tajikistan's offer to renovate and upgrade the Ainy airbase. President Pratibha Devisingh Patil's visit to Tajikistan in September 2009 was marked by her being the Chief Guest on the occasion of Tajikistan's Independence Day celebrations. During this visit, the Indian President made an announcement that Indian firms intended to invest US$ 28 million in the construction of a cement plant and the development of gas fields in southern Tajikistan.[14] Further, on July 2–3, 2012, India's External Affairs Minister S.M. Krishna visited Tajikistan. His visit to Dushanbe was the first by an Indian External Affairs Minister to the strategically located Central Asian Republic of Tajikistan in nine years. The next visit was paid by Indian Vice President Hamid Ansari on April 14–18, 2013 as part of revamping the Connect Central Asia Policy aimed at a greater political, economic and people-to-people engagement with the Central Asian nations.[15] Ansari has been the first Indian Vice-President to have ever visited the Central Asian country.

India's close strategic partnership with Tajikistan was elevated to a higher plane with the successful visit of Prime Minister Modi to Tajikistan from July, 12–13, 2015 and his meetings with President Rahmon. During the visit, the two sides decided to step up cooperation in the spheres of trade and economic ties, defence and connectivity. Both countries also reiterated their common resolve to expand and strengthen their fight against terrorism in the shared region. PM visited the India-Tajikistan Friendship Hospital in Qurgon Teppa and interacted with the patients. The PM also unveiled a bust of Rabindranath Tagore along with the Tajik President. During the visit, the two sides signed a Programme of Cooperation in the field of Culture for the period 2016–18. An MOU for setting up of computer labs in 37 schools of Tajikistan was also signed.[16]

During President Rahmon's visit, India and Tajikistan signed an agreement against terror financing and money laundering. Tajikistan supported India's candidature for the Shanghai Cooperation Organization and India's bid for permanent membership of the United Nations Security Council. Mr Rahmon, who also sought investment in the upcoming small and medium hydroelectricity projects, appreciated the signing of the trilateral Chabahar port agreement between India, Iran and Afghanistan as the project will provide connectivity to Tajikistan.The two sides indicated that the relationship was expected to deepen in 2017, which would mark the 25th anniversary of the establishment of diplomatic ties between the two nations.[17]

These visits have resulted in the signing of several agreements and MoUs in all areas of mutual concern including the economic and trade field. The following important agreements and MoUs have been concluded for the promotion of bilateral economic cooperation:

(i) The 1993 Agreements on Trade and Economic Cooperation; Economic and Technical Cooperation; Cooperation between the Commercial Bank for Foreign Economic Activities in Tajikistan and the State Bank of India (TSOB is a joint stock commercial Bank for Foreign Economic Activity started in 1992. Before independence, it functioned as a branch of the Soviet Vnesheconom Bank and specialised in foreign trade transactions).

(ii) The 1995 Agreement for setting up the Indo-Tajik Joint Commission for Economic, Scientific and Technological Cooperation and the Bilateral Investment Protection Agreement.

(iii) The 2001 Agreement on long-term cooperation in Trade and Economic Cooperation and the Agreement for Cooperation in the Field of Industry and Air Services.

(iv) The 2003 MoU on setting up a fruit-processing unit, the Tourism Agreement, an MoU on Cooperation in the IT sector and an MoU on establishing an IT Centre.

(v) The 2006 MoU on Energy Cooperation.

(vi) The 2010 Agreement on Cooperation in the Field of Agriculture which has been the main document for the development of bilateral cooperation in such areas as exchange of information in joint programmes for scientific agriculture research and technology, animal husbandry, commercial activity, joint ventures for production of agricultural products and processing.

(vii) The 2012 MoU on cooperation in the field of textiles between the Ministry of Energy and Industry, Tajikistan and Ministry of Textiles, India; Agreement on Mutual Cooperation between the Ministry of Labour and Social Protection of Population, Tajikistan and the

Ministry of Labour and Employment, India; Agreement between the Ministry of Health and Family Welfare, India and the Ministry of Health, Tajikistan.

(viii) Programme of Cooperation (POC) between the Ministries of Culture of India and Tajikistan in the field of culture for the years 2016–18.

(ix) Exchange of Note Verbale (NV) on setting up of computer labs in 37 schools in Tajikistan.

In addition, India also supports Tajikistan's accession to the WTO to promote its economic relations. On August 3, 2012, Minister of Economic Development and Trade, Sharief Rahmzoda and Indian Ambassador, Asith Bhattacharjee signed a protocol supporting Tajikistan's accession to the WTO.

India–Tajikistan Economic Cooperation

The elevation of India–Tajikistan bilateral relations to the level of a "Strategic Partnership" provided a much-needed boost to cooperation in a wide spectrum of areas including political, economic, education, health, human resource development, defence, counter-terrorism, science and technology, culture and tourism. The two countries already have consultative mechanisms: (a) India-Tajikistan Joint Commission on Trade, Economic, Scientific and Technical Cooperation (b) Joint Working Group on Counter Terrorism and (c) Foreign Office Consultations. These institutional mechanisms helped a lot in promoting economic cooperation between the two sides. In addition, in 2001, a Joint India–Tajikistan Commission on Economic Cooperation was established which has since been involved in the activation of beneficial economic collaboration.[18] However, it was the Bilateral Investment Promotion Agreement signed during the visit of President Rahmon to New Delhi in December 1995 that cleared the way for Indian investments in Tajikistan. The Indian companies started investing in different Tajik sectors (Table 6.1).

Table 6.1: Indian Investment in Tajikistan

S.No.	*Names of major Indian Companies investing in Tajikistan*	*Main sectors ofIinvestment with Description*
1	CHL International	Developer of the Sheraton Dushanbe Hotel
2	Marvis Ltd.	Exploration of natural gas
3	KEC/RPG	Construction of long power transmission line

Source: Department of Industrial Policy & Promotion, Ministry of Commerce and Industry, Government of India.

Another major development that took place again in 1995 was the establishment of the India–Tajikistan Joint Commission on Trade, Economic, Scientific and Technical Cooperation. It has so far held eight meetings. On December 7–14, 2001, the first session of this Joint Commission was held in New Delhi in which a joint protocol was signed. From May 27 to June 1, 2003, the second session of the Joint Commission took place in Dushanbe. The third session was held in Delhi from 31 July to 1 August 2006 under the Co-Chairmanship of G.K. Pillai, Commerce Secretary and then Special Secretary, Department of Commerce from the Indian side and Hakim H. Soliev, Minister for Economy and Trade of the Republic of Tajikistan from the Tajik side.[19]

While the fourth session of this Joint Commission was held in Dushanbe on October 10–11, 2007, the fifth session was held in New Delhi on November 19–21, 2008. In the fifth session, the Tajik delegation was led by Gulomjon Bobozoda, Minister for Economic Development and Trade and the Indian side was chaired by the Commerce Secretary G K. Pillai. The sixth session was held on May 16–17, 2011 at Dushanbe in which the Indian side was led by P.K. Chaudhery, Addl. Secretary and the Tajik delegation was led by Farrukh Hamraliev, Minister of Economic Development & Trade.[20] In the seventh session, Tajikistan suggested New Delhi to consider the Transit Agreement between Governments of Tajikistan, Afghanistan, Pakistan and India. Since the proposed agreement had a multidimensional character, the Indian side stressed that the matter shall be considered by the foreign ministry.The eighth session was held on January 13 and 14, 2016, in Dushanbe. During the meeting, the two sides reviewed the status of the seventh session of the IT-JCM and agreed to continue the work for the execution of the remaining action points mentioned in the Protocol. At the end of the session, the two sides signed a new protocol, which includes an Action Plan for enhanced trade, investment and economic relations between India and Tajkistan.

India and Tajikistan decided to initiate negotiations for concluding a new Bilateral Investment Treaty, MOUs for Cooperation in the Field of Traditional Medicines and Medicinal Plants and the setting up of an AYUSH Academic Chair in one of the reputed universities of Tajikistan. The two sides reiterated their support to the International North–South Transport Corridor and the development of the Chabahar port in Iran and hoped that these initiatives will help in addressing the connectivity issues between the two countries. The two countries also decided to work together for the inclusion of India in Pakistan-Afghanistan-Tajikistan Transit Trade Agreement.[21]

Cooperation in the Framework of Regional Development

India's efforts to strengthen economic ties with Tajikistan have also been complemented by India–Iran and India–Afghanistan relations. These countries are pulling together their resources to build industry and infrastructure, including pipelines. This is evident from the Indian government's bid for iron ore blocks in the rich Hajigak mines in Afghanistan apart from a proposal to set up a steel plant there. In November 2011, Afghanistan awarded four of the five blocks at Hajigak iron ore deposit to a consortium of seven Indian firms led by the state-owned Steel Authority of India Limited (SAIL). Similarly, India, as discussed in Chapter Two, is engaged in the construction of the Chabahar port in Iran that would be connected by the Zarang–Delaram Highway that India had built in the mid-2000s. This would help revive the economy of both Tajikistan and Afghanistan. In the process, India would also have a stronger economic engagement with a broader region. Tajikistan is also likely to join the Customs Union of Russia, Belarus and Kazakhstan in the future. It could be useful for India to have a smooth accessibility to the region.[22]

Cooperation in Energy Sector

Tajikistan has the greatest hydropower potential in the region, and not many countries across the world match the potential of the country. Though hydropower is Tajikistan's greatest economic source, this potential has largely been untapped. The hydropower potential of Tajikistan is estimated at 527 billion Kwh per annum, but less than 6 percent of this capacity is being used for hydropower production. The Tajikistan government aims to exploit the hydropower potential to support the domestic market and also export power to its neighboring countries in Asia. Further, the Governments of Afghanistan, Iran and Pakistan have expressed their interest in importing electricity from Tajikistan. In fact, Tajikistan has a capacity of producing 4.4 gigawatts (GWe) of electricity, about 90 percent of which is hydroelectric. A significant fraction of the hydroelectric capacity is used in aluminium production. According to the official report of *Tajikistan's National Strategy for Energy Sector Development 2006-2015*, the country was estimated to reach a production of 35 billion Kwh of hydroelectricity in 2015. Tajikistan does not produce oil, gas, or coal of its own, but hydroelectricity.

With a high and under-invested hydroeletricity sector, Tajikistan offers decent opportunities to the Indian investors. According to an MoU signed by the two countries, a Centre of Information Technology was opened in

Dushanbe in August 2008. The same year, the National Hydro Power Cooperation (NHPC) through CHL International and Bharat Heavy Electricals Limited (BHEL) undertook renovation of the Indian government-funded Varzob-I hydropower plant.[23] Two units of the Varzob-I with an uprated capacity of 2×4.75 MW were successfully commissioned on December 28, 2012 and were formally handed over by BHEL to Tajikistan on January 31, 2013.[24]

Earlier, an Indian company KEC/RPG completed the construction of a 116-km long power transmission line from Sangtuda-1 hydropower plant to the Afghan border in October 2010. A two-member team from BHEL visited Tajikistan from May 19 to 23, 2008 and held negotiations with AKDN's "Pamir Energy" and the World Bank for the supply of a 7MW generator on a commercial basis to Pamir Energy.[25] This project was completed in 2011. A Singapore-based Indian Company, Marvis Pvt. Ltd., obtained 4 gas fields in southern Tajikistan in 2008 and started producing gas from two of its wells. The same year, the Valpro Group from India signed a Memorandum of Intent with the Tajik Ministry of Energy for setting up a power plant based on captive coal mines at Shurab and Fan Yagnob.[26] However, due to a financial crisis, the investments got delayed. Two Indian companies—KEC International Ltd (KEC) and RPG Transmission—have won an ADB-funded contract for the construction and commissioning of the 118 km Regional Power Interconnection (Project LOT 1, 220 KV) line connecting Tajikistan to Afghanistan on a turnkey basis and the project will be finished by the middle of the year.[27] A number of other Indian companies such as the Abhijit Group, Soma Enterprises, etc., are looking at various commercial opportunities in Tajikistan's mining and hydropower sectors. The Khoday Group from Bangalore has also proposed the construction of Hydropower stations to the Government of Tajikistan.

Cooperation in Construction and Hotel Industry

In the construction sector, some Indian companies won contracts for the repair of air strips at the Khujand and Dushanbe airports (Tanya Construction Company). Following President Patil's visit to Dushanbe in September 2009, it was announced that some Indian firms intended to invest US$ 28 million in the construction of a cement plant and the development of gas fields in southern Tajikistan.[28] However, these plans have not been implemented. On the other hand, the CHL International group of India constructed the Sheraton Dushanbe Hotel. The company was allotted nearly 2.2 hectares of land in Dushanbe for constructing this hotel and high rise apartments.[29] Three Indian restaurants (Ashoka, Anahita and Delhi Darbar) operate in Dushanbe, while one restaurant-cum-hotel is located at Khorog which is owned by the Delhi Darbar.

Cooperation in the Field of Agriculture

Agriculture, as in India, is the main economic sector in Tajikistan. As mentioned earlier, both countries signed an agreement on cooperation in the agricultural sector in October 2010[30] Tajikistan occupies a prominent place in the world for the production of dried fruits, in growing fresh vegetables and fruits, cotton and legumes. By applying innovative technology and rich experience of the Indian enterprises to grow cotton in Tajikistan, it can boost mutual cooperation between the two countries.[31] During Vice President Ansari's visit to Dushanbe in April 2013, while India sought Tajik help in gaining expertise on better management of the cotton crop, it was also agreed to set up an Entrepreneurship Development Centre in Tajikistan.[32] At the same time, Tajikistan invited investment and cooperation in its agriculture sector from India.[33] Under the 'Connect Central Asia' policy, India has made commitments to supply agricultural machinery and implement a package of small development projects.

Cooperation in Food-Processing Industry

India has been assisting Tajikistan in its economic development, capacity-building and humanitarian needs. A grant of US$ 0.6 million was extended by the Government of India to set up a Food Processing Plant in Dushanbe. Hindustan Machine Tools (International) Ltd. from the Indian side and Dushanbe Contract Prom (DCP) from the Tajik side were the executing agencies. The plant was commissioned on January 26, 2005 and handed over to the local government in Dushanbe for commercial operation. The plant has been commercially since July 2007. The label on the products acknowledges the technical contribution of HMT (I). With the aim of strengthening the all-round bilateral relationship under its 'Connect Central Asia' policy, India has recently offered to undertake a series of new development projects in Tajikistan, including the setting up of a fruit and vegetable processing plant.[34]

Cooperation under ITEC Programme

As of now, 844 slots for ITEC and 296 ICCR (Indian Council of Cultural Relations) scholarships are being utilised by Tajik candidates to study in India.[35] Tajikistan is one of the largest beneficiaries of India's ITEC programme. After the visit of President Patil to Tajikistan in September 2009, the number of ITEC slots was increased from 70 to 100 per year. The ITEC training slots were further increased to 150 from 100 during President Rahmon's visit to India in September 2012. In 2015–16, 125 ITEC slots were allotted to Tajikistan.

Indian Assistance to Tajik Projects

In 1995, India extended a credit line of US$ 5 million to the government of Tajikistan to set up a joint venture with a private Indian company "Ajanta Pharma" for the production of pharmaceuticals. The joint venture, "Tajik Ajanta Pharma" could not take-off due to the inability of the Tajik side to provide working capital. The Government of India converted the principal amount along with the accrued interest of US$ 3.37 million into a grant during the visit of Prime Minister Vajpayee to Dushanbe in November 2003. The Indian government disbursed a grant of US$ 6,00,000 to set up an Information Technology Centre in Tajikistan with Centre for Development of Advanced Computing (CDAC) in India as the executing agency. The Centre was inaugurated on July 18, 2006 and started functioning from November 2006 under the name Bedil India-Tajikistan Centre for Information Technology (BITCIT). India also gave a grant to set up an "India-Tajikistan Modern Engineering Workshop" at the Tajikistan State Technical University (TTU) in Dushanbe. The workshop was inaugurated on June 2, 2011.[36]

During the visit of President Rahmon to India in September 2012, as part of its ongoing developmental partnership with Tajikistan, India announced new developmental projects including an IT Centre of Excellence; an enetwork, including tele-education and tele-medicine; medical centres; language laboratories; an Entrepreneurship Development Institute; supply of agricultural machinery and the implementation of a package of small development projects [SDPs]. Earlier, India had also provided a grant of US$ 2mn ($1 mn cash and $1mn in kind, i.e., power cables, generator and pump sets) to overcome a crisis due to the unprecedented harsh winters during January–February 2008. In June 2009, a US$ 200,000 cash assistance was given by India to overcome damages caused by the heavy rains and floods during April–May 2009. Also, after the flashfloods in Kulyab on May 7, 2010, India donated a cash assistance of US$ 200,000. After an outbreak of polio in Tajikistan, 2 mn doses of oral vaccines were provided through UNICEF in November 2010. Recently, on 28 December 2013, India gifted a high quality ambulance to the Governor of the Khorog city of the Gorno Badakshan Autonomous Region (Pamirs).[37]

India–Tajikistan Trade Relations

Compared with India's trade with other CARs, the India–Tajikistan trade is very small. This is evident from Table 6.2 which gives the total trade turnover including imports and exports between the two countries. The total bilateral trade stood at a meagre US$ 1.53 million in 1996–97 which grew to US$ 4.09 million in 2000–01. The two-way trade between the two sides in 2005–06 further grew to be valued at US$ 12.09 million. This consisted of India's exports to Tajikistan valued at US$ 6.20 million and India's imports from Tajikistan worth US$ 5.89 million. But again, it was not an impressive bilateral trade figure. In order to widen trade and economic relations between the two countries, India agreed to hold a meeting of the business forum of both the countries during the forthcoming visit of the President of the Republic of Tajikistan to India in August 2006. Tajikistan too agreed to hold a similar forum in May 2007 in Dushanbe. Both sides also underlined the importance of establishing long-term

Table 6.2: India-Tajikistan Bilateral Trade, 1996-2016 (In US$ million)

Year	*Export from India*	*Growth Percentage*	*Percent Share in Total Exports by India*	*Imports from Tajikistan*	*Growth Percentage*	*Percent Share in Total Imports by India*	*Total Bilateral Trade*
1996-97	0.73	NA	0.0022	0.80	NA	0.0021	1.53
1997-98	1.12	54.27	0.0032	NA	NA	NA	NA
1998-99	0.51	-54.62	0.0015	2.53	NA	0.0060	3.04
1999-00	2.38	368.87	0.0065	2.33	-7.73	0.0047	4.71
2000-01	3.55	49.22	0.0080	0.54	-76.71	0.0011	4.09
2001-02	1.22	-65.54	0.0028	1.34	145.97	0.0026	2.56
2002-03	8.65	606.14	0.0164	0.08	-93.91	0.0001	8.73
2003-04	4.47	-48.34	0.0070	3.95	4,756.14	0.0051	8.42
2004-05	6.59	47.54	0.0079	4.09	3.37	0.0037	10.68
2005-06	6.24	-5.38	0.0061	5.89	44.11	0.0039	12.13
2006-07	7.46	19.54	0.0059	7.95	35.08	0.0043	15.41
2007-08	12.40	66.20	0.0076	9.81	23.38	0.0039	22.21
2008-09	16.71	34.73	0.0090	17.47	77.97	0.0058	34.18
2009-10	15.71	-5.94	0.0088	16.85	-3.50	0.0058	32.56
2010-11	18.31	16.49	0.0073	23.02	36.59	0.0062	41.33
2011-12	21.28	16.22	0.0070	8.86	-61.53	0.0018	30.14
2012-13	35.16	65.25	0.0117	12.86	45.15	0.0026	48.02
2013-14	54.27	54.37	0.0173	0.86	-93.34	0.0002	55.13
2014-15	53.71	-1.04	0.0173	4.39	412.50	0.0010	58.09
2015-16	22.26	-58.55	0.0085	9.98	127.43	0.0026	32.24

Source: Based on Export-Import Data (1997-98 to 2015-16) collected from Directorate General of Foreign Trade (DGFT), Department of Commerce, Ministry of Commerce & Industry, Government of India.

cooperation in the field of industry and agreed to make efforts to achieve this goal, especially in view of the great potential for cooperation in the manufacturing sector in textiles, chemicals, construction materials, mining and processing of light metals.[38] The possibilities of setting up joint ventures in the territories of both countries in identified areas were also considered.

Both sides lament the poor trade figures. In 2007–08, the total trade turnover was around US$ 22.21 million— a significant increase from US$ 8.42 million in 2003–04. The total trade of both the countries stood at US$ 41.33 million at the end of the first decade of the 21st century, i.e., in 2010–11, representing a giant 18 percent leap. Yet, in overall terms, the bilateral trade represents an insignificant less than 0.01 percent of India's trade with the rest of the countries. In 2013–14, although the total trade further grew to reach US$ 55.13 million, it remained an imbalanced trade as India's exports to Tajikistan was much more (US$ 54.27 million) in comparison to India's imports from that country (US$ 0.86 million).

The India–Tajikistan trade on a large scale is done by "suitcase traders" who visit India as tourists. They purchase leather goods, pharmaceuticals and woollens for retail sale in Tajikistan. But bilateral trade between the two sides is not at any significant level. Trade is hampered by the circuitous route for transportation of goods (India to Bandar Abbas by sea route, from Bandar Abbas to Tajikistan by land via Turkmenistan and Uzbekistan). However, on April 17, 2013, while returning to India from his visit to Tajikistan, Vice President Ansari said that India and Tajikistan are working on finding an easy route for enhanced bilateral trade; "the present approach routes for trade are complex, time-consuming and difficult. These are some things to which we have to live with till something better comes up."[39] Indeed, the problem everywhere is one of connectivity, though there is a great scope for micro, small and medium industries where the Indian expertise and experience can come closer. The two countries agreed on opening up a trans-Afghan corridor to facilitate easy access to trade to and from landlocked Tajikistan. The proposed trade route will come via Afghanistan and Pakistan.

Since India does not share borders with any of the Central Asian republics, Modi had been stressing the themes of connectivity as well as invoking India's cultural linkages with Central Asia during each stop including Tajikistan. "We share deep historical, cultural and civilizational links. Tajikistan is nearest to India among all Central Asian countries. We are separated by a narrow corridor. Our linguistic links are the closest in Central Asia... We discussed measures to tap the rich potential in trade and commerce and to encourage joint ventures and investments," Modi said after meeting President Rahmon.[40]

The major items of India's exports to Tajikistan are pharmaceuticals, iron, steel, tea, coffee, chemicals, meat and meat products, textiles and clothing and the major imports are aluminium, cotton, dry fruits, vegetables, organic chemicals and essential oil. Some of the prominent items of India's export and import baskets can be seen through Tables 6.3 and 6.4.

Table 6.3: Main Indian Exports to Tajikistan during 2015-16 (In US$ million)

S.No.	*Commodity*	*Value*	*Percent Share of India's Total Export to Tajikistan*
1	Pharmaceutical products	13.54	60.83
2	Meat and edible meat offal	3.7	16.62
3	Articles of iron or steel	1.55	6.96
4	Coffee, tea, mate and spices	0.62	2.79
5	Electrical machinery and equipment and parts thereof; sound recorders and reproducers, television image and sound recorders and reproducers,and parts	0.43	1.93
6	Articles of apparel and clothing accessories, knitted or corcheted	0.41	1.84
7	Sugars and sugar confectionery	0.33	1.48
8	Organic chemicals	0.29	1.30
9	Articles of apparel and clothing accessories, not knitted or crocheted	0.27	1.21
10	Nuclear reactors, boilers, machinery and mechanical appliances; parts thereof	0.25	1.12
	Total Export of top 10 items	21.39	
	Total Export	22.26	
	India's Global Export	262,290.13	

Table 6.4: Main Indian Imports from Tajikistan during 2015-16 (US$ million)

S.No.	*Commodity*	*Value*	*percent Share of India's Total Imports from Tajikistan*
1	Ores, slag and ash	9.72	97.39
2	Lac; gums, resins and other vegetable saps and extracts	0.2	2.00
3	Edible fruit and nuts; peel or citrus fruit or melons	0.04	0.40

S.No.	Commodity	Value	percent Share of India's Total Imports from Tajikistan
4	Electrical machinery and equipment and parts thereof; sound recorders and reproducers, television image and sound recorders and reproducers, and parts	0.01	0.10
5	Optical, photographic cinematographic measuring, checking precision, medical or surgical inst. and apparatus parts and accessories thereof	0.01	0.10
	Total import of top 5 items	9.98	
	Total import	9.98	

Potential Areas of Indian Investment

A number of promising sectors in Tajikistan offer investment opportunities for Indian investors. These include agriculture, mining, transport and infrastructure, hydropower as well as health, tourism and education. A diversified economic base of India and a large pool of trained manpower further give incentives for forging beneficial partnerships with Tajik companies. In recent times, Tajikistan has already invited India to explore the huge untapped hydropower potential in the country as part of its efforts to explore new fields of partnership between the two sides. India, on its part, has expressed its desire to increase cooperation between Indian and Tajik enterprises through Indian investments into the light industry of Tajikistan.

More than 40 Indian pharmaceutical companies do business in Tajikistan and a few of them have their representatives there. In July 2013, a delegation of the Khoday's Group of Industries visited Tajikistan to finalise several projects in different fields and consider new proposals for further cooperation between the two sides. The Confederation of Indian Industries (CII) has identified some sectors like the mining industry and energy for investment opportunities in Tajikistan.[41] So far as the mining industry is concerned, Tajikistan has rich deposits of silver, gold and antimony. There is a potential for growth in the mining sector as over 400 mineral reserves of around 70 different minerals have been discovered in Tajikistan. Konimansuri Kalon is one of the biggest silver minefields in Tajikistan. The field has deposits of about 1 billion tonnes of ore with the content of silver (49 gm/tonne of ore), lead (0.49 gm/tonne of ore), and zinc (0.38 gm/tonne of ore).[42]

In the energy sector, Tajikistan has identified certain priority investment projects in the fields of hydropower and heating stations. These projects would require an investment of over US$ 5 billion. The government has also developed schemes of integrated use of the country's hydropotential and construction of power transmission lines. In this regard, the Tajikistan government has allocated an amount of US$ 472.2 million for the development of the country's energy sector.[43] The funds would be utilised for rehabilitation of existing facilities as well as construction of new generating capacities and new power transmission lines. The government also plans to increase electricity rates in the country, which would reduce the quasi-fiscal deficit, thus helping the country to attract investment projects in the energy sector. There are plans to offer incentives to investors to promote the production of energy from other sources. This may attract Indian investors willing to participate in the energy-related projects.

To sum up, as India aspires to play a stronger role in Central Asia, its defence and security ties with Tajikistan should be matched with adequate economic cooperation and financial support for the cash-stripped Tajik government. Without achieving this balance, India will remain only a marginal player in the region. Besides, to consider Indian engagement with Tajikistan as solely aimed at ensuring energy security or curbing Islamist extremism would be a narrow, if not an inaccurate, assessment of India's interests in Tajikistan. As an *India-Tajikistan Bilateral Brief* highlights, "a desire to help diversify the Tajik economy and to address humanitarian concerns drives India's engagement with Dushanbe as strongly as does realizing India's energy demand or mitigating shared security and geo-strategic concerns."[44]

REFERENCES

1. Patnaik Ajay, 'India-Tajikistan Relations: Prospects of a Regional Development', in, *The State in Eurasia: Local and Global Arenas*, A. Sengupta and S. Chatterjee (eds), New Delhi: KW Publishers, p. 28.
2. Rasulov, Gafur, 'Foreign Investments in the Economic Developments of Tajikistan', in *Post-Soviet States: Two Decades of Transition and Transformation*, A. Patnaik, and Tulsiram (eds), New Delhi: KW Publishers, p. 86.
3. Patnaik, op. cit., p. 29.
4. Ibid., p. 30.
5. 'Tajikistan', 13 February 2014, URL: http://silkroad.ccpit.org/ccpit/website/201402001/en/news_detail.jsp?id=F0F0D1CCA997D899E040A8C048013331 &sid= F0F0D1CCA969 D899E040A8C048013331&curpager=1
6. Patnaik, op. cit., p. 30.

7. EBRD, 'Public Procurement Policy Workshop in Dushanbe, Tajikistan', 2011. URL: http://www.ppi-ebrd-uncitral.com/index.php/en/tajikistan/ppworkshopdushanbe
8. US Department of State, Bureau Of Economic and Business Affairs, '2014 Investment Climate Statement', June 2014. URL: http://www.state.gov/e/eb/rls/othr/ics/2014/228606.htm
9. EBRD, op. cit.
10. 'India's Relations with Tajikistan: Beyond the Airbase', *Tajikistan Monitor*, 28 February 2011. URL: http://tjmonitor.wordpress.com/2011/02/28/india_in_tajikistan/
11. Roy, Meena Singh, 'Pratibha Patil's Visit to Tajikistan: Enhancing Goodwill, Trust and Mutual Confidence', IDSA Comment, 2009. URL: http://www.idsa.in/idsastrategiccomments/PratibhaPatilsVisittoTajikistan_msroy_230909
12. 'India's Relations with Tajikistan: Beyond the Airbase' op. cit.
13. Bandyopadhyay, Lopamudra, 'India and Tajikistan: Towards a New Strategic Partnership', Global India Foundation, 2012. URL: http://www.global indiafoundation.org/Indiapercent20Tajikistanpercent5B1percent5D.pdf
14. Patnaik, op. cit., p. 25.
15. 'India, Tajikistan to hold Wide-Ranging Talks on Terror, Trade', 15 April 2013. URL: http://articles.timesofindia.indiatimes.com/2013-04-15/rest-of-world/38555245_1_afghan-wakhan-corridor-hamid-ansari-trade-ties
16. Ministry of External Affairs, Government of India, *Annual Report*, 2015-2016, pp. 55.
17. 'Tajikistan, India Step Up Security Ties'. URL: http://www.thehindu.com/news/national/Tajikistan-India-step-up-security-ties/article16897179.ece.
18. Ministry of Foreign Affairs of Republic of Tajikistan, 'Tajikistan Diplomacy: The Past and the Present', vol.1, Dushanbe, 2009, p. 26. URL: http://mfa.tj/files/kitobkhona/tajikistan_ diplomacy_the_past_and_the_present_1/tajikistan_diplomacy_the_past_and_the_ present_en.pdf
19. Ministry of Commerce and Industry, Government of India, 'Trade Promotion Programme - Focus CIS: Major Events Held in 2006-2007'. URL: http://commerce.nic.in/trade/international_tpp_cis_10.asp
20. Embassy of India, Dushanbe, 'Country Brief of Tajikistan' op. cit.
21. Embassy of India, Dushanbe, Tajikistan, '8th Session of India-Tajikistan Joint Commission on Trade, Economic, Scientific and Technical Cooperation'. URL: http://www.indianembassytj.com/index.php?itfpage=newsevent&itemid=25.
22. Patnaik, op. cit., p. 31.
23. 'India-Tajikistan Relations', January 2013. URL: http://www.mea.gov.in/Portal/ForeignRelation/tajikistan_bilateral_brief.pdf
24. Ministry of External Affairs, Government of India, *Annual Report, 2012-2013*, pp. 39-40.
25. *Annual Economic and Commercial Report-2008*. URL: http://www.tradeindia.com/newsletters/country_focus/country_focus_10_march_2009_dushanbe.html
26. Ibid.
27. Ministry of External Affairs, Government of India, *Annual Report, 2012-2013*, pp. 39-40.

28. 'India's Relations with Tajikistan: Beyond the Airbase', op. cit.
29. Embassy of India, Dushanbe, op. cit.
30. 'India-Tajikistan Relations', 8 March 2013. URL: http://www.gktoday.in/india-tajikistan-relations/
31. 'India-Tajikistan Relations', January 2013. http://www.mea.gov.in/Portal/ForeignRelation/tajikistan_bilateral_brief.pdf accessed on 5/08/2013.
32. 'India, Tajikistan stress Stakes in Afghan Peace', *The Hindu*, 16 April 2013.
33. 'Tajikistan invites Indian Investment in Agriculture, Mining', *Hindustan Times*, 16 April 2013.
34. Roy, Meena Singh, 'India and Tajikistan: Building a Long-Term Strategic Partnership', IDSA Comment, 18 September, 2012. URL: http://idsa.in/idsacomments/IndiaandTajikistan BuildingalongtermStrategic Partnership_MeenaSRoy_180912
35. 'India-Tajikistan Relations', July 2014. URL: http://www.mea.gov.in/Portal/Foreign Relation/Tajikistan_July_2014.pdf
36. 'India-Tajikistan Relations', op. cit., January 2013.
37. 'India-Tajikistan Relations, op. cit., July 2014.
38. Ministry of Commerce & Industry, Government of India, 'India, Tajikistan to Strengthen Trade and Economic Cooperation', August 1, 2006, URL: http://commerce.nic.in/pressrelease/pressrelease_detail.asp?id=1751
39. 'India, Tajikistan working on an Easy Route for Trade: Hamid Ansari', *The Economic Times*, 17 April 2013. URL: http://articles.economictimes.indiatimes.com/2013-04-17/news/38616144_1_top-tajik-leadership-cross-border-terrorism-afghan-wakhan-corridor
40. 'Narendra Modi arrives in Tajikistan to Cap Off Central Asia Visit'. URL: http://www.livemint.com/Politics/hZZqhoxtlkNq7wv3NK850O/Narendra-Modi-arrives-in-Tajikistan-to-cap-off-Central-Asia.html
41. *A Strategy Paper for CIS Countries: India-CIS Roadmap 2020*, FT (CIS) Division, July, 2012, pp. 276-77.
42. Ibid.
43. Ibid.
44. Prasad, Kailash K. Prasad and Rani D. Mullen, 'India-Tajikistan Bilateral Brief', India Development Cooperation Research (IDCR) Project, Bilateral Brief no. 5, December 5 (last updated 15 May 2014), 2013. URL: http://idcr.cprindia.org/blog/india-tajikistan-brief-0

7

India and Turkmenistan

Turkmenistan, formerly known as Turkmenia, is the third largest of the five Central republics with a population of seven million. Located towards the southernmost part of Central Asia, Turkmenistan is physically isolated from the other four Central Asian Republics by a vast expanding Karakum or Garagum (Black Sand) desert which is one of the world's largest sand deserts with an area of approximately 1,38,966 sq. miles (3,60,000 sq. km). It covers almost 80 percent of Turkmenistan's terrain of approximately 4,92,100 sq. km. Turkmenistan though is well connected to its neighboring Republics by air, railways, road network and bridges over Amudarya River. However, inspite of its large geographical size, Turkmenistan is the least populated country among the CARs. Consequently, population density is confined to a few core areas. It is bounded by the Caspian Sea in the west, Kazakhstan in the north, Uzbekistan in the east, and Iran and Afghanistan in the south. It has a long border touching Afghanistan (918 km), Iran (1200 km), Kazakhstan (379 km) and Uzbekistan (1,621 km). Thus, its location particularly on the Caspian Sea along with Kazakhstan makes it of geostrategic significance in the Central Asia region. In addition, it possesses the world's fourth largest reserves of natural gas resources and it is expected that the Turkmen natural gas production over the next decade will turn the country into a major supplier of the fuel.[1]

Turkmenistan declared its independence on October 27, 1991 and became a member of the Commonwealth of Independent States (CIS) on December 21, 1991 along with ten other former Soviet republics.[2] Saparmurat Niyazov became the first President of the new republic and remained so till his death in December 2006. Under his leadership, Turkmenistan proclaimed itself as a secular democratic country. In matters of foreign policy, Niyazov's Presidency was instrumental in evolving a distinct foreign policy, i.e., the status of "Permanent Neutrality", which made it stand out in the region. On December 12, 1995, the United Nations General Assembly recognised Turkmenistan's status as a neutral state. This was interpreted by President Niyazov as not practising "self-isolation" but taking a "positive" and "constructive position".[3] It has adopted a policy to promote mutually beneficial non-discriminatory relations with its neighbouring countries to ensure a conflict-free environment conducive to stability and the economic development of the country.

Despite having a declared "neutral status", Turkmenistan did not remain in isolation and joined a few multilateral institutions like the International Monetary Fund (IMF), the World Bank, European Bank for Reconstruction and Development (EBRD), Asian Development Bank (ADB), the United Nations (UN), etc. Currently, Turkmenistan is a member of the UN and its agencies, it is an "Associated Member" in CIS, ECO, OIC, and of NATO, i.e., Partnership for Peace Programme, OSCE, NAM, IMF, etc. While the country is closely working with the UN and its bodies like UNESCO, UNHCR and other regional and international bodies, its association with organisations like the EBRD, IMF and the World Bank is "extremely limited".[4] Turkmenistan has kept itself out of most of the regional groupings. It did not sign the Collective Security Treaty of 1992 despite joining the CIS soon after its independence, and moreover, from 2005, it has remained just as an associate member of the CIS. It is not a member of the SCO, CSTO and EurAsEc though it has been participating in the SCO summits as a guest.

Turkmenistan held its first multi-candidate Presidential elections on February 11, 2007 following the death of President Niyazov on December 21, 2006. Gurbanguly Berdimuhamedov, a former Deputy Prime Minister and the Minster of Health & Medical Industry, was elected as the country's new President by securing 89.2 percent of the total votes polled and has since then remained in power as he was re-elected for a second term with a massive mandate of 97.14 percent in the elections held on February 12, 2012. The death of President Niyazov brought about a few policy changes in the foreign policy thinking of Turkmenistan.[5] The priorities of Turkmenistan in the area of international relations are defined in the document entitled "The Basic Directions for Realisation of Foreign Policy Strategy of Neutral Turkmenistan for 2008-2012" which was ratified by the President of Turkmenistan on March 20, 2008.[6] In the domestic economic sphere, the new government under Berdymuhamedov established a State Agency for Statistics. It has initiated a series of reforms such as the unification of the country's dual currency exchange rate, ordering the redenomination of its currency manat, the reduction of state subsidies for gasoline and initiating the development of a special tourism zone on the Caspian Sea.[7]

The developments in the past few years indicate that the country under the Presidency of Berdymuhamedov is becoming "diplomatically active". Berdimuhamedov's frequent visits to foreign countries are setting a trend of active diplomacy. The country is following "selective engagement", mainly in the economic sphere to cooperate with other countries. While earlier, Turkmenistan' efforts to engage with the outside world were targeted more towards diversifying the country's energy markets and confining to bilateral economic cooperation, today it is cooperating with countries such as Turkey, France and Russia in constructing facilities and infrastructure on its soil. The country has leased its sectors in the Caspian Sea for exploration to a number of countries like the UAE, the US, Russia, China and Germany and it has welcomed them to build pipelines as well.[8]

Steps have also been initiated to improve business environments favourable for foreign investors as well as small and medium enterprises. In July 2012, the World Bank elevated Turkmenistan from a "lower middle income" country to an "upper middle income" country to reflect the country's recent robust economic growth.[9] In order to attract foreign investment; Turkmen authorities have adopted and implemented a new Foreign Investment Law that brings Turkmenistan's investment regime closer to the best international practices. As a result, a number of international oil and gas companies have started exploring opportunities in the country. To facilitate international trade, Turkmenistan has modestly liberalised international trade by reducing import duty and excise taxes. However, wider opinion is that the reforms must be deepened as the trade system appears to be still very restrictive because almost all trade transactions (domestic and foreign) have to be registered with the Turkmen State Commodity Exchange. The development of small and medium enterprises (SME) has also been supported by various positive measures. The Law on Support of Small and Medium Enterprises adopted in 2009 simplified the clumsy procedures for registering a business, offered a range of tax breaks and eased import restrictions for certain goods.[10] The tax code was amended to simplify the tax system which reduced tax rates for small and medium enterprises. In February 2010, a high level "Commission on SME support" was established for promoting SME development.[11]

Economic Situation of Turkmenistan

Due to largely being a desert country, Turkmenistan's economy remains dependent on intensive agriculture in irrigated oases as well as on the sizeable gas and oil resources. The two largest crops are cotton and wheat, consumed domestically and are also exported, exports of raw cotton has been declining, whereas wheat has been in the list of export goods since last 5 years. Although agriculture accounts for roughly 10 percent of the GDP, it continues to employ nearly half of the country's workforce. Agricultural products include cotton, grain and livestock. Small businesses are flourishing construction, repair and other services are in the hands of private sector. Agriculture is subsidized but private farmers do the major part in producing, processing and sale of agri-products. Turkmenistan is an important supplier of raw materials, especially natural gas, petro-chemicals and wheat. Other natural resources of the country include salts, potash, iodine, urea, etc.

Since Turkmenistan is a landlocked country, it is dependent on other countries for trade. Therefore, Turkmenistan was positively oriented towards the countries that gave it a channel to reach international markets. During 1998–2005, Turkmenistan suffered from a continued lack of adequate export routes for natural gas and from obligations on extensive short-term external debt.[12] At the same time, however, total exports rose by an average of roughly 15 percent per year during 2003–08, largely because of higher international oil and gas prices. New alternate route of pipelines to China and Iran, which came in to operation in late 2009 and early 2010, have given Turkmenistan additional export routes for its gas, though these new routes have not offset the sharp drop in export revenue due to decreased gas exports to Russia since early 2009.

Post-Niyazov, Turkmenistan's relations with its neighbours are still primarily dependent on economic considerations, especially with regard to energy issues. Turmenistan seeks to reduce its dependence on Russia to export gas to international markets as the pipelines connecting Turkmenistan to the international markets traverse through Russia, giving Russia a stronger bargaining position. This has impelled countries like the US and China to establish strong ties with Turkmenistan. The completion of the Central Asia–China gas pipeline, i.e., Turkmenistan-Uzbekistan-Kazakhstan-China, commissioned in 2009 is a major development in the region, giving Turkmenistan and the region an alternative to the Russian pipeline system. The US is engaging Turkmenistan for the success of pipelines like the Nabucco which would give Turkmenistan access to European markets bypassing, Russia. The Republic in 2009 agreed to sell 10 billion cubic metres of gas annually to the Nabucco pipeline but the pipeline is yet to be materialised.[13]

Key Economic Indicators of Turkmenistan

(a) Foreign Exchange Reserves: US$ 13.62 billion (31 December 2015 est.)
(b) Exchange Rate of Local Currency (New Turkmenistani Manat): 3.5 per US$ (2015).
(c) Inflation Rate (2015): 16percent (2015 est.)
(d) External Debt: US$ 454.7 million (31 December 2015)
(e) GDP (2015): US$ 35.68 billion
(f) GDP per Capita (2015): US$ 16,400 (PPP)
(g) Real GDP Growth (2015): 6.5percent
(h) Sector-wise Distribution of GDP (2015 est.): agriculture (13.1 percent), industry (48.4 percent), Services (38.5 percent)
(i) Population below poverty line: 0.2percent (2012 est.)
(j) Unemployment: 11percent (2014 est.)
(k) Main industries: natural gas, oil, petroleum products, textiles, food processing
(l) Exports: US$ 10.38 billion (2015 est.)
(m) Export goods: gas, crude oil petrochemicals, textiles, cotton fibre
(n) Main export partners: China (68.5 percent), Turkey (4.9 percent) (2015 est.)
(o) Imports: US$ 8.198 billion (2015 est.)
(p) Import goods: machinery and equipment, chemicals, foodstuffs
(q) Import partners: Turkey (24.9 percent), Ukraine (7 percent), Russia (12.3 percent), China (10.9 percent), UAE (9.1 percent), Kazakhstan (5.1 percent), Germany (4.6 percent), Iran (4.4 percent) (2015 est.)

The main natural resources of Turkmenistan include petroleum, natural gas, sulphur salts, potash, iodine and urea, etc. According to Turkmenistan official figures, Turkmenistan's resource base is approximately 71.64 billion tons of oil equivalent, including 53 billion tons located in onshore fields and 18.21 billion tons in the Caspian Sea. In November 2015, the China National Petroleum Corporation (CNPC) reported that the accumulated volume of natural gas exported from Turkmenistan to China reached 121bcm. The State Committee of Statistics of Turkmenistan reported a total production of 76.2 bcm in 2014. The British firm Gaffney, Cline, and Associates conducted an audit of the country's Galkynysh gas field and concluded that it holds 28.2 trillion cubic meters of natural gas, making it the second-largest natural gas field in the world. According to Turkmenistan's State Statistics Committee, Turkmenistan produced about 11,589 million tons of oil, including gas condensate, in 2014. According to official figures, the Turkmenbashy Complex of Oil Refineries produced 270 thousand tons of liquefied petroleum gas (LPG) in 2014. The country produced 53.5 billion cubic metres (bcm) of gas in 2002 on the background of domestic consumption standing at 10 bcm. At the same time it exported 43.5 bcm of gas. In 2004, the country's natural gas production was 58.57 bcm and export was 42 bcm. Turkmenistan remains the second largest natural gas producer in the former Soviet Union after Gazprom. Its natural gas production in 2011 was 59.5 bcm as against the post-Soviet peak-production of 66.1 bcm in 2008.[14] Turkmen gas exports in 2011 included 10 bcm to Russia, another 10 bcm to Iran and 14 bcm to China. The dramatic drop of natural gas production in the post-2008 period can be explained by Gazprom's unwillingness to buy large quantities of Turkmen gas during the period of decreased energy demand in the European Union.[15]

But encouraging results came in 2012, when natural gas production increased to more than 69 bcm apart from oil production which registered a figure of 11 million tonnes.[16] According to the Ministry of Foreign Affairs of Turkmenistan, the programme on the development of oil and gas complex of Turkmenistan insists on increasing gas production up to 250 billion cubic metres and oil production up to 110 million tonnes by the year 2030.[17] Previously Turkmenistan use to rely heavily on Russia for its exports route through pipelines running through Russian territory, the Russian route is almost non existent now as new route to China and Iran took the main center stage in gas export from Turkmenistan gas fields and oil industry. Among other major exports are liquefied natural gas (LNG) and polypropylene. Turkmenistan is expected to play a significant role in the global oil and gas sector due to the following reasons:[18]

1. Huge hydrocarbon reserves in its Caspian Sea depths, with the government's target to triple natural gas production by 2030;
2. Strategy for mutually advantageous international cooperation pursued by the government of Turkmenistan; and
3. Developed export markets and development of new pipeline projects, including Turkmenistan-Afghanistan-Pakistan-India (TAPI) gas pipeline.

Development of India–Turkmenistan Relations

Turkmenistan's border-sharing with Afghanistan makes the country strategically important for India to actively engage with it. The deteriorating security situation in Afghanistan, and Turkmenistan's ability to deal with the Taliban have been important factors in developing cordial relations with Turkmenistan. From the purpose of energy security, Turkmenistan's rich oil and gas resources, its proximity to India and the country's relative stability under the leadership of President Berdimuhamedov as compared to the Middle Eastern countries has increased its significance in recent times.[19]

The year 2017 marked the 25th anniversary of the establishment of diplomatic relations between India and Turkmenistan. India formally recognised Turkmenistan's statehood on December 26, 1991. The formal relationship between the two countries was established on April 20, 1992, with the first visit of the then President of Turkmenistan, Saparmurat Niyazov to India. During the visit, a set of documents were signed, which laid the basis for the establishment of a bilateral relationship.[20] Following this, India established its embassy in Ashgabat, the capital of Turkmenistan, on January 30, 1994 and has had a resident Ambassador in Ashgabat since then.[21] A year later the diplomatic mission of Turkmenistan was established in New Delhi.

The Indian Prime Minister P.V. Narasimha Rao paid a three-day official visit to Turkmenistan on September 19–21, 1995. It was the occasion when he was conferred an honorary membership of the Turkmen Academy of Sciences. The Turkmen leadership cherished India's non-political and non-ideological objectives in Turkmenistan and held the view that this is a positive point towards a stable and meaningful partnership between the two republics.[22] The Prime Minister Rao praised the neutral attitude of the Turkmen Republic as well as the secular and modern temper of the Turkmen people. On the other hand, President Niyazov,[23] assured his support to India's bid for a permanent membership in the UN Security Council. Niyazov's opposition to attempts by Pakistan and other actors to politicise the Central Asian regional fora and the formation of an Islamic Emirate further reflected the commonality in attitude and interests of the two countries. Niyazov also held the view that the issue of Kashmir should be resolved in accordance with the Shimla Agreement of 1972.[24]

During Prime Minister Rao's visit, five major agreements were signed, which are as follows:[25]

1. Cooperation between the Foreign Offices of both the countries apart from providing training to Turkmen diplomats in India;
2. Extension of a Cultural Exchange Programme in education, science and technology till December 1996;
3. Encouragement and protection of bilateral investments;
4. Setting up of a joint commission on trade and economics; and
5. Extending a second credit line of US$ 10 million in addition to the US$ 5 million extended in March 1995 for purchasing items for and from joint ventures.

The Indo-Turkmen Joint Communiqué spoke of the concern of both the republics over the continued resort to terrorism and a hostile propaganda in the South Asian context—the first such forthright expression by any Central Asian Republic.[26]

The visit of the Foreign Minister of Turkmenistan to New Delhi in June 1996 added a new dimension to the Indo-Turkmenistan relations. The visiting Turkmen Foreign Minister addressed a special gathering of the Indian strategic community, organised by the Institute for Defence Studies and Analyses (IDSA) in New Delhi and called for an urgent need to resume a regular Track-II dialogue between India and Turkmenistan in order to examine new opportunities and options for bilateral relations. The first Indo-Turkmenistan bilateral dialogue jointly organised by the IDSA and Turkmenistan's Foreign Ministry in Ashgabat on October 18, 1996 was the first of its kind with any Central Asian Republic, which proved to be a major step in the direction of promoting understanding on the key issues of national and international peace and security.[27]

President Niyazov came to India for his second official visit that took place on February 25–26, 1997. India's External Affairs Minister, Jaswant Singh, visited Turkmenistan in May 1999. Agreements on the setting up of a Working Group on Energy and a protocol for the development of cooperation between the Ministries of Foreign Affairs of the two countries were signed during this visit. Foreign Office Consultations amongst India and Turkmenistan were held in New Delhi in April 2000.[28]

On October 18, 2005, Rajiv Sikri, Secretary East (Eurasian Division) of the Ministry of External Affairs, Government of India, visited Ashgabat and held a number of high-level meetings. His negotiations with the Turkmen delegation covered a wide range of issues including cooperation in oil and gas, fuel and energy, transportation, textile, agriculture, science, education, culture and healthcare sectors. The Indian envoy stressed that the bilateral relations had grown slowly but steadily because of the historical and cultural ties between the two countries and the people of both the countries besides the policy of peace, friendship, good neighbourhood and cooperation actively being pursued by Niyazov.[29] Both the sides expressed readiness to expand interaction in education through the implementation of joint educational and research programmes. Creation of joint training centres was discussed. One such training centre now works successfully in Turkmenistan. In 2008, India's Vice President Hamid Ansari visited Turkmenistan where he discussed with the Turkmen leaders issues related to oil and gas pipelines. , He also received assurances from the Turkmen leaders about a strong support for India's membership in the United Nations Security Council.

At present, both countries are providing each other mutual support in the international arena, expanding multilateral cooperation in the framework of the international structures. The first state visit of President Berdimuhamedov to India from 24 to 26 May 2010 offered an excellent opportunity to improve the relationship further and opened fresh areas for cooperation. Since then, regular exchanges of ministerial level visits have been taking place between the two countries. The last visit from the Turkmen side was that of Deputy Prime Minister and Foreign Minister,Rashid Meredov from 21 to 22 January 2013 and from the Indian side, of the Indian Vice-President Hamid Ansari visited Ashgabat and Mary to attend International Conference devoted to 20th Anniversary of Neutrality of Turkmenistan and ground breaking ceremony of TAPI, accordingly. The Indian External Affairs Minister Mrs. Sushma Swaraj visited Ashgabat in April 2015 and co-chaired India-Turkmenistan Inter-governmental Commission.

PM Modi visited Turkmenistan from July, 10–11, 2015. During the visit, several agreements to expand and strengthen cooperation in the field of defence, chemical products, science and technology, sports, tourism, yoga and traditional medicine and Foreign Service Institutes were signed including a joint statement. A Yoga and Traditional Medicine Centre was inaugurated in Ashgabat and Mahatma Gandhi's bust was unveiled by the Hon'ble PM in Ashgabat during the visit. It was agreed to expand cooperation in the energy and transport sectors.[30]

Bilateral Agreements

Turkmenistan is interested in promoting a trade and investment relationship with India, as the latter's economy has grown rapidly in the aftermath of the global financial crisis. So far, India and Turkmenistan have signed 35 international documents, laying the legal foundations of a bilateral cooperation, including three agreements signed at the top level, 19 documents signed at the inter-governmental level and 13 documents signed at the inter-agency level.

Some of the noteworthy treaties and agreements include the following:

- India and Turkmenistan have implemented w.e.f. April 1, 2011 an agreement on visa-free entry for Diplomatic Passport holders.
- An agreement on trade and economic cooperation between India and Turkmenistan was signed in May 2010.
- Bilateral Investment Promotion and Protection Agreement signed in September 1995 which was ratified on February 27, 2006.
- Agreement on Avoidance of Double Taxation and the Prevention of Fiscal Evasion with respect to taxes on income and on capital was signed in February 1997 which became operational in July 2002.
- Agreement between Chamber of Commerce and Industry of Turkmenistan and the India–CIS Chamber of Commerce signed in September 1996 to develop cooperation between the economic, commercial and financial organisations of the two countries.
- A Trilateral Transit Agreement among India, Iran and Turkmenistan was signed, the first meeting of which was held in Delhi on January 31, 2000.
- Agreement on Air Services signed on February 7, 2000.[31]

MoU on Improvement and Modernisation of the Turkmen–India Training-and-Industrial Centre in Ashgabat was signed on April 8, 2015. These are the lists of the MOUs and agreements signed during the visit of PMModi in Ashgabat on July 11, 2015.

- Memorandum of Understanding on Supply of Chemical Products between the Indian Public Sector Undertaking 'Rashtriya Chemicals and Fertilizers Limited' and the Turkmen State concern 'Turkmenhimiya'.
- Memorandum of Understanding between the Foreign Service Institute of the Ministry of External Affairs of the Republic of India and the Institute of International Relations of the Ministry of Foreign Affairs of Turkmenistan.
- Agreement between the Ministry of Youth Affairs and Sports of The Republic of India and the State Committee For Sport of Turkmenistan on Cooperation in the Field of Sports.
- Programme of Cooperation in Science and Technology between

the Government of the Republic of India and the Government of Turkmenistan for the period 2015–2017.

- Memorandum of Understanding between the Government of the Republic of India and the Government of Turkmenistan on Cooperation in Yoga and Traditional Medicine.
- Memorandum of Understanding between the Government of the Republic of India and the Government of Turkmenistan on Cooperation in the Field of Tourism.
- Agreement between the Government of the Republic of India and the Government of the Republic of Turkmenistan on Cooperation in the field of Defence.[32]

Institutional Basis for Engagement

The Inter-Governmental Commission (IGC) on Trade, Economic, Scientific and Technological Cooperation is the main institutional structure that since its inception has been involved in promoting ties between the two countries. The IGC has been meeting regularly since 2006. Simultaneously, a Joint Working Group on Energy has also been set up. The third meeting of the India–Turkmenistan IGC was held in February 2010 in Ashgabat. The fourth meeting of the IGC was held on January 21–22, 2013 at New Delhi which was attended by Deputy Chairman of Cabinet of Ministers (DPM) and Foreign Minister Rashid Meredov from the Turkmen side while the Indian side was represented by Minister of State for External Affairs, E. Ahmed. The fifth meeting of India-Turkmenistan IGC was held in Ashgabat in April 2015, and was co-chaired by Indian External Affairs Minister Sushma Swaraj and Turkmenistan Deputy Prime Minister R. Meredov. The 6th IGC is scheduled to be held in August 2017. The IGC meetings comprehensively reviewed the status of bilateral relations in areas such as energy, trade and economic cooperation, transport and connectivity, civil aviation, information technology, science and technology, cultural, educational, consular, counter-terrorism, and visa issues. The Turkmen side also agreed to form a joint Working Group on Trade and Economic Cooperation which was tasked to meet early and discuss measures to increase the bilateral trade and identify areas of cooperation. A protocol of this fourth meeting of the IGC was also signed by the two co-chairs.[33] But the most important issue which was the focus of the IGC meeting was of the strategic TAPI gas pipeline project. Both sides agreed to take necessary steps for the early realisation of the project.[34] It may be noted that the TAPI project which will come into operation in 2022 (revised projected time period) has made significant progress since the state visit of President Berdimuhamedov to India in May 2010.The 5th meeting of the Inter-Governmental Commission on Trade, Economic, Scientific and Technological Cooperation was held in Ashgabat on April 8, 2015. Hon'ble Smt. Sushma Swaraj led the Indian side. During the 5th IGC, both sides signed an MoU on the upgradation of the Turkmen–India Industrial Training Centre (TIITC) by HMT, besides holding wide-ranging discussions on bilateral cooperation across the sectors.[35]

Joint Ventures

According to the official reports of Turkmenistan, in the last 2–3 years, 12 Indian companies and 11 investment projects were registered in Turkmenistan. Joint ventures between Indian and Turkmen construction companies are taking place for the past few years and they are becoming partners in infrastructural development projects. Other joint ventures in the areas of juice making and wool processing sectors are also going well.

Various trade bodies like CII, FICCI, ASSOCHAM, etc. are sending regular business delegations to Turkmenistan to expand the bilateral trade. An Indian scientific delegation representing the Central Electronics Limited (CEL) and the Council for Scientific and Industrial Research (CSIR) visited Turkmenistan in June 1998 to explore the possibilities of cooperation in the solar energy sector.[36] A delegation from the Indian Oil Corporation also visited Turkmenistan and held discussions with Turkmenistan's Deputy Minister of Oil and Gas Industry. A three-member delegation from the Punjab Agri-Export Corporation visited Turkmenistan in November 1998 with a proposal to set up joint commercial farming for which a Protocol of Intent was also signed.[37] An India centric exhibition was held in Ashgabat Expo Center in May 2015 for the first time with participation of number of Indian companies to showcase their industries and services.

India also offered to build Information Technology and Educational Infrastructure for Turkmenistan. Offering the low-cost tablet "AKASH" to Turkmen students during his September 2012 visit to Turkmenistan, the then Indian Minister for Communications & IT, Kapil Sibal, said that a joint venture between Indian and Turkmen companies can be formed which may manufacture the low-cost tablet in India.[38] The Indian side will design the necessary hardware and software for the tablet fulfilling the needs of Turkmenistan. Besides supplying the low-cost tablet to Turkmenistan, the joint venture company can market the product to other international markets too. In May 2012, the Turkmen government signed an agreement on the purchase and sale of natural gas from India's GAIL Ltd.[39] Work on the establishment of an international consortium is being conducted under the auspices of the Asian Development Bank. There have also been reports that the ONGC Videsh Ltd (OVL) Company is also exploring opportunities to invest in the economy of Turkmenistan and is interested in developing the largest gas field in the country.[40]

During the visit of PM Modi, a Memorandum of Understanding between the State Concern "Turkmenhimiya" and the Indian PSU Rashtriya Chemicals and Fertilizers Limited was signed to provide a framework for long-term sourcing of urea from Turkmenistan.[41]

Cooperation in Drugs and Pharmaceuticals

A Joint venture between Turkmenistan and the Indian Pharmaceutical Company Turkmenderman-Ajanta Pharma Ltd. was established in December 1998 in Ashgabat which is still functioning. It has an ultra-modern plant which manufactures 70 different types of medicines. India contributed US$ 5 million for the whole project. India is in a position to supply a number of commodities in the chemicals, petrochemicals and pharmaceutical sector. The Indian chemicals industry is well developed and it has had a consistent growth.[42] The industry is highly heterogeneous comprising many sectors like inorganic and organic chemicals, dyes and dye-intermediates, drugs and pharmaceuticals, petro-chemicals, pesticides etc. The Indian side can offer Turkmenistan petrochemical items like HDPE, PVC, PSF, PFY, NEY, MEG, LEB, etc. for exports.[43] Seventy percent of the bulk drug requirements similarly are produced domestically and a 100 percent requirement of formulations is made through indigenous production.[44]

Cooperation in the IT Sector

The Turkmen–Indian Industrial Training Centre has been functioning in Ashgabat since December 2002. Machine tools worth over a million US dollars have been gifted to the Centre by the Government of India under the ITEC programme. More than 250 Turkmen citizens have availed the training facilities under the programme. India provides scholarships every year under the General Cultural Scholarship Scheme. At present, around 100 students are studying in India under this scheme. In October 2011, the India–Turkmenistan Centre for Information Technology (ITCIT) was established in Asghabat in accordance with a Memorandum of Understanding signed between the two sides in February 2010 during the visit of Minister of State for External Affairs Preneet Kaur to Turkmenistan. India provided a grant of Rs 40.38 million for the establishment of ITCIT.[45]

Having an expertise in IT skills, India shares its expertise for the development of information and communication technology, telecommunication network, e-governance, etc., with Turkmenistan.

On September 19, 2012, during his meeting with Sapardurdy Toyliev, Turkmenistan's Deputy Chairperson of the Cabinet of Ministers of Education and Information Technologies, Sibal reiterated India's support in building the infrastructure for providing better education through ICT application and services. Promising to provide technology and capacity-building initiatives, Sibal offered India's help in setting up an Educational Satellite which will be interconnected to the National Knowledge Network through which professors from top Indian universities could deliver direct lectures to the Turkmen students.[46]

Cooperation in Science and Technology

An Indian scientific delegation representing the Central Electronics Limited (CEL) and the Council for Scientific and Industrial Research (CSIR) visited Turkmenistan in June 1998 to explore the possibilities of cooperation in the solar energy sector.[47] Cooperation in science and technology particularly in seismic studies as well as in combating desertification has been initiated between them as well.[48] During Sibal's visit to Turkmenistan in September 2012, both sides underlined that India can help Turkmenistan in setting up its satellite system, OFC network, GPS network for navigation for the shipping industry, etc.[49]

Cooperation in Tourism

The tourism sector is now one of the priority sectors for the Government of Turkmenistan. The government launched its most ambitious project Avaza NTZ in 2007, with an aim to attract US$ 4 billion foreign investments in the project. The project is the first free economic zone in the country. In addition to the Avaza zone, the natural landscapes, rich historical and cultural heritage of Turkmenistan reflect the nation's potential to become a major tourist centre in the region. The government aims to exploit this potential and make tourism as one of the key sectors of the economy.

By investing in Turkmenistan's tourism sector, Indian investors can take advantage of the expected growth in the sector. The country's Avaza zone offers a range of projects for investment opportunities. These include seaside resorts, building hotels, spas, restaurants, sport complexes, managing hotels, providing tourist entertainment and sport activities, catering and tourism services. Further, the advantageous incentives offered by the Government of Turkmenistan can facilitate the investors to mobilise their funds in the region.

India–Turkmenistan Connectivity

A significant agreement signed between the two countries was the agreement on the transport corridor, which was signed on February 22, 1997 between India, Iran and Turkmenistan. This agreement linked the Indian port of Mumbai with the Iranian Bandar Abbas terminal, through which the containers move across Iranian Mashhad and Sarakhs to Tejen in Turkmenistan, moving further east across the Turkmen cities of Mary and Turkmenabat to Bukhara-Navoy-Samarkand and Tashkent (in Uzbekistan) and reaching beyond other Central Asian Republics like Kazakhstan, Kyrgyzstan and Tajikistan.

The North–South Railway Corridor Project which was initially expected to be completed by 2013 connects Turkmenistan with Iran and Kazakhstan. The railway[50] will link Iran to Turkmenistan and then to Uzbekistan and Kazakhstan and will connect the CIS countries with the Indian Ocean and high seas and the Persian Gulf's littoral states. The primary agreement on the construction of the rail link among Iran, Turkmenistan and Kazakhstan was signed between the Presidents of Turkmenistan and Kazakhstan in April 2007 and its final agreement was signed in a summit meeting in Tehran in September 2007 by the three Presidents.[51] The total route of the railway is 1,000 km, of which 90 km would be in Iran, 700 km in Turkmenistan and 210 km in Kazakhstan. The railway facilitates the transportation of goods from the Central Asian countries to the Persian Gulf. This route was completed in 2014 and is functioning since 3 December 2014 and intensively used by Kazakhstan to reach Persian Gulf.

Turkmenistan is also connected to the North–South Transport Corridor, which connects the ports on the western coast of India with Russia connecting Europe and Central Asia via Iran by a combined sea–land route. As regards air connectivity, Turkmenistan Airlines operates 8 flights every week—2 flights in the Ashgabat–Delhi sector (Saturday and Sunday) and 6 flights to Ashgabat–Amritsar (all days except Friday). The flying time from Delhi to Ashgabat is shorter than that from Delhi to Kanyakumari. Turkmenistan Airlines proposes to start another two flights a week on the Ashgabat-Goa-Ashgabat sector in 2014. Increased connectivity in this region will undoubtedly benefit both India and Turkmenistan and will also boost bilateral trade.[52]

Cooperation under ITEC Programme

India is training young professionals of Turkmenistan under the ITEC (Indian Technical and Economic Cooperation) programme. In 2015–16, 40 ITEC slots were offered to young Turkmen professionals.[53] Turkmen students also avail the opportunity to study in Indian universities under the ICCR (Indian Council for Cultural Research) Scholarships programme. Since 2009, 20 ICCR scholarships are being offered to the Turkmen students every year. A Hindi Chair is functioning in the Turkmen National Institute of World Languages in Ashgabat. Experts and scientists from various centres of Turkmenistan are regularly visiting India to gather research materials for manuscripts on the bilateral relations and to know more about the history of the India–Turkmenistan relations.[54] In 2012, India offered its help in setting up international schools in Turkmenistan. During his September 2012 visit to Turkmenistan, Sibal said that the Central Board of Secondary Education International (CBSEI) schools may be set up in Turkmenistan where the students can be imparted education by Indian teachers who may be deputed from India to Turkmenistan for this purpose.[55]

Energy Cooperation

In 2008, India signed an MoU framework with Turkmenistan on cooperation in the oil and gas sector. Before signing of the MoU, the Turkmen President stated: "participation of large Indian companies and enterprises in the realization of oil-gas projects in [the] territory of Turkmenistan will serve for [the] two countries' benefits".[56]

The India–Turkmenistan energy cooperation is moving smoothly, particularly in the implementation of the TAPI project, which proposes to deliver gas from the Galkynysh gas fields of Turkmenistan to Pakistan and India via Afghanistan. Once completed, the project could change the entire region. There has been remarkable progress on the project till date. In 2010, while the then Indian Petroleum Minister, Murli Deora described the TAPI gas pipeline project as the new "Silk Route" between Central Asia and South Asia, the then Indian Prime Minister, Dr Manmohan Singh pronounced it as the "Pipeline of Peace" for the region.[57] The implementation of the TAPI project will bring Central Asia and South Asia much closer in an enduring energy partnership for peace, development and prosperity for the people of the region. TAPI is expected to provide India 60 percent of 33 bcm of gas annually. The Galkynysh deposits, which contain 28.2 tcm of gas, can supply India with the necessary volumes of gas.[58]

In Turkmenistan, Modi pushed for the early realisation of a gas pipeline starting from that country and running through Afghanistan and Pakistan onwards to India (TAPI) as well as for connectivity between India and Turkmenistan. "The most significant initiative in our relationship is the TAPI gas pipeline. This could transform regional economic cooperation and bring prosperity along the route... We underlined the need to implement the project quickly," Modi said.[59]

The TAPI pipeline starting from Turkmenistan's Galkynysh gas fields passing through Herat and Kandahar will follow Afghanistan's ring road. The pipeline would extend to the cities of Quetta and Multan in Pakistan and connect to the Indian city of Fazilka at the Indo-Pak border. Its total length would be approximately 1,735 km. The US$ 10 billion-TAPI pipeline's first supplies are planned for 2017, however due to many inevitable issues and events its now projected to be complete by 2022. The TAPI pipeline offers benefits to all four participating countries and has the potential to enhance regional cooperation. Turkmenistan that currently exports gas to Russia, China and EU will now have an alternative for exporting its energy resources to other countries too. Pakistan and India will be able to use Turkmen gas to address their energy deficits.[60]

Regionally, the TAPI pipeline will provide new business opportunities for the gas and engineering industries. ADB is the leading stakeholder of the project. Oil and gas firms such as Chevron, Exxon, Gazprom and GAIL are part of the project. The Afghan National Army will face challenges in defending the TAPI pipeline. The Afghan government promised to provide a minimum of 7,000 security personnel to guard the pipeline in Afghanistan alone. However, currently, the difficult security conditions in Afghanistan and the unresolved issues between India and Pakistan are becoming inhibiting factors for the project, but the recently intensified contacts among the four participants of this project, especially between India and Turkmenistan, indicate growing prospects for the TAPI project. Physical connectivity and access to energy resources is one of the important elements of the India–Turkmen bilateral partnership, but not exclusively. India and Turkmenistan are increasing their bilateral cooperation with each other in different sectors with the energy sector being a priority and TAPI is a key project in this sphere.[61]

India–Turkmenistan Trade Relations

Table 7.1 shows that the total bilateral trade between the two countries in 1996–97 stood at US$ 1.65 million which increased three-fold to US$

3.83 million in 2000–01. In the decade 2001–2010, the total bilateral trade between the two countries which stood at US$ 6.30 million in 2001–02 grew to US$ 35.89 million in 2010–11, thus reflecting a continuous increase over the years. In the past two years of the present decade, the bilateral trade has again shown an increasing trend and stood at US$ 78.25 million and US$ 87.73 million in 2012–13 and 2013–14 respectively, though these are not impressive figures. Besides, all these years, the trade figures have remained imbalanced. It is always India's exports that remain more than its imports from Turkmenistan.

Table 7.1: India-Turkmenistan Bilateral Trade, 1996-2016 (In US$ million)

Year	*Export from India*	*Growth Percentage*	*Percent Share in Total Exports by India*	*Imports from Uzbekistan*	*Growth Percentage*	*Percent Share in Total Imports by India*	*Total Bilateral Trade*
1996-97	1.38	NA	0.0041	0.27	NA	0.0007	1.65
1997-98	1.68	21.64	0.0048	0.02	-92.68	0.0000	1.70
1998-99	1.93	14.69	0.0058	0.11	442.05	0.0002	2.04
1999-00	5.64	192.88	0.0153	0.38	263.2	0.0008	6.02
2000-01	2.71	-51.95	0.0061	1.12	192.34	0.0022	3.83
2001-02	4.35	60.51	0.0099	1.95	73.32	0.0038	6.30
2002-03	10.29	136.55	0.0195	5.40	177.85	0.0088	15.69
2003-04	19.21	86.64	0.0301	9.34	72.77	0.0119	28.55
2004-05	15.26	-20.60	0.0183	10.87	16.37	0.0097	26.13
2005-06	18.83	23.43	0.0183	12.35	13.68	0.0083	31.18
2006-07	33.99	80.51	0.0269	11.95	-3.27	0.0064	45.94
2007-08	36.09	6.19	0.0221	8.55	-28.42	0.0034	45.64
2008-09	41.40	14.70	0.0223	12.10	41.51	0.0040	53.50
2009-10	36.15	-12.67	0.0202	10.00	-17.37	0.0035	46.15
2010-11	26.16	-27.65	0.0104	9.73	-2.72	0.0026	35.89
2011-12	43.95	68.04	0.0144	19.46	100.03	0.0040	63.41
2012-13	69.92	59.08	0.0233	8.83	-57.20	0.0017	78.25
2013-14	73.63	5.30	0.0235	14.10	69.35	0.0031	87.73
2014-15	91.98	24.94	0.0296	13.05	-7.51	0.0029	105.03
2015-16	68.53	-25.50	0.0261	46.97	260.03	0.0123	115.50

Source: Based on Export-Import Data (1997-98 to 2015-16) collected from Directorate General of Foreign Trade (DGFT), Department of Commerce, Ministry of Commerce & Industry, Government of India.

India exports electronic goods to Turkmenistan, alongwith machinery and equipment, silk products, meat products and sugar. Exports from Turkmenistan to India are mainly raw cotton, inorganic chemical, scrap metal, etc. (Tables 7.2 and 7.3).

Despite not-so-encouraging economic and trade relations, India and Turkmenistan have a lot of potential to cooperate with each other in areas of mutual concern and benefit. It may be pointed out that though there are

Table 7.2: Main Exports to Turkmenistan during 2015-16 (US$ Million)

S.No.	*Commodity*	*Value*	*Percent Share of India's Total Exports to Turkmenistan*
1	Meat and edible meat offal	33.68	49.15
2	Pharmaceutical products	17.94	26.18
3	Nuclear reactors, boilers, machinery and mechanical appliances; parts thereof	8.66	12.64
4	Rubber and articles thereof	1.48	2.16
5	Electrical machinery and equipment and parts thereof; sound recorders and reproducers, television image and sound recorders and reproducers, and parts	1.22	1.78
6	Iron and steel	0.82	1.20
7	Organic chemicals	0.49	0.72
8	Miscellaneous chemical products	0.49	0.72
9	Optical, photographic cinematographic measuring, checking precision, medical or surgical inst. and apparatus parts and accessories thereof	0.47	0.69
10	Miscellaneous edible preparations	0.37	0.54
	Total Export of top 10 items	65.62	
	Total Export	68.53	
	India's Global Export	262,290.13	

Table 7.3: Main Imports from Turkmenistan during 2015-16 (In US$ Million)

S.No.	*Commodity*	*Value*	*Percent Share of India's Total Imports from Turkmenistan*
1	Mineral fuels, mineral oils and products of their distillation; bituminous substances; mineral waxes	38.27	81.48
2	Cotton	4.49	9.56
3	Salt; sulphur; earths and stone; plastering materials, lime and cement	2.14	4.56
4	Inorganic chemicals; organic or inorganic compounds of precious metals, of rare-earth metals, or radi. Elem. Or of isotopes	1.71	3.64
5	Plastic and articles thereof	0.22	0.47
6	Wool, fine or coarse animal hair, horsehair yarn and woven fabric.	0.13	0.28
	Total import of top 6 items	46.96	
	Total Import	46.97	

around 2,000 Indian nationals in Turkmenistan, comprising mainly junior engineers/technicians (working in the oil and gas industry), most of the Indian nationals in Turkmenistan reside in only three main clusters: approximately 1,450 Indians at Yolotan/Mary area, 500 Indians in Ashgabat and remaining about 50 at Hazar/offshore Caspian Sea region. There are no Indian Associations, Indian students or Indian restaurants in Turkmenistan.[62] India and Turkmenistan, thus, need to review and re-energise their efforts to manage the new set of challenges, to ensure their security and to improve connectivity with each other. There is a tremendous scope for improving relations between the two countries, for satisfying their immediate as well as long term needs. From the point of view of building a stable, prosperous and peaceful Asia, it is important to increase a dialogue with each other and to establish people-to-people contact, and, therefore, both the countries need to participate in the development of the region together for establishing a mutually beneficial partnership and cooperation to set the movement of growth.[63] Undoubtedly, energy-rich Turkmenistan can be a major factor in ensuring India's energy security.

REFERENCES

1. Daly, John C. K., 'Turkmenistan builds on its Relationship with Latvia", *Eurasia Daily Monitor*, 5 (195), 10 October, 2008. URL: http://www.jamestown.org/single/?tx_ttnewspercent5Btt_newspercent5D=34013&no_cache=1#.U-PRWvmSxnk
2. Mueller, Barbara, *Dynamics of International Advertising: Theoretical and Practical Perspectives*, New York: Peter Lang Publishing, 2011, p. 8.
3. Sarma, A.S., 'Turkmenistan's Foreign Policy after Niyazov: Looking Beyond 'Positive Neutrality", in *The State in Eurasia: Local and Global Arenas*, A. Sengupta and S. Chatterjee (eds), New Delhi: KW Publishers, 2013, p. 177.
4. Pomfret, Richard, 'Turkmenistan's Foreign Policy', *China and Eurasia Forum Quarterly*, 6 (4), 2008, p. 20.
5. Sarma, A.S., *India and Central Asia: Redefining Energy and Trade Links*, New Delhi: Pentagon Press, 2010, p. 80.
6. 'Turkmenistan at a Glance', Embassy of Turkmenistan, Washington DC, 2012. URL: http://turkmenistanembassy.org/turkmenistan-at-a-glance/
7. Yushanova, Sofiya, 'What are the Effects of 2007-09 Global Economic Crises on Turkmenistan's Economy', in *Post-Soviet States: Two Decades of Transition and Transformation*, A. Patnaik and Tulsiram (eds.), New Delhi: Oscar Publications, 2013.
8. Sarma, op. cit., p. 189.
9. 'Turkmenistan – Economy', URL: http://www.globalsecurity.org/military/world/centralasia/turkmen-econ.htm
10. Sarma, op. cit., p. 80.
11. 'Bridging the Economic Policies Programme for Turkmenistan (AAP 2010)'. URL: http://killefitconsult.files.wordpress.com/2011/06/turkmenistan-tor-100153.pdf

12. Central Intelligence Agency (US), 'Turkmenistan'. URL: https://www.cia.gov/library/publications/the-world-factbook/geos/countrytemplate_tx.html
13. Sarma, op. cit.,", p. 189.
14. Bochkarov, Danila, 'Turkey, Turkmenistan and the Dream of Trans-Caspian Energy Supplies', *Turkish Review*, June1, 2013. URL: http://www.turkishreview.org/newsDetail_getNews ById.action?newsId=223315
15. Ibid.
16. Ministry of Foreign Affairs of Turkmenistan (2013), 'Economy'. URL: http://www.mfa.gov.tm/en/tukrmenistan/economy
17. Ibid.
18. *A Strategy Paper for CIS Countries: India-CIS Roadmap 2020*, FT (CIS) Division, July, 2012, pp. 278-279.
19. Bandyopadhyay, L., 'Turkmenistan's Foreign Policy: A Comparation of the Niyazov and the Post-Niyazov Regimes", in *The State in Eurasia: Local and Global Issues*, A. Sengupta and S. Chatterjee (eds), New Delhi: Maulana Abul Kalam Azad Institute of Asian Studies, Kolkata/KW Publishers Pvt Ltd: 2013, p.170-171.
20. Sahai P.S., 'India and Central Asia: Establishment of Diplomatic Relations and Beyond', in *South-Central Asia: Emerging Issues*, Kuldeep Singh (ed.), Amritsar: Guru Nanak Dev University, 2005, p. 42.
21. www.indianembassy-tm.com
22. Puri, M.M., 'Central Asian Geopolitics: The Indian View', *Central Asian Survey*, 16 (2), 1997, p. 250.
23. Holley, David, 'Turkmen President Niyazov dies at 66', *The Baltimore Sun*, 22 December, 2006. URL: http://articles.baltimoresun.com/2006-12-22/news/0612220138_1_ turkmenistan-gas-russia
24. Puri, op. cit., pp. 250-251.
25. Ibid., p. 251.
26. Ibid., p. 251.
27. Stobdan, P., 'India-Turkmenistan Relations in Perspective', *Strategic Analysis*, 19 (9), 1996, pp. 1266-1267.
28. 'India-Turkmenistan Relations', January 2014. URL: http://www.mea.gov.in/portal/foreignrelation/turkmenistan_january_2014.pdf
29. Mavlonov, I.R., 'India's Economic Diplomacy with Central Asian Nations and the Economic Development of the Region', *Dialogue*, 7 (3), p. 34.
30. Embassy of India, Ashgabat, Turkmenistan, 'India-Turkmenistan Relations'. URL: http://www.eoi.gov.in/ashgabat/?0760?000
31. Sarma, op. cit., p. 52.
32. Ministry of External Affairs, Government of India, 'List of Agreements/ MOUs signed during the Visit of Prime Minister to Turkmenistan'. URL: https://www.mea.gov.in/outoging-visit-detail.htm?25457/List+of+Agreements+ MOUs +signed+during+the+Visit+of+Prime+Minister+to+Turkmenistan.
33. MEA, GoI, 'Fourth Meeting of India-Turkmenistan Inter-Governmental Commission', Jan 22, 2013. URL: http://mea.gov.in/press-releases.htm?dtl/21119/Fourth+Meeting+of+IndiaTurkmenistan+InterGovernmental+Commission

34. 'India, Turkmenistan agree to fast track TAPI project', 22 January 2013. URL: http://www.thehindubusinessline.com/government-and-policy/india-turkmenistan-agree-to-fast-track-tapi-project/article4332972.ece
35. 'India–Turkmenistan Relations'. URL: http://mea.gov.in/Portal/Foreign Relation/Turkmenistan_2015_07_02.pdf.
36. Mavlonov, op. cit., p. 32.
37. 'India-Turkmenistan', URL: www.indianembassy.org
38. Ministry of Communications & Information Technology, Government of India, 'India Offers to Build Information Technology and Educational Infrastructure for Turkmenistan', September 19, 2012. URL: http://pib.nic.in/newsite/erelease.aspx?relid=87848
39. Hasanov, Trend H., 'Turkmen-Indian Intergovernmental Commission on Economic Cooperation convened in New Delhi', January 21. URL: http://en.trend.az/regions/casia/turkmenistan/2110218.html
40. Ibid.
41. Ministry of External Affairs, Government of India, 'List of Agreements...', op. cit.
42. Chandra, Amiya, 'Turkmen-India Cooperation for Peace and Development', *Strategic Analysis*, 19 (9), 1996, p. 1239.
43. Ibid., pp.1239-40.
44. Ibid., p. 1240.
45. Ministry of External Affairs, Government of India, 'Visit of Minister of State for External Affairs Smt. Preneet Kaur to Turkmenistan', February 10, 2010. URL: http://mea.gov.in/press-releases.htm?dtl/1190/Visit+of+Minister+of+State+for+External+Affairs+Smt+Preneet+ Kaur+to+Turkmenistan+regards
46. Ministry of Communications & Information Technology, Government of India, 'India Offers...' op. cit.
47. Mavlonov, op. cit., p. 32.
48. Sarma, op. cit., p. 51.
49. Ministry of Communications & Information Technology, Government of India, 'India Offers...', op. cit.
50. Asian Development Bank, 'North-South Railway Project: Project Data Sheets (PDS)', 24 July, 2014. URL: http://www.adb.org/projects/43441-013/details
51. 'Tehran Starts Last Phase of Iran-Turkmenistan Railway Project', September 10, 2012. URL: http://www.railpage.com.au/f-p1918567.htm
52. Kundu, N.D., 'India & Turkmenistan Relationship: From Silk-Route Connection to the Contemporary Era', 2013. URL: http://www.southandcentralasia comment.org/wp-content/uploads/2012/12/India-Turkmenistan.pdf: p. 8.
53. 'India-Turkmenistan Relations', January 2014. URL: http://www.mea.gov.in/portal/foreignrelation/turkmenistan_january_2014.pdf
54. Ibid., p. 8.
55. Ministry of Communications & Information Technology, Government of India, 'India Offers...', op. cit.
56. *A Strategy Paper for CIS Countries*, op. cit., pp. 278-279.
57. 'TAPI project will be the new Silk Route, says Deora', *The Hindu*, 12 December 2010.
58. Kundu, op. cit., p. 8.

59. 'Narendra Modi's Visit brings Central Asia Back in Focus'. URL: http://www.livemint.com/Politics/7iJD1gvVb9VWUoIiPLHjQK/Narendra-Modis-visit-brings-Central-Asia-back-in-focus.html.
60. Ibid., p. 4.
61. Ibid., p. 8.
62. 'Overview of India-Turkmenistan Relationship', July 2013, http://www.indianembassy-tm.org/bilateral.html
63. Kundu, op. cit. pp. 8-9.

8

India and Uzbekistan

Uzbekistan occupies a unique position from a geostrategic and geopolitical point of view due to its borders touching all the other four states of Central Asia along with Afghanistan. Sharing not just borders but having ethnic overlaps with all the other neighbours, Uzbekistan is the most populous and centrally located country in the region enjoying a position in Central Asia only next to Kazakhstan. Like India, it has been the pivot of Central Asian civilisation and state systems. But it has bilateral disputes with most of its neighbours on a range of issues including borders and river waters. Its central place among the Central Asian Republics has helped it to emerge as the hub of transit corridors. However, Uzbekistan does not enjoy preponderance in the region as does India despite being doubly landlocked.[1]

Economic Situation of Uzbekistan

Though Uzbekistan is generally a dry, landlocked country, its location between the two giant Central Asian rivers—Syr Darya and Amu Darya—makes it a highly fertile zone and the cradle of the largest population in the region (29.5 million as of 2013). More than 60 percent of the population lives in densely populated rural communities, and hence it has a strong agricultural base which is the main economic activity of its people. Around 11 percent of the land is intensely cultivated in irrigated river valleys.[2] Uzbekistan has a diversified agricultural crop production which is dominated by cotton and wheat, which makes it now the world's second largest cotton exporter and fifth largest producer country.[3] The country benefitted much from a bumper cotton crop in 2010 amidst record high prices.

Fergana valley in the eastern part of Uzbekistan is not only important cotton, silk and wine region but also a crucial site of oilfields. Western Uzbekistan has large natural gas deposits where minerals like gold, coal, lead, zinc, copper, tungsten, molybdenum, fluorspar and uranium are also found. Remittances from citizens working abroad, especially in Kazakhstan and Russia, contribute greatly to Uzbekistan's economy.[4] Uzbekistan has moderate reserves of natural resources including petroleum and natural gas and other mineral resources such as uranium, silver, copper, lead, zinc, tungsten and molybdenum. Its gold production ranks among the highest in the world, a large part of which is exported. Export of hydrocarbons, including natural gas and petroleum, provided about 40 percent of foreign exchange earnings in 2009.

While pursuing its foreign economic relations, Uzbekistan has successfully carried out its "open door policy" by trying to ensure the following:[5]

1. Development of trade and economic relations irrespective of ideological principles;
2. Equal and mutually beneficial cooperation based on both bilateralism and multilateralism;
3. Giving priority to international law over national law, recognition of the GATT and WTO principles and rules as applied to the stage-by-stage liberalisation of the trade regime in the process of integrating into the international organisations;
4. Reasonable trade-off between competition and cooperation; and
5. Providing "Most Favoured Nation" treatment to countries and individual foreign investors that bring in latest technology to the country.

In 2003, the government of Uzbekistan accepted Article VIII obligations under the IMF, providing for full currency convertibility. However, strict currency controls and tightening of borders have lessened the effects of convertibility and have also led to some shortages that have further stifled the economic activity. The Central Bank often delays or restricts convertibility, especially for consumer goods. Potential investment by Russia and China in Uzbekistan's gas and oil industry as well as increased cooperation with South Korea in the realm of civil aviation may enhance growth prospects.[6] In November 2005, the Russian President, Vladimir Putin, and the Uzbek President, Islam Karimov, signed an "alliance" agreement which included provisions for economic cooperation. Since then,

Russian businesses have shown an increased interest in Uzbekistan, especially in mining, telecom, oil and gas.

In 2006, Uzbekistan took steps to rejoin the Collective Security Treaty Organisation (CSTO) and the Eurasian Economic Community (EurAsEC), which it subsequently left in 2008; both Organisations are dominated by Russia. In the past, Uzbek authorities had accused the US and other foreign companies operating in Uzbekistan of violating Uzbek tax laws and had frozen their assets, with several new expropriations during 2010–2012. At the same time, the Uzbek Government actively courted several major US and international corporations by offering attractive financing and tax advantages, and landed a significant US investment in the automotive industry including the opening of a powertrain manufacturing facility in Tashkent in November 2011. Although growth slowed down in 2009–10, Uzbekistan has seen few other effects from the global economic downturn, primarily due to its relative isolation from the global financial markets.

Until 2012, Uzbekistan had registered its GDP growth of over 8 percent per year for several years, driven primarily by state-led investments and a favourable export environment for its main commodities—natural gas, cotton and gold, and some industrial growth. However, growth slipped slightly in 2013 to 8 percent as a result of lower export prices due to continuing European recession. Even though the figure looks impressive due to wage and pension increases, high public investment spending and large remittances may help the country to keep the growth rate near 8 percent in 2014 and 2015 as well.[7] However, Uzbekistan's economy advanced 7.8 percent in 2016 compared to an 8 percent growth recorded in 2015 reflecting a weaker external environment and slower growth in the industry.

Key Economic Indicators

(a) Foreign Exchange Reserves: US$ 16 billion (2015 est.)
(b) Foreign Exchange Reserves: Exchange Rate of Local Currency (Uzbekistani Soums): 2,569.6 per US$ (2015 est.)
(c) Inflation Rate (2012): 10 percent (2015 est.)
(d) External Debt: US$ 13.92 billion (31 December 2015)
(e) GDP (2015): US$ 187.9 billion
(f) GDP per Capita (2015): US$ 6,100 (PPP)
(g) Real GDP Growth (2015): 8 percent
(h) Sector-wise Distribution of GDP (2015 est.): agriculture (19.2 percent), industry (33.6 percent), services (47.2 percent)

(i) Population below poverty line: 17 percent (2011 est.)
(j) Unemployment: 5 percent (2015 est.)
(k) Main industries: textiles, food processing, machine building, metallurgy, mining
(l) Exports: US$ 11.35 billion (2015 est.)
(m) Export goods: energy products, cotton, gold, mineral fertilisers, ferrous and non-ferrous metals, food products, machinery, automobiles
(n) Main export partners: Switzerland (25.8 percent), China (17.6 percent), Kazakhstan (14.2 percent), Turkey (9.9 percent), Russia (8.4 percent), Bangladesh (6.9 percent) (2015 est.)
(o) Imports: US$ 11.81 billion (2015 est.)
(p) Import goods: machinery and equipment, foodstuffs, chemicals, ferrous and non-ferrous metals
(q) Import partners: China (20.8 percent), Russia (20.8 percent), South Korea (12 percent), Kazakhstan (10.8 percent), Turkey (4.6 percent), Germany (4.4 percent) (2015 est.)

Development of India–Uzbekistan Relations

At the beginning of the 20th century, relations between India and Uzbekistan were determined by the trade and economic relations between the two republics. Politically, mutual understanding has helped develop relationships between Uzbekistan and India to fathom the gravity and fight such menaces as terrorism, separatism and other problems. Both countries share similar views on a range of issues and have worked together to develop close cooperation in the expansion of their economic sphere.

The political and diplomatic relations were established soon after the Declaration of Independence was adopted by Uzbekistan in June 1990. The visit of the President of the Republic of Uzbekistan, Islam Karimov to India on August 17–19, 1991 was in fact the first for the new leadership reflecting the cordiality of mutual relations between the political leaders of the two countries.[8] The visit of President Karimov was also fundamental in the development of Trade and Economic Cooperation between Uzbekistan and India. Trade relations between the two countries came to be governed by the Agreement on Trade and Economic Cooperation signed in Tashkent in May 1993 during the Indian Prime Minister P.V. Narasimha Rao's visit. It deals with the normal features of trade agreements such as mutual Most Favoured Nations (MFN) status, promotion of economic, industrial, scientific and technical cooperation, including in the field of training of personnel, active participation of small and medium-sized enterprises in bilateral economic cooperation and counter-trade.[9] During Prime Minister Rao's visit to Uzbekistan, an Indo-Uzbek Treaty on the Principles of Inter-state Relations and Cooperation was also signed besides an announcement of "the setting up of an 'India Chair' at the University of World Economy and Diplomacy in Tashkent, opening of an Indian Cultural Centre in Tashkent, donations of medicines and medical equipment worth Rs. 40 lakhs, a credit of US$ 10 million for joint ventures, project exports and purchase of capital goods from India and donation of equipment for receiving Doordarshan programmes for telecast on Uzbek Television".[10]

The second official visit of President Karimov to India took place in January 1994 which gave a new dimension to the India–Uzbekistan economic and trade relations. The agreement signed between India and Uzbekistan on May 18, 1999 on the promotion and mutual protection of investments, further created a legal base for the development of a mutual investment process. It was in May 2000, during the third official visit of Karimov to India, that the Uzbek Ministry of Foreign Economic Relations and Confederation of Indian Industry signed a Memorandum of Understanding and Cooperation. Also, basic agreements regulating external economic relations between the economic entities of the two countries were signed. On April 8, 2005, Karimov paid a fourth official visit to India during which a number of inter-governmental documents in all major spheres of priority directions of cooperation were identified. The next important visit was of the Indian Prime Minister Dr Manmohan Singh, who paid a return visit to Tashkent on April 25, 2006. During this visit, the two sides discussed various regional, national and international issues such as the fight against terrorism and extremism, trade and economic activities and cultural cooperation. In addition, the two sides exchanged opinions on the development of military cooperation. During Karimov's fifth visit to India on May 17–18, 2011, the relations between the two countries were elevated to the level of strategic partnership. In all, 34 documents, including a joint statement establishing strategic partnership between India and Uzbekistan, were signed during the visit.[11]

In the first-ever visit of an Indian Vice President to Uzbekistan, on May 21–24, 2013, Hamid Ansari was accompanied by four members of the parliament. During this visit, an MoU for the upgradation of the Jawaharlal Nehru Centre for Information Technology was signed.[12] This Indo-Uzbekistan IT Centre based in the Tashkent University of Information Technology was inaugurated in April 2006 by the then Indian Prime

Minister Dr Singh during his visit to Uzbekistan. These high-level visits have resulted in the establishment of close political ties at the highest level between the two countries which has further been strengthened by signing almost 74 bilateral documents in the form of Agreements/MoUs/Treaties/Protocols/Work Plans, etc., that have laid a solid foundation of bilateral ties over the past two decades.[13] Uzbekistan firmly supports India's entry as a permanent member of the UN Security Council, and welcomes India's participation as an observer in the Shanghai Cooperation Organization (SCO). Both the countries are also actively cooperating within international structures like the UN, SCO, ADB and others. The relations between the two countries are developing on the basis of a consistent and practical partnership which aims at producing the best results in achieving the prosperity of the people of the two sides while working towards global peace and stability.

Further, on July 6–7, 2015, Prime Minister Modi visited Uzbekistan during his first visit to the Central Asian countries and held talks with President Karimov on key bilateral and regional issues including the situation in Afghanistan as the two countries inked three pacts to boost cooperation between their foreign offices and in the field of culture and tourism. Both the leaders discussed ways to enhance strategic, economic and energy ties apart from reviewing key regional issues including the situation in Afghanistan. The two leaders also discussed ways to implement the contract for the supply of uranium from mineral-rich Uzbekistan signed earlier. The pact was signed for the supply of 2,000 metric tonnes of the yellow cake. They also explored various initiatives to further enhance connectivity between the two countries and in this context, Modi briefed Karimov about the International North–South Transport Corridor (INSTC) and proposed that Uzbekistan consider becoming a member. Modi also sought the Uzbek President's support for India joining the Ashgabat Agreement.[14]

India–Uzbekistan Economic Cooperation

Since the independence of the Central Asian Republics, both India and Uzbekistan have been focusing on the development of mutually beneficial and fruitful cooperation between them in the field of economic and trade relations. In 1992, a Joint Indo-Uzbekistan Inter-Governmental Commission on Trade, Economic, Scientific and Technological Cooperation was established to explore the areas of bilateral interest and suggest substantive measures to synergise the efforts of the two sides in those areas. Since then the Inter-Governmental Commission (IGC) holds its meetings in Tashkent and Delhi alternately.[15] The First meeting of the IGC was held in New Delhi on July 27–28, 1993 during which agreements were signed on cooperation in science and technology, tourism, avoidance of double taxation and a protocol on cooperation between the Foreign Ministries of the two countries.

The second meeting of the IGC was held in New Delhi on November 22, 1994 in which the Uzbek Deputy Prime Minister Utkir Sultanov and the then Union Commerce Minister of India led the respective delegations. An Indo-Uzbek credit agreement for the utilisation of a credit line of US$ 10 million was signed in addition to an MoU which envisaged closer interaction between government agencies in specific sectors including trade and economic cooperation, banking, technical education, etc. Two sub-commissions on trade and commerce and science and technology were constituted to address specific issues in the areas of mutual interest. The third meeting of the IGC was held in Tashkent during the Indian External Affairs Minister's visit to Tashkent in March 1996. The fourth meeting of the IGC was held in New Delhi on February 18–19, 1999.[16] The fifth meeting took place during the visit of the Indian Minister of State for Commerce and Industry to Tashkent on January 8–12, 2005. The IGC meeting was held in Tashkent on January 11, 2005 which reviewed the bilateral cooperation in trade, economic, scientific and technological fields. The areas identified for cooperation included transportation, construction, Information Technology (IT), consultancy, food processing, textiles, pharmaceuticals, mining, joint ventures, culture and human resources. A protocol between the two sides was signed at the end of the meeting.

The sixth meeting of the IGC was held at New Delhi on March 7–8, 2006, under the co-chairmanship of Jairam Ramesh, the then Minister of State for Commerce and Alisher Shaykhov, Minister of Foreign Economic Relations, Investments and Trade of the Republic of Uzbekistan. Further, the seventh meeting of the IGC was held in Tashkent on April 13–14, 2007, under the co-chairmanship of Jairam Ramesh and Abdulla Aripov, Deputy Prime Minister of the Republic of Uzbekistan.[17] At the ninth meeting on May 1-5, 2011,[18] both sides confirmed the importance of strengthening political dialogue and holding consultations on the expansion of economic relations, particularly in areas such as small business and entrepreneurship, mining industry, machine building, textile, health, science, information technology and agriculture.[19] The Inter-Governmental Commission (IGC) on Trade, Economic, Scientific and Technological Cooperation has met ten times, and the last session was held in New Delhi on 04–05 March 2014.[20]

Joint Ventures

With Uzbekistan now being one of the fastest growing economies in the ECA region and the middle-income countries during the period 2008–2012,[21] there is tremendous potential for Indian business opportunities, especially through joint ventures. According to the database of the State Statistics Committee of Uzbekistan, the main activities of enterprises with Indian investment involve manufacturing of consumer goods, processing of leather and agricultural products, production of pharmaceuticals, textiles, detergents, tourism, wholesale and retail trade, etc.[22]

There are currently 65 enterprises with Indian capital, of which 10 are with 100 percent Indian capital.[23] They work in such areas as production of consumer goods, pharmaceuticals, processing of leather products, agriculture goods, production of textile goods, etc. Five of these enterprises are in the pharmaceuticals sector.[24] The first Indo-Uzbek joint venture was 'East Butterfly' for the manufacture of stainless steel kitchenware. The joint ventures in the pharmaceutical sector, which are already operational, are Surkhan-Ajantha Pharma Ltd., Core Pharmsanoat Ltd., Gufic-Avicenna Ltd. and Reddy Pharma Ltd. One more joint venture is Rusan Pharma Ltd. which is still in the initial stage. Another joint venture is being set up by Premier Explosives Limited, Secunderabad with M/s. Navoiazot in Nukus for the manufacture of industrial explosives and detonators. In the construction sector, M/s Tata Projects Ltd. constructed a modern hotel (Hotel Le Meridien) in Tashkent in 1996. An Indian company M/s Larson and Toubro has constructed another two hotels, one each in Samarkand and Bukhara.[25]

On April 26, 2006, India's Ministry of Petroleum and Natural Gas entered into an agreement for cooperation in the oil and gas sector with Uzbekneftegaz (UNG), the national petroleum holding company of Uzbekistan.[26] The Gas Authority of India Limited (GAIL) and Uzbekneftegaz have also signed a Memorandum of Cooperation to jointly pursue gas sector projects covering exploration and production, gas processing/Liquefied Petroleum Gas (LPG), production of petrochemicals as well as the training of personnel.[27] Along with Uzbekneftegaz, GAIL also plans to set up an LPG plant in western Uzbekistan, which will produce LPG for consumption in the domestic market of Uzbekistan.[28] The facilities will cost 50–60 million US dollars each and have a production capacity of

1,00,000 tonnes annually. An Uzbek gas distribution company, Uztransgaz, which is also a subsidiary of the Uzbekneftegaz, has requested GAIL to assist in the development of Compressed Natural Gas (CNG) and its distribution in Tashkent, Samarkand and Bukhara. Both the companies have also expressed a desire to work on the setting up of an ethane extraction unit and construction of a 60-km-long transportation pipeline.[29] the Ashok Minda Group of India established a joint venture with Uzavtosanoat and formed the "OzMinda LLC" in March 2010 in the Free Industrial Economic Zone, Navoi, with a total investment of US$ 9 million. The company is producing the driver information system and security systems for automobiles. The major customer is GM Uzbekistan.[30]

A number of forums and exhibitions have been organised to strengthen the India–Uzbekistan relationship in spheres such as fuel and energy, mining, geological searching, etc. The Federation of Indian Chambers of Commerce and Industry (FICCI) signed an agreement to establish a Joint Business Committee with the Chamber of Commodity Producers and Entrepreneurs of Uzbekistan.[31] In 2000, the Ministry of Foreign Economic Relations of Uzbekistan and the Confederation of Indian Industry (CII) signed a Memorandum of Understanding (MoU) on bilateral cooperation.[32] The Director General of the Federation of Indian Export Organisations (FIEO) led a product specific business delegation to Uzbekistan on July 18–22, 2004 comprising of Indian companies having interest in the areas of silk, cotton processing, agro products, tea, exports of jewellery, gold and diamond mining, etc. the Tea Board of India, Moscow office, participated in the Food Expo-Uzbekistan held at Tashkent on November 23–25, 2004. The same year a delegation of Women's Committee of Uzbekistan led by Rano Kh. Abdullaeva visited New Delhi to attend an international symposium of women entrepreneurs.

The third Indian Trade Exhibition was organised by the India–CIS Chamber of Commerce and Industry in October 2006 in Tashkent, in which more than 60 major Indian companies took part. The exhibition attracted a large number of Uzbek entrepreneurs, industrial houses and companies which held negotiations with their Indian counterparts for bilateral trade and investment in Uzbekistan.[33] Quite effective was the exhibition "India Minitech" which was held in Tashkent in July 2008. The exhibition presented 50 Indian firms and companies, including such well-known companies as Seam Projection Technologies, Tishya Gems, Pacon Industries, Singh Technical Works, Modern Industries, Raksha Packaging, Madro Agro Industries, Kanwal Food and Spices and so on. From the Uzbek side, the

National Bank of Uzbekistan, "Microcredit", "Pahta-bank", "Galla-bank" and "Asaka" bank attended this event.[34] The aim of the exhibition was to adopt modern technologies for the development of small business and entrepreneurship and for further strengthening cooperation with India. The event also stimulated entrepreneurs to open their own business, creating opportunities for their activity and increasing job opportunities. Around 331 contracts were signed in the framework of the exhibition that lasted for almost a week.

On October 15, 2010, a delegation of the Republic of Uzbekistan, consisting of the representatives of Cabinet Ministers, the Ministry of Foreign Economic Relations Investment and Trade, the State Joint Stock Company "O'zbekyengilsanoat" and the Indian businessmen working in Uzbekistan came to India. The main purpose of the visit was to present investment opportunities in the light industry as well as meeting with representatives of the Indian textile companies interested in investing in the light industry of Uzbekistan.[35] More recently, from February 8 to 12, 2014, the Chamber of Commerce and Industry of Uzbekistan in cooperation with the Pharmaceuticals Export Promotion Council of India organised a visit of the Indian business delegation to Uzbekistan.[36] The delegation included heads and representatives of enterprises which produce pharmaceuticals products, including vitamins, vaccines, anti-virus, anti-cancer drugs and other pharmaceuticals. They considered the issues of developing mutual cooperation and strengthening relations among the business circles of the two countries.

Despite having a number of joint ventures in Uzbekistan, India could offer new joint ventures in the automobile ancillary components, especially for small and medium cars; in the production of jewellery and other minerals; in small-spinning weaving (textile factories); in upgrading the telecommunication sector and hotel industry. The output through joint ventures could be exported to India as well as other countries. Once the exports from Uzbekistan to India is built up the freight rates will come down considerably due to the availability of the return cargo.[37]

Scientific and Technological Cooperation

The Uzbek–Indian scientific and technological interaction is based on the inter-governmental agreement on cooperation between the two countries in the field of science and technology which was signed on July 29, 1993 in New Delhi. Following this agreement an "Indian-Uzbek Center for Promotion of Scientific and Technological Cooperation" was set up in

1995 in Tashkent for the practical and successful realisation of joint scientific and technological programmes. In accordance with the terms of the agreement, a Working Programme for cooperation in Science and Technology was signed in May 1998 which was followed by the signing of another Working Programme in March 2004 between the State Committee of the Republic of Uzbekistan for Science and Technology (SCST) and the Department of Science and Technology (DST), Ministry of Science and Technology, Government of India.[38] This provided joint workshops and conferences in areas of bilateral interest, such as exchange visits of scientific and technological personnel; training of young Uzbek scientists in Indian institutions and implementation of joint research projects in areas considered to be significant for the economic development of the two countries.

The Indian–Uzbek Centre for Promotion of Scientific and Technological Cooperation carries out activities in the priority directions of cooperation as determined by the SCST and the DST such as agriculture, medicine, pharmacology, ecology, computer science (including software for computers), physics, energy sciences (including solar energy), theoretical problems of science and technology, etc.

Cooperation in the Textile Sector

Uzbekistan is not only the largest but also the most industrialised cotton producer in Central Asia. With a production of over one million tonnes per annum and four percent share of the total world production, one can see the impact of cotton monoculture in Uzbekistan. Large-scale cotton exports worldwide make textiles a promising area of cooperation between India and Uzbekistan.[39]

In order to attract foreign investment in the textile sector, since 2006, the Uzbek government has been offering a wide range of legal and tax benefits which has been highly successful. This has also opened new possibilities for investment cooperation with Indian companies. The Indian textile company Spentex bought two textile mills near Tashkent in August 2006 with an investment of US$ 81 million. Spentex also acquired one more textile company in Fergana in 2007 and made a further investment of US$ 6 million.[40] So far, Spentex has invested more than US$ 88 million in Uzbekistan, and is one of the largest investors in the textile sector of Uzbekistan.[41] At that time, the buoyant Indian textile industry encouraged Uzbekistan to attract substantial Indian investments by giving liberal sops. Since Tashkent was looking at attracting about US$ 300 million investments from the Indian textile companies in the next three years, it urged the Indian companies to tap investment opportunities in Uzbekistan.[42]

Over the years, enthused by the achievements of their Uzbek counterparts, the Indian companies have actively been seeking cooperation and exchange of expertise and scientific data in textile industry and sericulture. In June 2007, a 16-member delegation from Tirupur, a city in Tamil Nadu known for its knitted garments, visited Uzbekistan with a view to establish a joint venture or takeover.[43] On October 15, 2010, an Uzbek delegation consisting of representatives of the Cabinet Ministers, the Ministry of Foreign Economic Relations Investment and Trade, State Joint Stock Company "O'zbekyengilsanoat" and Indian business working in Uzbekistan visited India with a view to assess opportunities for investment in the light industries of Uzbekistan. On May 18, 2011, during President Karimov's visit to India, a Memorandum of Understanding between India's Ministry of Textiles and Uzbekistan's Ministry of Foreign Economic Affairs, Investments and Trade for Cooperation in the Textile Sector was signed.[44] The MoU, which aimed at developing the capacity of textiles and clothing industry in both countries, included cooperation in cotton, sericulture and fashion industries.

Further, a presentation of Uzbekistan's Light Industry took place in New Delhi in April 2013. The event was aimed at presenting investment proposals in the development of textile and silk industry. Uzbekistan offered favourable conditions for foreign investment and developing industrial potential. At the same time, the Ministry of Textiles of India signed a Memorandum of Understanding with Uzbekistan supported by the Indian Council for manufacture of silk products.[45] The document was signed at the second session of the Uzbek–Indian Joint Working Group on Cooperation in the textile industry. Both sides also agreed to promote cooperation in trade and investment in the textile sector as Uzbekistan has created favourable conditions for foreign investors and the development of industrial potential. It has also plans to significantly enhance cotton processing capacity that would be an added advantage for the Indian investors.

Cooperation in the Field of Solar Energy

The Uzbek–Indian programme on cooperation in solar energy is based on the experience of solar power installations and provides the realisation of joint scientific researches, experiments and engineering works on the development and construction of Solar Furnace in India with the help of Uzbek experts. The programme is being conducted under the aegis of the

Institute of Material, Academy of Science of Uzbekistan and the International Centre of Power Metallurgy and New Materials (ICPMNM) in Hyderabad. The cooperation under the programme is carried out in the direction of joint research of physical properties of high temperature, especially clean materials and development of similar materials on the Large Solar Furnace of the Institute of Material. In 1999, the solar furnace with a concentration diameter of 2 metres and with power of 1.5 kwt, developed by the Institute of Material, was handed over to the ICPMNM for the development of scientific–technological works in India in the field of solar power on a complimentary basis.[46]

Cooperation in the Field of Agriculture

The Republic of Uzbekistan, which has large areas of fertile land, pastures and considerable water resources, occupies the second place in karakul production and the fifth place in both cotton and silk production in the world. Wheat is the most important foodgrain in the country followed by barley. Livestock is an integral part of the agricultural system in the country. In 2006, about six million tonnes of foodgrains and 3.7 million tonnes of raw cotton were produced in Uzbekistan. The Uzbek authorities have shown interest in cooperating with Indian scientists in the breeding of early maturing and highly productive varieties of cotton and also on breeding new varieties of grain-legume crops such as chickpea, lentil, pea, vetch and berseem, etc.[47] An MoU for cooperation in the field of agriculture was signed in 2000 under which the Work Plan for 2007 was prepared which covered the period up to 31st March 2009.[48]

On January 17, 2007, the International Ecoforum on "Reorienting Agricultural Researches to achieve Millennium Development Goals: International and Regional Experience" held in Tashkent was a continuation of the Consultation Meeting organised by the Global Fund for Agricultural Research (GFAR) jointly with the Indian Council for Agricultural Research (ICAR). The Ecoforum adopted the Tashkent Declaration in the presence of the then Indian President A.P.J. Abdul Kalam during his visit to Uzbekistan. The Declaration included the following directions for bilateral cooperation in the field of agriculture:[49]

1. Regional and international partnership in agriculture;
2. Focus on household food and nutrition security;
3. Post-harvest technology and value addition for increased income;
4. Improving crop productivity;
5. Researches for the use of dry bottom of the Aral Sea for agriculture;

6. Conservation of valuable genetic resources; and
7. Environmentally efficient use of natural resources.

There has been cooperation on improving the technology of cultivation of rice by the sprout way and it has been generated and executed. A complex set of materials on technology and the technique of sprout way and two hand-operated mechanisms of rice-sprouting for application in the field in Uzbekistan were supplied by India on a complimentary basis. At present, the concerned Uzbek agencies are carrying out large-scale experiments on the application of the new technology in different regions in Uzbekistan. The partner links between the Institute of Plants Protection of Uzbekistan and the Central Institute of Cotton Growing of India were established in order to conduct a joint study of the application and practice of biological methods of plant protection. Within the framework of the given programme, the scientists of the two countries have exchanged new effective methods of plant protection without the use of chemical preparations.

In order to share experiences and scientific–technical information, two seminars were held in Tashkent on advanced technologies and in India on agricultural research in 1996 and 1999, respectively. The issues concerning mechanisation of cotton-growing, rice-growing and gardening were discussed in the seminars. The seminars recommended cooperation in such areas as material, power, laser technologies, rice and cotton-growing, gardening, soil-growing and agro-chemistry, irrigation, genetic fund of plants and genetic researches. The recommendations became the basis for realisation of a number of major joint projects.[50] An MoU for cooperation in the field of agriculture was signed in 2000 under which a Work Plan for 2004 was also signed, to be extended up to December 31, 2005. There has been an agreement between the Uzbek Scientific Production Centre of Agriculture and the Indian Council for Agricultural Research for joint graduate and doctoral programmes for training researchers.[51] The India–Uzbekistan bilateral cooperation in the field of agricultural research and education has been on ever since.

Cooperation in Chemical and Petrochemical Industries

The chemical sector is one of the basic segments of Uzbekistan's economy as it is expected to create a base for the economy to achieve long-term and sustainable development. The chemical sector of Uzbekistan produces several chemicals including fertilisers, organic and inorganic compounds, artificial fibres, polymers, and chemical reagents used in energy, gold and chemical industries. Most of the chemical companies in the country are part of the State Joint-Stock Company, UzKimyoSanoat.[52]

Uzbekistan has identified the chemical sector as amongst its priority sectors under the Anti-Crisis Programme. During 2011–2015, seven large projects in the chemical industry were expected to be implemented in Uzbekistan by India with an aim of developing this sector. It is to be noted that about US$ 1.6 billion investments would be involved in these projects, of which US$ 1.2 billion would be financed through foreign credits and investments. The remaining investments would be financed by UzKimyoSanoat, the Fund for Reconstruction and Development of Uzbekistan and commercial banks.[53]

Further avenues for an active Indo-Uzbekistan cooperation are unfolding in the chemical and petrochemical industries. A Memorandum of Cooperation between the UzKimyoSanoat and the Indian company Coromondel has been signed to undertake the study of and implement the following:

1. Cooperation in the reconstruction and modernisation of the existing urea plant with an annual capacity up to 330 thousand tonnes per year with a Joint-Stock Company "Ferganaazot", and to export urea to India;
2. Cooperation in the area of plant protection products such as herbicides, fungicides, etc. based on the JV "Electrohimzavod"; and
3. Explore the possibility of enrichment of ore of the Kyzylkum phosphate complex for the further processing of nitrogen, phosphate, potassium fertilisers and so on.

Cooperation in the Field of Information Technology

Within the framework of the programme on joint development and the introduction of computer training programmes in the education system, an agreement was reached to study the prospects of application in Uzbekistan of the experience of the Indian side for the organisation of computer courses at various levels. An intensive exchange of experts between the two countries has been carried out and training and retraining courses for experts have been organised on information technology, automation, management and other disciplines. In 1999, special courses for the enterprises in village districts for the chiefs of regional scientific and technical centres of Uzbekistan were also conducted.[54]

The inauguration of the Jawaharlal Nehru Centre for Information Technology in Tashkent on April 26, 2006 was a landmark development in cooperation in the IT sector. Earlier, under an MoU signed in October 2004 for establishing the Indo-Uzbek Centre for Information Technology, India provided Uzbek authorities a grant of 30 million rupees besides offering technical assistance. With this grant, the building identified for the Indo-Uzbek Centre for Information Technology in the Tashkent University of Information Technology (TUIT) was renovated and eight faculty members of TUIT underwent six months' advanced training in Information Technology from August 2005 to February 2006 at C-DAC in Pune. Experts from C-DAC installed the equipment and conducted the training courses.[55]

The India–Uzbekistan Working Group on Information Technology held its first session in New Delhi on January 24, 2011 and discussed the opportunities and prospects of cooperation.[56] On May 22, 2013, an MoU was signed between India and Uzbekistan on the upgradation of the Jawaharlal Nehru Centre for Information Technology in Tashkent.[57] The decision to upgrade this centre was taken during President Karimov's visit to India in May 2011. A team from C-DAC had earlier visited Uzbekistan in 2012 to examine the possibilities of upgrading the centre, which was expected to be completed during 2013–14. An MoU for the upgradation of the IT Centre was signed during the visit of the Vice President in May 2013 and the upgradation was completed in 2014.[58]

Cooperation under the ITEC Programme

Uzbekistan has become a beneficiary of India's ITEC Programme since 1993 and over the years this programme has gained wide popularity in Uzbekistan. In 2011, the slot was raised to 150 annually, a hike from the earlier slot of 120.[59] This is the highest number of ITEC slots allocated to any country. Under the ITEC Programme, the areas of training include information technology, English for professionals, management, journalism, diplomacy, small business planning, remote sensing and hotel management administration, banking and finance, education and human resource development, entrepreneurship, textile mill management, water resource development, NGOs and civil society, etc. The ITEC slot utilisation from Uzbekistan remained close to 100 percent during 2009–2011. Since 1993, more than 1,100 Uzbek experts and specialists have been trained in India in diverse areas.

Energy Cooperation

Uzbekistan occupies the leading position in gas, oil and gas condensate. The proven resources in Uzbekistan are 3 trillion cubic metres of gas and about 94.8 million tonnes of oil. According to the data of "Uzbekneftegas", the estimated reserves of Uzbekistan are about 5.9 trillion cubic metres of gas and more than 800 million tonnes of oil. The annual extraction of gas in Uzbekistan is 60 billion cubic metres. The main suppliers of natural gas and oil are Bukhara and Khorezm regions (Bukhara-Kiva), Ustyrt, Surkhandarya and Fergana regions and the shelves of the Aral Sea. The implementation of new projects in the shelves of the Aral Sea can increase the natural gas and oil potential of Uzbekistan.[60]

The India–Uzbekistan cooperation in the sphere of energy security remains one of the main directions of interaction between the two countries. In order to achieve close cooperation between India and Uzbekistan in the energy sector, various agreements concluded between the two sides, particularly between the Uzbekneftegaz on the one side and the Indian Ministry of Oil and Gas Industry, Gas Authority of India Limited as well as ONGC Videsh Ltd (OVL) on the other side, have been working properly. The position of Uzbekistan concerning the participation of Indian capital in the oil and gas sector of Uzbekistan was defined by President Karimov, who guaranteed Indian participation by offering oil and gas blocks in the state on equal management basis (50 : 50) as given to Russia, China, South Korea and the European countries.[61]

In addition, India seems to be very close to importing uranium from Uzbekistan. The issue came up for discussion during talks in Tashkent on September 14, 2013 between the then visiting India's External Affairs Minister, Salman Khurshid and his Uzbek counterpart Abdulaziz Kamilov. The agreement reportedly was not a civil nuclear deal but a contract like the one with Kazakhstan, under which India was to import a little over 2,000 tonnes of uranium by 2014,[62] though it still needs to be seen how this agreement gets implemented. However, the state-owned Uzbek mining major NMMC (Navoi Mining & Metallurgy Combine), one of the world's top ten uranium and gold producers, had agreed to supply 2,000 metric tonnes of uranium ore concentrate to India over a period of four years (2014–2018).[63]

Other Areas of Cooperation

India has also invested in the reconstruction of the Uzbek railway infrastructure. During the visit of the Indian Minister of State for Commerce Jairam Ramesh in 2007, India expressed its interest in gold mining in Uzbekistan which is the fourth largest producer of gold in the world while India is the world's largest importer of the metal. The Uzbek government has agreed to consider a proposal from the Indian MMTC/National Mineral Development Cooperation (NMDC) for gold exploration, which would include development of the gems and jewellery sector.[64] An Indian company, Larsen & Toubro, completed the turnkey construction of a 500-bed international class hotel at Samarkand, a 440-bed international class hotel at Bukhara and the refurbishment and modernisation of a tobacco factory at Urgut, Samarkand.[65]

In the field of civil aviation, the Indian Air Force has been working with the Tashkent Aircraft Production Association (TAPC) and has even purchased some planes. To enhance mutual cooperation in the aircraft industry, India has purchased six Ilyushin-78 aircrafts from the TAPC named Chkalov. Indian aircraft are being regularly serviced at the Chkalov aircraft plant in Tashkent.[66] In the field of civil aviation, both countries have established a strong partnership. In particular, "Uzbekistan Airways" successfully works with Indian specialists and operates regular flights from New Delhi and Amritsar.[67] India and Uzbekistan have signed agreements under which Uzbek Airways supplies machinery and cargo services to India that includes remittances of revenues earned by Uzbekistan Airways from its flights to India, of both cargo and passengers.

India-Uzbekistan Trade Relations

The India–Uzbekistan trade relations are governed by the Agreement on Trade and Economic Cooperation signed in May 1993. The Agreement provides for mutual MFN treatment, promotion of economic, industrial, scientific and technical cooperation, including in the field of training of personnel, active participation of small and medium sized enterprises in bilateral economic cooperation and counter-trade, etc. The same year, the two countries also signed an Agreement on the Avoidance of Double Taxation. In May 1999, they concluded another agreement on Bilateral Investment Promotion and Protection. According to the State Statistics Committee of Uzbekistan, India has occupied the 15th place among countries that are the trading partners of Uzbekistan, covering 0.7 percent of the total trade turnover of the country.[68]

The growth of trade turnover has been connected with both the growth of export of goods from Uzbekistan to India as well as an increase of imports of necessary raw materials and other goods from India. In comparison with 1992, the trade turnover increased by 12 times in 2000. While exports increased by almost 10 times, imports increased by virtually 15 times. In

2001, the total trade turnover between the two countries was US$ 19.98 million, with exports of US$ 10.52 million and imports of US$ 9.46 million. The major exports from India are pharmaceuticals, tea, plant and machinery, surgical items and services including payments for technology transfer by Indian joint ventures. On the other hand, exports of commodities from Uzbekistan have included non-ferrous metals, machinery and equipment and agricultural produce. However, more than 95 percent of Uzbekistan's exports to India are shown as 'Services' in the figures published by the Uzbek authorities. This requires attention in terms of coordinating the trade statistics between the two countries.[69]

For the past one decade or so, the mutual trade turnover between the two countries has grown substantially but not constantly. Table 8.1 presents an empirical profile of trade between India and Uzbekistan for the periods 1996–97 and 2013–14. While in 1996–97, the bilateral trade between the two sides stood at a meagre US$ 10.74 million, in 2008–09, it reached up to US$ 116.27 million. After decreasing in 2009–10 and 2010–11, it again registered a sharp growth in 2011–12 with an impressive figure of US$

Table 8.1: India-Uzbekistan Bilateral Trade, 1996-2016 (In US$ million)

Year	*Export from India*	*Growth Percentage*	*Percent Share in Total Exports by India*	*Imports from Uzbekistan*	*Growth Percentage*	*Percent Share in Total Imports by India*	*Total Bilateral Trade*
1996-97	8.14	NA	0.0243	2.60	NA	0.0067	10.74
1997-98	17.59	116.23	0.0506	2.71	4.05	0.0065	20.30
1998-99	12.83	-27.04	0.0386	1.67	-38.44	0.0039	14.50
1999-00	9.94	-22.56	0.0270	12.97	678.13	0.0261	22.91
2000-01	9.39	-5.47	0.0211	10.58	-18.4	0.0209	19.97
2001-02	6.53	-30.45	0.0149	17.27	63.16	0.0336	23.80
2002-03	5.08	-22.32	0.0096	20.54	18.96	0.0335	25.62
2003-04	15.14	198.33	0.0237	27.70	34.82	0.0354	42.84
2004-05	21.35	40.97	0.0256	31.46	13.59	0.0282	52.81
2005-06	24.44	14.49	0.0237	26.13	-16.93	0.0175	50.57
2006-07	29.69	21.51	0.0235	33.91	29.74	0.0183	63.60
2007-08	40.32	35.79	0.0247	16.2	-52.23	0.0064	56.52
2008-09	45.53	12.93	0.0246	70.74	336.77	0.0233	116.27
2009-10	54.03	18.65	0.0302	29.97	-57.63	0.0104	84.40
2010-11	60.42	11.83	0.0241	20.63	-31.18	0.0056	81.05
2011-12	89.39	47.94	0.0292	37.04	79.61	0.0076	126.43
2012-13	124.90	39.73	0.0416	31.85	-14.02	0.0065	156.75
2013-14	114.07	-8.67	0.0364	31.50	-1.11	0.0070	145.57
2014-15	170.44	49.43	0.0549	55.86	77.37	0.0125	226.31
2015-16	94.64	-44.48	0.0361	45.26	-18.99	0.0119	139.89

Source: Based on Export-Import Data (1997-98 to 2015-16) collected from Directorate General of Foreign Trade (DGFT), Department of Commerce, Ministry of Commerce & Industry, Government of India.

126.43 million which further grew in 2013–14 to stand at US$ 156.75 million. When the value of bilateral trade is taken on a yearly basis, the India–Uzbekistan trade grew by 29 percent to touch the figure of US$ 259.5 million in 2013 (January–December), according to the Ministry of Foreign Economic Relations, Investments and Trade of the Republic of Uzbekistan.[70] As of the first five months of 2014, the volume of bilateral trade increased by 8.4 percent to a total of US$ 114 million.

Table 8.2: Main Indian Exports to Uzbekistan during 2015-16 (In US$ million)

S.No.	*Commodity*	*Value*	*Percent Share of India's Total Export to Uzbekistan*
1	Pharmaceutical products	47.86	50.57
2	Nuclear reactors, boilers, machinery and mechanical appliances; parts thereof	13.02	13.76
3	Vehicles other than railway or tramway rolling stock, and parts and accessories thereof	7.6	8.03
4	Articles of apparel and clothing accessories, not knitted or crocheted	4.33	4.58
5	Electrical machinery and equipment and parts thereof; sound recorders and reproducers, television image and sound recorders and reproducers, and parts	2.96	3.13
6	Optical, photographic cinematographic measuring, checking precision, medical or surgical inst. and apparatus parts and accessories thereof	2.88	3.04
7	Articles of apparel and clothing accessories, knitted or corcheted	2.58	2.73
8	Organic chemicals	1.83	1.93
9	Ceramic products	1.61	1.70
10	Coffee, tea, mate and spices	1.41	1.49
	Total Export of top 10 items	86.08	
	Total Export	94.64	
	India's Global Export	262,290.13	

Uzbekistan is the second largest country after Kazakhstan in terms of the total trade value for India among the Central Asian Republics. This in itself is a noticeable feature because access to Uzbekistan from India is not easy at present considering the doubly landlocked situation of Uzbekistan. The shortest and the most direct route through Pakistan and Afghanistan is not usable due to political–military reasons and the state of turbulent relations between India and Pakistan. Hence, the cost of transportation is

Table 8.3: Main Indian Imports from Uzbekistan during 2015-16 (In US$ million)

S.No.	*Commodity*	*Value*	*Percent Share of India's Total Imports from Uzbekistan*
1	Fertilisers	18.08	39.95
2	Edible vegetables and certain roots and tubers	16.84	37.21
3	Lac; gums, resins and other vegetable saps and extracts	5.88	12.99
4	Lead and articles thereof	2.19	4.84
5	Silk	0.67	1.48
6	Oil seeds and olea. Fruits; misc. Grains, seeds and fruit; industrial or medicinal plants; straw and fodder	0.58	1.28
7	Raw hides and skins (other than furskins) and leather	0.53	1.17
8	Salt; sulphur; earths and stone; plastering materials, lime and cement	0.2	0.44
9	Plastic and articles thereof	0.13	0.29
10	Other base metals; cermets; articles thereof	0.13	0.29
	Total import of top 10 items	45.23	
	Total Import	45.26	

high as are the tariffs at several points which have to be paid when the goods cross from one country to another. These tariffs need to be reduced by introducing a phased transition to what may be envisaged as the North Asian Free Trade Area. India can also seek the support of Uzbekistan in joining the Economic Cooperation Orgnanization (ECO), a regional grouping of Pakistan, Afghanistan, Turkey and Iran founded in 1985 to which the Central Asian Republics were admitted in February 1992.[71]

India's Investments in Uzbekistan

After signing the Bilateral Investment Promotion and Protection agreement in 1993, India granted a credit of US$ 10 million to Uzbekistan for financing the projects on the Uzbek imports of equipment, goods and services from India. This credit was utilised for financing the supply of equipment for tea packaging and modernising the tea factory in Samarkand, for the production of tomato ketchup in a factory in Tashkent and for the production of medicines by the Surhan-Ajanta joint venture as well as for the production of kitchenware by the Uzbek–India joint venture named as "East Butterfly".[72] In 1994, India gave another credit of US$ 10 million, out of which US$ 2.8 million was financed for the furnishing of a hotel in Bukhara. On May 2, 2000, the third Indian credit of US$ 10 million was disbursed to finance a modernisation project of the Buvaida yarn-spinning factory in Uzbekistan.[73] The government of Uzbekistan has been able to utilise US$ 12.5 million out of the first two credit lines and as the third credit line remained unutilised, the Indian credit line was closed in July 2004.[74]

The several measures that have been taken for improving the investment environment in Uzbekistan have significantly increased the volume of foreign direct investment (FDI). India is one of the largest investors in Uzbekistan's economy. Between 2007 and 2010, the Indian FDI in the Uzbek economy totalled US$ 33.5 million.[75] Currently, there are as many as 72 enterprises operating in Uzbekistan, which have been established with the direct participation of Indian companies and investment. Among these 26 are joint ventures and 10 are enterprises with 100 percent Indian capital. Some of the distinguished enterprises, such as Diamond Uzbekistan International in the tourism sector, Emsam Trading in the construction and tourism sectors, Multi Channel Impex Ltd. in the cotton processing and commerce sectors are making valuable contributions to the development of Uzbekistan's pharmaceutical, tourism, construction and other industries.[76]

In July 2006, Spentex Industries Ltd. acquired Tashkent To'ytepa Tekstil Ltd., an Uzbek government spinning company with a combined capacity of 2,20,000 spines and 236 air jet looms, for US$ 81 million. This made Spentex India's largest spinning enterprise with an installed capacity of over 5,70,000.[77] However, ironically in 2012, Spentex "lodged its claim with the Government of Uzbekistan in pursuance to Investment Agreement to the tune of US$ 100 million to compensate it for its losses in terms of its commitments...Spentex believes that the Government of Uzbekistan would honor its commitments to repose and build the trust of a vast community of foreign nationals for investments".[78] There are several other Indian companies that are still interested in investing in textiles, pharmaceutical and the oil and gas sectors in Uzbekistan.

India has been making determined efforts to promote Indian products in Uzbekistan. It is evidenced by the fact that India Trade Promotion Organization held an Indian Trade Exhibition in Tashkent from September 14 to 20, 1995. Over 84 leading companies from India displayed a diverse range of products covering engineering equipment, machinery and accessories, electrical and electronic equipment, automobiles, kitchen equipment, hospital equipment, petrol pumps, stainless steel castings, cables, pipes, welding electrodes, telecommunication equipment, chemicals, pharmaceuticals, bicycles and bicycle parts, sanitary fittings, household appliances, electrical appliances including batteries, rubber products, leather board sheets, leather garments, textiles, woollens, fabrics, footwear, handicrafts, medicines, stationary, TV cabinets, non-ferrous metal articles, plywood, wood enamels, paper and paper boards, coolers, cosmetics, toiletries, consumer goods, home furnishings, toys, lenses, sports goods, spirits and beer. Leading corporate giants like TATA Exports Ltd., Maruti Udyog, Avon Cycles, US Global Corpn. Ltd., Usha International Ltd., Malhotra Global Eximp. Ltd., Kirlosker Bros. Ltd. and several other companies together with a few state organisations participated in this exhibition with favourable results. It was estimated that they generated business worth Rs. 106 crore.[79]

In August 2013, a presentation on the economic potential and investment climate of Uzbekistan was organised at the Embassy of Uzbekistan in New Delhi with the support of the Indian Ministry of Commerce and Industry and in collaboration with the Export Promotion Council of machinery goods.[80] The Indian business groups highly appraised the advantages the Uzbek economy has to offer, such as rich raw stocks, favourable geographical location of being at the crossroads of the large regional markets, sophisticated transport and logistics system, a diversified industrial base, scientific, intellectual and human resource potential of the country, the legal framework and the system of benefits for foreign investors. Such events hold significance in attracting Indian investments in Uzbekistan.

Future Prospects for India–Uzbekistan Cooperation

Though the Indo-Uzbek cooperation has shown an enormous potential for growth and progress, India has not yet made a stronghold in the Uzbek market. Since both the countries have expressed their willingness to work for the promotion of peace and prosperity in the 21st century, an Uzbek scholar suggests the following steps to be taken in the future:[81]

1. Maintaining high-level contacts and bilateral summits;
2. Institutionalising consultations on foreign policy issues;
3. Continuing bilateral efforts for strengthening regional security;
4. Cooperating closely by starting initiatives like multilateral forums so as to contribute to stability in a culturally diverse and rapidly transforming Asia vis-à-vis the world globalisation process; and

5. Creating supportive structures for both private as well as public businesses to utilise existing credit lines more efficiently and providing the capacity to cope up with the existing financial and investment realities.

Another scholar recommends the following measures for improving the bilateral economic relations between India and Central Asia on one hand and the Indo-Uzbek economic partnership on the other:[82]

1. Conducting a Feasibility Study on the Central Asia–India Economic Cooperation Agreement in general and the Uzbekistan–India Free Trade Agreement in particular;
2. Signing of an MoU between Trade Point in India and Competent Institution in Uzbekistan;
3. Constituting an Expert Group to study the possibilities of India providing technical advice to Uzbekistan on Central Banking Functions and Commercial Banking Operations;
4. Increasing the inter-governmental exchange of technical experts related to science and technology projects aimed at economic development;
5. Initiating joint ventures in the areas of cotton, textiles and garments, automobiles, bicycles, food processing, telecommunications, etc.;
6. Cooperation in the area of Services such as database creation and dissemination, consultancy services, infrastructural services, etc.;
7. Considering multi-entry visa provision in Uzbekistan in order to make it a window to other Central Asian countries.

An Indian expert on Central Asia too outlines some of the future prospects for cooperation between India and Uzbekistan, which are as follows:[83]

1. India needs to create strong economic, political and security linkages. A two-pronged approach needs to be adopted: firstly, India needs to be economically relevant to the Central Asian Republics and secondly, it can collaborate with Iran, China and Afghanistan to extend its connectivity with the CARs thus improving its trade and economic ties with the region.
2. India needs to support any regional economic initiative to make the Central Asian region an important part of the trade network in the entire South Asian region.
3. India should play an active role to back the Central Asian Republics as observer nations in the SAARC group. Similarly, the Central Asian Republics should back India's membership in the Economic Cooperation Organisation (ECO), which would strengthen India's

economic ties with the Central Asian Republics as well as with Pakistan, Afghanistan, Iran and Turkey.

4. India should increase its public health and ecological assistance to the CARs, besides giving main emphasis on building infrastructure (roads, transport systems and communications), industrial activities, construction sector, financial and banking institutions.
5. More Indian investment in the pharmaceutical sector may augur well for both India and Uzbekistan.
6. As Uzbekistan is interested in introducing new data processing techniques into electronic management, banking and financial sectors, India's success in IT could contribute immensely to this.
7. Tourism is another area of cooperation between the two republics. Both the countries have world-famous tourist sites to attract tourists from inside the country, from the region and also from other parts of the world.
8. As the largest democracy in the world, India can contribute to the democratisation process, civil society and media in Uzbekistan. India's electoral process could be a role model for that country.
9. There is a strong demand for Indian tele-serials, documentaries and films in the CARs. These can be dubbed in Russian or the local languages and made available to the Central Asian audience.

The existing ties between India and Uzbekistan can be taken to new heights if India goes beyond the articulated polices and draws a roadmap of cooperation in the economic field. There is an ample scope for cooperation between the two countries, so the need is to realise that and put the efforts on the right track through astute policymaking.

REFERENCES

1. Pandey, S.K. Pandey, 'India's Approach to Regional Cooperation in South Asia and Its Relevance for Uzbekistan', in *Perspectives on Bilateral and Regional Cooperation: South and Central Asia*, R. Malhotra, S.S. Gill and N. Gaur (eds), Chandigarh: CRRID, 2013, p. 117.
2. Sahgal, A. and V. Anand, 'Strategic Environment in Central Asia and India', 2010, p. 38. URL: http://www.silkroadstudies.org/new/docs/publications/1004Joshi-V-Strategic.pdf
3. Chandra, Amiya, 'Economic Cooperation: Potential and Prospects', *Building a Common Future: Indian and Uzbek Perspectives on Security and Economic Issues*, P. Stobdan (ed.), New Delhi: Knowledge World, 1999, p. 172.
4. 'Uzbekistan: Economy'. URL: http://www.infoplease.com/encyclopedia/world/uzbekistan-economy.html

5. Abduraxmonovich, A.O., 'Economic Cooperation between India and Central Asian Republics with Special Reference to Uzbekistan', *RIS Discussion Papers*, RIS # 53/ 20003, Tashkent: University of World Economy and Diplomacy, 2003, p. 2.
6. *The CIA World Fact Book 2010*, New York: Skyhorse Publishing, p. 728.
7. ADB, 'Uzbekistan: Economy', *Asian Development Outlook 2014*, Manila, 2014. URL: http://www.adb.org/countries/uzbekistan/economy
8. Rakhimov, Mirzhoid, 'Foreign Policy of Uzbekistan: Bilateral and Multilateral Dimension', in *The State in Eurasia: Local and Global Issues*, A. Sengupta and S.Chatterjee (eds), New Delhi: KW Publishers, 2013, p.141.
9. Mavlonov, I.R., 'India's Economic Diplomacy in Central Asia: A New Architecture for Interegional Cooperation', *South and Central Asia: Quest for Peace and Cooperation*, R. Malhotra et al. (eds), Chandigarh: CRRID, 2013, p. 35.
10. 'The Indo-Uzbekistan Relations', *The Indian Analyst*, 7 May 2007. URL: http://www.whatisindia.com/issues/uzbekrel/indo-uzbekrel_info.html
11. 'Joint Statement issued on Strategic Partnership between India and Uzbekistan during the visit of Uzbek President Islam Abduganievich Karimov, May 18, 2011', India's Foreign Relations-2011: Documents, Public Diplomacy Division, Ministry of External Affairs, New Delhi: Geetika Publishers, p. 1268.
12. 'India-Uzbekistan Relations', July 2014. URL: http://www.mea.gov.in/Portal/ForeignRelation/Uzbekistan_July_2014.pdf
13. Potapova, Nelya Y., 'Uzbek-India Relations: Realities and Prospects', in *Perspectives on Bilateral and Regional Cooperation: South and Central Asia*, R. Malhotra, S.S.Gill and N. Gaur (eds), Chandigarh: CRRID, 2013, pp. 155-156.
14. 'India, Uzbekistan ink Pacts to boost Cooperation'. URL: http://www.thehindu.com/news/national/prime-minister-narendra-modis-visit-to-uzbekistan/article7392482.ece.
15. Teshabaev, Fatih, 'Uzbek-India Relations', in *Central Asia since Independence*, K. Warikoo and Mahavir Singh (eds), New Delhi: Shipra Publications, 2004, p.174.
16. Abduraxmonovich, op. cit., p.12.
17. Ministry of Commerce and Industry, Government of India, 'Trade Promotion Programme - Focus: CIS'. URL: http://commerce.nic.in/trade/international_tpp_cis_10.asp
18. 'India-Uzbekistan Relations', op. cit
19. Zakirova, Saiyora A., 'A Status Report on Indo-Uzbek Economic Cooperation', in *Perspectives on Bilateral and Regional Cooperation: South and Central Asia*, R. Malhotra, S.S.Gill and N. Gaur (eds), Chandigarh: CRRID, 2013, p.183.
20. Embassy of India,Tashkent, 'Uzbekistan: India-Uzbekistan Relations'. URL: http://eoi.gov.in/tashkent/?2615?000.
21. 'World Bank Group-Uzbekistan Partnership: Country Program Snapshot', April 2014. URL: http://www.worldbank.org/content/dam/Worldbank/document/Uzbekistan-Snapshot.pdf
22. Tabal, G.A., 'Salience of Synergy in Uzbek-Indian Ties', in *Perspectives on Bilateral and Regional Cooperation: South and Central Asia*, R. Malhotra, S.S. Gill and N. Gaur (eds), Chandigarh: CRRID, 2013, p.150.
23. 'Business Circles of India are paying Visit to Uzbekistan', *Uz Daily*, 11 February 2014. URL: http://www.uzdaily.com/articles-id-26651.htm

24. Bhat, Bilal, 'Matrix of National Initiatives: Perspectives on Cross Leveraging India and Uzbekistan Relations', in *Perspectives on Bilateral and Regional Cooperation: South and Central Asia*, R. Malhotra, S.S. Gill and N. Gaur (eds), Chandigarh: CRRID, 2013, p. 362.
25. Abduraxmonovich, op. cit., p.13.
26. *Teri Energy Data Directory & Year Book 2005-06*, New Delhi: The Energy and Resources Institute, 2007, p. 81.
27. 'India, Uzbekistan sign 7 MoUs', 26 April 2006. URL: http://www.rediff.com/money/2006/apr/26mou.htm
28. Katakey, Rakteem, 'GAIL in Talks with Uzbekistan for Gas', *Business Standard*, 22 July, 2007.
29. Ibid.
30. 'India-Uzbekistan Relations', op. cit.
31. Teshabaev (2004), op. cit., pp. 174-175.
32. Ibid., p. 175.
33. 'Uzbekistan-India', *World Mass Communication*, 11 (26), February 2007, p. 13.
34. Potapova, op. cit., p.156.
35. Ibid., p.157.
36. 'Business Circles...'.
37. Chandra, op. cit., pp.183-185.
38. 'India-Uzbekistan Relations', op. cit.
39. Sarma, A.S., *India and Central Asia: Redefining Energy and Trade Links*, New Delhi: Pentagon Press, 2010, p. 42.
40. 'India-Uzbekistan Relations', January 2012. URL: http://www.mea.gov.in/Portal/ForeignRelation/Uzbekistan-January-2012.pdf
41. Rakhimov, op. cit, pp. 47-48.
42. 'Indian Textile Cos to invest $ 300 mn in Uzbekistan', *The Economic Times*, 18 December 2006.
43. Sarma, op. cit, p. 45.
44. Ministry of External Affairs, Government of India, 'Factsheet of Agreements signed during the State Visit of the President of Uzbekistan', 18 May 2011. URL: http://mea.gov.in/bilateral-documents.htm?dtl/5180/Factsheet+of+Agreements+signed+during+the+State+ Visit+of+the+President+of+Uzbekistan
45. 'Uzbekistan and India signed a Memorandum on Cooperation in the Field of Textile', 13 April 2013. URL: http://www.thetextileicon.com/blog/2013/04/13/uzbekistan-and-india-signed-a-memorandum-on-cooperation-in-the-field-of-textile/
46. Abduraxmonovich, op. cit, p.14.
47. 'Uzbekistan-India', *World Mass Communication*, pp. 17-18.
48. 'India-Uzbekistan Relations', op. cit.
49. 'Uzbekistan-India', op. cit., p. 18.
50. Abduraxmonovich, op. cit., p.15.
51. 'Uzbekistan-India', op. cit., p. 18.
52. *A Strategy Paper for CIS Countries: India-CIS Roadmap 2020*, FT (CIS) Division, July, 2012, p. 283.
53. Ibid.

54. Abduraxmonovich, op. cit., pp.15-16.
55. 'Uzbekistan-India', op. cit., p. 14.
56. 'India-Uzbekistan Relations', op. cit..
57. 'India, Uzbekistan warn against Outside Interference in Afghanistan', 22 May 2013. URL: http://www.siasat.com/english/news/india-uzbekistan-warn-against-outside-interference-afghanistan
58. 'India-Uzbekistan Relations'. URL: https://www.mea.gov.in/Portal/ForeignRelation/Uzbekistan_July_2016.pdf.
59. Sheraliyev, Oybek R., 'Central Asia Mirrors India's Geo-Economic Interests', in *Perspectives on Bilateral and Regional Cooperation: South and Central Asia*, R. Malhotra, S.S. Gill and N. Gaur (eds), Chandigarh: CRRID, 2013, pp.138-139.
60. Urazdoboeva, Sojida, 'Some Aspects of Indian Energy Interests in Central Asia', *India's Engagement with Central Asia with focus on India-Uzbekistan Relations*, in Jyotsana Bakshi (ed), Tashkent: University of World Economy and Diplomacy, 2007, pp.185-186.
61. Ibid., p. 187.
62. 'India Close to Importing Uranium from Uzbekistan', *The Economic Times*, September 14, 2013. URL: http://articles.economictimes.indiatimes.com/2013-09-14/news/42062415_1_ chabahar-port-uzbekistan-uzbekistan
63. 'India widens N-fuel Base, signs up Uzbek Firm for Uranium Supplies'. URL: http://indianexpress.com/article/business/business-others/india-widens-n-fuel-base-signs-up-uzbek-firm-for-uranium-supplies/.
64. Sarma, op. cit., p. 46.
65. Ibid., p. 46.
66. Kundu, N.D., 'Hamid Ansari's Visit to Turkmenistan and Kazakhstan', April 24, IDSA Comment, 2008. URL: http://www.idsa.in/idsastrategiccomments/HamidAnsarisVisitto TurkmenistanandKazakhstan_NDKundu_240408
67. Tabak, Gulzade A., 'Salience of Synergy in Uzbek-India Ties', in *Perspectives on Bilateral and Regional Cooperation: South and Central Asia*, R. Malhotra, S.S. Gill and N. Gaur (eds), Chandigarh: CRRID, 2013, p. 362.
68. 'India-Uzbekistan Relations', op. cit. URL: http://eoi.gov.in/eoisearch/MyPrint.php?2615?001/0020
69. Abduraxmonovich, op. cit., p.13.
70. Azizov, Demir, 'Indian Ambassador completes Diplomatic Mission in Uzbekistan', 12 July, 2014, URL: http://en.trend.az/regions/casia/uzbekistan/2293598.html
71. Shri Prakash, 'India Uzbekistan Relations during the 1990s and Future Prospects', in *Central Asia since Independence*, K. Warikoo and Mahavir Singh (eds), New Delhi: Shipra Publications: 2004, p. 186.
72. Teshabaev, op. cit., pp. 175-176.
73. Ibid., p. 176.
74. Indian Embassy in Tashkent, op. cit.
75. 'Uzbekistan and India have Similar Approaches to Global, Regional Issues'. URL: http://thebluemoonmedia.com/uzbekistan-and-india-have-similar-approaches-to-global-regional-issues/
76. Uzbekistan, The Extraordinary and Plenipotentiary Diplomatist Special, Embassy of Uzbekistan, New Delhi, 2006, p. 13.

77. Ibid., p. 40.
78. Fergana International Information Agency, 'Uzbekistan: Indian Investor lodges US$ 100 Million Complaint against the Uzbek Government', 31 May, 2012. URL: http://enews.fergananews.com/news.php?id=2294
79. Uzbekistan, *EIU Country Report,* December 2000, p. 5.
80. 'Economic and Investment Potential of Uzbekistan highlighted in India', 27 August 2013. URL: http://news.uzreport.uz/news_4_e_108262.html
81. Teshabaev, op. cit., p. 176.
82. Abduraxmonovich, op. cit., p. 18.
83. Roy, Meena Singh, "'India-Central Asia Relations: Changing Dynamics and Future Prospects', in *South-Central Asia: Emerging Issues,* Kuldip Singh (ed.), Amritsar: Guru Nanak Dev University, 2005, pp. 54-97.

9

Quantum Leap

Currently and in immediate future the Central Asia Region does not seems to be a strategic market for the US & the EU firms due to a geographic remoteness, their relatively smaller population, lower level of household incomes making their manufactured product expensive in comparison to China, obscured trade regime as well as high transactions cost of doing business in the region in comparison to the advantage that Russia & China enjoys. Their main interests in Central Asia are energy resources, regional stability and issues related to Foreign policy & security in Afghanistan and the Central Asian strategic geo-political relevance with Russia. From the US & EU firm's perspectives, the Central Asian market is not a strategic one since many of European export items are not affordable for most consumers in the region. China, Turkey and to a certain extent Russia have been quite successful in foreign trade in Central Asia, where as Iran & India despite their continuous efforts have not been able to make any substantial gains. India's trade with Central Asian nations is barely 1 percent of the overall Chinese trade with these nations; this shall set the scale of comparison.

Russia by its historical, political as well as geographical linkage with the Central Asian nations had an inherent advantage, hence its trade relationship is far ahead than any of the other country in the world. However this over dependence on Russia, and Russia trying to leverage its position and domination of this erstwhile Soviet Era region, is causing discomfort and pushing these CARs to open up and diversify their foreign policy as well as foreign trade. Taking advantage of this situation China and Turkey were able to expand their exports to the region and its export structure is very diversified as it includes apparel, clothing accessories, textile yarn, fabrics, footwear, plastic, rubber items, iron, steel, metalworking, power generating and other industrial machinery, road vehicles including automobiles, telecommunication and office equipment, home appliances, consumer chemicals, fertilizers, furniture and selected food items. Between 80 and 90 percent of Chinese exports to Central Asia consist of finished, diversified goods. Overall export structure of China and especially Turkey matches very well with the import baskets of Central Asian countries and its projected and anticipated that exports from these countries will further increase their share in the market.

There is a great lesson to be learnt from the China experience which demonstrates how the Chinese built on their relationship with the Central Asian neighbors, despite overcoming the greatest of the obstacle of being dubbed as pariah by the erstwhile Soviet Union in their propaganda and the common perception of it being anti-Islam. China's concealed its multi-vector objectives in the region by forwarding only the economic agenda. China had its hand on the delicate nerve of the Central Asian nations and that was the need of these nations to be supported and funded financially. With no baggage of ideology or moralistic stance towards the CARs, China very shrewdly encashed on the CAR's urgent need of capital.

Prior to the collapse of the Soviet Union, the generally bad state of Sino-Soviet relations had impeded direct relations between Central Asia and China. Establishing direct bilateral relations with Beijing has required overcoming several extremely negative clichés of China put about by Soviet propaganda, clichés that reinforced Central Asian societies' already long-standing apprehensions of their large neighbor. An old Central Asian tradition, handed down through centuries-old oral epics, presents China as a distant but recurrent enemy of Turkic peoples and as an historical opponent of Islam. However, in two decades only, Beijing has become one of Central Asian countries main partners.[1] Initially Beijing's concern was to sign demarcation treaties, demilitarize the borders, and prevent the strengthening of Uyghur separatism as well as about the risks of conflict linked to the non-resolution of territorial borders with their Central Asian neighbors , however they were quick to realize the importance of the Central Asian region and adapted rapidly, created a policy framework to occupy the vacuum created by sudden demise of Soviet Union, and strengthened their relationship with CARs by either luring, offering or supporting through financial funding. In 2001 the Shanghai Cooperation Organization (SCO), out of the Shanghai Group, was created. This organization helped to ease long-standing tensions between the newly independent Central Asian Republics and Chinese worlds, to put in place cooperative mechanisms for former Soviet states to discover their Chinese neighbor. Chinese government moved to establish themself vigorously on the Central Asian market, mainly in hydrocarbons, extractive industries or mining, infrastructures, and communications, there by securing their long-term interests in energy as well as raw material supply chain to support their domestic manufacturing. With its vision on future since 2005 Beijing has been trying to establish ways to promote its language and culture and to train Central Asian elites according to the Chinese model, the opening of several Confucius Institutes in the CARs capitals (aimed to teach Mandarin language) is the "soft power" card that the Chinese government handily played. Despite China's initially negative overall image in Central Asia, the Middle Kingdom has succeeded in improving its reputation with soft-power diplomacy, and drastically changed the economic and strategic given on the Central Asian arena.[2] Today China is a force and a major stakeholder in Central Asia, it can be easily be stated that it is the second most influential external actor in the region, surpassing Russia in economic terms, but not strategic or cultural ones, where Russia still holds influence.

The invasion of Central Asian markets by Chinese goods that has seriously damaged national production and the growing number of Chinese farmers buying up Tajik land are strengthening the popular opposition to a feared "Chinese expansionism". Moreover, the wage gap between Chinese and Central Asian workers engaged in infrastructure-building represents another dangerous factor, which is fuelling local discontent and creating a potential threat to the political stability and security of the weaker states, namely Kyrgyzstan and Tajikistan[3]. China's growing presence and influence in Central Asia has raised controversies and is not limited to changing the international environment of the new states, or structuring their economic development. It also partially structures the domestic orders, social changes, and national narratives of the latter. Beijing has made it possible to act as a catalyst for indirect political debates on the choices made by governments[4], it fosters a reorganization of the social fabric by giving rise to new professional niches that present themselves as "go-betweens" between China and Central Asia; it is an object of academic knowledge, and of expertise, and has entered into the popular imaginary[5]. Exactly how China will intensify its presence in Central Asia is going to depend partly on the approaches and attitudes of the

Central Asian states themselves. The Central Asian states are at once desirous of the growing Chinese presence, wanting to take advantage of its economic dynamism and geo-strategic influence, but also fearful of its potential demographic and cultural clout.

China's position within the SCO also raises numerous questions, and opinions on this issue diverge accordingly. The majority of experts agree that the Organization's statutes make it impossible to curb Chinese expansion in the region and view the SCO as an instrument that directly serves Chinese interests and works to justify Beijing's activities in the region in the eyes of the international community. The expression, "China's soft hegemonism", was proposed by the KISI former expert, Murat Laumulin, especially through the geopolitical influence but also through the economic investments, in Central Asia seems realistic.[6] There is growing discomfort within the CARs with China, and many of them feel that with every passing year, the influence of China and its control over CAR nations would be much beyond Russia not only in economic or trade policies but also on political, social, cultural and religious fabric of these nations. They are trying to weigh out options where they can escape from two heavy weight grind stones i.e. China & Russia. The US & the EU though have strategic interest in the energy sector and is more concerned with foreign policy & security alignment, trade and economics as general has been out of their sight for various reasons. Iran, Turkey, Pakistan & India are eyeing a more robust role; however the possibility of India providing an alternative to Russia & China iron grip over CARs is most likely. However for that both India & the CAR nations have to look beyond the traditional, slow and irregular approach of engagement.

India and Central Asian Republics will have to take a leap of faith, if they wish to pursue a meaningful pursuit for strengthening & developing their trade relationships. What it requires is to look beyond the obvious challenges of not having a direct physical access connecting the two regions, and similarly other obvious challenges like other security and terrorism etc. Both India and Central Asian republics need a Quantum leap in their bond, association, their desire to find alternative and innovative solutions to the challenges. Being in constant trance of inaction and waiting for magic to happen is nothing short of miracle. The extent of accessibility between countries, whereby bilateral trade is a function of the distance between the countries and their joint income, it is not only the direct physical access that matters, though it is not to discount that it has a major role to play in any strong trade relationship, there are equally other important factors which are challenges and needs immediate attention. The inherited colonial heritage is still a major influencer and an important factor in determining India's direction of trade, till date we are obsessed by the Western world and the Americas or to say we trade more with developed nations rather than focusing on developing or less-developed countries.[7]. Only recently we have started focusing on our immediate neighborhood and on to our eastern side. Similarly there are many factors which can be magnet to trade for both nations, though currently these factors are either ignored or need to be relooked into for building a strong trade foundation. Indian strategy towards trade needs to be realigned and modified to help India gain any meaningful foothold in the Central Asian countries.

Following are few of the ideas; suggestions and recommendations which can help India improve its trade relationship with Central Asia and can stretch up to its potential. India has been late entrant in the "new Great Game" already laid out between China & Russia, and cannot afford to be a bystander and let them overwhelm itself to inaction or at best reaction. What is required at this of point is a disruptive, aggressive, focused and multipronged strategy by India, which is truly reflective of its intentions and its growing stature in global world.

1. AMENDMENT IN INDIAN TRADE STRATEGY TOWARDS CENTRAL ASIA

The most positive aspect of Indo-CA (Central Asian) is the goodwill present within the two sides. India shares a very good rapport and has always been welcomed and well supported by Central Asia nations. India has till date maintained neutrality and has chosen a path of dialogue for resolving any issue. The political contact and connect has been omni-present irrespective of any government change. Despite the best intentions at both sides the trade relationship has not progressed much, all efforts put in this direction has been awfully slow and held hostage to political compulsions. Whatever strategy India has to strengthen their trade relationship with Central Asia, it is not delivering the desired results. A paradigm shift is necessitated in India's approach to Central Asia. Fundamental changes will have to be introduced and a fresh, proactive and aggressive approach would need to be undertaken and practiced.

Paradigm Shift

(a) Economic interest to lead

One of the most important shifts that India needs to undertake is to allow economic engagement and partnership to lead other political engagement and security objectives. In absence of any deep economic foundation, the prospect of strategic partnership is diluted and staggered and it would be similar to riding a blind horse, where one is guaranteed to fall. Economics shall be the glue to security and foreign policy. The Central Asian nation is leaning towards China and Russia for this basic fundamental reason, otherwise it has so much to fear from both the nations. In near future unless these nations are unable to balance out their overdependence on China and Russia, they would slowly be consumed and that would be a far more serious consequence for India. India's reluctance to muddy the water is going to provide opportunity to many other nations to take the advantage away. Pakistan is one such nation, and with China as its all-weather friend, the possibility of it becoming a more reliable partner to Central Asian countries is much higher, especially when it is opening and welcoming China's Silk route and CPEC route which would also provide the Central Asian nations the access to sea routes.

Whereas till date India is unable to break away from sibling rivalry with Pakistan, India will have to delink the security aspect (not to suggest that it's not important) from its economic & trade objectives. If the trade objectives are critical and important, then the onus lies on the trade policy makers and the political class to find innovative solutions to overcome the obstacles and achieve the trade objectives. Out-dated defensiveness and in trade negotiations must give way to pragmatism and new resolve. The attitude of both the government and administration must change towards each other and deeper understanding and respect must evolve towards Geo-political, Economical & Security limitations. Ahead of the Chinese President hijacking the Silk Route initiative and using it for China's dominance and spread of China influence over Central Asia, the concept was ignited by the US by Hillary Clinton, and it had India's undeniable support and backing. With the US presence and engagement in Afghanistan, it had supported the Silk route which was different from the one Chinese have suggested and the US was banking upon India to take some lead over it. However that opportunity slipped due to political inaction and now the Chinese are trying to leverage it to their benefit both economically & strategically.

India will have to set the economic agenda along with the Central Asian nations and will have to create a blue print to achieve it. The myth of landlockedness and inaccessibility will have to be demystified, be it by engaging Iran, Afghanistan more proactively or finding an amicable solution with Pakistan. If Pakistan is not an alternative, then the entire focus must be shifted from imports to exports, shift from goods trade to services trade.

(b) Shift from Import orientation to exports or establishing offshore manufacturing base in CARs

Currently the focus of Indo-Central Asia trade relationship is on imports of hydrocarbon and other precious minerals from the Central Asia region, this focus needs to re-adjust to promoting exports from India. The simple argument is that for India to start importing oil and minerals from Central Asia needs a presence of easy accessible trade route, which unfortunately for last 22 years is still to happen and may take another 8 to 10 years to materialize going by the past experience. The stake holders have been in talks and have been committing, however little is changing on the ground and precious time is being lost. India can ill afford to wait that long to establish any reasonable trade relationship. The required shift is required for simple reason, that India can exports finished or semi-finished goods to the Central Asia by existing routes, however such goods would need to be identified as they shall be able to compete within the market on cost as well as quality. The policy will need to re-align with this objective and Government at each side shall find mechanism to reduce trade barriers for Indian goods to Central Asia. If the duties, customs, transactional costs etc. needs to be re-worked out, then immediate attention shall be paid to it.

Another alternative to the issue of inaccessibility of Indian Goods in Central Asia could be to promote Indian manufacturers to setup their base in Central Asia in Special Manufacturing Zones (SMZ), where in the product manufactured and supplied to Central Asian nations shall be tax free. The Central Asia nations have vast tract of lands which could be specifically committed to Indian manufacturing unit for setting up of these SMZ. These SMZ are in reality Mega Industrial Parks with complete infrastructure, the infrastructure could be provided by the Central Asia national government. India can undertake such agreement with any one nation or apply the approach to all five CARs. Even if India is able to setup its base in one of the nation, it will be able to spread its footprint all across Central Asia, Russia, West Asia and Europe. This could be the fastest means of achieving the Indian trade objective. Chinese exports are dominating the Central Asian region and it is slowly killing the industry there. The Indian and the Central Asian entrepreneurs shall be encouraged to form joint ventures and collaborate, so that the Indian manufacturing industry is able to establish it base in these nations. Not only helping and increasing the employment of local workforce in CARs, but would also help in bringing down the costs. This way India and Central Asia would mutually benefit. As setting up of the manufacturing base in Central Asia can help industry to be closer to raw material source as well as through it, the Indian entrepreneurs are able to expand their product reach deep in Russia, West Asia and Europe. Currently many of the product categories remain untouched by the Indian traders for Central Asia, specifically for perishable food items, or by manufacturers for food processing etc. The proximity of the Indian manufacturing units to the agricultural production base will help both Indian as well as the Central Asian nations to develop their agriculture based industry. The product consumption and product loyalty pattern in Central Asian nations is different from the western nations or from India. The pattern is to buy what is visible and easily identifiable; most of the purchases are walk-ins. The proximity of Indian manufacturing would help their products to be easily visible, available and build on some product loyalty. The component of walk-in purchase is also helpful as it helps company recover their costs fast and remain less at risk With Indians setting up their manufacturing they would be able to bring in desired technologies, it will also help the Central Asian nations to build further more industries, services around to support Indian manufacturing. It will also encourage local domestic growth as well betterment of basic services like retail, healthcare, education, recreation, banking and logistics. India would gain from extending its manufacturing footprint in central Asia as well as from development of support infrastructure and services that would grow in India as well as other friendly neighboring nations like Iran. Scalability and Capacity is a big enabler, if the Indian manufacturing Industry is able to prosper in Central Asia, automatically the physical transportation routes will start becoming shorter or more economically feasible.

Central Asian nations are rich in hydrocarbons & precious minerals, the Indian mining industry can undertake the similar approach as suggested for Indian manufacturing. Even though India may have less direct supply of the minerals mined, but it would be free to export them to other nations through Central Asian land routes and their rail networks.

(c) *Swing concentration from goods to services trade*

The biggest difference between service and produced goods is that while a produced or manufactured good can be stored for later consumption by its consumer, the service gets consumed while getting produced. It means that for a service to be consumed the consumer and the service provider must be in either close proximity or connected with telecommunications. Another distinct advantage is that for providing a service the necessary infrastructure can be easily planned and provided for, and the cost of the infrastructure is comparatively less in comparison to the large industrial setups required for production of goods. Its requirement of space is also considerably less and the business model is also more organized then the manufacturing or production. Servicing is much more dependent on human connect, hence the training, communication and necessary skill set becomes critical. For establishing an efficient system, trained personnel have to be in control of the system. India is already an established service export nation and is amongst the top 6 service provider nations. The advantage that India has is not only because of cost efficiency in terms of infrastructure costs and HR cost, but also the level of exposure, experience and innovation that already has happened in India. In the coming future, Indian service sector and its exports is going to be the key driver of Indian growth. Technology & Telecommunications have been a great leveler. Being less capital intensive, more skill & knowledge dependent and heavily in favor of human resource requirement, it provides India an edge in comparison to production and manufacturing sector. The Central Asia nations can take advantage from India's experience and there is vast scope of cooperation between India & Central Asian nations. The services sector is hugely diverse and caters to a wide set of skill and technology levels. Some of the sectors with potential for mutually beneficial bilateral trade in services include: Healthcare, Business and Professional services; Telecommunications services; Logistics & Transport Services; Financial Services; Energy-related services; Travel services; Tourism & Hospitality; Research and Development; Computer and related services; Academics, Entertainment, Recreation & Audiovisual Services, Environmental and agricultural services etc.

The demand for services is growing at a fast pace in Central Asia, and the current system has not been able to keep up with the growing demand gap. India can partner with CARs to bridge this gap at the same time enabling the service sector to grow and become the major driver of growth in these nations. There is urgency for India and Central Asia nations to firm up a policy framework for services. However the foundation of any policy framework is credible data and research. Lack of empirical research in the area of services export remains the biggest hurdle along with lack of reliable, timely and easily interpretable data. The data that is more widely available do not currently encompass all forms of trade in services. Moreover, there is a lack of distinction in data collection procedure between goods and services within each sub-sector such as telecommunications and IT. What is required is trade data on services at a more disaggregated level which is consistent with value-added and employment data and is comparable across time. Given the heterogeneity of services, formulation of separate indices shall be considered. Also, the services sub-sector definitions in India do not match with international definitions which make it difficult to do cross-country analysis. There is an urgent need to have clear definition of sub-sectors, based on international definitions like the UNCPC. Since services sector is heterogeneous it is important to identify the most important trade barriers faced by different services sub-sectors and then undertake sector-specific reforms.

The service trade between India and Central Asia nations is not so heavily dependent upon the physical accessibility to the land locked nations. Though there are challenges in service trade, but they can be more easily resolved. The first challenge is to provide easy movement for people providing services, for which the visa reforms become essential. The second challenge is to provide cost efficient and easy air connectivity, currently the air connectivity is very limited and India is yet to take any major initiative on it. Unless the air connectivity is not increased there are very less chances for India to gain on service exports to Central Asia. Third challenge is of HR practices, money remittances, social security, repatriation laws and their compliances; this can be easily resolved to mutual satisfaction, however this requires urgent attention. Fourth is of a secured, safe habitat and harassment free and non-discriminatory work space, which is a major concern for Indian entrepreneurs as well as professionals. Language is another challenge encountered by the Indians, for which the Indian government must contemplate and prepare so that Indians are able to respond to the challenge. There are multiple languages spoken & practiced in the Central Asia, however Russian is common language of communication in foreign trade. Language Programme can be introduced in School & Colleges, especially professional colleges.

Expansion of Indian Service exports in the Central Asia nations is solely possible if one is able to adapt to the local concerns and is able to customize their service in manner that it matches their expectations. . Digital communication platforms, Cloud computing & artificial intelligence, 3D printing and robotics are going to transform manufacturing and services and the Central Asia will not remain untouched by it. India can have a first mover advantage in the Central Asia digital & IT world, by setting & integrating itself in their system & culture. IT & Digital services are also influencing the way of governance, they are integral nowadays for smooth & transparent functioning of governments. They help anticipate, plan and respond through new Intelligent Integrated Service Grids, which look into transport, water, power, communications, security, government to citizen (G2C), government to government (G2G), and government to business (G2B) interaction and other essential services like sanitation, municipal solid waste management services for the city. India itself has faced these issues in the recent times, it has gone through the learning curve and it's a reality that India experienced first-hand that it is not necessary that the systems and the planning adopted by the west or more developed nations to resolve their challenges would get the desired result for a developing nation, where the challenges would be so vast and shift so slow. India itself being a developing nation would much better placed to understand the challenges of Central Asia nations and shall be able to partner with them for efficient solution.

(d) Private investment to lead

One of the major reasons for trade relationship not moving to potential is the absence of private investment by entrepreneurs at both sides. The current businesses are majorly government supported. Serious efforts have been lacking by individual exporters to research the Central Asian markets for their potential to Indian exports or imports. The potential is present for the big boys of the Indian manufacturing and service industry as well as the mid & small players. There are multiple reasons for the same, for which both Indian and the Central Asia nations will have to undertake reforms and action. To start with serious efforts will have to be made in by the governments in both sides to provide a certain level of assurance for level playing field to Indian traders, though in trading certain degree of risk is always present, however that risk currently seems too high and discouraging private investors to initiate. There is a perception that the Central Asia nations trade policy and regulations are complex, intricate, heavy-handed and under influence of political interference. At the macro level, the countries in general are characterized by a poor regulatory environment and standards regime. Many public sector decision-makers are unfamiliar with the realities of market economics, and are unaware of how rules, regulations and different policy decisions could affect the private sector. On their side, many businessmen have a strong aversion to what is seen as a heavy-handed government presence in the market and lack of practical implementation mechanisms, including public/private partnerships. It's critical to break this mold of negative perception. The encouragement to them could be through simplifying the Visa requirements and making their business travel hassle free, providing them incentives for their trade through schemes targeted to promote new traders, setting up of an Indian bank to facilitate and fasten the business transaction, providing clarity in documentation and standardizing it at all ends, encourage all customs related, export-import trade related transactions and documents on line and minimizing the human contact to avoid any foul play or delays. Increase air connectivity and promote tourism. Initiate small trade with help of allowing and promoting courier trade (or baggage trade i.e. that the air passenger is permitted to carry tradable goods to a certain maximum limit without hassles), so that small trade openings for various product categories can be initiated.

The big manufacturing units and business companies like Reliance, Tata, Escorts, Wipro, Infosys, Shapoorji, L&T, Britannia, Parle, Bharti, Godrej, Munjal (Hero), Biocon, TVS, Bajaj etc. shall be encouraged to setup their bases in Central Asia and the governments shall participate actively to bring confidence in them to venture into Central Asia. The opportunity lies in every Central Asia nation and in almost all categories. The Pharmaceutical industry exports seem to dominate the scene currently when it comes to the major products that flow from India to Central Asia. Since a market for Indian medicines and vaccines has been established, this market can be deepened further. Another product of India that appears to be popular in the Central Asian markets is frozen and processed meat. There is ample opportunity for processed food production in Central Asia as much of their economy is still Agri-based. The Central Asia nations can help by providing necessary basic infrastructure or allot land in specially demarcated zones, which shall be able to provide a greater degree of flexibility and freedom required to undertake and setup these industries. The Central Asian nations can also encourage Indian industrialists and business houses by providing them tax breaks, exemption from duties/ customs etc. for necessary infrastructure setup and getting in state of the art technology in Central Asia. The Indian Government can link in their support by grants or extending a line of credit or loans for promoting these business houses to set their offshore bases in Central Asia. This would not only encourage growth and employability in Central Asia, but can help Indian Industry to locate near raw source of material, especially Industries dependent on Hydrocarbons as well as huge power requirements as Central Asia is rich in minerals, oil and natural gas. The setting up of Indian manufacturing bases in Central Asia would also automatically push for Indian service sector to establish their bases in Central Asia especially construction, engineering & professional services, ITC, insurance, logistics, Travel & tourism etc.

All this is feasible only if the Central Asia nations bring in necessary reforms in their policies towards Indian manufacturing units, as well as ensure that the business interests of Indian companies are well safeguarded and provided with continuous government support & backing.

(e) Public investment for strategic collaboration and JVs

The mega projects in energy & power sector, minerals and oil exploration etc. are ideal for forging collaborations and joint ventures amongst the Government supported public entities like ONGC, SAIL, BHEL, BSNL, CIL etc. The initial push for trade would come from the public companies and then only the private investment is going to flow in. The Indian government and the Central Asia nations have shown the intent, however nothing substantial is visible on the ground to attract more business. It is important for the Central Asia nations to promote and provide ample opportunity to the Indian public companies. In the initial phase profits or revenue shall not be the sole guiding figure. If the Central Asia nations wish to balance out the domination and monopolies of China and Russia, then they will have to sweeten the deal and provide ample opportunity to the Indian Public companies. The objective has to be long-term and must be evaluated from the added benefits that the Central Asia nations may derive strategically and through other means. It is in the interest of Central Asian nations to open up their market for the Indian companies as the level of neutrality and fair play would be far more with India, then China or Russia, which try to dominate them. Special purpose Vehicles (SPV) can be formed, with active participation from government to ensure and safeguard the interest of both nations and to promote trade and development in Central Asia.

IT parks, Industrial parks, Transport infrastructure, Metro or monorail projects, Hydel power etc. are ideal for planning, designing, construction or operations to be undertaken under SPV initiatives setup especially for these purposes. It is well demonstrated that India has better understanding on cost minimization and value for every penny put in.

Country Specific Trade Strategy

One size fit all approach is not suitable and cannot be adopted. Instead of formulating a general trade policy for a region, it is advisable to formulate and have country specific trade strategies. Each of the nations in Central Asia has a different challenge, different opportunities and sovereign mindset. A country like Kazakhstan is far more integrated with foreign trade and is involved in multiple multilateral treaties with Russia and China and those treaties influence its trade relationship with India and ease of conducting business with India. At the same time the challenges of Kyrgyzstan and Turkmenistan are much different than Kazakhstan. The degree of political interference and heavy handiness in trade is also varying and they need different approach.

It would be in the interest of India to constitute a separate team of experts, chosen from the stake holders as well as the best talent available to formulate and lead the trade strategy for each of the specific nation. There could be a Trade Governing Body (TGB) to overview the progress as well keep a birds eye perspective on Trade growth and objectives met for each of the nation as well for the Central region. The team and the TGB shall be full time body functioning and working towards common goal every single day of their employment and not get into the habits of committees and sub committees which will be meeting once or twice in a year. There cannot be a more telling indifference in India's approach viz a viz with China, that today India's trade with Central Asia is merely 1 percent of China's trade with them. There has to be a radical change in India's approach towards trade with Central Asia. The conventional way of forming committees and assigning them the task to suggest and recommend policies within a short duration of time, period, and merely passing on their suggestions and demands to the Government, is not going to increase Indian Exports in Central Asia nations. Similarly just by providing further financial incentives to push trade is also not going to get desired results and is unsustainable in the long run. Aggressive trade and investment promotions and growth plan needs a far more determined, professional and hands on approach for day to day dealing and decision making with Central Asia nations & Indian administration. The Government must seriously consider rejigging the existing organisation structure looking after the Indian trade and exports and forming country specific teams and TGB. This body shall be well structured, with defined organisation chart and goals, a clear captain (who is accountable for the win or loss of team) and officials with expertise in international trade law, international trade marketing, international commercial and trade practices, expert negotiators, research scholars and data analytics. The team can be formed from identifying brilliant talent from various Government & Exporters trade associations for next five to ten years to ensure continuity and accountability. This body shall be un-biased, full time non-political, and must be aligned with stiff targets to be achieved. This country specific team shall have professionals well versed with Indian Manufacturing & Trade scenario as well up-to-date with Central Asia trade scenario and its challenges. They shall be the co-ordinating agency for various trade exports promotion bodies and must help strategies, provide direction and resolve issues related to them. They spearhead at ground level the tasks of trade negotiations with Central Asia Republic's administration, remove trade barriers for Indian exports, challenge legally on unfair practices, and create roadmap for promotion of Indian products & services in these nations.

2. MAPPING THE OPPORTUNITIES

Central Asia Market Mapping, Analysis and creation of data bank for, raw produce, consumer & capital goods and for services export is critical for the Indian exporter. The updated information on same shall be available on line to Indian exporters. The information shall be collated in manner that it's easy to cross reference and is actionable. It should be a precise ready reckoner with customised services to exporters for their queries and support required specific to Central Asia. Indian exporters have to struggle, when it comes to trade data and the analysis of it. As the existing trade between India and Central Asia is not substantial, the genuine effort to research, collect data and its analysis is based on secondary data and is not very encouraging. The data currently provided on various Indian sites in respect to Central Asia is either all together missing or at sharp contrast with each other and cannot be reliably depended upon. Much of this data is years old, collected 3-4 years back, where as in current situation the trade scenario can change every season in major trading nations like the US, EU, Japan etc. and annually for regions like Central Asia and Africa.

In previous chapters, the potential sectors and product categories have been suggested as the stepping stones to the Central Asia markets.

Individual sectors and opportunities have been listed nation wise in Chapter 4 for Kazakhstan, Chapter 5 for Kyrgyzstan, Chapter 6 for Tajikistan, Chapter 7 for Turkmenistan and Chapter 8 for Uzbekistan. Never the less there are other opportunities that lie within these nations for exporters and manufacturers at all levels and across sectors, opportunities that may appeal to the large manufacturing and business houses and opportunities that might be of interest to MSME players. These opportunities may be missed as there is no data available to infer on them. For the same the mapping shall be undertaken by the Indian Government separately for the Goods and Services, nation wise, city wise, sector wise, and product-wise.

This requires a serious planning from Indian Administration if they intend to capture some considerable market share in Central Asia. They will have to map each of the major cities for that respective nation and identify the exports opportunity for Indian traders; they will have to work their strategy around on focus city and focused export sectors. One of the ways to categorize cities would be to group them as:

- Hot spots in a nation, these could be the 1-2 cities where Indian exports may be available and have gained a certain visibility. The chances of pushing exports in these cities would be considerable high as there is already a certain level of acceptance in the market. The approach should be to build strongly on Indian product visibility, aggressive marketing as well as celebrity (local, Indian and Russian) endorsements. These cities shall act as fresh launch pads for new Indian opportunities.
- Warm Spots, these could be the next 2-5 cities where India would need to concentrate really hard as they offer the potential and increase in Indian products in these cities. These shall be developed as landing pads; it means the emphasis would have to increase Indian companies and product visibility & presence in these cities. They would require special attention by the Indian government and Indian mission in that respective CAR.
- Cold Spots, these would be the balance of cities, where India has no presence though potential may be there. These will require special scouting efforts from Indian government and traders. They may not be critical to immediate push in trade, but they will play a strong role in long term.

Sector-wise

Each of the nation and city needs to be mapped sector wise to identify, which are the sectors, where in the imports is required, what is the gap between demand and supply in those sectors, which country is dominant in each of the sector in each of the city, and finally India shall list down the sectors or sector in which it can fulfill the gap or edge out competition. Such data bank would need to be created and analytical study would have to be undertaken. Once the actual potential for Indian exporters is gauged by minutely understanding the Central Asian nation's requirement, then the Indian government shall craft its policy accordingly and engage with CARs administration to forge a meaningful trade relationship.

The top 5 sectors where India shall be able to penetrate and wishes to be substantial player across all the Central Asian nations can be categorized as Platinum sectors, the next 10 sectors as the Gold and the next 10 sectors as Silver. India's focus shall be on the service sector as the chances of it achieving success is very high. India must firstly pick the low hanging fruits, though they may not be very profitable. The motivation to export in the top 5 sectors shall be enhanced through tax breaks, incentivizing or providing some other advantage or an edge.

The Indian Government and Indian exporters will have to clearly understand the quality, price and service benchmark. The same is true with environmental & phyto-sanitary restrictions and compliances. Unless Indian products don't excel in the above, there is little chance that they will be able to garner any market share. Currently the Central Asia markets are gutted with Chinese products and few of the sectors are dominated by the Russian and EU manufacturers. There is wide gap available between the low quality but low priced Chinese products and high quality and high priced European products, India have to find the right position for itself after the thorough study. These studies can't be expected to be undertaken by the exporters directly (though they do undertake their own market research before investing); the Indian Government must sponsor such studies and identification of sectors where India can excel. It's possible to dominate a sector, for example Chinese have been able to capture consumer goods and consumer electronics market in Central Asia. So much so, that even the Russian goods, or products produced in locally are not able to match their price point. The Chinese have deeply invested in same and have studied it well. The idea is to carefully analyze the requirements of the sector and match it, unless such gap analysis are undertaken and efforts made through creating proper infrastructure and human resources for same, increasing Indian exports is a tough task. Such gap analysis can't be undertaken by exporters, the Indian government and various Indian export trade bodies will have to invest into such initiatives.

Service export sectors like Tourism & Travel, Engineering & Architectural services, Medical & wellness tourism, Data analytics, Entertainment & Recreation content design & creation, Animation & FX etc. can be few of the sectors where India may be able to establish themselves and attain a competitive advantage. India ranks sixth place currently amongst the top ten exporters of service in the world. Technology, innovation, creativity and speed of delivery are rapidly redefining services, digitization and internet has helped in collapsing distances and help Indian exporters provide solutions and services to their clients in the remotest parts of the world. What is critical is that stakeholders, investors and policy-makers are up-to-date with the current statistics in the Indian services landscape to be best equipped thereafter in strategizing for the future and tapping the Central Asia market.

Product-wise

Each of the sectors has some hero products, which constitute majority of share in a sector imports. These products have to be identified and evaluated against similar Indian products or product category. The gaps in quality, pricing, compliances, packing etc. would have to be minutely analyzed. The benchmarking would have to be undertaken.

All the data collected and analyzed scientifically would open new frontiers for Indian exporters. Sectors and products where India has potential get missed in absence of proper data base to support it. Data is the foundation of strategy, of marketing, for R&D and to understand the gaps. Data gives birth to innovation, and it unveils new strengths which could have been hidden till now. Data is the proof that one needs to quantify a success or a failure. Data analytics and its simplification for Indian manufacturer and exporters is an important task that Indian Government and Indian trade bodies will have to undertake. They will have to backup exporters, make it easier for Indian manufacturers to identify niches for their products in Central Asia markets, across nations.

3. NEW LOGISTIC ROUTE

China is selling a dream to the world in the form of One Belt One Road (OBOR) initiative or Belt & Road initiative or simply put the New Silk route. It is a reality that currently many of the nations are not convinced and are opposing it altogether, many have the reservations about its route details, project transparency, its economic viability as well as the tendering processes, many have taken objection to it from environmental aspect and many see to it as the ambition of China to spread its dragon wings across the world. Still there are a large number of nations who are lapping up to that dream, and they are all together bound by common characteristics of being either under-developed or developing nations, facing resource and infrastructure scarcity, and China is offering them incentives to join him in the dream. The same is true for the Central Asia Republics too. Being landlocked and short on infrastructure to support their trade and economic growth, short on funds, they are welcoming China openheartedly to undertake the Silk Route through Central Asia. The Central Asia nations, view it as an access route to EU markets, an access route to sea ports. They believe that this initiative will help, local manufacturing industry, setting new services industry and push economic growth domestically as well as help in increasing their export to the world. There is no denying that China has committed huge funds for the project and is very actively trying to push it, the task is also bit easier with China sharing physical boundary with Central Asia. Yet the other side of this initiative is that the project is driven from China's own need to get more market access for its manufacturing units, its own need to secure raw material as well as driven from objective of energy security. With the last economic slowdown, China realized that their existing exports and development model is not sustainable for long, as there are huge manufacturing capacities lying unutilized, adversely impacting its own domestic growth & development. It realized that its existing export market has saturated and that it is facing stiff resistance from other nations for its violation of trade spirit. China has slowly but steadily destroyed the manufacturing capacities of the nations where it has exported be it the US or the Central Asia. China's sole objective is self-interest which it is cloaking very beautifully and presenting to the world.

India alternative routes to the Central Asia had been discussed already in Chapter 3, Titled Transportation Routes and the possibility of their being operational before the operations of the Silk Route is very high. However the role and potential of already discussed routes is limited and needs to be expanded. Also the Proposed connectivity projects have largely remained on paper and any progress has been at a snail's pace, which needs to be completed at urgent pace.

The southern peninsula of India protrudes into the Indian Ocean, which helps India to establish close contact with West Asia, Africa, and Europe from the western coast and with Southeast and East Asia from the eastern coast. India shares a good relationship with all nations except for Pakistan & China, though with the later India has substantial trade relationship. India has an advantage of connecting world to a much larger extent then China, if we integrate land and maritime routes. India can provide the shortest possible route to the South East Asia and South Asia. India can be the gateway to Central Asia nations to expand their exports especially in energy and minerals, along with providing access to Indian and other South-East & South Asian markets for the goods manufactured and exported from Central Asia. Russia, EU, West-Asia all can gain access to these markets through India. India is already working with SARC countries for establishing a road network.

As a part of its "Connect Central Asia" policy, India plans to operate up to 14 direct flights to Dushanbe. To begin with, both India and Tajikistan will launch four flights each. The announcement was made prior to the Indian Prime Minister in his 2016 visit to Tajikistan, and till date awaiting action. India needs to be consistent and match its intent; the said airline connectivity is in reality waiting from 2007 and much before that. If it's going to take 10 years for Air connectivity then possibility of other land transport corridor is absolutely rare. Air connectivity will not only help boost tourism, but also provide accessibility to the Indian Service sector, especially tourism, hospitality, healthcare, engineering & professional services, ITC etc. , but will also help in setting up Cargo Terminal through which India and Central Asia countries can undertake trade in perishable goods, expensive machinery & capital goods, etc.

Logistics encompasses Transportation and is much more than just transporting goods. Logistic includes all the processes that get involved from sourcing of raw material and its delivery to the factory floor, for a finished good to be delivered at the doorstep of the consumer or client. The economic structure of Central Asia is one of low density and long distances. The combined population of the Central Asia countries is approximately 63 million, spread unequally over a relatively large geographical area, including large deserts and high mountainous, with limited connectivity. The development of the region as well as the future trade growth will be dependent on the logistical network. India historically has evolved out of this similar situation, where majority of its population resided in the rural portions with no connectivity or logistical support. Yet Indian distribution system is one of the efficient ones and its efficiency has further improved many notches with easy availability of internet & telecommunications. Mobile connectivity and smart phones have revolutionised the way of commerce and logistics in India. Central Asia can gain from India's experience and improve its logistical infrastructure with its help.

The proportion of logistics expenditure in the final cost is generally around 5–10 percent of the actual production cost of the product depending upon distance and ease of accessibility. However in the case of land locked nations with large distance from the oceanic route, the cost of logistics could go as high as 50–70 percent of the actual production cost of the product. Logistics can be a big differentiator especially for Central Asia Region, which not only is vast land locked region but is also tough with hilly terrain, deserts and few water bodies. The logistical solution for country like Uzbekistan, which is doubly land-locked, is far more critical. India's focus should be on establishing the Logistics infrastructure in the Central Asia Republics. Warehousing chains, Cold storage chains, distribution networks, courier services, movers and packers, transportation fleets, inland container depots or dry ports etc. are few of the opportunities and services where Indians can excel and it will help in controlling and reducing the costs for Indian shipments etc. Many of the successful startups that have been implemented in India can be easily extended to Central Asia.

4. BUSINESS FOLLOWS TOURISM

Ever since the humans moved out of their habitat, there had been two reasons one was food (business) and another was his desire to see more, know more (tourism). Explorers would venture out to search new worlds and once they saw the opportunity they ventured out to do business and trade with them. Business follows tourism, India and Central Asia must aggressively pursue and encourage Tourism as it encourages people to people contact, brings better understanding of the culture, believes and social norms. It builds a positive goodwill among people from two nations. Many of these tourists would be businessmen, manufacturers, traders, professionals, entrepreneurs and service providers and they will come in close contact with their counterpart in the other nations and hence increasing curiosity and once convinced about it will finally establish trade or business relationship.

Both India as well as Central Asian Republics has excellent tourism potential. Globally Tourism and Hospitality industry has emerged as one of the key drivers of growth among the services sectors. Tourism is an employment generator and a significant source of foreign exchange for the country, apart from being an economic activity that helps local communities. In tourism, service trade transpires when foreign tourists visit a country and utilise services provided by partakers in the sector. Tourism is one of the top generators of foreign exchange and its performance influences directly other sectors such as hospitality, food and beverage, retail and recreational services. Both India as well as CARs needs to generate more employment, and this sector can help achieve twin benefit. Indian service providers can collaborate and help setup new hotels, resorts and other such hospitality services, which may appeal to Indian traveller. Indians have the tendency to be fussy about their food especially if they are vegetarians, Indian hospitality entrepreneurs have deep understanding of them, and they can establish Indian fine dining and other such facilities. Language barrier can be brought down by trained interpreter, which will also help further in establishing agents for business dealings. Ticketing, local transportation, operations and maintenance of the hotels, event management, recreational events, performing arts & cultural shows that can help bring the two societies together and bond, finally leading to trade.

For tourism to be encouraged between India and Central Asia, the facilitation centres shall be setup in all the nations to issue Travel Visas or Visa on arrival, i.e. e-visa or on-line visa. Currently Tajikistan is the only Central Asian nation, which is extending the facility of Visa on arrival for Indians. India has already extended the Visa on arrival facility to 180 countries of the world, and India must also take the first step to extend the facility to all Central Asian Republics for their citizens travelling to India. Air-conectivity between major cities in India and the capitals of the five CARs must be improved and established for promoting easy accessibility of these cities to the Indian tourists.

Promote Indian and CARs destinations in popular soap operas, reality shows, events and other soap programmes in Central Asia countries and in India. The reality shows as an entertainment medium is already well established, such shows can be planned in tourist locales as well the mixing of the contestants to generate interest and awareness about tourist destinations in the CARs and in India. Participation in international events: Events and exhibitions are an effective platform to promote tourism services (offered by firms) in each other country. Events held by the government (in various countries) and trade bodies could be leveraged. Extensive marketing and promotional campaigns across all key markets through all media platforms including the use of a professional public relations agency, to connect stakeholders and educate the market. Customised and targeted campaigns can be created to reach niche tourists through social media, radio and outdoor mediums.

Healthcare, Wellness and Medical Tourism

Healthcare is not only crucial from the perspective of providing good health to the citizens, but is one of the key parameter which drives the economic & social growth of the country. A healthy society ensures high productivity, longer and healthy life, a happier, literate and socially secure country. It stimulates consumption and production. In India, healthcare sector is the fifth largest employer among all the sectors, with medical education sector being one of the largest in the world. Indian doctors, their knowledge and skills are well recognised worldwide. The alternate medicine practices like Ayurveda, Siddha, Unani, and Naturopathy & Homoeopathy are also strong in India. The awareness level as well as service levels in the healthcare ecosystem as seen tremendous positive change and is witnessing emergence of new service delivery models through use of innovative technologies and telecommunication systems. The focus of the people has shifted from providing cure for ailments to maintaining an overall wellness/ fitness level. The Internet of Things (IoT) has helped integrating technology, gadgets and wearable detectors to collect health data of the person/ patient and communicate with physicians in real time. There is clear visible shift from the old traditional way to a new innovative approach. It has opened new access to diagnosis, transformed patient-physician relationship. It has helped create new business models for delivery of healthcare. Old traditional business models and operating processes may no longer deliver the expected services to the rising demands of patients.

The consumption of healthcare services is growing globally, evolving with new trends, such as medical tourism and e-health. New pattern has developed with patients from developed nations like the US travelling for health services to developing nations like India, owing to the low costs, easy information availability on the internet and relatively smaller waiting periods. Many countries are also providing healthcare services through the telemedicine mode to countries in need of the same. Emerging markets, such as India, Thailand and Malaysia, are driving the supply side of cross border healthcare services.[8]

India has emerged as a hub for medical tourism with quality healthcare services at an affordable price. Over the last decade India has seen a quantum jump in people coming to India from Iran, Iraq, and Afghanistan, West Asian countries, Africa, EU, US and other developed nations for medical services. To them India offers an attractive value proposition with multispecialty private healthcare services is being provided to them at a fraction of the costs in comparison to their home countries, without or a lower waiting times in hospitals for admission & treatment in comparison to their own nation. India's cost arbitrage gives it an advantage over other countries offering similar services, such as Dubai, Singapore and Malaysia, and save about 30 to 70 percent of their costs by getting services in India. The presence of highly qualified and worldwide recognised doctors, nurses and other healthcare staff make Indian healthcare services attractive to them. India has attained leadership position in complex medical procedures & skills in advanced healthcare in cardiovascular, eye, neurological, and organ transplants procedures with a high success rate.

Telemedicine, offshoring transcriptions, diagnosis consultations are few of the other services where India excels, its digital innovations and technology are revolutionising the entire healthcare sector. The role of technology and telecommunication is being incorporated in every aspect of the healthcare delivery value chain. The global healthcare market recognises India as amongst the leading hubs in Asian countries for offshoring transcription services owing to its infrastructure, availability of skilled manpower and a favorable economic environment. The healthcare system in Central Asia nations has limitations in serious ailments and are lacking in comfort and in technology when compared with Global standards. These services are much cheaper in India and popular among medical tourists from across the world. Air ambulances are required and can be an excellent business opportunity and a bridge between India and the CARs healthcare system as well as promote more medical tourism in India.

5. OVERCOMING TRADE BARRIERS

Nearly three decades after independence, significant barriers to international trade continue to afflict the Central Asian region. The leaders of the Central Asian countries have adopted diverse economic strategies which have led to divergence in trade policies, ranging from quite liberal (Kyrgyzstan) to relatively restrictive (Uzbekistan). This can be seen as one obstacle to harmonization of regional trade and cooperation. One of the key reasons for cold response by the Indian traders and manufacturers is complexity of in transactional documentation for trade and their facing significant trade barriers, particularly for oceanic trade, which makes Central Asia one of the world's most expensive, time consuming, and bureaucratically encumbered regions with which to trade.

Central Asia is clearly at a disadvantage with respect to oceanic trade, being landlocked within the world's largest landmass. Surface transport & Rail transport is the mode of choice for extra regional trade. For India due, the transport & rail connectivity is not an available choice as Pakistan & China cutoff India's route to Central Asia, hence only possible solution is through Iran, which involves Oceanic transport for Indian exports. Hence geography as well as governmental actions (policy) would seem to impact the cost, time and documents required for import and export. Being landlocked and distant from ports, it increases the time for import and export, and increase transport costs. Crossing an additional international boundary (Iran / Afghanistan) would also add another layer of required documents. Tariffs and other taxes increase cost, and additional required documents raise bureaucratic obstacles as well as add time and perhaps the cost.

With both geography and policy impacting the Indo- CARs Trading, as well as presenting significant barriers to international trade, it would seem advantageous for CARs to attempt to ameliorate some of these barriers. With geographical barriers largely intransient, the trade policy arena offers particular opportunities for improvement (relaxing trade barriers) by reduction in the number of documents required to import and export as well bringing down the tariffs. Lowering the number of documents required to import and export, across the region, would yield shorter import and export times, as well as possibly lessening the cost of international trade. Fewer documents would also decrease the opportunity for corruption and other non-transparent uncertainties, improving the overall regional performance and efficiency in the import and export of goods.

Awareness level and sensitivity towards phyto-sanitary, environment and other International standards occupational safety & health is still low. Slowly but steadily the region is waking up to them as more and more its coming in close contact with other world, especially with the EU, where the sensitivity towards these issues is quite high and requires very strict compliance. While we must push aggressively our traditional goods into the Central Asian market, there is no denying of the fact that in due course, a jungle of technical standards, environmental, veterinary and sanitary regulations would evolve in these markets also which would need to be complied with if we are looking into these markets in terms of future projections. The major non-tariff barriers against India in the developed markets like in terms of import policy; standards, testing, labeling and certifications; export subsidies; disadvantages due to regional trading blocs/preferential trading arrangements; child labour; new policy instruments and anti-dumping measures will slowly but surely affect these markets also and we must tune ourselves for an enlarged Eurasian market which includes Central Asia as well.

In order to raise our industry to internationally, established quality standards, including the ISO 9000 and ISO 14000 series of quality standards, need to be met with. To compete with the Western and other multinationals in the Central Asian markets, it is time to further strengthen the newly established Quality Council of India.

Central Asian countries have adopted diverse custom regulations, with their divergent trade policies and different trade tariffs within the same region, ranging from quite liberal (Kyrgyzstan) to relatively restrictive (Uzbekistan). While tariffs are not particularly restrictive by global standards, tariff structures are complex and changes are not transparent or predictable and non-tariff measures are extensive and pervasive. The EAEU attempted to have some level of harmonization, however not all the Republics our part of it. It would be in the interest of international trade if the Central Asian Republics could expedite the adoption of appropriate customs laws and give wide publicity to their liberal customs regime. Their signing some of the international conventions on customs will also generate reassurance and promote international trade. Kyrgyz Republic and Tajikistan became WTO members in 1998 and 2013 respectively and Kazakhstan is close to the accession, it would be in the regions interest if balance two can join the WTO. WTO membership is a significant instrument to strengthen and accelerate structural reforms at the domestic level and go beyond simple trade liberalization, helping the

Central Asian Countries to move to a more open and market oriented model of economic development. It signals a readiness for reforms and commitment to globalization. It enables countries to adhere to multilateral rules, thus raising confidence among investors.

As the tariff structure of the Iran route presently includes mostly the cost of return of empty containers from destination to the port of Bandar Abbas, it is necessary to provide for return consignments in order to bring down the costs. Some Indian traders are already importing containerisable goods from Central Asia.

6. DISMANTLING LANGUAGE BARRIER

Central Asia, as similar to India is cauldron of many languages. Each of the Republic have their own official language, Kazakh is the official language in Kazakhstan, Kyrgyz is the language of Kyrgyzstan, Tajik is the official language in Tajikistan, Turkmen is the language of Turkmenistan and Uzbek is the official language of Uzbekistan. Apart from the official languages there are numerous dialects and other minority languages spoken in these countries. Russian language is the common bond amongst these nations and is the de facto lingua franca throughout these former Soviet Central Asian Republics. Russian is spoken by 95 percent of population in Kazakhstan, it has the equal status to Kyrgyz language in Kyrgyzstan, it is widely spoken and well understood in Tajikistan, and around 12 percent to 14 percent of population speaks and understand in Turkmenistan & Uzbekistan. Russia has the designated status as the "Language of inter-ethnic communication".

English as language is still limited to very few, though attempt is being put in to study the language. English, the language which was an advantage for the Indians has no relevance and unfortunately the emphasis on other international languages such as Russian is not so prevalent within India. Hence the communication barrier becomes one of the main obstacles in the Trade communication. The English language played a very important role in spread and acceptability of the Indian service exports. India needs to take some corrective policy decision towards Russian and other foreign languages, so that the Indian Industry has the capability to make inroads into other nation service sectors.

India must encourage Indian Engineering, Technical, Medical & other professional colleges to undertake extensive student exchange programmes with Russia, Central Asia and other nations. Not only the same would provide international exposure to the students but will also accustom them with their culture, working and professional ethics, improve and enhance their communication skills and make the confident about overcoming any kind of foreign challenge.

Communication skills in Russian Language can be taught through short term courses, or as a secondary subject in the school or college curriculum. Professional trainers shall be hired to impart Russian language skills. Translators, especially well versed with business communication, technical idioms and legal communication & writing in Russian language would be required. India had a long relationship with Russia, and still many of the Indian imports happen from Russia both for Goods & Services. The experience of dealing with Russian in Russian must be shared across all the major metropolitan city colleges and premier institutes like IIT etc.

India and Central Asian Republics can partner in language training in each other nations for which various schools of language of Indian Universities can be considered as channel partners. India and CARs member states could look at intensifying educational linkages, in the English and Russian languages especially in scientific, technical and higher education through use of IT enabled services such as e-education.

7. FINANCIAL INSTITUTIONAL INFRASTRUCTURE AND AID

Market-oriented diversification requires a supportive macro- and microeconomic environment, which at present is not at its optimum level in Central Asia Region. Kazakhstan & Kyrgyzstan are somewhat still ahead than Uzbekistan and Turkmenistan.

The Central Asian economy is dependent on exports of its natural resources and the development of the SME sector is extremely slow, in absence financial institutions that can help them with finance. Banking, Financing, Micro Financing, Insurance sector all need serious push and there is ample opportunity available in the Central Asia Region. However for that the Central Asian nations would have to introduce large scale reforms and open up their economy. The CARs being natural resource rich nations can only milk them to a certain limit, unless the other sectors like services, manufacturing, agriculture don't start contributing high share to GDP, they will fail in the long run. Access to finance is one of the key constraints on the creation and growth of SMEs in the Central Asian region. The SME segment also faces structural problems due to state control in the economy at large, and in some cases large cash based shadow economy which is unable to meet the collateral and credit conditions of potential lenders. Moreover, throughout the region there are widespread problems in the business environment and regulatory constraints, some of which were further aggravated by the response to the global financial crisis.

In the last two decades, China has actively increased its presence in Central Asia through investments in energy and infrastructure. China has been actively investing in oil and gas pipelines, roads and railways, and accompanying infrastructure. Both China and Russia – provide financial and development aid to the CARs as it largely serves their own national and geopolitical interests. The major part of which is provided by state-controlled corporations or companies those are close to their respective governments. Both have taken advantage of the situation and tried to unduly influence and manipulate the CARs economic growth. As both the nations are more keen on exports of Hydrocarbon and precious minerals and other natural resources from the CARs, they have very little interest in the development of the SMEs or other sectors.

Given Kazakhstan's and Kyrgyzstan's membership of the Eurasian Economic Union, the EU cannot offer them negotiations on free trade agreements, as it has done with Georgia, Moldova and Ukraine. The same limitation in terms of opportunities for free trade arrangements with the EU applies to Turkmenistan and Uzbekistan, which are not WTO members and have not completed basic market reforms. Thus, the potential EU toolkit of policies that could support economic and political transition in Central Asia is limited. The IMF, World Bank, various UN agencies and the Asian Development Bank, have provided major financial and technical support to modernisation in Central Asia, particularly in terms of eradicating poverty and infrastructure investment. This has included IMF, World Bank and Asian Development Bank lending on concessionary terms to Kyrgyzstan and Tajikistan. Turkmenistan's and Uzbekistan's relationships with the IMF and World Bank are less developed because of their non-market economic systems and information closeness.

India being far more neutral and having larger goal then just pure economics and committed towards the cultural and social upliftment of the Central Asian nations, can fill in the gap and must provide financial aid to the them. The existing level of aid is not at all relevant when compared with investments pumped in by China & Russia. For any meaningful foothold, India will have to extend a much larger Line of Credit to the Central Asia nations. India can link it with aid for development of

Tourism, Logistic infrastructure development or for setting up Institutes and Healthcare projects. India has good expertise in IT & Telecommunication, and it can link in its aid with development and interconnecting of the region through internet.

The banking infrastructure and financial institutions are either missing or at very rudimentary level. India can help by collaborating with the CARs to setup an effective banking system. India has evolved through some of the hiccups that the CARs are facing, and today they are one of the safest banks with well streamlined processes as well as policies. CARs can benefit out of India's experience. These financial institutions can help in formulating and rolling out financing schemes for SMEs, providing insurances as well as loans to general citizens of the CARs. Establishing Indian bank in CARs will also help Indian trade grow.

8. MARKETING AND PROMOTIONS

Various export & trade promotion bodies (councils) have been setup by the Indian government to market and promote Indian products and services. These bodies are quite active and have been trying to get Indian exporters more exposure and encouraging them to be more aggressive in capturing more market share. There have been some rewards to these efforts being put in and Indian exports have been growing worldwide. Nevertheless the results are far from the expectations in the Central Asia region and the growth pace has been much slower than anticipated. This means that government and export promotion councils must have a relook in their approach and modify. Unless the export rate does not grow in leaps and bounds, India's trade with CARs is going to be dismally low

Following are few of the recommendations

- Outdoor medium is a very cost efficient medium, and has the flexibility of being customized to local requirements. Such mediums shall be used to market Indian goods and create awareness, reassure about quality and service.
- Radio is another medium, which has the flexibility of size and customisation to target selected audience. Sponsorship, new radio programmes on awareness about India, and its products shall be aired. Build positive perception about India and Indian products & services. International & Russian Celebrity, local celebrity endorsements as well engaging Indian celebrities to promote India and Indian goods.

- Establishing chain of experiential centres for encouraging locals to try out and experiment with Indian products, cuisines, handicrafts, consumer goods etc. These centres can double up as market research as well as distribution points. The trade bodies can invest in these chains along with local investors keen to partner them.
- Hold India centric events, fairs, trade meets etc. and engage with all stake holders (community to community engagement), entertainment, cultural programmes, exhibitions and DIY (do it yourself) camps etc. Showcase India's achievements, contributions and their commitment to local community. This is required to offset any negative backlash, and to win their hearts.
- Hold more training meets, buyer seller meets etc. in India as well as in CARs to encourage domestic manufacturers and service providers to venture out in CARs markets.

REFERENCES

1. Discussing China: Sinophilia and sinophobia in Central Asia; http://www.sciencedirect.com/science/article/pii/S1879366515000251#
2. Luba v. Hauff, "A Stabilizing Neighbor? The Impact of China's Engagement in Central Asia on Regional Security," DGAPanalyse, no. 3, April 2013. Aleksandra Jarosiewicz, Krzysztof Strachota, "China vs. Central Asia. The achievements of the past two decades," OSW Studies, No. 45
3. The Rise of China in Central Asia; http://www.limesonline.com/en/the-rise-of-china-in-central-asia
4. https://zn.ua/international/drakon-na-kryshe-mira-_.html
5. Discussing China: Sinophilia and sinophobia in Central Asia; http://www.sciencedirect.com/science/article/pii/S1879366515000251#
6. Murat T. Laumulin, "Na grani blefa i real'nosti", Analytica, June 13, 2006, http://www.analitika.org/article.php?story=20060613225246616
7. http://www.ejbe.org/EJBE2012Vol05No09p021SUVANKULOV-GUC.pdf
8. "Medical Tourism: Treatments, Markets and Health System Implications: A scoping review", Neil Lunt, Richard Smith, Mark Exworthy, Stephen T. Green, Daniel Horsfall and Russell Mannion, Directorate for Employment, Labour and Social Affairs, Page 9, accessed 032916;

10

Conclusion

Going through the foregoing chapters, one can see that despite its geographical proximity and economic potential as well as increasing strategic interest, India seriously lags behind other regional actors in Central Asia. China, in particular, is the key regional actor that for a long time now has been posing serious challenges to India's outreach in Central Asia. It has already developed exceptionally good political and economic relations with virtually all of India's neighbours, thereby strategically encircling India. In Central Asia too, China has made deep inroads in terms of investments. This is so because in comparison to India China has geo-economic advantage in Central Asia due to sharing a long border of more than 1500 kms with Kazakhstan, more than 850 kms with Kyrgyzstan and more than 400 kms with Tajikistan. Turkmenistan and Uzbekistan are also easily accessible through the land route. China's primary thrust has been to make use of Central Asia's huge mineral resources for its economic own development as well as to provide the much desirable consumer goods to Central Asia in addition to protecting itself against the menace of the three evils: separatism, extremism and terrorism from its Uighur minority operating from the Central Asian territories. Moreover, China has sought to build connectivity with the Central Asian Republics (CARs) through networks of rail, road, oil and gas pipelines. It was in this context that in 2012 India launched its "Connect Central Asia" Policy, which is a broad-based approach covering political, security, economic, and cultural connectivity. The primary goal behind the "Connect Central Asia" policy was, as the name suggests, re-connecting with the region which has a long shared history with India. Such a policy was formulated keeping in mind both the geostrategic compulsions as well as energy concerns that highlight geo-economic importance of Central Asia.

No wonder then that India's ongoing engagement with Central Asia remains a vital part of New Delhi's policy towards its extended neighborhood. Although centuries-old historical and cultural ties are the foundation of India's relations with Central Asia, energy security is a key driver today in their overall relationship. This relationship, however, is not driven merely by an exclusive objective of India's access to resources but consists of a broad-based strategy of engaging with Central Asia, based on political, strategic, economic, cultural and multilateral elements. Such a strategy is in line with India's "Connect Central Asia" policy. This includes an all-embracing template to diversify and deepen the relationship between the two sides that includes increasing the frequency of high-level visits, forging strategic partnerships with the Central Asian Republics, comprehensive economic engagement, partnership in the development of energy and natural resources. The new-fangled "Connect Central Asia" policy was very much required given the fact that in the last two and half decades or so, the close relations have not been translated into strong trade and investment relations.

By exploring various dimensions of India-Central Asia relations, in particular the economic dimension, this study verily observes the limited presence of Indian enterprises in the individual Central Asian Republics as well as the not-so-impressive trade figures as the overall trade flow between the two regions stood at US$ 819 million in 2015–16. This indicates that economic and trade relations between the two regions remain below the full potential. There are several reasons for this, though the main reason has been identified as India's lack of a direct overland access to the region. This has resulted in a slow growth of India's trade with the CARs since the establishment of their diplomatic relations. Whereas the volume of trade in 1996-97 was recorded at US$ 31 million, it has increased to the tune of only US$ 819 million in 2015-16, i.e., an increase of barely US$ 788 million over a long period of 20 years. However, India still maintains a positive trade balance with Central Asia and over half of its trade to the region is with Kazakhstan (55 percent) followed by Uzbekistan (20 percent), Turkmenistan (10 percent), Kyrgyzstan (9 percent) and Tajikistan (6 percent). What indeed points to the reality is that the average trade between India and Central Asian Republics during the period 2000–2012 has been just 0.1 percent of India's overall trade which attests to the fact that efforts for economic cooperation between the two regions have not been to the full potential. Although during 2013–14, India's trade with Central Asia increased sharply to reach US$ 1238 million; it was only with Kazakhstan that the bilateral trade had grown. While Kazakhstan's share in India's total trade with Central Asia stood at US$ 914.5 million, other republics (Kyrgyzstan, Tajikistan, Turkmenistan and Uzbekistan) together had a share of US$ 323.56 million only. During 2014-15, the overall trade between India and Central Asia further increased though on a diminutive extent to reach at only US$ 1380 million. However, during 2015–16, a decrease in bilateral trade with almost all the Central Asian Republics resulted in bringing down India's trade figure with Central Asia to the tune of US$ 819 million. That means that in comparison to China which has over US$ 50 billion trade with CARs the overall Indian trade with Central Asia has remained meager. Although trade has picked up considerably in the last couple of years with Central Asia, it is more country-specific than region-specific. Even with Kazakhstan, the largest country of the region, the trade with competing countries has grown manifold on account of investment and aid flowing from these countries to Kazakhstan.

Yet, India's endeavors to woo the Central Asian Republics have been a partial success, which can be gauged from the number of visits of important dignitaries from each of the CARs, the establishment of institutional mechanisms to direct their bilateral relationship towards a fruitful goal and increasing Indian business ventures in the varied sectors of the Central Asian economy. Moreover, there has been a remarkable increase in India's presence and achievements in some areas such as IT and the energy sector. Despite an overwhelming presence of rival competitors who enjoy a greater degree of geopolitical advantage than India, one can observe a great degree of complementarity of economic interests that these countries share which make India's efforts to constantly knock at the Central Asian door understandable. India's presence as an additional factor in the Central Asian economic space has a more nuanced meaning for all the Central Asian Republics as it is in tune with their national development strategies from varied perspectives. In this regard, Prime Minister Narendra Modi's visit to all the five Central Asian Republics was a decisive shift from the past, which scripted a new chapter in India's relations with the region. The visit gave a fresh momentum to the new economic and strategic engagement of India with the region. It was more so because this was the first comprehensive visit by an Indian Prime Minister since P.V. Narasimha Rao went on a goodwill tour of the CARs within a few years of their liberation. Narasimha Rao undertook visits to four of the five CARs, specifically Kazakhstan and Uzbekistan in 1992 and Turkmenistan and Kyrgyzstan in 1995. The first visit by an Indian Prime Minister to Tajikistan was undertaken by Atal Behari Vajpayee in 2003. In addition to Tajikistan, Vajpayee also visited Kazakhstan in 2002, combining this visit with his participation in the first Conference on Interaction and Confidence Building Measure in Asia (CICA) held in Almaty the same year. The former Prime Minister Dr. Manmohan Singh paid a visit to Uzbekistan in 2006 and to Kazakhstan in 2011.

However, Modi's six-day tour, followed by a visit to Ufa in Russia to attend the SCO-BRICS summit, which confirmed India and Pakistan as full members of the SCO, was a fresh unveiling of India as a regional and global power. Its key outcome was upgrading the India-Central Asia relations to a new level by expanding economic and trade links with emphasis on energy and transport connectivity and making India visible as a neutral third vector, poised to deploy its soft power in a regional geopolitical and economic landscape dominated respectively by Russia and China. Two key processes coinciding with Modi's visit shore up the prospects for a comprehensive Indian engagement: Firstly, it was the lifting of international economic sanctions on Iran which is a major channel in the India-initiated project of building connectivity with the CARs via sea route from the Chabahar port and by rail route from Chabahar through Afghanistan to landlocked parts of Central Asia. Secondly, the SCO-BRICS summit announced the accession of India and Pakistan as full members of the SCO from 2016 which Modi attended along with an informal summit of the Eurasian Economic Union (EAEU) that establishes India as a firm player in Eurasia. Modi's visit, thus, provided a new strategic direction for India's "Connect Central Asia" policy being pursued discreetly.

Since India is seen as a neutral power in Central Asia, this is useful for the CARs from the viewpoint that allows this landlocked region to have access to a diversified market for their products in the Indian subcontinent. On the other side, the Indian presence as a neutral power in Central Asia does not pose any threat, both economic as well as strategic, to the CARs while engaging a larger number of regional and global competitors in their market space. These competitors need to be dexterously balanced by the CARs in which India could play the role of an additional factor. At the same time, India's historical and cultural linkages coupled with its stable, democratic and secular credentials with a dynamic economy close to the Central Asian geopolitical space is seen as a viable direction to relate to in the long term. India's stronger presence in the region is quite possible since most of the regional states have made it a priority to diversify their diplomatic activities. Concretely, the Central Asian regimes are being courted by Japan, South Korea, Malaysia, Turkey, the EU and other important players in East and South-East Asia so as to lessen their reliance on China. In this context, India is seen as a better alternative to costly Western products as well as to the cheap but low-quality Chinese products. India also represents a technologically advanced country in many areas such as the ICT and space technologies that are relevant in the context of modern communication systems.

Another significant point that has emerged from this study is that India's primary drive towards Central Asia so far has been based upon the long-term objective to establish its stronger presence in this resource-rich region. The need for energy security for its fast growing economy and to diversify its energy procurement sources have been the main geo-economic reasons for India's constant efforts to reconnect with Central Asia. It is, therefore, obvious that in future, energy routes will significantly determine the regional unions and geopolitical situation not only in Central Asia but also in the world as a whole. The conclusion of the TAPI project, in the future, will certainly result in the strengthening of the value and priority of southern direction pipeline routes which forms an important basis for India's direct relationship with the Central Asian countries. In this connection the route of the future pipeline from Central Asia to India is extremely important in India's evolving relationship with the Central Asian countries. On the transport front, as Central Asia is envisioned to be connected with the wider world via different sets of transport projects driven by major regional powers, in the long run, the Central Asia market would be accessed through any of these means. Because of the need to bypass the political and geographical barriers on trade routes linking India with Central Asia, New Delhi has pinned its hopes on the completion of the International North–South Transport Corridor (INSTC) project which will be a meticulous achievement of India's strategic planning to overcome its indirect access to the Central Asian market.

Such a projection, therefore, demands that for the time being, India should concentrate on actively consolidating its position strongly in Afghanistan and Iran which hold the key for stability in Central Asia. India's contribution in these two countries closer to the Central Asian Republics will be of crucial advantage in the long run. Besides, India has already made significant progress by concluding a three-nation pact (India-Iran-Afghanistan) for renovating the strategic port of Chabahar, development of the International North-South Transport Corridor (INSTC) and agreeing to accede to Ashgabat Agreement. On 23rd March 2016, The Union Cabinet, chaired by the Prime Minister Shri Narendra Modi, has given its approval for India to accede to the Ashgabat Agreement[1], an international transport and transit corridor facilitating transportation of goods between Central Asia and the Persian Gulf. The Ashgabat Agreement has Oman, Iran, Turkmenistan and Uzbekistan as founding members. Kazakhstan has also joined this arrangement subsequently. Accession to the Agreement would enable India to utilise this existing transport and transit corridor to facilitate trade and commercial interaction with the Eurasian region. Further, this would synchronise with India's efforts to implement the International North South Transport Corridor (INSTC) for enhanced connectivity. India's membership of Shanghai Cooperation Organization (SCO) as also of the Eurasian Economic Union (EAEU) would go a long way in bridging the gap. Another regionally important transportation project between India and Central Asia is the US-initiated New Silk Road Project which aims at directing Central Asia's main transportation arteries southwards to pass through Afghanistan and reach Pakistan and Indian markets. Recently, Trump administration has resuscitated the New Silk Road Project that is being seen as countering China's One Belt, One Road (OBOR) initiative. The US has also clarified that this New Silk Road refers to a suite of joint investment projects and regional trade blocs that have the potential to bring economic growth and stability to Central Asia and India seems to be a potential participant in this project. Though the US too is supportive of Indian participation in the project, the proposed corridor project is still in its embryonic stage, and even if successfully realised, it suffers from India's old geopolitical dilemma that this route still would continue to pass through "unreliable" Pakistan's territory. Even though the importance of these trade and transportation routes cannot be denied, their demand is from the policymakers of the countries involved, who want to make all-out efforts to realise the goals for the greater benefit of the individual countries as well as the entire region.

This study clearly indicates that in order to emerge from the shadows of regional and overarching global powers, the CARs would not let go untapped the opportunities that the new worldwide economic interdependencies are investing in them, for pursuing their national development agenda with a great degree of autonomy. At the same time, they are aware of the fact that not a single country in the world, not even the ones that are abundantly provided with fuel energy resources, can develop their resources without participating in the integrating international processes. This is particularly vital for countries with a transitional economy, where the following are needed for their stable development: wide influx of foreign investments; presence of external market demands of the manufactured goods; provision for secure and fair transport and transit of the energy holders via the territory of third countries; and working towards realisation of an agreeable political line at the international markets for energy holders. Increased regional cooperation and connectivity from Central Asia through Afghanistan to South Asia would help in the broader objective of integrating Afghanistan into a regional trade and transit network. This would encourage all stakeholders to participate in Afghanistan's development which in turn could promote its stability. When resource-rich Central Asian States look for a wider choice of trading partners and there is stability in the intervening territories, the large-scale use of trade and economic opportunities via ports on the Indian Ocean could well become a reality. Significantly, due to the evolving economic inter-dependency and integration of the Eurasian space, India has proposed a Comprehensive Economic Cooperation Agreement (CECA) to integrate India's markets with the unifying Eurasian space, including the Central Asian Republics.

While the geopolitical challenge to surmount Pakistan's hostility has, for the time being, constrained India's direct access to the CARs via a shorter route, another challenge India faces is to compete with the Chinese economically in the Central Asian market. These remain the central dilemma of the Indian policymakers to strategise on a long-term basis for an Indian foothold in the region. Even though India's growing attention to the region is in no small part a response to the changing dynamics of the major powers' relations with Central Asia. Augmented Chinese investment and its tactful engagement, Russia's economic downturn and the ensuing decline in remittances to Central Asia, and the reduced US military focus on Afghanistan have all pushed India to concentrate more on Central Asia than it has ever been. In this context, an increased involvement of China in Central Asia from the economic point of view is of particular importance. In 2013, Chinese President Xi Jinping undertook a ten-day visit to the Central Asian Republics and signed an estimated US$ 48 billion worth of investment and loan agreements covering energy, trade and infrastructure. This investment was intended to set a stage for China's ambitious OBOR initiative that aims at connecting Asia and Africa with Europe through a transportation network of six economic corridors, a project that could potentially reshape the geo-economics and geopolitics of Eurasia as a whole. However, there is no denying that connectivity projects must be based on acceptable international norms, effective governance, transparency in reforms and respect towards sovereignty and territorial integrity of the nations. The China-Pakistan Economic corridor (CPEC) as part of China's OBOR initiative, has made it difficult for countries like India to accept such vision that indicates significant threat across the priorities. Indian concerns about the CPEC are justified as this corridor runs through Pakistan-occupied Kashmir. That is why the project like Chabahar is viewed by numerous analysts as a strategic move by India not only to bypass Pakistan but also to counter China in implementing its OBOR strategy through CPEC. China, on the other hand, may not see the Chabahar project pessimistically as more connectivity will benefit China given that it is one of the largest trading partners of almost every country in the region. Both China and Russia have also expressed interest in future integration between the EAEU and the OBOR. If it does take place, most CARs might pursue enhanced strategic and economic engagement with India in order to balance their dependence on Russia and China in accordance with their multi-vector foreign policies.

Nevertheless, a viable economic and trade relationship between India and Central Asia is the key concern today as New Delhi believes in taking all possible measures to help the trade levels rise to their full potential. As already pointed out, the single biggest obstacle to a larger trade figure is clearly the lack of direct surface connectivity routes, though one can also see an information deficit, which aggravates the connectivity deficit. Insufficient information on trade and investment opportunities has also constrained economic relations that require linking both the connectivity and information deficits. Following India's new membership in the SCO the India-SCO cooperation is of paramount importance so far as the issue of connectivity is concerned. In this regard, Prime Minister Modi's speech at the recently concluded SCO Astana summit (8-9 June 2017) is a positive indication as he stressed on enhancing connectivity in the region, saying it was the key to more trade and investment but, at the same time, he made it clear that sovereignty and territorial integrity should be the key factors in such cooperation. "For connectivity initiatives and for success and approval of the projects, sovereignty and regional integrity must be respected while inclusivity and sustainability are essential," Modi said. It, therefore, appears that by indirectly flagging key concerns with Pakistan and China he has offered some space to the Chinese to pay serious attention to India's concerns over the CPEC. Notwithstanding such concerns of India, the future trajectory of the India-Central Asia relations points to the following:

- Firstly, it needs to be underlined that despite numerous challenges and the ongoing flux in the ambient region due to varied interests, India's relation-ship with Central Asia is going to only deepen and diversify in the days ahead.
- Secondly, the geo-economic aspect of the relationship and win–win out-comes in the economic arena will become more visible in the years to come.
- Thirdly, while economics will be a key driver, India's relationship with Central Asia as part of its extended neighborhood will acquire greater strategic depth, which will manifest itself in increasing defence and security cooperation. This is logical and inevitable as the expansion of economic interests will involve a concomitant increase in consultation and collaboration to deal with a host of challenges including terrorism and drug-trafficking.
- Fourthly, in engaging with Central Asia, India will have to factor the role of players like China and Russia on the one hand, and the roles of other powers like the US on the other hand. The multiplicity of external powers in the region could open up new avenues of cooperation, if handled with tact and foresight.
- Fifthly, India's active engagement with the SCO Energy Club, the Eurasian Economic Union and the Asian Energy Strategy as proposed by Kazakhstan could become a game changer. India's SCO membership could play a bigger role in ensuring greater energy cooperation between energy producers and consumers by linking Central Asia and South Asia, wherein Iran can be instrumental in facilitating the SCO Energy Club by becoming a major energy trading hub through the opening up of its Chabahar port.
- Sixthly, how India handles its relationship with Central Asia will have a vital bearing on the continued emergence of India as a global player. This in turn will influence the collective destiny of an emerging Asia and an emerging Asian century.

As far as the economic dimension of the India–Central Asia relations is concerned, this study argues that India's economy needs Central Asian energy, mineral and other resources in order to sustain its growth, stability and security concerns. Being late for over two decades to actively engage with the Central Asian countries, India now seems to be quite determined to compensate for the lost time. Hence, it is knocking at Central Asia's door to get its portion of energy and mineral resources, invest in the regional countries and establish trade routes bypassing Pakistani territory. The whole study provides the following recommendations to be taken into consideration both by India and each of the five Central Asian Republics in order to enhance their economic and trade relations, both bilaterally as well as collectively:

- Switch, swap and counter-trade are the most prevalent modes of trading due to the lack of a classical Western marketing model. It requires the visibility of the product and the presence of the producer/trader, both of which have been sadly missing from the Indian side. Our agencies and apex bodies could undertake these roles by locating themselves there. It is recommended that Indian organisations such as the State Trade Corporation (STC) and Minerals and Metals Trading Corporation (MMTC) enter into such agreements with suitable clients in the Central Asian Republics for enhanced visibility and off-the-shelf delivery.
- While we must push aggressively our traditional goods into the Central Asian market, there is no denying of the fact that in due course, a jungle of technical standards, environmental, veterinary and sanitary regulations would evolve in these markets also which would need to be complied with if we are looking into these markets in terms of future projections. The major non-tariff barriers against India in the developed markets like in terms of import policy; standards, testing, labeling and certifications; export subsidies; disadvantages due to regional trading blocs/preferential trading arrangements; child labour; new policy instruments and anti-dumping measures will slowly but surely affect these markets also and we must tune ourselves for an enlarged Eurasian market which includes Central Asia as well.
- In order to raise our industry to internationally, established quality standards, including the ISO 9000 and ISO 14000 series of quality standards, need to be met with. To compete with the Western and other multinationals in the Central Asian markets, it is time to further strengthen the newly established Quality Council of India.
- Central Asia is a region for big players because tremendous opportunities exist in terms of exploitation of petrochemicals, oil exploration, hydrocarbons and mining of ferrous and non-ferrous items as well as setting up a telecommunication network, building of hotels and tourist resorts, joint ventures in power engineering, gold mining and jewelry production, non-ferrous metallurgy, etc.

At the same time, tremendous opportunities exist for cooperation between small and medium enterprises in areas such as processing of cotton yarn, food, silk garments, refrigeration, caning and packaging, development of hybrid seeds and shipbuilding, etc. Hence, adequate resource mobilisation on the part of India will be required for entering into joint venture partnerships.

- Boilers, Machinery & Mechanical equipment's
- Electrical machinery & appliance
- computer hardware and software
- leather tanneries and garment factories
- light commercial vehicles

• Similar opportunities exist for setting up joint ventures in the priority areas such as:

(a) Pharmaceuticals

o India is said to be the "Pharmacy of the world". India being itself a developing country, with huge population which needs new medications, new medicines etc. at much cheaper cost than what the multinational companies offer. This is true for every developing, poor nation in the world including the CARs. Indian pharmaceutical companies have been able to develop generic medicines at the fraction of costs to the Americans and are now exporting it worldwide. The CARs & India can collaborate and must setup conducive environment, through clear policy framework, so that the Pharmaceutical industry can work together and benefit from each other's expertise. The two government can become facilitators for new joint ventures to setup and boost jobs, research and production efficiency. The scope and potential is tremendous on both ends. The bilateral agreements between India & CARs in Pharmaceuticals and Healthcare itself can be a big game changer.

(b) Chemicals industry

o Chemical industry not only serves as the major backbone of Indian agriculture and industrial sectors, but also adds to India's foreign reserves by way of exports to several countries across the globe. 34 percent of India's export earnings come from its chemical industry which is currently the third largest producer in Asia in major chemical categories including agrochemicals, polymers and plastics, dyes and various organic and inorganic chemicals. Chemical exports of India comprise several product groups such as inorganic and organic chemicals, plastics and petrochemicals, drugs and pharmaceuticals, dyes and pigments, pesticides and agrochemicals, fine and specialty chemicals, and fertilizers. Organic chemicals and pharmaceuticals are the two top exports of India. There is considerable scope for Indian companies as well as the CARs chemical companies to collaborate or form joint venture. Both the nations have considerable requirements which they can mutually fulfill.

(c) Agricultural produce, Food processing, dairy & poultry products and Coffee, Tea, Tobacco, Spices, Cucumber & Jerkins, Fish, Poultry & Meat etc.

(d) Rubber & plastic products

- o The Indian rubber & plastics industry produces and exports a wide range of raw materials, natural rubber, plastic-molded extruded goods, polyester films, molded/soft luggage items, writing instruments, plastic woven sacks and bags, polyvinyl chloride (PVC), leather cloth and sheeting, packaging, consumer goods, sanitary fittings, electrical accessories, laboratory/medical surgical ware, tarpaulins, laminates, fishnets, travelware, and others. The Indian industry offers excellent potential in terms of capacity, infrastructure and skilled manpower. It is supported by a large number of polymer producers, and plastic process machinery and mould manufacturers in the country. There is scope of establishing such industry in CARs.

(e) IT and ITES

- o India is the world's largest sourcing destination for the information technology (IT) industry, accounting for approximately 67 percent of the USD 124-130 billion market. More importantly, the industry has led the economic transformation of the country and altered the perception of India in the global economy. India's cost competitiveness in providing IT services, which is approximately 3-4 times cheaper than the US, continues to be the mainstay of its unique selling proposition (USP) in the global sourcing market. India is also gaining prominence in terms of intellectual capital with several global IT firms setting up their innovation & incubation centres in India. The Indian IT and ITeS industry is divided into four major segments—IT services, business process management (BPM), software products and engineering services, and hardware. India is the topmost off-shoring destination for IT companies across the world. Tremendous opportunities are available for collaboration between India and CARs.

(f) Audio-visual Services

- o The Indian media and entertainment industry comprises various segments which include television, print, films, radio, music, animation, gaming and visual effects, and digital advertising. India has co-production treaties with ten countries. To promote joint productions, coproduction agreements have been signed with Italy, Germany, Brazil, UK, France, New Zealand, Poland, Spain and Canada. India-CARs may examine the prospects of cooperation in film and animation projects.

(g) Telemedicine

- o Telemedicine, teleradiology followed by tele-diagnostics, tele-pathology, bioinformatics and continual remote monitoring, is a promising opportunity segment. Telemedicine potentially eliminates a number of other costs, including travel expenses for specialists and patient transfers. Bilateral engagements in the health sector can be established to overcome the problem of inadequate healthcare infrastructure, i.e., understaffed clinics and undertrained practitioners. Indian Hospitals have successfully established a large number of telemedicine facilities in various countries. Capacity building in areas such as healthcare is at the core of India's relationship building with developing nations.

(h) Collaboration in the field of Traditional Medicine and Healthcare services:

- o Traditional medicine (TM) refers to health practices, approaches, knowledge and beliefs incorporating plant, animal and mineral-based medicines, spiritual therapies, manual techniques and exercises, applied singularly or in combination to treat, diagnose and prevent illnesses or maintain well-being. Traditional Medicine can also have an impact on infectious diseases. India has well-developed systems of traditional medicine, including medicinal plants which have potential in the global health scenario. In order to augment the use of traditional systems of medicine, the Government of India formulated a National Policy on

Indian Systems of Medicine & Homeopathy in the year 2002. The Indian Systems of Medicine and Homoeopathy (Ayurvedic, Yoga & Naturopathy, Unani, Siddha and Homeopathy (AYUSH)) cover both the systems which originated in India and abroad, but which got adopted and adapted in India in the course of time. It is estimated that 65 percent of the population in rural India use Ayurveda and medicinal plants to help meet primary health care needs. India has 15 agro-climatic zones, 47,000 plant species and 15,000 medicinal plants that include 7,000 plants used in Ayurveda, 700 in Unani medicine, 600 in Siddha medicine and 30 in modern medicine. In India, Ministry of AYUSH enters into cooperation agreements to strengthen, promote and develop Cooperation in the field of Traditional Indian Systems of Medicines. Such international cooperation facilitates capacity building, training, exchange of information, exchange of experts, health manpower development, and technical support in establishing laboratories/hospitals and research in mutually identified areas, on the basis of equality, reciprocity and mutual benefit. It provides opportunities for sharing and emulating best practices and learning from each other, to address the health challenges faced by the country. The research and other delegation could visit research and educational institutes in India and drug manufacturing units where top class quality is maintained at every level.

(i) Higher Education

- o Prominent amongst the service sectors is the provision of education services, especially higher education services. Over the past few decades, the global economy has shifted from being a manufacturing centric to a knowledge driven one and as countries move up the ladder of development, the contribution of hi-tech manufacturing and high value added services to the GDP increases. The role of higher education in providing these skill sets is indisputable. Success in leveraging knowledge and innovation is only possible with a sound infrastructure of higher education. The emergence of India as a service based, knowledge driven economy has put the spotlight on human capital. Higher education is essential to build a workforce capable of underpinning a modern, competitive economy. India, today, has a total of more than 600 universities, 43 central universities, 299 state universities, 30 institutions of National importance, 45 technical institutes, 13 management institutes, 4 information technology institutes, 6 science and research institutes and 3 planning and architecture institutes. India has much to offer in cross border supply of education services. E-learning and Distance learning on the internet is gaining importance and is helped by development of MOOCs platforms. IGNOU has gained good reputation abroad in marketing education programmes at extremely cost competitive rates compared to similar courses from developed countries. IGNOU is already a recognized distance education provider in the gulf region—Dubai, Abu Dhabi, Sharjah, Doha, Muscat and Kuwait. Its courses are being offered in Mauritius, Maldives, Seychelles, Nepal and Sri Lanka. Thus, there exists a potential of providing education services over the internet to CARs by institutions in India. Many professional bodies in India are also offering courses through the distance education mode.

(j) Professional Services

- o Accountancy & Auditing Services: The Institute of Chartered Accountants of India (ICAI) is a statutory body established under the Chartered Accountants Act, 1949 (Act No. XXXVIII of 1949) for the regulation of the profession of Chartered Accountants in India. During its 68 years of existence, ICAI has achieved recognition as a premier accounting body is now the second largest accounting body in the whole world. The CAs in India are trained in International Financial Reporting Standards (IFRS), Forensic Accounting, Fraud Detection, Valuation, Enterprise Risk Management, Business Finance, International Taxation, International Forex and Treasury Management, Derivatives, Arbitration, Information Systems Audit, Computer Accounting and Auditing Techniques and host of other niche capabilities which make them truly combat professionals suited to handle any complex business situation. Suggestion for Possible Collaboration between India and CARs could identify accountancy sector as a potential area for services cooperation.
- o Engineering, Architectural and other Technical services are

other service sectors where the CARs & India can have trade agreement and choose to work on few of the key projects. India can also offer scholarships as well as permit training and retainership for CARs students in Indian professional services.

- The necessary physical infrastructure is available for transit trade through Iran. There is an excellent infrastructure in terms of roads throughout Central Asia and Iran. The Irano-Hind Shipping Company, a joint venture between the Islamic Republic of Iran Shipping Line (IRISL) and the Shipping Corporation of India (SCI) is already offering competitive tariffs for this route. We need to publicise this route as well as engage ourselves in a more proactive manner with the Government of Iran to improve ship turnaround and transport facilities from Iran.
- In the light of increasing reliance on road transportation, it is necessary that suitable highway stations are set up at appropriate locations along the inter-state highways. Such highway stations will enable truckers to park their vehicles during temporary halts and obtain essential services besides providing for the security of goods.
- There is a need to further strengthen the transport services sector from India and promote the institution of MTOs in the Central Asian region. The private sector has immense possibilities for entering this field.
- Reliable and up-to-date road and rail maps for the Central Asian states are not readily available. There is a need for urgent action for making such maps available.
- It would be in the interest of international trade if the states could expedite the adoption of appropriate customs laws and give wide publicity to their liberal customs regime. Their signing some of the international conventions on customs will also generate reassurance and promote international trade. As the tariff structure of the Iran route presently includes mostly the cost of return of empty containers from destination to the port of Bandar Abbas, it is necessary to provide for return consignments in order to bring down the costs. Some Indian traders are already importing containerisable goods from Central Asia.
- The providing of a facility to link export and import cargo would go a long way in the reduction of tariff costs as well as further popularising this route. The recommendation for container consolidation stations and setting up of joint ventures for freight forwarding are steps in this direction.

- The increase of trade will also have a direct effect on further usage and popularisation of this route. In order to promote further trade, there is a need to improve the trading infrastructure in these markets for the Indian businessmen. In this context, India's relations with Iran and the actualisation of key connectivity projects could play a critical role in turning around the situation.
- Absence of a strong viable banking infrastructure in the Central Asian region is a major barrier to trade and investment. One such recommendation is the opening of more joint venture banks between the Indian banks and their counterparts in Central Asia. Indian banks can expand their presence if they see a favorable policy environment. The establishment of such banks will not only improve the trading environment between India and this region, it would also set the stage for promoting further joint ventures. The Punjab National Bank already has a representative office in Almaty and the State Bank of India has a representative office in Tashkent. There is a need to set up Wholly Owned Subsidiaries/ Joint Ventures (WOS/JV) of Indian banks in Central Asia.
- In this somewhat uncertain and emerging trading regime, physical presence and visibility are prerequisites for effective and safe trading. Indian entrepreneurs are best advised to physically locate agencies and ventures in Central Asia to practice a 'cash and carry' model.
- The trading environment would also improve with a better provision of insurance cover as well as the availability of detailed rules and regulations prevailing in these markets to Indian entrepreneurs. Warehousing facilities for Indian trade are another means of increasing India's exports to this region which will affect "cash and carry" transactions.
- Thus, in order to effectively promote India's trade with Central Asia, we need to strengthen our institutional/infrastructural support. We need to provide credit facilities through the Exim Bank and other banks. We should also endeavor to set up a custom bonded warehouse/display centre. Steps should be taken to enhance the cover of the Export Credit Guarantee Corporation of India (ECGC) on India's exports. We need to operate our airline carrier to all the Central Asian Republics and also rationalise freight rates and terminal handling charges which are reported to be invariably higher for exports to Central Asia as compared to those available for other destinations. Other promotional measures include repeated participation by the India Trade Promotion

Organisation (ITPO) in the prominent trade fairs, conclusion of mutual recognition agreements between the Quality Council of India and its Central Asian counterparts, roving departmental store promotions as well as "Made in India Roving Exhibitions," etc.

- Under the Export Promotion Scheme (Chapter 3 of Import-Export Policy) of the Directorate General of Foreign Trade, Ministry of Commerce, Government of India, exports to the Central Asian Republics have been included in the Focus Market Scheme for post-export incentives. Under the scheme, exporters from India to Central Asian markets are entitled to the issuance of a strip (due to the landlocked status of the CAR markets) worth 3–4 percent of the FOB value of the exports to this region. They can utilise this strip for the import of duty-free materials. However, the entitlement for the Central Asian market is almost at par with other countries listed in the Focused Market Scheme. As this is a relatively new market with a huge transport bottleneck, the incentive needs to be higher for this market. Again, it is believed that a post-export incentive under Chapter 3 is being pruned down. We must, somehow, find a way to retain incentives for exports to this region in the new policy formulation under some other schemes.
- The projected Shanghai Cooperation Organization Free Trade Area, to be in place by 2020 to economically integrate all members of the SCO, is also an attractive proposal for New Delhi. Experts believe that it could be more lucrative than the West's offer to admit India to the Asia-Pacific Economic Cooperation (APEC) forum. India's full-fledged accession to the SCO is a positive outcome in this direction, as it will be more closely integrated economically with Central Asia, Russia and China in terms of market access and flow of goods and services to these countries.
- In order to overcome obstacles like limited land connectivity and the comparatively modest size of the Central Asian markets, India must intensify its diplomatic efforts within the framework of its "Connect Central Asia" policy.

Emergence of an interesting Central Asian regional dynamics demands India to ensure that "Connect Central Asia" policy should not just remain on paper but it should be realized in practice in the best possible manner. If New Delhi manages to do that, this policy can prove to be a game changer in times to come as India's stature will surely rise in the international system.

As India seeks to engage the Central Asian region through multilateral projects such as INSTC, SCO and EAEU the possibility of cooperation with China on OBOR cannot be summarily rejected. This is so because India would also like to build up connectivity to the main European markets passing through Eurasia. Moreover, the geo-economics of Chabahar, CPEC, and OBOR may push policymakers to recalculate their strategies. For, all such initiatives must be linked together in the long run in order to be economically viable and successful. The CPEC too will not be able to see the light of the day if it does not have access to the huge Indian market. It is, therefore, crucial for India to deal with China smartly rather than just showing reluctance to joining the OBOR.

REFERENCES

1. Press Information Bureau, http://pib.nic.in/newsite/PrintRelease.aspx?relid=138309

ANNEXURES

Annexure 1: Proposed map for China's One Belt One Road (OBOR) initiative

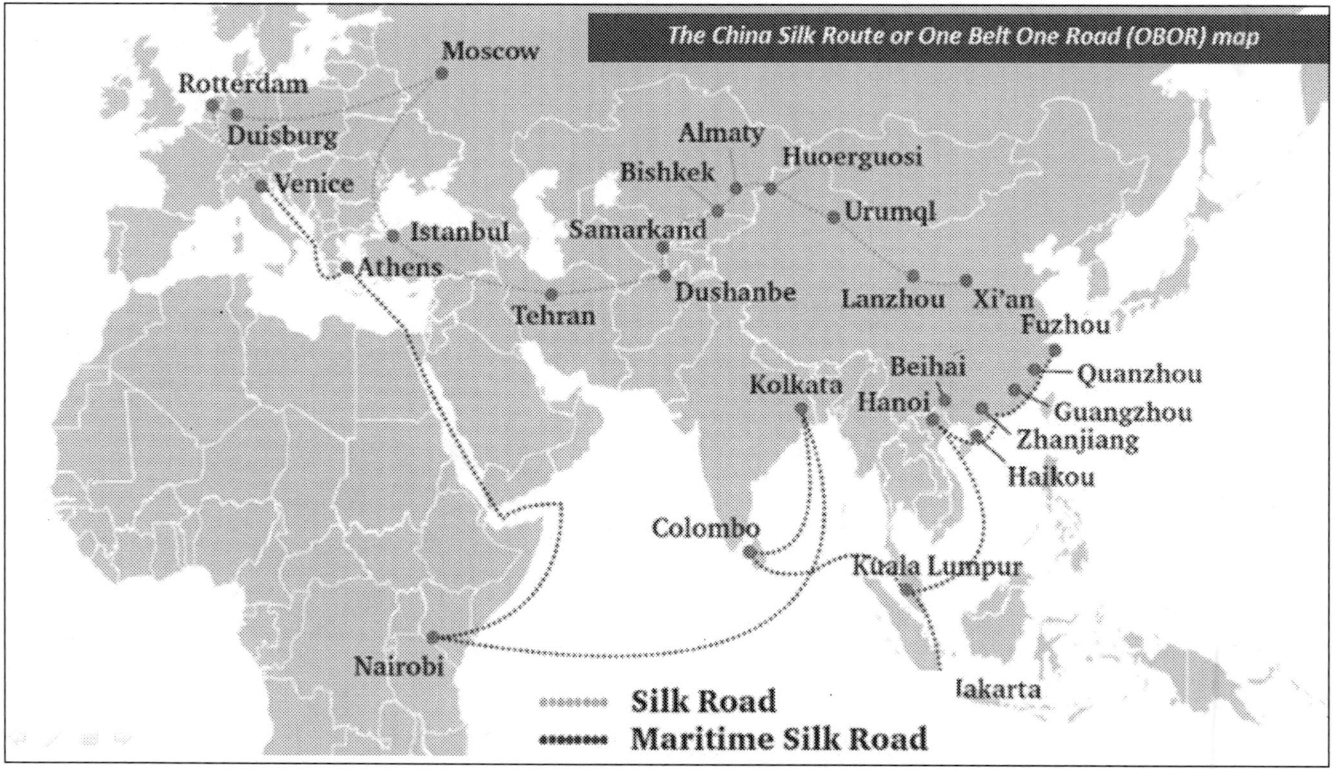

Source: PWC Presentation on China New Silk Route, https://www.linkedin.com/pulse/connected-eurasia-emerging-oppurtunities-expanding-corridors-masood

Annexure 2: Proposed Oil & Natural Gas Pipeline from Iran & Turkmenistan to India

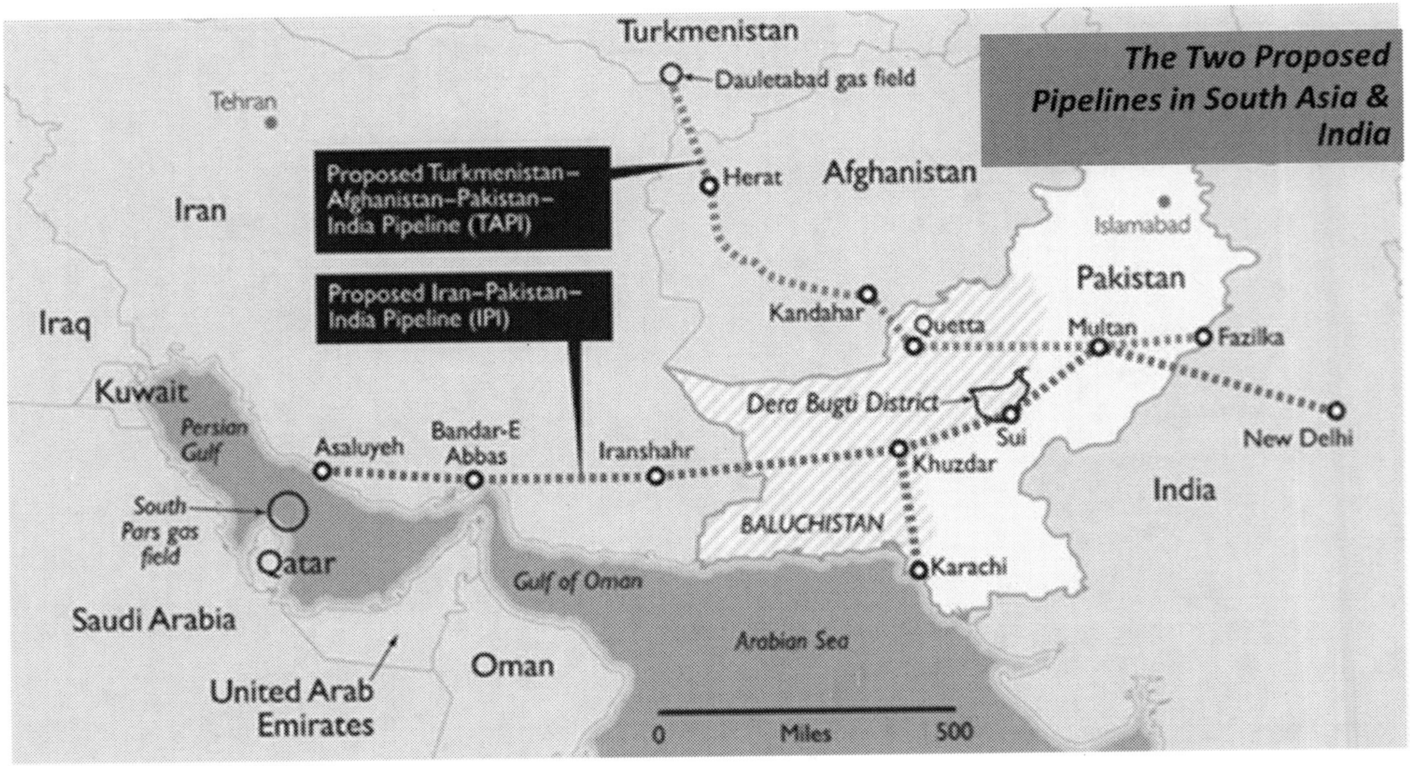

Source: http://www.heritage.org/sites/default/files/~/media/images/reports/2008/bg2139_map1sm/bg2139_map1.jpg

Annexure 3: Proposed map for TAPI 1814 Km pipeline to India from Turkmenistan

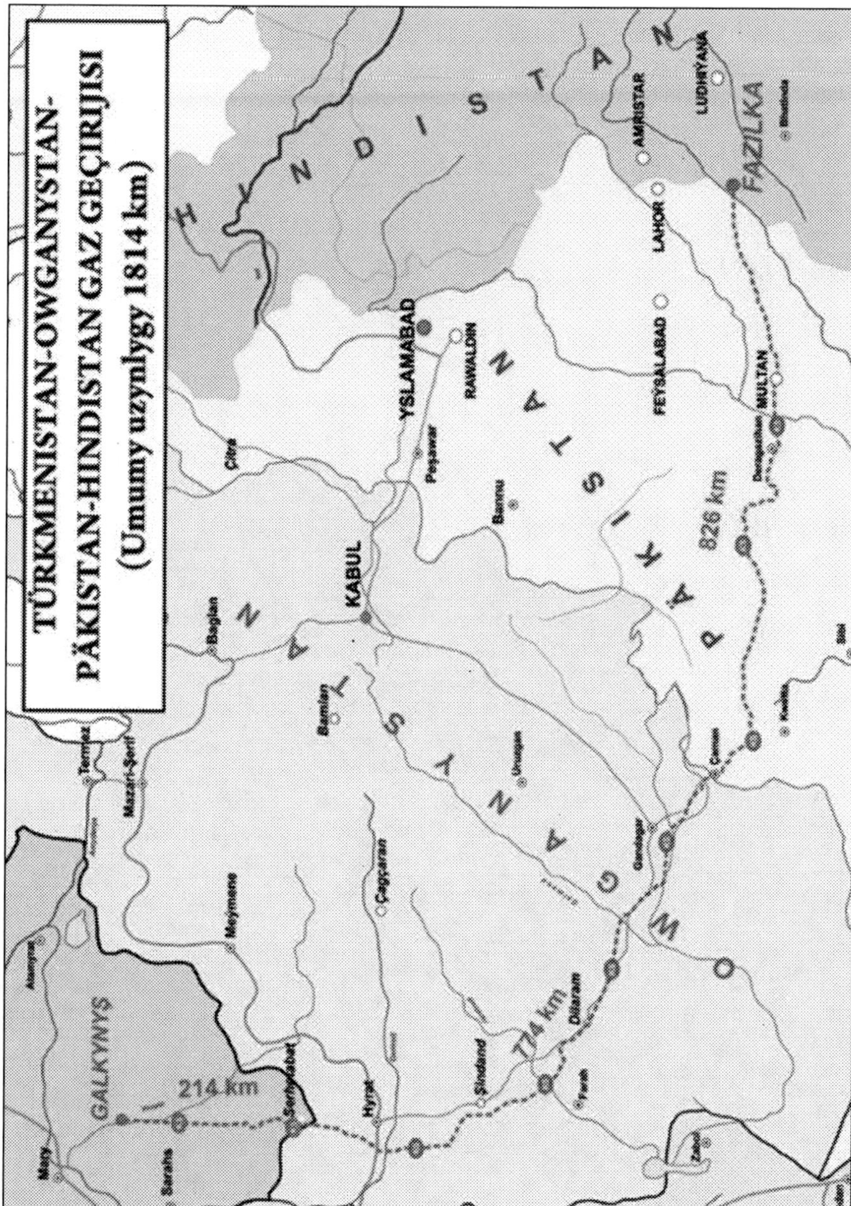

Courtesy: Turkmenistan Official Source

Annexure 4: Proposed International North-South Transport Corridor & other Trade Routes connecting to Europe & Central Asia

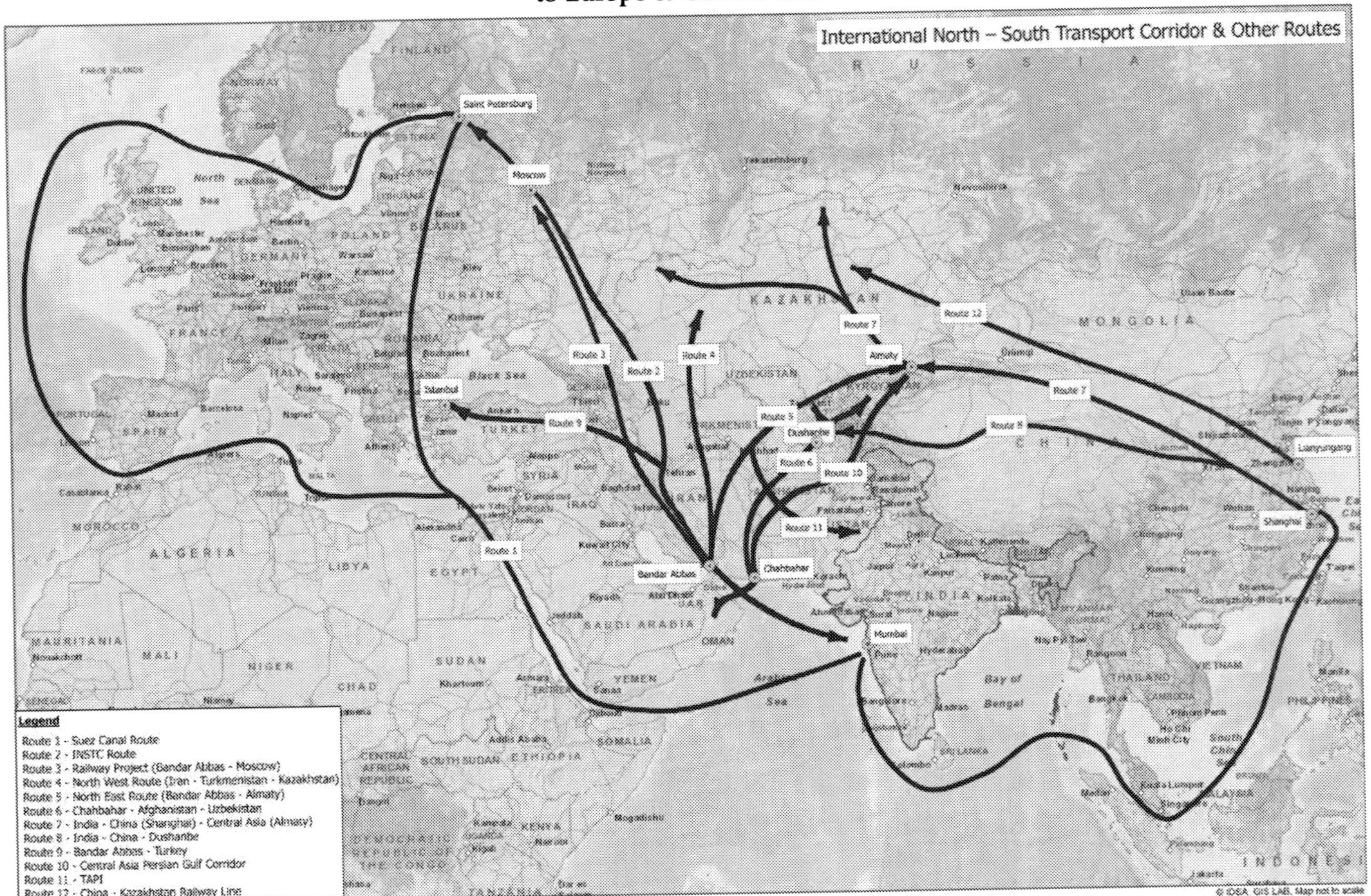

Source: GIS Lab, Institute for Defence Studies and Analyses, New Delhi, http://www.idsa.in/issuebrief/InternationalNorthSouthTransportCorridor_msroy_180815

Annexure 5: India Route Link to Central Asia through Chabahar Port in Iran

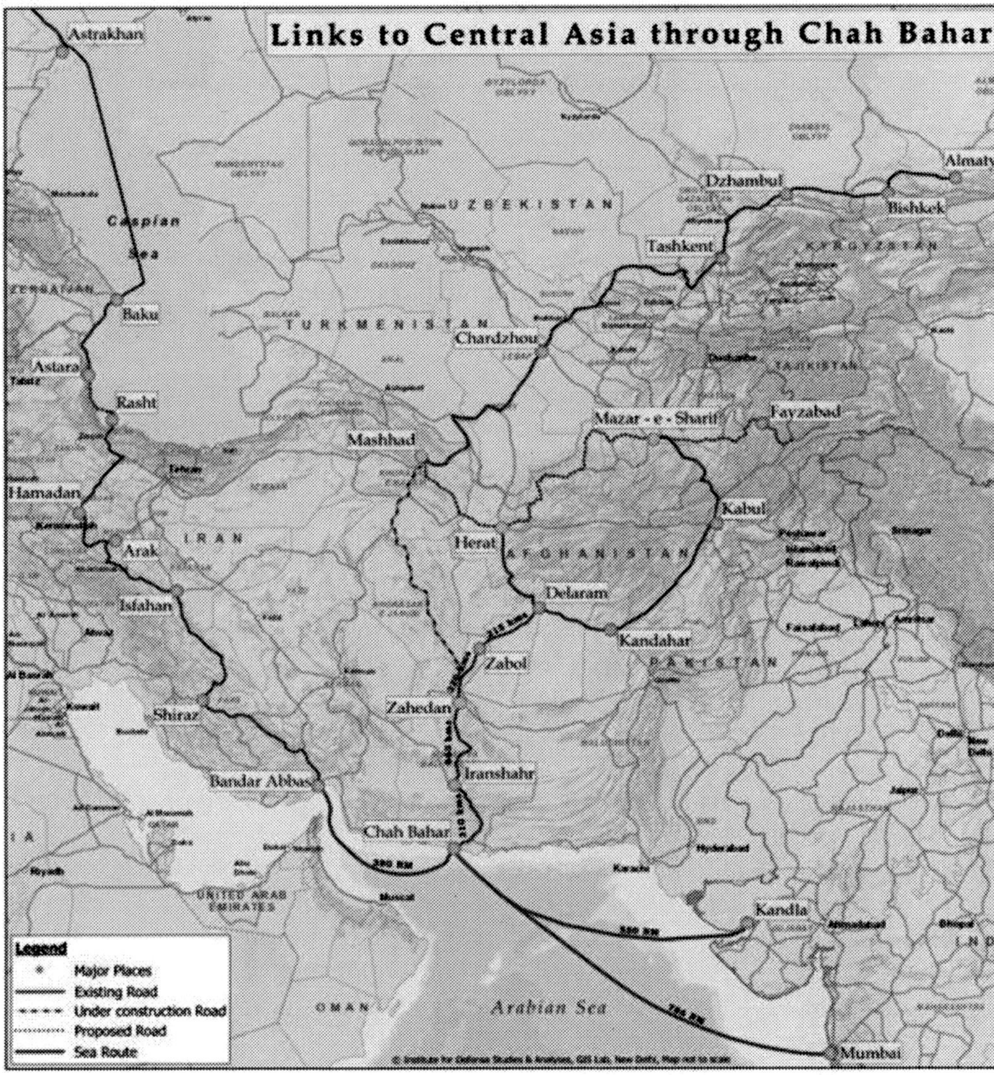

Source: https://www.quora.com/If-India-and-Pakistan-have-had-good-relations-and-open-borders-who-would-be-at-loss

Select Bibliography

Abduraxmonovich, A.O., 'Economic Cooperation between India and Central Asian Republics with Special Reference to Uzbekistan', *RIS Discussion Papers*, RIS#53/20003, Tashkent: University of World Economy and Diplomacy, 2003.

Adams, Terence, 'Caspian Energy Development', in *The Caspian: Politics, Energy and Security*, Shirin Akiner (ed.), London and New York: Routledge, 2004.

Adhikari, Sudipta, *Political Geography*, Jaipur & New Delhi: Rawat Publications, 1997.

Rashid, Ahmed Taliban, Islam, Oil and the New Great Game in Central Asia, London: I.B. Tauris., 2000

Akcali, P., 'Kyrgystan: Back to Being "The Island Democracy"', in *The State in Eurasia: Local and Global Arenas*, A. Sengupta and S. Chatterjee (eds), New Delhi: KW Publishers, 2013.

Akiner, Shirin, 'Asian Energy Projects in Caspian Basin', in *Central Asia and South Asia: Energy Cooperation and Transport Linkages*, K. Warikoo (ed.), New Delhi: Pentagon, 2011.

Akiner, Shirin (ed.), *The Caspian: Politics, Energy and Security*, London: Routledge, 2004.

Alam, Mohammad Monir (2000), 'Central Asian Republics: Quest for Security since Independence', *Contemporary Central Asia*, 4 (3), 2000.

Amirahmadi, Hooshang, 'Pipeline Politics in the Caspian Region', in *The Caspian Region at a Crossroad: Challenges of a New Frontier of Energy*, Hooshang Amirahmadi (ed.), Houndmills: Palgrave Macmillan, 2000.

Askarbek, Mambetaliev E., 'Central Asia: Trends in Geopolitics', *Contemporary Central Asia*, 10 (1), 2006.

Atabaki, Touraj and John Kane (eds.), *Post Soviet Central Asia*, London and New York: Tauris Academic Studies, 1998.

Azhar, Muhammad, 'The Emerging Trade Relations Between India and Central Asia', in *Nationalism in Russia and Central Asian Republics*, Shams-ud-din (ed.), New Delhi: Lancer Books, 1999.

Bakshi, Jyotsana, 'Sino-Russian Strategic Partnership in Central Asia: Implications for India', *Strategic Analysis*, 25 (2), 2011.

Bakshi, Jyotsana (ed.), *India's Engagement with Central Asia with focus on India-Uzbekistan Relations*, Tashkent: University of World Economy and Diplomacy, 2007.

Bal, Suryakant Nijanand, *Central Asia: A Strategy for India's Look-North Policy*, New Delhi: Lancer Publishers, 2004.

Bandyopadhyay, L., 'India and Tajikistan: Towards a New Strategic Partnership', Global India Foundation, 2012. URL:http://www.globalindia foundation.org/Indiapercent20Tajikistanpercent5B1percent5D.pdf

Bandyopadhyay, L., 'Turkmenistan's Foreign Policy: A Comparation of the Niyazov and the Post-Niyazov Regimes', in *The State in Eurasia: Local and Global Arenas*, A. Sengupta and S. Chatterjee (eds), New Delhi: KW Publishers, 2013.

Bashiri, Iraj, 'Central Asia: An Overview', 1999. URL: http://www.angelfire.com/rnb/bashiri/CentAsia/CentAsia.html

Bek-Ali, 'Kazakhstan-India Trade and Economic Relations', in *Contemporary Kazakhstan: The Way Ahead*, A. Mohanty and S. Swain (eds), New Delhi: Axis Publications, 2009.

Bhardwaj, Sanjay, 'India-Central Asia Relations: Quest for Energy Security', in *South-Central Asia: Emerging Issues*, Kuldeep Singh (ed.), Amritsar: Guru Nanak Dev University, 2005.

Bhardwaj, Sanjay, 'India's Thrust for Energy Security: Need for India-Central Asia Cooperation', *Contemporary Central Asia*, 10 (3), 2006.

Bhat, Bilal, 'Matrix of National Initiatives: Perspectives on Cross Leveraging India and Uzbekistan Relations', *Perspectives on Bilateral and Regional Cooperation: South and Central Asia*, R. Malhotra, S.S. Gill and N. Gaur (eds.), Chandigarh: CRRID, 2013.

Bhattacherjee, Kallol, "Tajikistan, India step up security ties",*The Hindu*, 18 December 2016, URL:http://www.thehindu.com/news/national/Tajikistan-India-step-up-security-ties/article16897179.ece.

Blank, S., 'Rethinking Asymmetric Threats', Carlisle Barracks, PA: Strategic Studies Institute, U.S. Army War College, 2003.

Brar, B., 'Images in the Mirror: India and "Central Asia in Transition"', in *South-Central Asia: Emerging Issues*, Kuldeep Singh (ed.), Amritsar: Guru Nanak Dev University, 2004.

Burnes, A., Travels into Bokhara: Being an Account of a Journey from India to Cabool, Tartary and Persia, London: John Murray, 1934.

Calabrese, John, 'Indo-Iranian Relations in Transition', *Journal of South Asian and Middle Eastern Studies*, 25 (5), 2002.

Capisani, Giampaolo R., *The Handbook of Central* Asia, London: I. B. Tauris, 2000.

Chacko, Joseph P., 'DRDO's Kyrgyz India Mountain Biomedical Research Centre inaugurated', 8 July, Frontier India, 2011. URL: http://

frontierindia.net/drdos-kyrgyz-india-mountain-biomedical-research-centre-inaugurated

Chadda, Maya, 'Indo-Russian Relations in the Post-Cold War Era, in *The Roles of the United States, Russia and China in the New World Order*, Hafeez Malik (ed.), New York: St. Martin's Press, 1998.

Chandra, Amiya, India-Central Asia Relations: The Economic Dimension, New Delhi: Pentagon Press, 2015.

Chandra, Amiya, 'India and Afghanistan: Renewing Economic Relations', in *Afghanistan: The Challenge*, K. Warikoo (ed.), New Delhi: Pentagon Press, 2007.

Chandra, Amiya, 'Economic Cooperation: Potential and Prospects', in *Building a Common Future: Indian and Uzbek Perspectives on Security and Economic Issues*, P. Stobdan (ed.), New Delhi: Knowledge World, 1999.

Chandra, Amiya, 'Turkmen-India Cooperation for Peace and Development', *Strategic Analysis*, 19 (9), 1996.

Cohen, Bernard Saul, *Geography and Politics in a Divided World*, London: Methusen, 1964.

Cohen, Stephen P., *India: Emerging Power*, London: Oxford University Press, 2006.

Cooley, Alexander, Great Games, Local Rules: The New Great Power Contest in Central Asia, New York: Oxford University Press, 2012.

Chatterjee, Bipul and Surender Singh, "An Opportunity for India in Central Asia", *The Diplomat*, 4 May 2015, URL: http://thediplomat.com/2015/05/an-opportunity-for-india-in-central-asia/.

Chaudhury, Dipanjan, "PM Modi's visit to Central Asia: India and Kazakhstan ink deals on uranium supply, defence",*The Economic Times*, 9 July 2015, URL: http://economictimes.indiatimes.com/news/defence/pm-modis-visit-to-central-asia-india-and-kazakhstan-ink-deals-on-uranium-supply-defence/articleshow/47996585.cms.

Crandall, Maureen. S., Energy, Economics, and Politics in the Caspian Region: Dreams and Realities, London: Praeger, 2006.

Cummings, Sally N., Understanding Central Asia: Politics and Contested Transformations, London: Routledge, 2012.

Daly, John C.K., 'The Aftermath of the Kyrgyz Revolution: The Lesser Players', *Oil Price.com: Source for Oil & Energy News*, 2010. URL: http://oilprice.com/Geopolitics/Europe/The-Aftermath-Of-The-Kyrgyz-Revolution-The-Lesser-Players.html.

Daly, John C.K., 'Kyrgyzstan's Kumtor Mine Becomes Political Football', 14 June 2013. URL: http://www.cacianalyst.org/publications/analytical-articles/item/12757-kyrgyzstans-kumtor-mine-becomes-political-football.html

Dave, Bhavna, "Resetting India's Engagement in Central Asia: From Symbols to Substance", *RSIS Policy Report*, January 2016, URL: https://

www.rsis.edu.sg/wp-content/uploads/2016/02/PR160202_Resetting-Indias-Engagment.pdf.

Debata, Mahesh Ranjan, 'Turkmenistan-Afghanistan-Pakistan-India (TAPI): Pipeline or Pipedream? in *Central Asian and South Asia Energy Cooperation and Transport Linkages*, K. Warikoo (ed.), New Delhi: Pentagon Press, 2011.

Denyer, Simon, 'China bypasses America's 'New Silk Road with Two of Its Own', *The Washington Post*, 14 October, 2013. URL: http://www.washington post.com/world/asia_pacific/china-bypasses-american-new-silk-road-with-two-if-its-own/2013/10/14/49f9f60c-3284-11e3-ad00-ec4c6b31cbed_ story.html

Dhaka, Ambrish, 'Geopolitical Linkages with Central Asia: A South Asian Perspective', in *India's Foreign Policy: Emerging Challenges and Paradigms*, B.C. Upreti, M.L. Sharma and S.N. Kaushik (eds.), New Delhi: Kalinga Publications, 2003.

Dhaka, Ambrish, *South Asia and Central Asia: Geopolitical Dynamics*, Jaipur: Mangal Deep Publication, 2005.

Dienes, Leslie, 'The Russian Oil and Gas Sector: Implications of the New Property System', *The National Bureau of Asian Research*, no. 4, 1996.

Dikshit, R.D., *Political Geography the Spatiality of Politics*, New Delhi: Tata McGraw-Hill, 2000.

Dorian, James P., 'Central Asia: A Major Emerging Energy Player in the 21st Century, *Energy Policy*, 34 (5), 2006.

Dwivedi, Ramakant, 'President Romanov's Visit to India', 25 April, 2006. URL: www.idsa.in/publications/stratcomments/RamakantDwivedi170806.htm.

Faye, Michael L. et al., 'The Challenges Facing Landlocked Developing Countries', *Journal of Human Development*, 4 (1), 2004.

Foshko, Katherine, Re-Emergizing the India-Russia Relationship: Opportunities and Challenges for the 21st Century, Mumbai: Gateway House, 2011.

Fuller, Graham E., *The Emergence of Central Asia: The New Geopolitics*, Ankara: Eurasia Studies TICA, 1990.

Ganguly, Sumit, 'India's Alliances 2020', in *South Asia in 2020: Future Strategic Balances and Alliances*, Michael R. Chambers (ed.), Carlisle Barracks, PA: Strategic Studies Institute, US Army War College, 2002.

Garrett, Crae and Zhibek, Aidymbekova, "Uranium Mining in Kazakhstan and Pervasive State Participation: A Canadian Comparative Perspective', American Chamber of Commerce in Kzakhstan, no. 32, 2008. URL: http://large.stanford.edu/courses/2010/ph240/sagatov1/docs/Uranium_Mining.pdf

Gidadhubli, R.G., 'Energy Resources of Central Asia and Geopolitics of Pipelines', in *Central Asian and South Asia: Energy Cooperation and Transport Linkages*, K. Warikoo (ed.), New Delhi: Pentagon Press, 2011.

Gidadhubli, R.G., 'Kyrgyzstan: Achievements and Problems', in, *The State in Eurasia: Local and Global Arenas*, A. Sengupta and S. Chatterjee (eds), New Delhi: KW Publishers, 2011.

Gommans, Jos, 'Mughal India and Central Asia in the Eighteenth Century', in *India and Central Asia: Commerce and Culture, 1500-1800*, Scott C. Levy (ed.), New Delhi: Oxford University Press, 2007.

Gopal, Surendra (ed.), *India and Central Asia: Cultural, Economic and Political Links*, Calcutta: Maulana Abul Kalam Azad Institute of Asian Studies, 2001.

Gujral, I.K., *A Foreign Policy for India*, New Delhi: External Publicity Division, Ministry of External Affairs, Government of India, 1998.

Gupta, S.P., 'Hindu Gods in Western Central Asia' in *India and Central Asia: Classical to Contemporary Periods*, J.N. Roy and B. B. Kumar (eds.), New Delhi: Concept Publishing Company, 2007.

Hagan, Charles B., 'Geopolitics', *The Journal of Politics*, 4 (4), 1942.

Harmatta, Janos (ed.), *History of Civilizations of Central Asia Vol. II*, New Delhi: Motilal Banarasidas Publishers, 1997.

Hiro, Dilip, Inside Central Asia: A Political and Cultural History of Uzbekistan, Turkmenistan, Kazakhstan, Kyrgyzstan, Tajikistan, Turkey, and Iran, New Delhi: Harper Collins, 2010.

Huasheng, Zhao, Security Building in Central Asia and the Shanghai Cooperation Organization, Sapporo: Slavic Research Center, 2004.

Hussain, Majid, *Evolution of Geographical Thought*, Jaipur and New Delhi: Rawat Publications, 2001.

Iwasaki, Ichiro, 'Industrial Structure and Regional Development in Central Asia: A Micro Data Analysis on Spatial Allocation of Industry", *Central Asian Survey*, 19 (1), 2000.

Jafar, Majid, 'Kazakhstan: Oil, Politics and the New Great Game', in *The Caspian: Politics, Energy and Security*, Shirin Akiner (ed.), London and New York: Routledge, 2004.

Jafarova, Aynur, 'Leasing Kazakhstan's Farmlands to Foreign Firms needs Legal Elaboration: Minister', 21 January, 2014. URL: http://www.azernews.az/region/63589.html

James, Preston E., *All Possible Worlds: A History of Geographical Ideas*, Indianapolis: Odyssey Press, 1972.

Jha, Shashikant, 'India and Russia: Challenges of Rediscovering the Past Linkages', in *India and Russia towards a Strategic Partnership*, Shams-ud-Din (ed.), New Delhi: Lancer's Books, 2001.

Jiali, Ma, 'Central Asia: Geostrategic Situation and Big Power Policies', *Contemporary Central Asia*, 3 (1), 1999.

Jorisch, Avi, 'Port of Damaged Goods: India's Dangerous Investment in Iran's Chabahar', *Forbes*, 16 September, 2013. URL: http://www.forbes.com/sites/realspin/2013/09/16/port-of-damaged-goods-indias-dangerous-investment-in-irans-chahabar/

Joshi, Nirmala, 'Indian and Russian Security Perspectives on Central Asia, in *India and Russia towards a Strategic Partnership*, Shams-ud-Din (ed.), New Delhi: Lancer's Books, 2001.

Joshi, Nirmala, 'Kyrgyzstan: The Road to Stability', 12 September, 2011. URL: www.gatewayhouse.in.

Joshi, Nirmala, Reconnecting India and Central Asia: Emerging Security and Economic Dimensions, New Delhi: Pentagon Press, 2011.

Joshi, Shashank, 'India's Af-Pak Strategy', *RUSI Journal*, 155 (1), 2010.

Kablukov, Evgeni, 'India and Central Asia: Cultural Relations in Middle Ages in *India and Central Asia: Classical to Contemporary Periods*, J.N. Roy and B. B. Kumar (eds.), New Delhi: Concept Publishing Company, 2007.

Kak, Kapil, 'Security Interests in Central Asia', in *Central Asia: Present Challenges and Future Prospects*, V. Nagendra Rao (ed.), New Delhi: Knowledge World, 2005.

Kalikova, 'Banking Systems in the Kyrgyz Republic', *Global Legal Resources*, 27 November, 2007. URL: http://www.hg.org/article.asp?id=4923.

Kapoor, Vijay, 'The Dynamics of Aggressive Islamic Fundamentalism in Central and South Asia: Emerging Challenges', *Himalayan and Central Asian Studies*, 4 (3-4), 2000.

Kassenova, Nargis, 'The Shanghai Cooperation Energy Club: Purpose and Prospects', in *Caspian Energy Politics: Azerbaijan, Kazakhstan and Turkmenistan*, Indira Overland, Heidi Kjaernet and Andrea Kendall-Taylor (eds),London: Routledge, 2009.

Kasymova, Valentina and Batyrkul Baetoy, 'The Kyrgyz Republic: The Present and Future of Interstate Cooperation in the Energy Sphere', *Central Asia and the Caucasus*, 6 (48), 2006.

Kaushik, Devendra, 'India and Central Asia: Past and Present Realities and Future Hope', *Contemporary Central Asia*, 1 (1), 1997.

Kaushik, Devendra, 'India and Central Asia: Renewing a Traditional Partnership', *South Asian Survey*, 5 (2), 1998.

Kaushik, Devendra, 'Islamic Fundamentalism in Central Asia: An Appraisal', *Himalayan and Central Asian Studies*, 4 (3-4), 2000.

Kaushik, Devendra, 'New Geopolitics of Hydrocarbon Resources: A Eurasian Perspective', in *Central Asian and South Asia: Energy Cooperation and Transport Linkages*, K. Warikoo (ed.), New Delhi: Pentagon Press, 2011.

Khan, Amina, 'Afghanistan: Still at a Standstill', *Strategic Studies*, 28 (1), 2008.

Khaydarov, A., 'Afghan Factor in India-Central Asia Relations', in *India's Engagement with Central Asia with Focus on India-Uzbekistan Relations*, Jyotsana Bakshi, (ed.),Tashkent: University World Economy and Diplomacy, 2007.

Khosla, I.P., *Energy and Diplomacy*, New Delhi: Konark Publishers, 2005.

Kormilitsyn, Fedor V., 'UNESCAP Experience on International Transport Corridors: Need for Balance of Developing Infrastructure and Transport

Facilitation', 2011. URL: http://www.comcec.org/userfiles/file/ulastirma/escap.pdf

Kumar, B.B., 'India and Central Asia: Links and Interactions', in *India and Central Asia: Classical to Contemporary Periods*, J.N. Roy and B.B. Kumar (eds) New Delhi: Concept Publishing., 2007

Kumar, Satish, 'The Post-Cold War International System: An Indian Perspective', *Strategic Analysis*, 21 (6), 1997.

Kundu, N.D., 'Hamid Ansari's Visit to Turkmenistan and Kazakhstan', IDSA Comment, April 24, 2008. URL: http://www.idsa.in/idsastrategic comments/HamidAnsarisVisittoTurkmenistanandKazakhstan_NDKundu_240408

Kundu, N.D., 'India & Turkmenistan Relationship: From Silk-Route Connection to the Contemporary Era', 2013. URL: http://www.southandcentral asiacomment.org/wp-content/uploads/2012/12/India-Turkmenistan.pdf

Laruelle, Marlène and S. Peyrouse (eds), Globalizing Central Asia: Geopolitics and the Challeges of Economic Development, Armonk: M.E. Sharpe, 2013.

Laruelle, Marlène and S. Peyrouse (eds), *Mapping Central Asia: Indian Perceptions and Strategies*, Surrey and Burlington: Ashgate, 2011.

Levina, Maria, 'Kyrgyzstan-India Business Forum held in Bishkek', *Times of Central Asia*, 2014. http://www.timesca.com/index.php?option=com_content&view=article&id=13568:kyrgyzstan-india-business-forum-held-in-bishkek&catid=79:economy-a-finances&Itemid=567

Levi, Scott, 'India, Russia and the Eighteenth-Century Transformation of the Central Asian Caravan Trade', in *India and Central Asia: Commerce and Culture 1500-1800*, Scott Levi (ed.), New Delhi: Oxford University Press, 2007.

Levi, Scott C., India and Central Asia: Commerce and Culture, 1500-1800, New Delhi: Oxford University Press, 2007.

Linn, Johannes F., 'Central Asia's Energy Challenge: Overcoming the Natural Resource Curse', August 11, 2008. URL: http://www.brookings.edu/research/opinions/2008/08/11-central-asia-linn

Lutfu, Sagbansu, 'Banking System in Kyrgyz Republic", *IBSU Scientific Journal*, 1 (1), 2006.

Mahalingam, Sudha, 'India-Central Asia Energy Cooperation', in *India and Central Asia: Advancing Common Interest*, K. Santhanam and R. Dwiwedi (eds), New Delhi: IDSA & Anamaya Publishers, 2004.

Mahapatra, D.A., 'North-South Corridor: Prospects of Multilateral Trade in Eurasia', March 14, 2012. URL: http://indrus.in/articles/2012/03/14/the_north-south_corridor_prospects_of_multilateral_trade_in_eurasia_15134.html

Makara, Peter and Anna Ritsatakis, Gaining Health: Analysis of Policy Development in European Countries for Tackling Non-Communicable Diseases, Denmark: WHO Regional Office for Europe, 2009.

Malik, Ishfaq and M.A. Mir, 'India's Trade Relations with Kazakhstan: Problems and Prospects', *Abhinav*, 1 (12), 2012. URL: http://www.abhinavjournal.com/images/Commerce_&_Management/Dec12/8.pdf

Malvlanov, I.R., 'Central Asia and South Asia: Diplomatic Potential of Uzbekistan and India for Sustainable Inter-Regional Economic Cooperation', in *India's Engagement with Central Asia with Focus on India-Uzbekistan Relations*, Jyotsana Bakshi (ed.), Tashkent: University of World Economy and Diplomacy, 2007.

Mandelbaum, Michael (ed.), Central Asia and the World: Kazakhstan, Uzbekistan, Tajikistan, Kyrgyzstan and Turkmenistan, New York: Council on Foreign Relations Press, 1994.

Mattoo, Amitabh, 'United States of America and Central Asia: Beginning of the Great Game', in *Central Asia the Great Game Replayed*: An *Indian Perspective*, Jyotsana Bakshi (ed.), New Delhi: New Century Publications, 2003.

Mavlonov, Ibrokhim R., 'Central Asia and South Asia: Potential of India's Multilateral Economic Diplomacy in Intra-Regional Co-operation', *Strategic Analysis*, 30 (2), 2006.

Milto, Marina, 'Prospects of Transnational Gas Pipeline Projects from Caspian Littoral States to South Asia', *Contemporary Central Asia*, 8 (1&2), 2004.

Mir, M.A., 'India-Kazakhstan Relations: Special Reference to Trade and Investment', in *Perspectives on Bilateral and Regional Cooperation: South and Central Asia*, R. Malhotra et al. (eds), Chandigarh: CRRID, 2013.

Mohanty, A. and S. Swain, (eds.), *Contemporary Kazakhstan: The Way Ahead*, New Delhi: Axis Publications, 2009.

Moore, Scott, 'Peril and Promise: A Survey of India's Strategic Relationship with Central Asia', *Central Asian Survey*, 26 (2), 2007.

Mueller, Barbara, Dynamics of International Advertising: Theoretical and Practical Perspectives, New York: Peter Lang Publishing, 2011.

Muni, S.D., 'India and Central Asia: Towards a Cooperative Future' in *Central Asia, the Great Game Replayed: An Indian Perspective*, Nirmala Joshi (ed.), Delhi: New Century Publications, 2003.

Muni, S.D. and Girijesh Pant, India's Energy Security: Prospects for Cooperation with Extended Neighborhood, New Delhi: Rupa, 2005.

Musaeva, Indira, 'Prospects of Kyrgy-India Economic Cooperation', in *India-Kyrgyzstan Relations: Perspectives and Prospects*, K. Santhanam and R. Dwiwedi (eds),New Delhi: Anamaya Publishers, 2008.

Pandey, S.K., 'Indo-Kyrgyz Relations: The Search for New Horizon', in *India-Kyrgyzstan Relations: Perspectives and Prospects*, K. Santhanam and R. Dwiwedi (eds),New Delhi: Anamaya Publishers, 2008.

Pandey, S.K., 'India and Central Asia: Alternative Trade Routes and Transit Options', *Geopolitics and Energy Resources in Central Asia and Caspian Sea Region*, Shams-ud-Din (ed.), New Delhi: Lancer Books, 2003.

Pandey, S.K., 'India's Approach to Regional Cooperation in South Asia and Its Relevance for Uzbekistan', in *Perspectives on Bilateral and Regional Cooperation: South and Central Asia*, R. Malhotra et al. (eds), Chandigarh: CRRID, 2013.

Pant, Harsh V., 'India in Afghanistan: A Test Case for a Rising Power', *Contemporary South Asia*, 18 (2), 2010.

Parker, Geoffrey, 'Western Geopolitical Thought In the Twentieth Century', *Coroom Helm*, London & Sydney, 1985.

Patnaik, Ajay, Central Asia: Geopolitics, Security and Stability, New York: Routledge, 2016.

Patnaik, Ajay, 'India-Tajikistan Relations: Prospects of a Regional Development', in *The State in Eurasia: Local and Global Arenas*, A. Sengupta and S. Chatterjee (eds),New Delhi: KW Publishers Pvt Ltd, 2013.

Patnaik, Ajay, 'Central Asia and India: The Post-Taliban Prospects', *Contemporary Central Asia*, 9 (2&3), 2005.

Patnaik, Ajay, 'Customs Union: Implications for India', in *Post-Soviet States: Two Decades of Transition and Transformation*, A. Patnaik and Tulsiram (eds), New Delhi: Oscar Publications, 2012.

Pattanayak, Satyanarayan, 'Oil as a Factor in Indo-Gulf Relations', *Strategic Analysis*, vol.25, no.3, June, 2001, pp. 465-480.

Perham, Steven, China's Borderlands: The Faultline of Central Asia, London: I.B. Tauris & Co, 2017.

Peyrouse, S., 'Domestic and International Articulation of the Indian Involvement in Central Asia', in *Mapping Central Asia: Indian Perception and Strategies*, M. Laruelle and S. Peyrouse (eds), Surrey: Ashgate, 2011.

Potapova, N.A., 'Uzbek-Indian Relations: Realities and Prospects'. in *Perspectives on Bilateral and Regional Cooperation: South and Central Asia*, R. Malhotra et al (eds), Chandigarh: CRRID, 2013.

Prakash, Mohan, 'Connecting Central Asia: A Roadmap for Regional Cooperation', Asian Development Bank, 2006. URL: http://www.unohrlls.org/UserFiles/File/LLDCpercent20Documents/MTR/ADBpercent20connecting-CA-roadmap.pdf

Prasad, Kailash K. and Rani D. Mullen, 'India-Tajikistan Bilateral Brief', India Development Cooperation Research (IDCR) Project, Bilateral Brief no. 5, December 5 (last updated 15 May 2014), 2013. URL: http://idcr.cprindia.org/blog/india-tajikistan-brief-0

Puri, M.M., 'Central Asian Geopolitics: The Indian View', *Central Asian Survey*, 16 (2), 1997, pp. 237-268.

Rakhimov, Mirzhoid, 'Foreign Policy of Uzbekistan: Bilateral and Multilateral Dimension', in *The State in Eurasia: Local and Global Arenas*, A. Sengupta and S.Chatterjee (eds), New Delhi: KW Publishers, 2013.

Rasulov, Gafur, 'Foreign Investments in the Economic Developments of

Tajikistan', in *Post-Soviet States: Two Decades of Transition and Transformation*, A. Patnaik and Tulsiram (eds), New Delhi: Oscar Publications, 2012.

Reznikova, Oksana, 'Transitional Corporation in Central Asia', in *Central Asia in Transition: Dilemmas of Political and Economic Development*, Borris Rumer (ed.), New Delhi: Aakar Books, 2003.

Roberts, John, 'Pipeline Politics', in *The Caspian: Politics, Energy and Security*, Shirin Akiner (ed.), London and New York: Routledge, 2004.

Roche Elizabeth, "Narendra Modi arrives in Tajikistan to cap off Central Asia visit",*Live Mint*, 14 July 2015, URL: http://www.livemint.com/Politics/hZZqhoxtlkNq7wv3NK850O/Narendra-Modi-arrives-in-Tajikistan-to-cap-off-Central-Asia.html.

Roche Elizabeth, "Narendra Modi's visit brings Central Asia back in focus", *Live Mint*, 15 July 2015, URL: http://www.livemint.com/Politics/7iJD1gvVb9VWUoIiPLHjQK/Narendra-Modis-visit-brings-Central-Asia-back-in-focus.html.

Roy, Allison, 'Strategic Reassertion in Russia's Central Asia Policy', *International Affairs*, 80 (2), 2004.

Roy, Arpita Basu, *Afghanistan: Towards a Viable State*, Gurgaon: Hope India Publications, 2000.

Roy, J.N. and B.B. Kumar, B.B. , *India and Central Asia: Classical to Contemporary Periods*, New Delhi: Concept Publishing Company, 2007.

Roy, Meena Singh, 'India's Interest in Central Asia', *Strategic Analysis*, 24 (12), 2001.

Roy, Meena Singh, 'India-Central Asia Relations: Changing Dynamics and Future Prospects', in *South-Central Asia: Emerging Issues*, Kuldeep Singh (ed.) Amritsar: Guru Nanak Dev University, 2005.

Roy, Meena Singh, 'Pratibha Patil's Visit to Tajikistan: Enhancing Goodwill, Trust and Mutual Confidence', IDSA Comment, 2009. URL: http://www.idsa.in/idsastrategiccomments/PratibhaPatilsVisittoTajikistan_msroy_230909

Roy, Meena Singh, 'India and Tajikistan: Building a Long-Term Strategic Partnership', IDSA Comment, 18 September, 2012. URL: http://idsa.in/idsacomments/IndiaandTajikistanBuildingalongterm Strategic Partnership_MeenaSRoy_180912

Rumer, Boris, ed., *Central Asia at the End of the Transition*, London: Routledge, 2016.

Rumer, Boris (ed.), *Central Asia: The Challenge of Independence*, Armonk: M.E. Sharpe, 2003.

Sachdeva, Gulshan, "Changing Dynamics Of India–Central Asia Ties", *Bishkek Project*, 5 April 2017, URL: https://www.bishkekproject.com/memos/24

Sachdeva, G., 'India's Objectives in Central Asia', at international conference on "US, China and the Future of Central Asia", New York University, New York, 6-8 February, 2012.

Sachdeva, Gulshan, 'Joint Venture and Export Routes in the Caspian Sea Region', in *Geopolitics and Energy Resources in Central Asia and Caspian Sea Region*, Shams-ud-Din (ed.), New Delhi: Lancer Books, 2000.

Sachdeva, Gulshan, 'India's Objectives in Central Asia', School of International Studies, Jawaharlal Nehru University, 2012. URL: http://uschinacenter.as.nyu.edu/docs/IO/23889/Sachdeva_Abs.pdf (accessed: 20 February 2013)

Sahai, P.S., 'India and Central Asia: Establishment of Diplomatic Relations and Beyond' in *South-Central Asia: Emerging Issues*, Kuldeep Singh (ed.), Amritsar: Guru Nanak Dev University, 2005.

Sahgal, A. and Anand, V., 'Strategic Environment in Central Asia and India', 2010. URL: http://www.silkroadstudies.org/new/docs/publications/1004Joshi-V-Strategic.pdf

Saipov, Z.S., 'Energy Diplomacy in Strategic Calculations of Central Asia', in *South and Central Asia: Quest for Peace and Cooperation*, R. Malhotra et al. (eds), Chandigarh: CRRID, 2013.

Sajjanhar Ashok, "India-Central Asia Relations: Expanding Vistas of Partnership", *ORF Raisina Debates*, 22 June 2016, URL: http://www.orfonline.org/expert-speaks/india-central-asia-relations-expanding-vistas-of-partnership/.

Sajjanhar, Ashok, 'Perspectives on India-Kazakhstan Relations: Challenges and Opportunities', in *Perspectives on Bilateral and Regional Cooperation*, R. Malhotra, S.S. Gill and N. Gaur (eds.), Chandigarh: CRRID, 2013.

Santhanam, K. and R. Dwiwedi (eds), *India and Central Asia: Advancing Common Interest*, New Delhi: IDSA and Anamaya Publishers, 2004.

Sarma, A.S, India and Central Asia: Redefining Energy and Trade Links, New Delhi: Pentagon Press, 2010.

Sarma, A.S., 'Turkmenistan's Foreign Policy after Niyazov: Looking Beyond 'Positive Neutrality", in *The State in Eurasia: Local and Global Arenas*, A. Sengupta and S. Chatterjee (eds), New Delhi: KW Publishers, 2013.

Schwirtz, Michael, 'Ethnic Rioting Ravages Kyrgyzstan', *The New York Times*, 2010. URL: http://www.nytimes.com/2010/06/14/world/asia/14kyrgyz.html.

Sengupta, Anita, 'Perceptions and Strategies: India's Relations with the Central Asian Region' in *Mapping Central Asia: Indian Perception and Strategies*, M. Laruelle and S. Peyrouse (eds), Surrey: Ashgate, 2011.

Sengupta, Anita, Heartlands of Eurasia: The Geopolitics of Political Space, Lanham: Lexington Books, 2009.

Shah, G.M., 'Economic Cooperation between Central Asia and South Asia: Prospects and Challenges', in *Perspectives on Bilateral and Regional Cooperation*, R. Malhotra, S.S. Gill and N. Gaur (eds.), Chandigarh: CRRID, 2013.

Shams-ud-Din, 'Caspian Sea: The Politics of Oil', in *Geopolitics and Energy Resources in Central Asia and Caspian Sea Region*, Shams-ud-Din (ed.), New Delhi: Lancer Books, 2000.

Shams ud-Din (ed.), Geopolitics and Energy Resources in Central Asia and Caspian Sea Region, New Delhi: Lancer Books, 2000.

Sharan, Shalini, 'Central Asia: India's Real Strategic Depth', 27 February, 2012. URL: http://csis.org/blog/central-asia-indias-real-strategic-depth

Sheraliyev, Oybek R., 'Central Asia mirrors India's Geo-economic Interests', in *Perspectives on Bilateral and Regional Cooperation*, R. Malhotra, S.S. Gill and N. Gaur (eds.), Chandigarh: CRRID, 2013.

Shiva Kumar et al., 'India-Central Asia Relations: Moving Towards Broader Development Partnerships', India Development Cooperation Research (IDCR) Project, Background Paper no. 4, 6 January, 2014. URL: http://idcr.cprindia.org/blog/india-central-asia-backgrounder

Shri Prakash, 'India Uzbekistan Relations during the 1990s and Future Prospects', in *Central Asia since Independence*, K. Warikoo (ed.), New Delhi: Shipra Publications, 2004.

Sibal, Kanwal, 'Devoid of Excitement, India-Russia Ties Have Remained Consistently Resilient', *Force*, January, 2012.

Sikri, Rajiv, 'Beyond Oil and Gas: India's Interests in Central Asia', *Global Envision*, 29 June, 2009.

Sikri, Rajiv, Challenge and Strategy: Rethinking India's Foreign Policy. New Delhi: Sage Publications, 2009.

Singh, Kuldeep, *South-Central Asia: Emerging Issues*, Amritsar: Guru Nanak Dev University, 2004.

Singh, Swaran, 'Sino-Central Asia Ties: Problems and Prospects', *Strategic Analysis*, 24 (6), 2000.

Sisodia, N.S. and Uday C. Bhaskar (eds), *Emerging India: Security and Foreign Policy Perspectives*. New Delhi: IDSA, 2005.

Skagen, Ottar, 'Survey of Caspian Oil and Gas Resources', in *The Caspian Region at a Crossroad: Challenges of a New Frontier of Energy*, Hooshang Amirahmadi (ed.), Houndmills: Palgrave Macmillan, 2000.

Sloan, Geoffrey, 'Sir Halford J. Makinder: The Heartland Theory Then and Now', *Journal of Strategic Studies*, 22 (2-3), June-September, 1999.

Sodiqov, Alexander, 'The Limits of India's Military Role in Tajikistan', *Eurasia Daily Monitor*, 9 (21), 31 January, 2012. URL: http://www.james town.org/single/?no_cache=1&tx_ttnewspercent5Btt_newspercent5 D=38953&tx_tt newspercent5BbackPidpercent5D=13&cHash=acfd2490783 e77efbb93047c0fb8561f

Song, Weiqing, China's Approach to Central Asia: The Shanghai Cooperation Organization, Abingdon: Routledge, 2016.

Soni, Sharad K., 'Book Review: *Mapping Central Asia: Indian Perceptions and*

Strategies, by Laruelle, Marlène and Peyrouse, Sébastien, eds. (2011), Surrey and Burlington: Ashgate', in *India Quarterly*, 69 (1), 2013.

Soni, Sharad K., 'Quest for New Asian Security: Regional Cooperation in Cultural Perspective', *Himalayan and Central Asian Studies*, 10 (1), 2006.

Soni, Sharad K., 'Changing Image of a Capital City: Relevance of OSCE Summit for Astana's International Recognition', in Materials of the Fourth Annual International Scientific Conference on Independence of the State and Capital of the Country: Connotation of Meanings, Astana: Elorda, 2011.

Soni, Sharad K., 'Kazakhstan OSCE Chairmanship and Regional Security', in Materials of International Scientific-Theoretic Conference on World Politics and Kazakhstan: Problems and Perspectives, Almaty, 2011.

Soni, Sharad K. and Vaishali Krishna, 'India and Central Asia: Quest for Reconnection', in Biswanath Chakraborty and Debasish Nandy (eds.), *An Outline of Indian Foreign Policy and Relations*, Kolkata: Mitram, 2016.

Sperling, Webber, 'NATO: From Kosovo to Kabul', *International Affairs*, 85 (3), 2009.

Sreedhar, 'Islamic Radicalism: Central Asia and Beyond', *World Focus*, vol. 21, 2000.

Srinivasan, N., 'Energy Cooperation between India and Its Neighbouring Countries', in *Energy and Diplomacy*, I.P. Khosla (ed.), New Delhi: Konark Publishers, 2005.

Srivastava, Deepti, 'Nuclear Fuel and Emerging Dynamics of Indo-Kazakh Relations', *Mainstream*, 48 (33), August 7, 2010. URL: http://www.mainstreamweekly.net/article2219.html

Stein, Tonnesson and Kolas Ashlid, 'Energy Security in Asia: China, India, Oil and Peace', Report to the Norwegian Ministry of Foreign Affairs, International Peace Research Institute, Oslo (PRIO), 2006.

Stobdan, P., 'Building A Strategic Partnership with Kazakhstan: A Blueprint For India's Central Asia Policy', *Journal of Social and Political Studies*, 5 (41), 2006.

Stobdan, P., 'India-Turkmenistan Relations in Perspective', *Strategic Analysis*, 19 (9), 1996.

Stobdan, P., 'Central Asia in Geo-political Transition', *Strategic Analysis*, 22 (1), 1998.

Stobdan, P., *India and Kazakhstan: Civilizational Explorations*, New Delhi: Heritage Publication, 2003.

Stobdan, P., Central Asia: Democracy, Instability and Strategic Game in Kyrgyzstan, New Delhi: Pentagon Press, 2014.

Stobdan, P. (ed.), *India-Russia Strategic Partnership: Common Perspectives*, New Delhi: Institute for Defense Studies and Analyses, 2010.

Tabak, Gulzade A., 'Salience of Synergy in Uzbek-India Ties', in *Perspectives on Bilateral and Regional Cooperation*, R. Malhotra, S.S. Gill and N. Gaur (eds.), Chandigarh: CRRID, 2013.

Tanchum, Michael, 'India's Central Asia Ambitions outfoxed by China and Russia', *East Asia Forum*, October 12, 2013. URL: http://www.eastasia forum. org/2013/10/12/indias-central-asia-ambitions-outfoxed-by-china-and-russia/

Tayal, S.R., 'Indian Foreign Policy: Engagement with Central Asia', in *India's Engagement with Central Asia with Focus on India-Uzbekistan Relations*, Jyotsana Bakshi (ed.), Tashkent: University of World Economy and Diplomacy, 2007.

Teshabaev, F., 'Uzbek-India Relations', in *Central Asia since Independence*, K. Warikoo and Mahavir Singh (eds), New Delhi: Shipra Publications, 2004.

Thomas, Timothy L., 'Russian National Interests and the Caspian Sea', *Perceptions*, December-February, 2000.

Tulsi Ram and Ajay Patnaik (eds.), *Eurasian Politics: Ideas, Institutions and External Relations*, New Delhi: KW Publishers, 2013.

Urazdoboeva, Sojida, 'Some Aspects of Indian Energy Interests in Central Asia', in *India's Engagement with Central Asia with focus on India-Uzbekistan Relations*, Jyotsana Bakshi (ed.), Tashkent: University of World Economy and Diplomacy, 2007.

Utegenova, Ailuna, 'OSCE Activities in Central Asia', *Himalayan and Central Asian Studies*, 10 (4), 2006.

Ved, Mahendra, 'Afghanistan: The Unfinished Task', *World Focus*, vol. 23, 2002.

Vohra, N.N. (ed.), Culture, Society and Politics in Central Asia and India, Delhi: Shipra Publishers, 1999.

Voropoeva, V. and V. Goryacheva, 'Kyrgyzstan on the Great Silk Road and Cultural Relationship with India', *Himalayan and Central Asian Studies*, 2 (3-4), 1998.

Wadhwa, R.K., 'Economic and Trade Relations between India and Russia', in *New Trends in Indo-Russian Relations*, V.D. Chopra (ed.), New Delhi: Kalpaz Publications, 2003.

Warikoo, K., 'Security Challenges in South and Central Asia', *Himalayan and Central Asian Studies*, 10 (1), 2006.

Warikoo, K., 'Strengthening India-Central Asia Cultural Ties', in *Emerging Asia in Focus: Issues and Problems*, P.L. Dash (ed.), New Delhi: Academic Excellence.

Warikoo, K., Religion and Security in South and Central Asia, London: Routledge, 2010.

Warikoo, K., 'India and Central Asia: Political Implication for Power Rivalries in Eurasia', in *India and Central Asia: Two Decades of Transition*, P.L. Dash (ed.), New Delhi: OUP, 2011.

Warikoo, K. and Mahavir Singh (eds.), *Central Asia since Independence*, New Delhi: Shipra, 2004.

Warikoo, K. (ed.), Central Asia and South Asia: Energy Cooperation and Transport Linkages, New Delhi: Pentagon, 2011.

Warikoo, K. (ed.), *Central Asia: Emerging New Order*, New Delhi: Har Anand, 1995.

Wu, Hsiu-Ling and Chien-Hsun Chen, 'The Prospects for Regional Economic Integration between China and Five Central Asian Countries', *Europe Asia Studies*, 56 (7), 2004.

Yadav, R.S., 'India and the Central Asian Republics', *World Focus*, vol. 20, 1998.

Yesdauletova, Ardak, 'Energy Security in Central Asia and India', *Contemporary Central Asia*, 11 (1), 2007.

Yuvshanova, Sofia, 'What are the Effects of 2007-09 Global Economic Crisis on Turkmenistan's Economy?' in *Post-Soviet States: Two Decades of Transition and Transformation*, A. Patnaik and Tulsiram (eds), New Delhi: Oscar Publications, 2013.

Zakirova, Saiyora A., 'A Status Report on Indo-Uzbek Economic Cooperation', in *Perspectives on Bilateral and Regional Cooperation: South and Central Asia*, R. Malhotra, S.S. Gill and N. Gaur (eds.), Chandigarh: CRRID, 2013.

Index